Compellence and the Strategic Culture of Imperial Japan

Compellence and the Strategic Culture of Imperial Japan

Implications' for Coercive Diplomacy in the Twenty-First Century

FORREST E. MORGAN

Westport, Connecticut
London

Library of Congress Cataloging-in-Publication Data

Morgan, Forrest E.
   Compellence and the strategic culture of imperial Japan : implications for coercive
diplomacy in the twenty-first century / Forrest E. Morgan.
       p. cm.
   Includes bibliographical references and index.
   ISBN 0–275–97780–3 (alk. paper)
   1. Japan—Foreign relations—1945–1989. 2. World politics—1945– I. Title.
DS889.5.M67 2003
327.52'009—dc21   2003045596

British Library Cataloguing in Publication Data is available.

Library of Congress Catalog Card Number: 2003045596
ISBN: 0–275–97780–3

First published in 2003

Praeger Publishers, 88 Post Road West, Westport, CT 06881
An imprint of Greenwood Publishing Group, Inc.
www.praeger.com

Printed in the United States of America

Copyright Acknowledgments

The author and publisher gratefully acknowledge permission to use excerpts from the
following material:
   Morinosuke Kajima, *The Emergence of Japan as a World Power, 1895-1925*. Rutland, Vt.:
Charles E. Tuttle Co., 1968.
   Munemitsu Mutsu, *Kenkenroku: A Diplomatic Record of the Sino-Japanese War, 1894–95*.
Edited and translated with historical notes by Gordon Mark Berger. Tokyo: University of
Tokyo Press, 1982. With permission of University of Tokyo Press and The Japan
Foundation.

To my beloved Susan

Contents

Figures and Tables

FIGURES

TABLES

Acknowledgments

I am indebted to several people and organizations for their help and support in conducting this study and producing the book that came out of it. I would not have been able to do this work without the tireless guidance of two mentors in particular. Professor Emeritus Thomas C. Schelling taught me the fundamentals of strategic thought and was ever available as a kind but insistently rational sounding board. His remarkable blend of brilliance and gentility inspired my efforts and will be the ideal on which I model all my future intellectual endeavors. Professor William Taft Stuart was an unfailingly enthusiastic champion of my cause. Serving as both teacher and friend, he patiently guided me through the seemingly arcane annals of cultural anthropology and never let me forget that rationality is in the eye of the beholder. I would like to thank the faculty and staff of the University of Maryland School of Public Affairs for supporting this project, one that was somewhat wide of their usual field of inquiry. I would also like to extend my special appreciation to Alan Vick and Daniel L. Byman at the RAND Corporation for exchanging ideas with me and allowing me access to parallel work they did on coercion theory. I would like to thank the United States Air Force School of Advanced Air and Space Studies for sponsoring this study and providing the time and resources for me to prepare the manuscript for publication. Most importantly, I would like to thank my wife Susan, my son Samuel, and my daughters Aubrey and Kara for their loving patience during the many hours I spent working on this project, hours that were rightfully theirs.

The following individuals read substantial portions of this manuscript and provided critical comments: Richard B. Andres, Daniel L. Byman,

James S. Corum, Ivo H. Daalder, Dennis M. Drew, Stephen T. Hosmer, John H. Miller, Kenneth M. Pollack, George H. Quester, Yoichiro Sato, Kori Schake, Thomas C. Schelling, Matthew R. Schwonek, William T. Stuart, Stansfield Turner, Alan Vick, and Barry D. Watts. All of these people provided insights that improved the product significantly. Any errors or oversights, however, are mine alone. I am entirely responsible for the contents of this book, and my work does not represent the views of the RAND Corporation, the University of Maryland, the School of Advanced Air and Space Studies, or the United States Air Force.

CHAPTER 1

Jousting in a Mirror

States often behave in ways that seem irrational to outside observers. In 1941 Japanese leaders were determined to go to war with the United States even though all tangible comparisons of power suggested such a conflict might be suicidal for Japan. Four years later, with Japanese naval strength and air power virtually destroyed, Tokyo tried to hold out for a negotiated peace while American bombers methodically burned 66 of Japan's largest cities, killing hundreds of thousands of Japanese citizens and putting millions more out of their homes.

Some analysts have suggested that Tokyo's seemingly irrational behavior before and during the Second World War can be attributed to Japan's martial culture, its proud tradition of military virtue and preference for death over humiliation or defeat. Yet, such a conclusion is difficult to sustain in light of Tokyo's submissive response to the 1895 triple intervention. In that episode Japanese leaders meekly complied when representatives from three European states "advised" them to return captured territory to China, territory for which the Japanese Imperial Army had shed blood and then occupied with 100,000 troops. Given such contradictory examples, how can culture explain Japan's strategic behavior?

This book is about compellence and strategic culture—that is, how culture affects the ways that states respond to coercive threat. More specifically, it examines three examples of how strategic culture conditioned the way Imperial Japan responded when other states tried to compel it to change its policies. The book then draws from those cases to help contemporary policy makers craft more effective strategies to curb the behavior of aggressive states.

Compellence is as old as human conflict. It is the process of forcefully persuading an adversary to do something he or she would not otherwise choose to do. Throughout history kings and statesmen have sought to impose their will on other actors in the international arena. Economic punishment and threats of force have been ready instruments of diplomacy, and compellence is the very purpose of war.

Coercive threat has become even more important in international relations since the end of the Cold War. The collapse of bipolarity unleashed a wave of instability throughout much of the world. At the same time, the end of the Soviet-American stalemate in the United Nations Security Council freed that body to sanction the efforts of states and coalitions to impress their will on actors who violate international standards of conduct. Iraq, Haiti, Bosnia, and Kosovo are but a few of the places where states have threatened or used force on behalf of the United Nations and other supra-national organizations to compel aggressive leaders to stop bullying their neighbors or abusing their own citizens. In sum, compellence is an increasingly important instrument of statecraft. As we feel our way into the twenty-first century, statesmen will be called upon ever more frequently to confront aggression and enforce international norms. Therefore, scholars, security analysts, and policy makers need to understand the theory and practice of compellence.

COMPELLENCE THEORY—ITS ROOTS AND LIMITATIONS

Ironically, though compellence has deep historical roots, systematic thinking about the theory behind it only began after the Second World War. Allied victory in that conflict was total; military strategy had triumphed. But as the flush of success faded and bipolar tensions emerged, the rising specter of nuclear conflict between the superpowers convinced many strategists that war could no longer be considered a rational policy option. The question became, how does a state maintain security and achieve policy objectives while averting a nuclear confrontation? Addressing this issue pushed strategic thought beyond the traditional confines of the military profession and into the domain of the "strategy intellectuals," a circle of civilian scholars and policy analysts.[1] It was in this rarified environment that compellence theory emerged from thinking about nuclear and conventional deterrence.

Alexander George and Richard Smoke describe deterrence as persuading one's opponent that the costs or risks of a given course of action he might take outweigh the benefits.[2] It involves using a coercive threat of force to maintain the status quo. This concept laid the groundwork for strategic thinking throughout the Cold War, but deterrence theory, with its goal of preserving a status quo, provided little guidance on how to achieve positive policy objectives. Consequently, in the late 1950s policy analysts began to explore the dynamics of coercive bargaining and other facets of strategic behavior. On March 10, 1959, Daniel Ellsberg delivered a lecture entitled "The Theory and Practice of Blackmail" in a Boston educational radio broadcast.[3] Later published and reprinted several times, it was probably the first work presented on what was to become modern compellence theory.

Although Ellsberg's work was illustrative, Thomas Schelling is the best known of the early compellence theorists, and he undoubtedly made the greatest contribution to this emerging field.[4] Like Ellsberg, Schelling applied concepts from game theory to analyze how interdependent actors in an international setting bargain with one another. In his 1960 book, *The Strategy of Conflict*, Schelling advanced the thesis that "most conflict situations are essentially *bargaining* situations" and a strategy for dealing with them should not be concerned with "the efficient *application* of force but with the *exploitation of potential force*" [italics in original].[5] Schelling's theory revolved around the premise that a coercer will achieve her aim if she can raise the opponent's expectation of pain to a level at which the cost he anticipates for further resistance outweighs the benefits he expects to gain. In essence, the coercer manipulates the adversary's sense of risk by issuing threats and, if necessary, using a measured amount of force, yet promises that she will withhold or end the pain as long as the adversary complies with her demands.

Although deterrence and compellence both involve coercion by manipulating the adversary's calculation of costs and benefits, they differ in several crucial respects. Deterrence is a threat intended to keep an adversary from starting something. Compellence is a threat intended to make him do something new or cease doing something he has already begun. Deterrence seeks to maintain the status quo, but compellence seeks to change it. Deterrence is more often passive—conditions are set, and the initiative of acting is left to the opponent—but compellence is active with the coercer seizing the initiative and attempting to force the adversary to change his behavior. Considering these differences, Schelling was dissatisfied with using the term "coercion" to describe his concept, because that word applies equally to passive and active forms of pressure. Consequently, he coined the term "compellence" to differentiate the active form of coercion from its more passive counterpart, deterrence.[6] Focusing on the coercer's power to hurt, Schelling's seminal work gave rise to the family of theories classified as *punishment*.

A second vein of compellence theory stems from the work of Alexander George, David Hall, and William Simons in their 1971 book, *The Limits of Coercive Diplomacy: Laos, Cuba, Vietnam*. Disturbed by America's compellence failures in the Vietnam War and generally puzzled by coercive diplomacy's inconsistent record of success, George and his co-authors conducted a focused comparison of three cases in an attempt to better understand the "many variables at play" in an actual compellence effort and to develop a "policy-relevant" theory, one designed to contribute to better foreign policy making.[7] Since 1971, George, working alone and in collaboration, has continued to develop and refine this context-oriented approach.[8] In their most recent work, *The Limits of Coercive Diplomacy* (second edition), George and Simons modify their description of contextual and process variables and factor in some historical work on ultimata.[9] Their use of the term "coercive diplomacy" is consistent with Schelling's definition of compellence except that it is limited to "defensive uses of the strategy—that is, efforts to persuade an opponent to stop or reverse an action."[10] With a strong focus on a variable called "asymmetry of motivation," George's framework and those patterned after it have come to be known as *balance of interest* theories.[11]

Returning to a more linear, utility-maximizing approach, Robert Pape characterized the compellence problem as a strategic choice between punishment and *denial*.[12] In a series of journal articles and a 1996 book, *Bombing to Win: Air Power and Coercion in War*, Pape asserts, as do most punishment theorists, that compellence results from a manipulation of the opponent's calculation of costs and benefits.[13] However, whereas punishment theories focus on raising the expected costs of the opponent's resistance, Pape's theory turns instead to denying the adversary the benefits of resistance by countering his military attempts to do so. Pape theorized that compellence only succeeds when the coercer counters the adversary's "strategy to achieve territorial objectives." Then and only then will the opponent concede to the coercer's demands in order to "avoid futile expenditure of further resources."[14]

While coercive diplomacy generally fell into disfavor after the Vietnam experience, Pape's work heralded a post–Cold War revival of interest in this field. In the new security environment, analysts and practitioners turned their attention once again to answering the question of how to compel adversaries to change their behavior.[15] These efforts are published under a variety of labels, but nearly all of them develop themes originating in the three schools of thought outlined previously—punishment, denial, and balance of interests. That should come as no surprise, as the classic approaches have yielded elegant theories that explain the outcomes of a considerable number of historical cases. Unfortunately, however, each of the leading theories leaves some cases unexplained, and there are a few cases that pose difficulties for all of them.

One source of these difficulties may lie in some overly simplistic assumptions that existing compellence theories make about the adversary's decision calculus. Most assume the opposing government is a unitary rational actor—that is, it makes decisions as if it were a single individual, fully aware of its interests and rationally weighing the potential costs and benefits of alternative responses to the coercer's demands. Such an assumption helps keep theories parsimonious, but it has serious shortcomings. A growing body of literature suggests that governmental decisions are rarely the products of a unitary actor, rationally calculating prospective costs and benefits. More often they are the outcomes of complex processes in which numerous actors with differing viewpoints and stakes in the issue negotiate a response to the challenge at hand. Decisions are the products of political "pulling and hauling," and the outcomes may not be purely rational in terms of costs and benefits to the state at large.[16]

However, a more serious problem may stem from the fact that existing theories also tend to assume that the adversary's perceptions of the geostrategic situation and each party's interests match those of the coercer. Simple intuition would suggest that opponents with different histories and widely dissimilar cultures would see the world through different lenses and weigh the same set of possible outcomes differently. Put bluntly, one would assume that *culture matters*. Yet, simple as it may seem, some scholars challenge that assumption. For instance, many realists assert that, in international arena, states seek and respond to power and power speaks a universal language, one not sensitive to the subtle nuances of national distinction.[17]

So does culture factor into strategic behavior? The answer to this question is vitally important, for if culture does affect the ways that states respond to coercive threat, planners will have to adjust for these differences when designing strategies for compellence.

WHAT STRATEGIC CULTURE THEORY PROMISED—AND WHERE IT FAILED

In the 1970s, an increasing number of scholars began exploring ideas in a newly emerging field of study—strategic culture. Strategic culture theorists contend that culture conditions how states conceive and respond to the strategic environment. The movement began when concern arose that American scholars, analysts, and policy makers might be "mirror-imaging" Western values in their analyses of Soviet strategies and intentions.[18] If so, they reasoned, American national security might be in peril—strategists might be jousting in a mirror.

RAND analyst Jack Snyder launched the strategic culture movement in 1977 with an analysis of Soviet limited nuclear warfare doctrine. Snyder tried to determine why Soviet leaders seemed to exhibit a "disposition to contemplate" the use of nuclear weapons. His study included a careful discussion acknowledging the danger of using simplistic descriptions of the sociocultural characteristics of Bolshevism to explain Soviet behavior in an overly deterministic way. Yet Snyder took a precipitous step—he coined the term "strategic culture" to describe a "body of attitudes and

beliefs that guides and circumscribes thought on strategic questions, influences the way strategic issues are formulated, and sets the vocabulary
and the perceptual parameters of strategic debate."[19] His initiative inspired others to build on this theme, but to Snyder's eventual dismay,
many of those who followed him painted strategic culture with a much
broader, more deterministic brush than he had originally intended.[20]

A considerable amount of scholarship has been devoted to strategic
culture since Snyder's inaugural effort.[21] One can divide this work into
two general categories based on methodological approach. The first can
be characterized as "broad descriptive." This body of literature has accumulated since the 1970s and, as the name implies, approaches the subject by doing broad historical analyses of patterns in the strategic behavior
of specific states, attributing culturally derived causes to those patterns,
then projecting them into the future.[22] The quality of this work varies
greatly. When done well it lays bare the roots of past strategic behavior
in ways that usefully shape student and policy maker expectations of the
future. However, even at its best, it provides only limited guidance for
developing strategies aimed at achieving specific security objectives in
specific geopolitical contexts. Done poorly it creates shallow stereotypes
that can misdirect policy makers to dangerously wrong expectations
based on tautological conclusions that adversaries will always behave in
the same ways they have in the past. When that happens, strategists continue jousting in a mirror—but instead of looking at their own reflections,
they simply substitute an image of their opponent's past.

The "analytical school" of strategic culture thought that emerged in the
1990s offers an alternative to this approach. Analytical scholars use more
narrow definitions of culture and more rigorous methods for testing its
effects on specific classes of strategic behavior as they explore cases in
which rational-actor models and realist-based definitions of interest fail
to adequately explain particular choices.[23] For instance, Elizabeth Kier asserts that the French conversion to a defensive military doctrine during
the interwar period was not the result of external structures or balances
of power. It was the policy outcome of conflicting civilian and military
subcultures that limited terms of conscription while simultaneously in-
flating military assessments of the length of training required to build an
effective offensive force.[24] Kier focuses on organizational culture and believes its effects on strategic behavior are driven not by biasing a state's
objectives, as many earlier theorists asserted, but by conditioning its
decision-making processes. In other words, Kier says culture does not
affect behavior by determining values leading to strategic preferences, but
by skewing the governmental processes that produce decision outcomes.[25]

Jeffrey Legro's work is another product of the analytical school. Legro
explored why combatants in the Second World War applied different
levels of restraint when attacking merchant shipping with submarines,

bombing civilians, and using poison gas. Asserting that realist expectations would suggest that combatants should have exhibited no self-restraint whatsoever, he concluded that the differences that did occur stemmed from divergences in military organizational cultures.[26] Like Kier, Legro asserted that organizational culture acts on strategic behavior by conditioning governmental processes; but, unlike Kier, he concluded that organizational culture also plays an important role in determining a state's strategic preferences, and this too affects decision outcomes.

Alastair Iain Johnston has done some of the most methodologically rigorous work on strategic culture to date. He used cognitive mapping in an effort to model the strategic culture of China, then compared predictions developed from his model with those derived from a realpolitik, dynastic-cycle model in a statistical analysis of the Ming Dynasty's tendency to use coercive diplomacy. Johnston defined strategic culture as "an integrated system of symbols (i.e. argumentation structures, languages, analogies, metaphors, etc.) that acts to establish pervasive and long-lasting grand strategic preferences by formulating concepts of the role and efficacy of military force in interstate political affairs, and by clothing these conceptions with such an aura of factuality that the strategic preferences seem uniquely realistic and efficacious."[27]

In pointing his conception of the culture-behavior linkage to grand strategic preferences, Johnston stepped away from the process-oriented relationships favored by Kier and Legro and returned to the value-driven linkage used by earlier theorists. Concerned that this might bring him perilously close to the same pitfalls of over-determination plaguing some of the broad-descriptive scholars, he attempted to build two safeguards into his approach: first, using statistical analysis of nearly 300 cases, he attempted to measure *tendencies* toward certain behaviors rather than being forced to attribute any particular outcome to the effects of culture. Second, he sought to avoid a tautological flaw he attributed to most earlier strategic culture studies, one he believed accounted for their tendency toward over-determination. According to Johnston, most earlier theorists defined strategic culture, the independent variable in their studies, as some pattern of strategic behavior—essentially, the same phenomenon they were measuring as their dependent variable. This defect made it impossible to explain how a relatively unchanging influence such as culture could account for any substantial variance in strategic behavior, the outcome being measured. Johnston attempted to avoid this trap by focusing his definition of strategic culture on attitudes, rather than habits, traditions, or other expressions of behavior. Nevertheless, even with these safeguards, Johnston's position that strategic culture consists of pervasive and long-lasting strategic preferences leaves less room for variance in strategic choice than do organizational culture-based explanations.

Moreover, carefully constructed as Johnston's study was, his results were less than conclusive. The outcome of his analysis suggested that China had not one, but two strategic cultures—the first, a symbolic, idealized system of values that Chinese elites used to rationalize their actions; the second, an operational set of ranked preferences that actually motivated strategic choice. Unfortunately, the operational strategic culture, which Johnston called the "parabellum model," mirrored realpolitik and was almost indistinguishable from the dynastic-cycle model to which he compared it.[28]

Ironically, though Johnston made a serious effort to avoid the pitfalls he attributed to earlier studies, some of his difficulties stemmed from a methodological shortcoming he shared with all other strategic culture work done to date. Johnston and the scholars before him, in their attempts to determine culture's effects on strategic behavior, have fashioned strategic culture as an independent variable.[29] Such an approach is flawed because culture does not act independently. Culture conditions behavior, but does not motivate it. Therefore, while it is standard practice in scientific inquiry to study a given phenomenon as an independent variable, doing so cannot yield reliable results in a study of culture's effects on behavior. Any attempt to measure strategic culture's effects as an independent variable sets a methodological trap in which the outcome is either over-determined, as in the case of so many earlier studies, or bifurcated, as in Johnston's findings.[30]

Johnston concludes that he discovered a "symbolic" strategic culture because the strategic treatises he analyzed failed to yield a model that matched the "standard image of Chinese strategic thought found in much of the secondary literature."[31] Yet, neither treatises nor academic conceptions constitute strategic culture in themselves. To relate either of them to strategic culture, one must posit a mechanism that plausibly explains how the symbols and values residing in those sources produce specific decision outcomes. More importantly, even if that connection is established, those symbols and values cannot be the sole determinants of strategic behavior. Decision makers do not respond to their strategic cultures; they respond to stimuli from the strategic environment. Cultural symbols and values condition those responses by providing decision makers interpretive context, but they do not determine them. Therefore, any study attempting to discover culture's effects on strategic decision making must ascertain how symbols, values, and even culturally derived social behaviors intervene in the decision-making process as political elites respond to the world around them. Until that is accomplished, security practitioners and students of strategy will continue jousting in a mirror.

HOW THIS BOOK BREAKS THE MIRROR

While no one has yet developed a strategic culture theory that can withstand analytical scrutiny, the potential that culture may indeed condition strategic behavior has interesting implications for compellence studies. Strategic culture concepts will never replace theories that explain coercive mechanisms more directly; however, when used to enhance other constructs, culture-based analyses offer richer sources of explanation for the peculiarities of an adversary's behavior than do more linear, rational-actor models standing alone. In other words, culture-based analyses can help us to understand more fully the perplexing outcomes of past compellence efforts that, theoretically, should have succeeded, but ultimately failed or achieved only marginal success.

With these possibilities in mind, I maintain that culture does indeed affect the ways that decision-makers respond to coercive threat, and in this book, I identify the mechanisms by which culture manifests those effects. To accomplish this task, I develop a theoretical framework positing how culture affects compellence outcomes and then conduct a culture-based comparative analysis of three cases in which coercers attempted to compel a state to change its behavior. The state in question is Japan during its imperial era—that is, 1894 to 1945. The three cases are: the 1895 triple intervention in which Russia, Germany, and France forced Japanese leaders to return the Liaotung Peninsula to China following the first Sino-Japanese War; the oil embargo in which the United States, in 1941, attempted to compel Japanese leaders to withdraw their military forces from China and end their aggression on the Asian continent; and the surrender of Japan in which American leaders compelled Tokyo to end the Second World War.

There are several reasons for focusing this book on Imperial Japan and these particular cases. The first is data availability. To determine culture's role in strategic decision making, one must carefully deconstruct and examine the reasoning target leaders used to reach their decisions. That presents a challenge. Twentieth-century history offers scores of compellence cases for scholars to investigate, but rarely can one examine the detailed records of how and why target governments responded in the ways they did, nor are the leaders of those states usually available for questioning after the fact. However, the American occupation of Japan following the Second World War provided authorities and scholars a rare opportunity to examine such evidence, and numerous Japanese officials testified at length about why they behaved in the ways they did before and during the war. Of course, those sources apply mainly to the second two cases, but diplomatic records and the personal memoirs of key leaders provide clear insights into Japanese thinking during the triple intervention as well.

Another reason for choosing Japan as the object of study is the notable distinctiveness of Japanese culture. Japan is one of the most homogeneous societies in the world. Physically separated from the Asian mainland and deliberately isolated from outside influences for most of the 300 years just prior to the period of this examination, Japanese culture is unique, and most of its traits are exhibited fairly evenly in all sectors of society. One of those traits, the tendency to glorify warrior virtues, has been cited frequently by journalists and historians to explain Japan's military fanaticism during the war. Unfortunately, more times than not, writers have used this rationale in ways that can be best described as romantic. This book deliberately examines the influence that militarism and other traits had on strategic decision making, but it does so in a more rigorous manner than the subjective approaches previous analysts have employed.

As for case selection, the triple intervention, oil embargo, and surrender of Japan provide a range of bounded diversity that is ideal for a study of this nature. All are classic examples of attempted compellence—Japanese leaders are forced to respond to coercive demands levied by hostile states—yet, the outcomes differ dramatically. The first effort is brilliantly successful, the second an abysmal failure, and the third a qualified success. Other differences are also interesting. One case revolves around an escalating series of economic embargoes. The other two involve military force—subtly threatened in one instance, applied without restraint in the other. Finally, the cases encompass all three types of coercive diplomacy as defined by Alexander George and William Simons: the oil embargo is an example of "Type A" coercion, an attempt to persuade an opponent to stop short of a goal; the triple intervention typifies "Type B," an effort to persuade an adversary to undo some action; and the surrender of Japan exemplifies "Type C," an attempt to convince a target state to make changes in its government.[32] Taken together, these cases offer opportunities to determine how culture conditioned Japanese responses to a variety of coercive threats, all considered within a logical framework of compellence.

ORGANIZATION AND METHOD

This study employs a deductive analytical framework. It begins in chapter 2 wherein I develop a conceptual model of strategic culture by linking the fundamental elements of strategic decision making—perception, strategic preference, and governmental process—to the cultural factors most relevant to those elements—symbols, values, and social behaviors. Unlike previous studies, this one fashions culture as an intervening variable, one that conditions a subject's responses to external stimuli without acting independently. Chapter 3 profiles the strategic culture of Imperial Japan by applying the model developed in the previous chapter to historical data and to the ethnographic work of scholars, Japanese and Western, in fields ranging from cultural anthropology to psychiatry. Then, relating this profile back to the model, it derives 15 hypotheses about how culture might condition the way imperial Japanese leaders respond to coercive threat. I use these hypotheses to compare and analyze case study results in chapter 7.

Chapters 4, 5, and 6 are case studies. Here, the approach is mostly inductive. Culture is a pervasive phenomenon, conditioning every aspect of the way people perceive and respond to the world around them; yet, the results of this conditioning are subtle and difficult to measure. Therefore, to capture strategic culture's effects, I examine each case in a great deal more detail and using a wider time frame than do most other policy analysts. Analysis begins with a thorough account of events leading to and resulting in the compellence outcome, avoiding analytical exposition as facts are brought to light. Then, I subject the case record to interpretations based on the two major classes of compellence theory—cost-benefit analysis (the basis of punishment and denial theories) and context-oriented theory (balance of interests)—before interpreting it in terms of strategic culture. As this book does not assert that strategic culture acts independently on an adversary's behavior, it does not attempt to refute competing theories or "prove" strategic culture's validity at their expense. Instead, I use the other theories to explain case events to the extent they are capable, but point out the areas in which they have difficulty. Then, I apply the strategic culture profile to interpret this "residual variance" and further refine the explanations offered by the other schools of thought.[33]

Chapter 7 conducts the comparative analysis using the hypotheses developed earlier. Here, I compare the effects of culture across cases and then develop findings, discuss their implications, and offer a conceptual approach for incorporating culture-based analysis into the strategy development process.

THIS BOOK CONFIRMS THAT CULTURE MATTERS ... AND MORE

Clearly, strategic culture affected the ways that imperial Japanese decision-makers responded to coercive threat. It did so by conditioning their perceptions, strategic preferences, and governmental processes, causing them to act in ways that cannot be fully explained by cost-benefit analysis or theories involving the balance of interest. One can see the effects of cultural conditioning in many aspects of Japanese behavior in all three cases, but several examples are dramatic. In the triple intervention, culture manifested itself most strongly in the way Japanese leaders seemed to interpret the world order as a Confucian hierarchy, one in which they outranked their Asian neighbors, but were subordinate to the Western powers. Thus, they meekly complied with the demands of those nations they believed, at that time, were superior to them. But 46 years later, when the coercive threat evoked in Washington's 1941 oil embargo forced Japanese leaders to choose between fighting a potentially suicidal war and abandoning their conquest of China, they chose to fight. Backing down on the China policy would have entailed shelving, if not altogether abandoning Tokyo's decades-old dream of building a continental empire, a goal the nation had long internalized as a core value. Finally, as Japan neared the brink of destruction at the end of the Second World War, culturally driven misperceptions, conflicting values, and peculiarities in the decision-making process confounded Japanese leaders' efforts to seek peace for months after they realized the war was lost and had secretly agreed to end it.

In addition to the culture-related findings, this study offers several general observations about compellence and other forms of coercion. First, though we tend to think of compellence in terms of discrete cases or episodes, it is actually but one possible phase in a complex, long-term relationship between two or more governments. This relationship extends across a spectrum of coercive interaction that includes deterrence, coercive diplomacy, compellence, and war. Coercive relationships are complex and dynamic: deterrence tends to be reciprocal, and when one state raises the stakes by attempting to compel another to change its behavior, the target of that effort almost always attempts to deter the coercer from carrying out its threat. Often, a compellence target resorts to compellent strategies of its own in an effort to unhinge the original coercer's designs.

All of this suggests that schemes aimed at compelling adversaries to change their behavior should be developed as phases or subsets of broader strategies designed to manage long-term coercive relationships. Moreover, given culture's pervasive role in shaping the way decision makers conceive and respond to the strategic environment, those who craft coercive strategies should employ thorough, culture-based analyses in all their efforts. With these findings in mind, this study closes with a discussion of one possible approach for incorporating such analyses in efforts to craft coercive strategies.

WHY THIS IS IMPORTANT TO POLICY MAKERS

This book's findings are relevant today, and they will be increasingly important as we advance in the twenty-first century. A few years ago, optimistic theorists heralded the end of the Cold War as the dawn of a new and golden age of international diplomacy, one in which the threat of force would become increasingly irrelevant in dealings between nations.[34] Unfortunately, events over the ensuing years suggest that, while the emerging strategic landscape may be new, it is hardly golden. The Gulf War was a sobering event. More importantly, the numerous instances since that conflict in which force has been threatened or used to cope with the instability that followed the breakdown of bipolarity suggest compellence will be more important, rather than less, in coming years. Coercion will remain a cornerstone of diplomacy and a key tool of international security policy.[35]

Culture-based analysis can improve coercive strategies in several ways.

Understanding an adversary's strategic culture will refine the way policy makers think about how that opponent perceives the international environment. It will help policy makers better understand the value structure an adversary uses to develop its national objectives and to calculate the costs and benefits of resisting compellent challenges to those objectives. Finally, it will increase their appreciation of what socio-governmental processes an adversary must employ to respond to a compellent demand. In sum, analyses of strategic culture can guide the development of more effective coercive strategies, strategies that will be vitally important in an increasingly volatile world.

NOTES

1. For an excellent history and theoretical development of postwar strategy, see Bernard Brodie, *Strategy in the Missile Age* (Princeton, N.J.: Princeton University Press, 1991). Also see Paul Gordon Lauren, "Theories of Bargaining with Threats of Force: Deterrence and Coercive Diplomacy" in Paul G. Lauren (ed.), *Diplomacy: New Approaches in History, Theory, and Policy* (New York: The Free Press, 1979), p. 186.

2. Alexander L. George and Richard Smoke, *Deterrence in American Foreign Policy: Theory and Practice* (New York: Columbia University Press, 1974), p. 11.

3. This was the first lecture in a series entitled, "The Art of Coercion: A Study of Threats in Economic Conflict and War." See Daniel Ellsberg, "The Theory and Practice of Blackmail," (RAND P-3883, 1968).

4. Actually, it can be debated whether Ellsberg or Schelling was first to write about coercive bargaining, because Ellsberg, in the published version of his "Blackmail" lecture, acknowledged an intellectual debt to Schelling's "An Essay on Bargaining," *American Economic Review* 46, No. 3 (June 1956): pp. 281–306.

5. Thomas C. Schelling, *The Strategy of Conflict* (Cambridge, Mass.: Harvard University Press, 1960), p. 5.

6. Schelling, *Arms and Influence* (New Haven, Conn.: Yale University Press, 1966), pp. 69–71.

7. Alexander L. George, David K. Hall, and William E. Simons, *The Limits of Coercive Diplomacy: Laos, Cuba, Vietnam* (Boston: Little, Brown and Co., 1971), pp. ix–xviii.

8. See Gordon A. Craig and Alexander George, *Force and Statecraft: Diplomatic Problems of Our Time* (New York: Oxford University Press, 1983) and Alexander L. George, *Forceful Persuasion: Coercive Diplomacy as an Alternative to War* (Washington, D.C.: United States Institute of Peace, 1991). George is also often published in works assembled by diplomatic historians such as Paul G. Lauren.

9. Alexander L. George and William E. Simons, *The Limits of Coercive Diplomacy*, 2nd ed. (Boulder, Colo.: Westview Press, 1994).

10. Ibid., p. 7. George prefers to apply the expression "blackmail strategy" to offensive uses of compellence.

11. This body of work is large and varied. To name but a few examples, it includes Robert E. Osgood and Robert W. Tucker, *Force, Order, and Justice* (Balti-

more, Md.: Johns Hopkins University Press, 1967); Andrew Mack, "Why Big Nations Lose Small Wars," *World Politics* 27 (January 1975): pp. 175–200; Robert Jervis, "Why Nuclear Superiority Doesn't Matter," *Political Science Quarterly* 94 (Winter 1979): pp. 617–33; and Glenn H. Snyder and Paul Diesing, *Conflict Among Nations* (Princeton, N.J.: Princeton University Press, 1977).

12. To Pape, "coercion" and "compellence" are synonymous, and he prefers to use the former. However, to avoid confusing readers (and because it is more precise), I will use the word "compellence" in the manner Schelling conceived, even when referring to Pape's work.

13. See Robert A. Pape, Jr., "Coercive Air Power in the Vietnam War," *International Security* 15, No. 2 (Fall 1990): pp. 103–45; "Coercion and Military Strategy: Why Denial Works and Punishment Doesn't," *The Journal of Strategic Studies* 15, No. 4 (December 1992): pp. 423–75; *Bombing to Win: Air Power and Coercion in War* (Ithaca, N.Y.: Cornell University Press, 1996); and "The Limits of Precision-Guided Air Power," *Security Studies* 7, No. 2 (Winter 1997/98): pp. 93–113.

14. Pape, "Coercion and Military Strategy," p. 439.

15. Notable examples include Richard H. Schultz, Jr., "Compellence and the Role of Air Power as a Political Instrument," and John Warden, "Employing Air Power in the Twenty-first Century," in Richard H. Shultz, Jr., and Robert L. Pfaltzgraff, Jr., (eds.), *The Future of Airpower in the Aftermath of the Gulf War* (Maxwell AFB, AL: Air University Press, 1992); John Warden, "Success in Modern War: A Response to Robert Pape's Bombing to Win," *Security Studies* 7, No. 2 (Winter 1997/98): pp. 170–88; Karl Mueller, "Strategies of Coercion: Denial, Punishment, and the Future of Air Power," *Security Studies* 7, No. 3 (Spring 1998); Matthew Waxman, "Coalitions and Limits on Coercive Diplomacy," *Strategic Review* 25, No. 1 (Winter 1997): pp. 38–47 and "Emerging Intelligence Challenges," *International Journal of Intelligence and Counterintelligence* 10, No. 3 (Fall 1997): pp. 317–31; Daniel Byman, Kenneth Pollack, and Matthew Waxman, "Coercing Saddam Hussein: Lessons from the Past," *Survival* 40, No. 3 (Autumn 1998): pp. 127–51; Lawrence Freedman (ed.), *Strategic Coercion: Concepts and Cases* (Oxford: Oxford University Press, 1998); and Daniel Byman, Eric Larson, Kenneth Pollack, and Matthew Waxman, *The Coercive Use of Airpower* (Santa Monica, Calif.: RAND, 2000).

16. For the seminal work in this area see Graham T. Allison, *Essence of Decision: Explaining the Cuban Missile Crisis* (New York: Harper Collins Publishers, 1971). For a detailed examination of how complex governmental processes frustrated U.S. compellence efforts during the Vietnam War see Wallace Theis, *When Governments Collide: Coercion and Diplomacy in the Vietnam Conflict* (Berkeley, Calif.: University of California Press, 1980).

17. Kenneth Waltz's formulation of neorealist theory has had a profound influence on the field of international relations and, in turn, security studies. Waltz and his many followers are explicit in asserting that the structure of the international system determines the nature of states and defines the possibilities for conflict and cooperation between them. See Kenneth N. Waltz, *Theory of International Politics* (Reading, Mass.: Addison-Wesley, 1979).

18. Ken Booth, *Strategy and Ethnocentrism* (New York: Holmes & Meier Publishers, Inc., 1979).

19. Jack Snyder, *The Soviet Strategic Culture: Implications for Nuclear Options* (RAND R-2154-AF, 1977).

20. Vague, pervasive definitions and overly deterministic linkages between culture and behavior had characterized much of the strategic culture work done to date. Frustrated with that trend, Snyder disavowed the strategic culture movement in 1990. He insisted the latter efforts had distorted his original concept, which was not linked to any sense of national distinctiveness but referred, instead, to a tendency of strategic approaches to persist beyond the conditions that gave rise to them. See Jack Snyder, "The Concept of Strategic Culture: Caveat Emptor" in Carl G. Jacobsen, ed., *Strategic Power: USA/USSR* (New York: St. Martin's Press, 1990), pp. 3–9.

21. For an exhaustive review of the strategic culture literature up to 1995, see Alastair Iain Johnston, *Cultural Realism: Strategic Culture and Grand Strategy in Chinese History* (Princeton, N.J.: Princeton University Press, 1995), pp. 4–22.

22. Notable examples include Russell F. Weigley, *The American Way of War: A History of United States Military Strategy and Policy* (Bloomington, Ind.: Indiana University Press, 1973); Colin Gray, *Nuclear Strategy and National Style* (Lanham, Md.: Hamilton Press, 1986) and *War, Peace, and Victory: Strategy and Statecraft for the Next Century* (New York: Simon and Schuster, 1990); and David R. Jones, "Soviet Strategic Culture," in Carl Jacobsen, ed., *Strategic Power: USA/USSR.* Most recently, Colin Gray has included a chapter on strategic culture in his *Modern Strategy* (Oxford: Oxford University Press, 1999) and Ken Booth and Russell Trood have edited a book entitled *Strategic Cultures in the Asia-Pacific Region* (New York: St. Martin's Press, 1999).

23. While this review focuses mainly on academic work done under the moniker "strategic culture," I should point out that a parallel body of literature called "constructivism" has emerged in the field of international relations. Proposing that shared norms and identities shape state behavior in ways that defy neorealist and neoliberal paradigms, much of this scholarship overlaps work done in strategic culture, and several scholars have published in both communities. For examples of constructivism in security studies, see Peter J. Katzenstein (ed.), *The Culture of National Security: Norms and Identity in World Politics* (New York: Columbia University Press, 1996). Also see Alexander Wendt, *Social Theory of International Politics* (Cambridge: Cambridge University Press, 1999); Thomas Risse, Stephen C. Ropp, and Kathryn Sikkink (eds.), *The Power of Human Rights: International Norms and Domestic Change* (Cambridge: Cambridge University Press, 1999).

24. Elizabeth Kier, *Imagining War: French and British Military Doctrine Between the Wars* (Princeton, N.J.: Princeton University Press, 1997) and "Culture and Military Doctrine: France Between the Wars," *International Security* 19, No. 4 (Spring 1995): pp. 65–93.

25. Kier, "Culture and Military Doctrine," pp. 79–80.

26. Jeffrey W. Legro, *Cooperation Under Fire: Anglo-German Restraint During World War II* (Ithaca, N.Y.: Cornell University Press, 1995).

27. Johnston, *Cultural Realism*, p. 36.

28. Ibid., p. x.

29. This methodological structure is explicit in Johnston's work and implicit in most of the studies that preceded him.

30. Actually, Johnston is but one of several authors who, on discovering that statements by policy elites frequently do not match operational doctrines, have concluded that states may have more than one strategic culture. For instance,

Reginald Stuart observed that U.S. politicians often play on the American popular self-image as a nation that abhors war, but one that will fight a moral crusade if sufficiently provoked. Yet, Stuart said this popular conception is largely mythical as the empirical record reveals that the United States frequently uses force in a Clausewitzean manner to achieve policy ends. He concludes that the United States has two strategic cultures—one moralistic and one based on realpolitik. Bradley Klein and Robin Luckham go even further in asserting that policy elites manipulate popular conceptions of strategic culture to their own nefarious ends. Klien describes strategic culture as a way in which states legitimize violence against putative enemies. Luckham, alternatively, takes ethnicity out of the argument, insisting strategic culture is a cross-national construct that strategists, statesmen, soldiers, and arms manufacturers use to justify global industrialization, militarization, and capitalization. See Reginald C. Stuart, *War and American Thought: From the Revolution to the Monroe Doctrine* (Kent, Ohio: Kent State University Press, 1982), pp. 282–94; Bradley Klein, "Hegemony and Strategic Culture: American Power Projection and Alliance Defense Politics," *Review of International Studies* 14 (1988): pp. 133–48; Robin Luckham, "Armament Culture," *Alternatives* 10, No. 1 (1984): pp. 1–44.

31. Johnston, *Cultural Realism*, p. 61.

32. To be more precise, the oil embargo encompasses elements of Type A and B coercive diplomacy. From the late 1930s until they resorted to the embargo, American leaders persistently attempted to persuade Japan to stop short of its goal of continental expansion. When Washington finally invoked the embargo, American leaders escalated to Type B coercion—trying to compel Tokyo to withdraw from China and thus undo an action already achieved. See Alexander L. George and William E. Simons, *The Limits of Coercive Diplomacy*, 2nd ed. (Boulder, Colo.: Westview Press, 1994), pp. 7–9.

33. In employing this method of analysis, I do not suggest that culture is a "residual cause" of state behavior, one that only has effect when other causes are absent. As I said, culture conditions every aspect of the way people perceive and respond to the world around them. However, the effects of culture can only be measured when they differ from those one would expect to see from other causes.

34. For instance, see John E. Mueller, *Retreat from Doomsday: The Obsolescence of Major War* (New York: Basic Books, Inc., 1989).

35. For an discussion on the growing emphasis on compellence in the post–Cold War world, see Richard H. Shultz, Jr., "Compellence and the Role of Air Power as a Political Instrument," in Richard H. Shultz, Jr., and Robert L. Pfaltzgraff, Jr. (eds.), *The Future of Air Power in the Aftermath of the Gulf War* (Maxwell AFB, AL.: Air University Press, 1992), pp. 171–91.

CHAPTER 2

Culture and Strategic Behavior

All notions of strategic culture are fashioned on the premise that culture somehow affects strategic behavior. While many people accept this supposition at face value, efforts to confirm and explain those effects are fraught with difficulty. First, manifestations of culture are hard to measure because the concept itself is a vague and troubled one. Much of this trouble stems from the breadth and ubiquitous nature of the various phenomena attributed to culture, but other factors have compounded the problem. In 1908, Franz Boas, one of the founders of American cultural anthropology, observed, "the field work of the anthropologist is more or less accidental and originated because other sciences occupied part of the ground before the development of modern anthropology."[1] This feeling of shared ground—or, more accurately, contested ground—has persisted throughout the twentieth century, so that the study of culture is one in which scholars in several disciplines have staked competing claims.[2] Due to this contentious scholarship, one can find hundreds of definitions of culture in diverse bodies of academic literature.[3]

Even so, these many definitions tend to merge on an understanding that culture is some collection of shared ideas that creates meaning within a social group, and many conceptions posit that cultural groups also share patterns of social behavior, that is, customs. Yet this convergence does little to set the boundaries of culture or explain what, if anything, it does. For culture seems to operate in multiple spheres simultaneously, even among the same individuals. People may share a national culture yet identify with regional subgroups that rally to different symbols. The same individuals may share ideas and customs with members of like socioeconomic, professional, or religious groups even when those groups cross regional or national boundaries. Given this complexity, it is sometimes difficult to attribute an individual's ideas or motives to any particular culture.

To complicate the issue further, it is hard to differentiate the inputs and mechanisms of culture from its outcomes and artifacts. Is culture both ideational and behavioral, or are the habits and customs so often depicted as culture merely behavioral artifacts of shared, value-laden ideas?[4] If culture does indeed encompass patterns of behavior, are these patterns also sources of culture, products of culture, or methods by which culture is transmitted from one generation to the next? Academic opinions divide on these questions, and some even maintain that culture is all of these things.[5] Such boundary issues are important if one is to avoid tautological flaws in analysis—just where does one draw the line between what a culture *is* and what culture *does?*

Disentangling culture from other purported causes of behavior may be even more difficult. Constructivists, such as Alexander Wendt, maintain that culture and related ideational constructs have much greater influence on strategic behavior than do such "rump" factors as physical and biological constraints or other structural elements in the political environment.[6] On the other hand, Jack Snyder argues that, "a rich body of research on war by anthropologists suggests that ideas and culture are best understood not as autonomous but as embedded in complex social systems shaped by the interaction of material circumstances, institutional arrangements, and strategic choices, as well as by ideas and culture."[7] That may be so, but even that literature is contentious regarding how much influence culture has on strategic behavior, vis-à-vis material-environmental and institutional factors, and how culture relates to such structural elements in decision-making processes.[8]

These many uncertainties present a formidable challenge for any attempt to determine how culture affects the ways that states respond to coercive threat, but the challenge is not insurmountable. This chapter develops a theoretical framework that bounds culture in terms of its relevance to strategic decision making and models its relationship to the behavior of states. It begins by examining the fundamental characteristics of culture, focusing on those elements most widely accepted by cultural anthropologists. It then buttresses this foundation with parallel work done by cognitive psychologists that explains how knowledge structures such as cultural symbols shape human perception and condition individual and group behavior. Yet, simply describing culture's effects on human behavior does not explain how it conditions the strategic behavior of states. Therefore, this chapter examines culture's role in translating personal preferences to organizational decisions and defines strategic culture by modeling how culture's ideational and behavioral elements intervene in governmental processes as a state formulates responses to stimuli arriving from the strategic environment. As this theoretical framework assembles, the boundaries of strategic culture will emerge and ways to differentiate its effects from those of other causes of strategic behavior will become clear.

A FUNDAMENTAL CONCEPTION OF CULTURE

Culture may be vague, but it is not mysterious. Though scholars disagree about precise definitions, even a brief survey of the academic literature reveals a common understanding of what culture is and allows us to make several generalizations about its fundamental characteristics. First, culture resides in patterns of thought—it is a way of thinking, feeling, and believing. It is a system of values and attitudes, preserved and transmitted through a commonly accepted set of symbols—that is, a collection of phrases, gestures, analogies, metaphors, argumentation structures, and other "vehicles of thought" that a self-identifying social group or "in-group" shares and interprets with similar meaning.[9] As such, culture provides a lens through which group members interpret stimuli from their environment, and it supplies the criteria by which they form preferences and structure priorities. Put more simply, by coloring an individual's perceptions and supplying the values he or she uses when deciding what is important, culture helps determine what outcome that person will prefer in a given situation.

Cultural is not congenital. People acquire patterns of thought from other members of the group through processes of formal and informal education.[10] Consequently, history is a central element in the development and evolution of culture. The repertoire of ideas that comprise culture is a shared interpretation of the common experiences of a group over time. As Kroeber and Kluckhohn wrote, " . . . culture is a precipitate of history. In more than one sense, 'history is a sieve.'"[11] Geography in turn plays an important role in the development of national and regional cultures, as climate, resources, fertility, and exposure to or insularity from security threats shape the history of every people.[12] Likewise, structural factors, such as resource availability, institutional strictures, and degrees of organizational autonomy, condition the cultures that develop in smaller groups. Many of these environmental factors may be relatively unchanging, and some are even fixed; yet culture is not rigid. As a group's experiences accumulate, its culture changes. These changes are rarely sudden—the evolution of culture is usually slow and often imperceptible—but it is important to understand that culture is not static. As Issa Boullata explains:

The culture of any human group is its collective experience in time. As the group moves in time from generation to generation, it continuously meets with new needs that challenge it. The response of the group shapes its experience of reality, which in turn, adds to its culture. The group learns to acquire new cultural elements and discard others, so that its culture continues to develop in the service of group survival and enhancement. Culture is thus continually changing and accommodating the group's institutions, beliefs, and values, to its ever-rising needs, both material and otherwise. Certain cultures may be more open to change than others. But there is no culture that does not change unless it is a dead culture— i.e., an archaeologically reconstructed culture of an extinct group.[13]

While the ideational piece of culture is undisputed, many anthropologists maintain that culture also resides in patterns of behavior.[14] They point to such culturally distinctive social institutions as religion, language, family structure, and even daily social interaction as evidence that behavior is a part of culture and not simply a product of cultural ideas.[15] Indeed, behavior may play an important subliminal role in the way people share those ideas. Nick Enfield argues:

Private representations, especially with relation to cultural practices, are not merely 'cognitive'. Practices are to a great extent, and perhaps primarily, *embodied*. [His emphasis.] Many practices must be learned by the body—consider what is involved in driving a car, plucking a chicken, or dancing. . . . While exotic rituals may indeed be rare, it is quite clear that the 'implicit routines of daily life' remain replete with elaborate ritual . . . Through such mundane and incessant but potent culture-specific ritual behavior (greeting, parting, proxemics, socialization routines, etiquette, phatic communion, discourse conventions, etc.), cultural knowledge and/or assumptions are indeed explicitly (but not always consciously) spelled out.[16]

Though such a position is far from universally accepted, identifying customs as a fundamental element of culture is useful for this study, as social interaction is integral to governmental decision making.[17]

Though culture is a difficult concept to define precisely, scholars largely agree on the general nature of the phenomenon in question, how it forms, how it is transmitted from one generation to the next, and how it changes. Culture is an interdependent collection of symbols, values, attitudes, beliefs, habits, and customs that a self-identifying group develops over time and shares through a common and evolving interpretation of its own historical experience. These shared ideas and behaviors lend meaning to events that people experience and condition their responses to those events by providing the values they use to rank alternative outcomes. Such generalizations are widely accepted, but one might question what empirical foundation they have beyond the "interpretive" ethnographic analyses that Clifford Geertz and other anthropologists have performed.[18] Interestingly, cognitive psychologists have done work that supports anthropology's conjectures about customs and symbols, and their efforts are grounded in controlled experiments.

SCRIPTS, SCHEMAS, AND THE POWER OF SYMBOLS

Cognitive psychology is a broad field of research that seeks to determine how the human mind works. Among the many questions that interest psychologists are how the mind detects, selects, and processes sensory information; how short- and long-term memories are structured and how they work; and how the mind handles such complex processes as language, imagery, and problem solving. While most research in this discipline has focused on understanding the mental functions and pathologies of individuals, starting in the early 1980s a growing number of scholars began examining the psychological roots of organizational behavior. As Richard Schott points out, "this effort has proved quite fruitful, for organizations are, next to the family, the central stage on which adult life is played out and individual psycho-dynamic characteristics displayed."[19] One should readily see the parallels between this work and culture studies and grasp its importance in providing a basis for understanding how culture conditions individual and group behavior.

Among the major issues that cognitive psychologists have debated is whether the mind processes information in a bottom-up format or one that is more top-down. The notion of bottom-up or molecular processing envisions the mind operating in a serial fashion detecting, selecting, processing, and storing one piece of information at a time. Conversely, top-down or modal processing concepts focus on "how the mind frames and interprets sensory experience, with special attention to what the individual brings to the interpretation of a situation and to the context in which it occurs."[20] Most psychologists now agree that the human mind's complex operations encompass both molecular and modal processing. Moreover, there is growing consensus that though some aspects of conscious thought may be serial, modal processing plays an important role in selecting which sensory stimuli the conscious mind will commit to its molecular processing functions—that is, in directing attention—and in providing the conscious mind interpretive templates that both filter and bias its serial processing operations.[21]

These complex filtering and interpretive processes have developed because the conscious mind's serial operation cannot handle the thousands of sensory inputs it receives each instant nor can it afford to recalculate anew all the complex machinations required to complete routine, repetitive functions. Each moment our minds are bombarded with multiple stimuli from our five physical senses, not to mention all the thoughts, memories, and fantasies that percolate at a semiconscious level, striving to be heard. The mind must have mechanisms for focusing its attention and concentrating its reasoning faculties. Likewise, everyday we do hundreds of repetitive functions, some as simple as tying our shoes, others as complex as ordering dinner at a restaurant. Rethinking all these activities at each iteration and consciously deciding each intermediary step would overwhelm our cognitive resources. To streamline these operations, we develop what psychologists call "scripts," preestablished mental constructs that spell out action sequences our minds call up when recognizing appropriate cues.[22] When an individual thinks of eating out, she does not consciously plan to open the restaurant door, select a table, open the menu, choose an entrée, et cetera.[23] The "eating-out" concept flashes to mind in one "chunk" of information. Through repetition, such actions become familiar—the mind stores information from experience and will recall a composite thought pattern when it detects a cue related to dining out. As a result, the reasoning process becomes more automatic as modal scripts focus and guide the conscious mind's serial operations.[24] Mental scripts largely explain the psychological workings of what anthropologists and sociologists call "habits" and "customs."

While the script concept is an important bridge between cognitive psychology and anthropology, a more fundamental knowledge structure linking culture to the mechanics of thought is what psychologists call a "schema."[25] Schemas are complex models or "cognitive maps" buried deep in our subconscious that "guide the processing of new information and the retrieval of stored information."[26] They are modal templates the mind uses to select, organize, and process sensory data. They bring patterns of past experience stored in memory to bear on current information, giving that information meaning. Schemas begin forming in early childhood starting with and building on such basic psycho-emotional knowledge structures as bonds to parents, gender roles, and racial stereotypes.[27] Over the course of a lifetime, individuals develop thousands of schemas providing a storehouse of canned understandings about a wide range of concepts. Indeed, David Rummelhart maintains that schemas are the very "building blocks of cognition . . . the fundamental elements upon which all information processing depends."[28] Most importantly, what psychologists call schemas by and large describes the knowledge structures underpinning those phrases, gestures, analogies, metaphors, argumentation structures, and other "vehicles of thought" that anthropologists call symbols.[29]

Given that schema and symbol are closely related terms, it is important to understand the ways that schemas constrain perception and bias rational thought. Like scripts, schemas serve as filters to limit the flow of data that the conscious mind apprehends.[30] When a sensory event stimulates mental function, the mind sorts and evaluates that data against patterns of information residing in its catalog of existing schemas. If some salient characteristic of the event appears to match one in an established pattern, it cues that schema and its programmed meaning becomes attached to the stimulus.[31] Beyond that, the mind draws additional pieces of information from the schema not present in the event itself, giving the individual, rightly or wrongly, a fuller understanding of what is happening.[32] On the other hand, if the incoming data do not match any existing schema, the mind frequently discards the information and it escapes conscious apprehension. In fact, schemas may be central operators in the classic defense mechanism of repression that Sigmund Freud first elaborated. Experiments have demonstrated that the mind seems to sublimate those patterns strongly connected with feelings of anxiety, guilt, or pain.[33] But a more serious problem, and one that probably occurs more frequently, is that incoming data may have traits that are substantially irrelevant, but prominent enough to capture attention, thus cueing inappropriate schemas. Then individuals misperceive the stimulus, fill in data gaps with incorrect information, and draw incorrect conclusions about what is happening.[34]

Such misconceptions are heightened when perceived events cue scripts and schemas that are laden with strong emotion. Indeed, psychologists are increasingly convinced that emotion (or "affect," as they call it) is an integral part of both memory and cognition. Many schemas seem to be stored with strong emotional elements imprinted on them. When those knowledge structures are cued, "hot cognitions" occur as the conscious mind experiences afresh the emotions associated with the events that created or reinforced those patterns.[35] In fact, research conducted in the field of neuroscience suggests that emotion plays so strong a role in mental function that associative learning and short-term memory are severely impaired when physical links between structures in the limbic system, the network that controls emotional arousal, are severed.[36] Such cognitive and neurological research on schemas supports the anthropological supposition that beliefs are strongly held, interrelated systems of emotion-laden symbols; likewise, attitudes may well be semiconscious cognitive networks associating those symbols with one's evaluation of the schematic meanings behind them.[37] If so, then the stronger an attitude's emotional content, the more resilient that pattern and its underlying schemas may be to changing in the face of contrary evidence.[38]

Yet, scripts and schemas, like habits, customs, and symbols, are not immutable—people learn and cultures change. With effort, you can learn to tie your shoes differently, and you can change your mental image of eating-out by regularly patronizing establishments that employ procedures with which you are unfamiliar. For instance, if you are normally an upscale restaurant diner, you can switch to all-you-can-eat buffets. For a while, your actions will be awkward and slow. You will likely make mistakes like knotting your shoelace or forgetting whether you are expected to pay before going through the buffet line or after you finish eating; but you can cast off old habits and learn new ones if you really want to.[39] Schemas change too. When the mind calls up an inappropriate schema and perceives an event incorrectly, the individual's wrong conclusions lead to inappropriate behavior and produce cognitive dissonance. If this happens repeatedly, the mind gradually modifies existing schemas or creates new ones to accommodate these experiences.[40] However, these fundamental knowledge structures are more resilient than scripts, so they change more slowly. Patterns embedded deep in the unconscious and reinforced throughout a lifetime are the most persistent. All of this suggests that, while individuals may be able to embrace or discard organizational cultures somewhat freely, thus accommodating movements from one organization to another, national cultures will be more enduring, particularly in societies that implant cultural symbols deep in their members' psyches through a lifetime of consistent religious indoctrination and orchestrated historical interpretation.

This does not suggest, however, that all members of a society will think exactly alike or react identically to the same stimuli, even in cultures with powerful symbols. Every individual has different interests and capabilities and has accumulated a unique series of personal experiences. As a result, people may share a common interpretation of prominent cultural symbols, but each person's mind will also contain innumerable scripts and schemas unique to his or her life experiences. In sum, culture does not determine behavior—ultimately, individuals and groups have free agency—but it does provide common lenses, values, and customs that tend to bind and harmonize their responses when shared scripts and schemas are cued. When an "out-group" actor in the strategic environment threatens a cohesive system of self-identifying in-groups—that is, a nationalist state—that threat may well cue some powerful, emotion-laden knowledge structures that those groups hold in common.

FROM CULTURE TO STRATEGIC CULTURE

While the foregoing discussion lays a theoretical foundation explaining how culture affects the ways that individuals and groups perceive and react to the world around them, it does not explain how these shared perceptions, preferences, and behaviors influence how states make strategic decisions. Such a linkage might be easy to envision if states were unitary actors—that is, if each government consisted of a single individual, perceiving the strategic environment through a single lens and acting on personal preferences drawn from his own culturally-shaped interpretation of his country's unique historical experience. However, that is rarely, if ever, the case. Ever-growing bodies of literature in the fields of government and organization theory maintain that, even in authoritarian regimes, state policies are rarely the products of a single actor. Rather, they are negotiated agreements between ever-shifting constellations of power brokers within the regime—elected or appointed political leaders, civil and military bureaucrats, legislators, interest groups, et cetera—each of whom brings different interests, perceptions, and preferences to the policy debate.[41] All of these individuals and groups may share a common set of cultural symbols and customs, but they also see the world through the narrower lenses of their own organizational cultures, and they all have personal and organizational interests to serve.

Therefore, in order to understand how culture conditions a state's strategic behavior, one must establish how it interacts in these complex governmental processes and affects their outcomes. The first step to such a determination is to compress the boundaries of culture into some finite set of factors that can be identified and, if not precisely measured, at least concisely described. The loose collection of symbols, values, attitudes, beliefs, habits, and customs that comprise the general conception of culture is too broad and vague to be of much analytical value. Moreover, as psychologists have discovered, these factors are not mutually exclusive. Attitudes and beliefs are interrelated systems of value-laden knowledge structures residing in varying levels of consciousness. Likewise, habits and customs are both scripted patterns of behavior, differentiated by little more than levels of complexity and awareness. Therefore, for the sake of analytical clarity, one can reasonably collapse these concepts down to their fundamental elements, the ones most deeply rooted in the human psyche: symbols, values, and customs. While such an approach may be reductionist, it is defensible because, not only are these three factors more easy to identify and describe than such ephemeral conceptions as attitudes and beliefs, they are less transitory in nature. Having pared the notion of culture down to a manageable construct, we can now examine how its elements interact in governmental decision-making processes. Then the mechanism by which culture conditions strategic behavior will become apparent.

In inquiries of this nature, it is sometimes helpful to examine the problem from the inside out—that is, to identify the abstract conceptual elements of governmental decision making, then to determine which factors of culture interact with them most directly.[42] Starting from the most general consideration, we must observe that the cardinal function relating culture to decision making is *governmental process*. Although it may seem too obvious to mention, governmental process is the engine of strategic decision in any state, regardless of its form of administration. If culture in some way influences a state's governmental process—and, for the sake of theory, one must presume it does—that influence will affect decisions the state produces. But it is not enough simply to say that culture conditions strategic behavior through this one intervening variable; we must identify the other variables involved in the linkage mechanism.

A second connection between culture and strategic behavior is *strategic preference*. Strategic preference is the prioritized list of desires decision makers develop, explicitly or implicitly, when considering conditions in the security environment that may impact their long- or short-term goals. For example, when a new political situation surfaces in a state's geographical region—let us say, a neighboring government falls, or one nation declares war on another—decision makers weigh these developments in terms of whether they enhance or jeopardize their own political and security objectives. The product of this evaluation, whether done formally or informally, is a prioritized list of outcomes each power broker would like to see result from that situation. This list of preferences is a key input to strategic decision making.

It is important to note that strategic preference is both an input for and a product of governmental process. At any given time, a state has a working set of strategic preferences that political elites consciously or unconsciously consider in their decision-making functions. These preferences in turn are modified through governmental processes, as new conditions develop, in order to take advantage of new opportunities or avoid new dangers. Therefore, strategic preference and governmental process are key intervening variables between culture and strategic behavior. But there is still one piece of the mechanism missing—*perception*.

Perception is the filter and lens through which decision makers interpret inputs from the environment around them. It defines the way they see their world. Perception lends meaning to external stimuli, thereby conditioning the evaluation of that data as political elites assess the impacts of new developments on their strategic preferences.[43] For instance, if a new government comes to power in a neighboring country, decision makers may calculate the resultant dangers or opportunities quite differently, depending on whether they perceive the new regime as politically compatible or incompatible, friendly or hostile, et cetera. Consequently, perception works in conjunction with strategic preference and governmental process in conditioning strategic behavior. But just how does this mechanism link to culture?

If one considers the general description of culture presented in the foregoing section, the linkage begins to emerge. First, culture determines how individuals and groups perceive the external environment. It establishes and defines the lexicon of symbols and signals by which members of a society acquire, transmit, and interpret knowledge. Policy elites cannot perceive the world around them or interpret stimuli arriving from the strategic environment without this mental catalog of knowledge structures. It literally defines the reality of their world. Culture also plays a role in defining strategic preferences. By drawing from religious, philosophical, and historical sources, it provides the value system that policy makers use to rank alternatives when they perceive opportunities or threats in the strategic environment. Finally, culture frames the patterns of social interaction that condition governmental processes. A particular government may be authoritarian or egalitarian, centralized or federated, but the ways that individuals and groups within that state relate to one another is largely determined by culture. Indeed, decision-making processes are particularly sensitive to social custom. Interpersonal dynamics in more egalitarian societies will differ greatly from those in which relationships are rigidly structured along hierarchical lines based on age, gender, class, or some other social discriminator. Likewise, societies that esteem charismatic leadership or majority rule will exhibit different governmental dynamics than those that value achieving consensus when facing important decisions. Fortunately, these kinds of traits lend themselves well to analytical profiling—with diligent effort, a strategic culture analyst can identify, map, and catalog most any prospective adversary's prominent symbols, values, and customs and draw some reasonable inferences of how that actor might respond to certain stimuli.

It is important to understand, however, that the mechanism linking culture to strategic behavior is not, in the real world, as straightforward as the foregoing description implies. No society is made up of a single, homogeneous culture; each is a "composite of varying and overlapping subcultures," representing differences in "locale, economic status, occupation, clique groups—or varying combinations of these factors."[44] Though perceptions and strategic preferences may be derived from symbols and values common to a greater culture, the interpretation of those elements may vary from group to group depending on their informational vantage points, other values and symbols that differentiate each subculture, and each group's stakes in any given decision. Once again, strategic behavior is an outcome of decisions negotiated in an often contentious process of political give and take, and conflicting subcultures contribute to that strife.[45]

Even so, there are factors that frequently mitigate variations between subcultures within a society. First, although perception and value interpretation may differ between domestic groups, these differences are usually small when compared to differences in perception and value across the boundaries of national cultures. Because each subculture perceives much of the information it receives using symbols drawn from the culture at large, the range of perception tends to be circumscribed similarly from group to group. Consequently, though different groups within a society may prefer different responses to a strategic challenge, they all tend to choose from the same set of alternatives, ignoring others that groups acculturated in dissimilar societies might consider viable. Finally, though interests may vary from group to group, serious external threats often unify those groups, prompting them to forego parochial concerns, at least for the duration of the crisis, to protect higher values held by the society at large. In sum, while political decisions may, indeed, be negotiated outcomes of competing groups, culture tends to homogenize the preferences and perceptions of those groups. Consequently, even when subcultures clash, the greater culture from which they are drawn conditions strategic behavior by circumscribing the range of strategic options a society conceives, harmonizing the valuation that contending leaders put on alternatives within that field, and structuring the terms of social interaction leaders use to choose from those alternatives.

Given this basic mechanism linking culture to strategic behavior, a working definition of strategic culture emerges by combining the relevant factors of culture with the intervening variables that link them to strategic behavior:

Strategic culture is an integrated system of shared symbols, values, and customs that, working through perceptions, preferences, and governmental processes, impose a degree of order on the ways that policy makers conceive and respond to the strategic environment.

This definition focuses on those elements of culture specifically relevant to strategic behavior. It defines strategic culture as a system of societal factors *and* the intervening variables through which they operate to influence strategic decision making. It is important to note, however, that while the foregoing discussion implicitly casts culture in the role of independent variable in order to derive the mechanism linking it to strategic behavior, culture does not act independently. While cultural symbols may color policy makers' perceptions of the external environment, they do not create that environment or produce the stimuli that arrive from there. While culturally rooted values may influence the formulation of strategic preferences, they do not invent the conditions calling for alternative options to prefer. Though culture-based patterns of social interaction may condition the governmental processes that generate strategic decisions, culture does not initiate those processes. In sum, culture does not drive behavior. Consequently, to conduct any serious examination of culture's role in strategic behavior, one must structure the analysis in a way that depicts that role most accurately. To do that, one must fashion culture as an intervening variable.[46]

MEASURING THE EFFECTS OF STRATEGIC CULTURE

Strategic culture intervenes between the variables that comprise stimuli from the strategic environment on the one hand, and a government's response to those stimuli on the other. As this book is about measuring the effects of this intervening variable on a government's response to attempted compellence, that response will be the dependent variable in each of the cases it examines. However, it is important to remember that this project involves measuring those effects from the perspectives of three different compellence theories; therefore, it will employ several different independent variables in various stages of interpretation in each examination.

For instance, when studying strategic culture's effect on the target's response to compellence from a standpoint of punishment theory, the independent variable consists of the compellent demand enforced by some form of punishment. The dependent variable is the government's response to that compellent demand, as conditioned by the intervening variable, strategic culture. As punishment and denial theories both suggest that political elites employ some form of cost-benefit analysis in their decision calculations, I can depict strategic culture's effects in a denial scenario using the same model. The only difference is that denial is substituted for punishment in the description of the independent variable (see Figure 2.1).

As Figure 2.1 illustrates, the target government can only act on the coercer's message through the linkage of strategic culture. To do that, the stimulus must be translated through a filter composed of cultural symbols into perceptions, and weighed in terms of the values held by that government's policy elites. (This operation is largely subliminal and can be quite rapid if information about the stimulus is readily available.) The government then begins the process of determining what response will best serve its strategic preferences. The formal structure of that process is a function of the target nation's form of government. Nevertheless, the individuals and groups involved in the decision-making process carry out their delib-

Figure 2.1
Model Relating Punishment or Denial to Compellence Outcome through the Intervening Variable, Strategic Culture

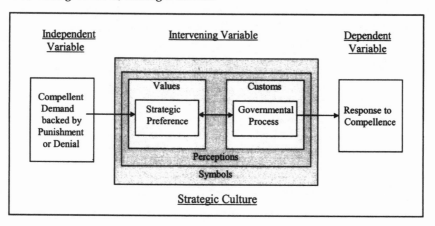

erations within a social framework created by the shared scripts that comprise their decision-making customs.

Efforts to link compellence inputs to outcomes using a balance of interest theory result in a model that is a bit more complex.[47] As Figure 2.2 illustrates, the linkage between strategic culture and compellence outcome remains the same; but, because balance of interest theories address a much broader range of factors than do punishment or denial theories, the model must be expanded to account for these additional process and contextual variables.

Figure 2.2 depicts this expanded model. The independent variable is still compellent demand, but the balance of interest theory forces one to consider how factors in the coercer's political situation—the clarity of that state's objectives, the terms it will accept in settlement, its leaders' strength and level of motivation, and its degree of domestic and international support—condition that demand. Interestingly, the theory also addresses contextual variables in the strategic environment and, more importantly, how target-state leaders perceive them. This model depicts that function in the gray box feeding into perceptions, where the strategic environment and

Figure 2.2
Model Relating Compellent Demand to Compellence Outcome through the Intervening Variable, Strategic Culture, with Process and Contextual Variables Addressed in Balance of Interest Theory

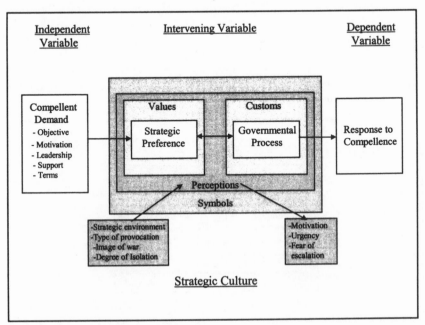

type of provocation as well as the target state's image of war and degree
of isolation all factor into that government's assessment of each party's
level of motivation and sense of urgency, and its own fear of escalation.
All these process and contextual variables, along with the independent
variable, are translated into the perceptions that constitute the target government's impression of the world as it weighs its strategic options and
decides how to respond to the coercer's demands.

It is important to appreciate the utility and analytical clarity these models provide. First, depicting strategic culture as an intervening variable
eliminates the confusion apparent in previous studies in which analysts
fashioned culture either as an independent variable, thus driving strategic
behavior in an over-determined manner, or as a pattern of strategic behavior itself, thus conflating their independent and dependent variables.
This theoretical construct also makes it possible to examine what effects
culture's behavioral elements have on decision outcomes without conflating those two classes of behavior—decision-making customs and resultant decisions—in a tautological mire. Finally, fashioning culture as a
variable that intervenes between stimuli arriving from the strategic environment and the state's responses to those stimuli enables analysts to
vary inputs to the models and thereby examine the potential impacts of
a range of independent variables. Such a capability makes it possible to
develop and test a variety of alternative coercive strategies. By applying
this theoretical construct to historical cases, a diligent analyst can disen-
tangle the effects of culture from other causes of strategic behavior by
carefully tracing the state's decision-making process and noting where
policy elites' perceptions, preferences, and ultimate decisions diverge
from objective rational expectations (or those drawn from values outside
the target society) and more closely resemble predictions drawn from a
strategic culture profile of that society's symbols, values, and customs.

Thus, having developed a bounded theoretical construct of strategic
culture, what remains for this book to accomplish is to identify those symbols, values, and customs that comprised the strategic culture of Imperial
Japan and then to determine whether such a profile can help explain the
ways that Japanese leaders responded to coercive threat. I embark on the
first of those tasks in the next chapter.

NOTES

1. Levi-Straus echoed this observation when he said, "How did anthropology
come into being? It made itself out of all kinds of refuse and left-overs from other
fields." See Robert Borofsky (ed.), *Assessing Cultural Anthropology* (New York: Mc-
Graw Hill, 1994), p. 2.

2. For more on culture's "contested ground," see Roger H. Keesling, "Theories
of Culture Revisited," in Borofsky, p. 308.

3. In 1950, A. L. Kroeber and Clyde Kluckhohn cited more that 150 separate definitions of culture drawn from the fields of anthropology, sociology, psychology, psychiatry, chemistry, economics, geography, and political science. Since then, the list has grown to include definitions from an even wider field including those from strategic culture theorists. See A.L. Kroeber and Clyde Kluckhohn, *Culture: A Critical Review of Concepts and Definitions* (New York: Vintage Books, 1963), p. 76.

4. For instance, is the obsessive bowing observed in some Asian societies a cultural trait in itself, or is it a behavior caused by a Confucian culture that values group harmony and confrontation avoidance? Early anthropologists such as Kroeber, Kluckhohn, and Jack Goody usually defined culture to include patterns of behavior. Some later scholars narrowed their definitions to ideational factors such as values and symbols. Likewise, early strategic culture theorists such as Ken Booth, Colin Gray, and David R. Jones tended to focus on patterns of behavior in their definitions while more recent analysts, most notably Alastair Ian Johnston, have deliberately excluded behavior from their strategic culture conceptions in order to avoid tautological relationships between their independent and dependent variables, culture and strategic choice.

5. Again, early anthropologists and strategic culture theorists set the boundaries of culture more broadly than did most later thinkers; yet, even as late as 1996, Kenneth Pollack wrote that cultural patterns of behavior such as "religion, language, family life, and tribal or other groupings . . . are simultaneously sources of culture, products of the culture, and methods for the transmission of culture." See Kenneth M. Pollack, "The Influence of Arab Culture on Arab Military Effectiveness," Ph.D. diss., Massachusetts Institute of Technology, 1996.

6. Alexander Wendt, *Social Theory of International Politics* (Cambridge: Cambridge University Press, 1999), p. 90. Also see Thomas Risse and Kathryn Sikkink, "The Socialization of International Human Rights Norms into Domestic Practice," in Thomas Risse, Stephen C. Ropp, and Kathryn Sikkink (eds.), *The Power of Human Rights: International Norms and Domestic Change* (Cambridge: Cambridge University Press, 1999), pp. 1–38.

7. Jack Snyder, "Anarchy and Culture: Insights from the Anthropology of War," *International Organization* 56, No. 1 (Winter 2002): pp. 7–45.

8. Ibid.

9. Charles Elder and Roger Cobb define symbols as "any object used by human beings to index meanings that are not inherent in, nor discernible from, the object itself." See Charles D. Elder and Roger W. Cobb, *The Political Use of Symbols* (New York: Longman, 1983), p. 28. For more on symbols, see Jacob Pandian, *Anthropology and the Western Tradition: Towards and Authentic Anthropology* (Prospect Heights, Ill.: Waveland Press, Inc., 1985), pp. 36–40; Michael Schmid, "The Concept of Culture and Its Place in Social Action," in Richard Munch and Neil J. Smelser (eds.), *Theory of Culture* (Berkeley, Calif.: University of California Press, 1992), pp. 89–91; and Claude Levi-Strauss, *Structural Anthropology*, trans. Claire Jacobson and Brooke Grundfest Schoepf (New York: Basic Books, Inc., 1963), pp. 186–205. For the influence of analogy on strategic decision making, see Yuen Foong Khong, *Analogies at War: Korea, Munich, Dien Bien Phu, and the Vietnam Decisions of 1965* (Princeton, N.J.: Princeton University Press, 1992) and Richard E. Neustadt and Ernest R. May, *Thinking in Time: The Uses of History for Decision Makers* (New York: The Free Press, 1986).

10. That is not to say that all scholars assert that genetic factors do not affect thought and behavior. Some maintain that human thought and behavior are the outcomes of both genetic predisposition and social acculturation. However, when addressing culture, they are specifically referring to patterns acquired in the socialization process. See Robert Boyd and Peter J. Richerson, *Culture and the Evolutionary Process* (Chicago: The University of Chicago Press, 1985).

11. Kroeber and Kluchhohn, p. 312.

12. Pollack, p. 38.

13. Issa J. Boullata, "Challenges to Arab Cultural Authenticity," in Hisham Sharabi (ed.), *The Next Arab Decade: Alternative Futures* (Boulder, Colo.: Westview Press, 1988), p. 148. Also cited in Pollack, p. 38.

14. See Jack Goody, "Culture and Its Boundaries: A European View," in Borofsky, p. 250.

15. On relationships between symbols, religion, and behavior see Clifford Geertz, "Religion as a Cultural System" and "Ethos, World View, and the Analysis of Sacred Symbols," in Clifford Geertz, *The Interpretation of Cultures* (New York: Basic Books, Inc., 1973), pp. 87–125 and 126–41.

16. Nick J. Enfield, "The Theory of Cultural Logic: How Individuals Combine Social Intelligence with Semiotics to Create and Maintain Cultural Meaning," *Cultural Dynamics* 12, No. 1 (2000): pp. 51–52.

17. Even among theorists who define culture to include behavior, there is some debate whether thought or behavior is the prime inducement in the formation of culture. For instance, Ward Goodenough, a pioneer in the development of modern cultural idealism, insists that culture is the end product of learning, not the result of behavior or various other factors. Conversely, Marvin Harris, the key proponent of the cultural materialist position, asserts that behavioral modes of production and reproduction probabilistically determine mental superstructures. This debate is largely irrelevant to this study, as most scholars acknowledge a circular effect; actions and ideas each affect the other in the evolution of culture. See Marvin Harris, *Cultural Materialism: The Struggle for a Science of Culture* (New York: Vintage Books, 1979), pp. 55–56, 265.

18. For a cogent explanation of anthropology's use of interpretive analysis, see Clifford Geertz, "Thick Description: Toward an Interpretive Theory of Culture" in Geertz, *The Interpretation of Cultures*, pp. 3–30.

19. Richard L. Schott, "Administrative and Organization Behavior: Some Insights from Cognitive Psychology" *Administration and Society* 23, No. 1 (May 1991): p. 55.

20. Ibid.

21. See Robyn M. Dawes, *Rational Choice in an Uncertain World* (New York: Harcourt Brace & Company, 1988), pp. 68–69; Mark K. Johnson and Steven J. Sherman, "Constructing and Reconstructing the Past and the Future in the Present," in E. Tory Higgins and Richard M. Sorrentino (eds.), *Handbook of Motivation and Cognition: Foundations of Social Behavior*, Volume 2 (New York: The Guilford Press, 1990), p. 485; Charles S. Taber, "The Interpretation of Foreign Policy Events: A Cognitive Process Theory," in Donald A. Sylvan and James E. Voss (eds.), *Problem Representation in Foreign Policy Decision Making* (Cambridge: Cambridge University Press, 1998), pp. 32–33.

22. Henri Zukier, "The Paradigmatic and Narrative Modes in Goal-Guided In-

ference," in Richard M. Sorrentino and E. Tory Higgins (eds.), *Handbook of Motivation and Cognition: Foundations of Social Behavior* (New York: The Guilford Press, 1986), p. 475.

23. Schank and Abelson used the restaurant example when they first introduced the script concept in 1977. It has become a classic and is probably the most widely cited illustration of how the mind develops and uses scripts. See Roger C. Schank and Robert P. Abelson, *Scripts, Plans, Goals, and Understanding: An Inquiry into Human Knowledge Structures* (Hillsdale, N.J.: Lawrence Erlbaum Associates, 1977).

24. Stephen J. Anderson and Martin A. Conway, "Representations of Autobiographical Memories," in Martin A. Conway (ed.), *Cognitive Models of Memory* (Cambridge, Mass.: The MIT Press, 1997), pp. 228–29; Johnson and Sherman, p. 485; Taber, pp. 34–35.

25. Scripts and schemas are the two most prominent concepts that psychologists have developed to describe the many knowledge structures the mind may use to sense, sort, process, store, and recall information. Other concepts include cases, classes, categories, frames, scenes, programs, memory organization packets (MOPs), meta-MOPs, and thematic organization packets (TOPs). While most psychologists accept the concepts of "script" and "schema" in a general sense, researchers do not fully agree on just how many different knowledge structures exist; wherein the unconscious, semiconscious, and conscious realms of long- and short-term memory each reside; and how they relate to one another hierarchically. For the purposes of this study, it is sufficient to sort knowledge structures into two broad categories and use the term "script" to describe those that record sequences of behavior and "schema" to describe more deeply embedded thought patterns that store the meanings of ideas. For more on the hierarchical arrangement of knowledge structures see Anderson and Conway, pp. 228–30; Ryan Beasley, "Collective Interpretations: How Problem Representations Aggregate in Foreign Policy Groups," in Sylvan and Voss, pp. 82–83; Taber, pp. 34–35; Joel Weinberger and David McClelland, "Cognitive versus Traditional Motivational Models: Irreconcilable or Complementary?" in Higgins and Sorrentino, pp. 570–71.

26. Pamela Johnston Conover and Stanley Feldman, "How People Organize the Political World: A Schematic Model," *American Journal of Political Science* 28 (1984): p. 96; Schott, p. 60.

27. Conover and Feldman, p. 97; on schemas and racial stereotypes, see Edward E. Jones, *Interpersonal Perception* (New York: W.H. Freeman and Company, 1990), pp. 86–107.

28. David Rummelhart, "Schemata: The Building Blocks of Cognition," in Rand Spiro, Bertram Bruce, and William Brewer (eds.), *Theoretical Issues in Reading Comprehension* (Hillsdale, N.J.: Lawrence Erlbaum Associates, 1980), pp. 33–34.

29. Paul J. Hanges, Robert G. Lord, and Marcus W. Dickson, "An Information Processing Perspective on Leadership and Culture: A Case for Connectionist Architecture," *Applied Psychology: An International Review* 49, No. 1 (2000): pp. 133–69; and Claudia Straus and Naomi Quinn, *A Cognitive Theory of Cultural Meaning* (New York: Cambridge University Press, 1997). For a discussion on the conceptual similarities between scripts, schemas, and analogies, see Khong, pp. 25–29.

30. Conover and Feldman, p. 97; Johnson and Sherman, p. 485.

31. Dawes, pp. 69–70; Taber, p. 35; Zukier, pp. 471–72. Also see Hanges et al., pp. 133–69.

32. Conover and Feldman, pp. 96–97; Dawes, pp. 69–70; Susan T. Fiske and Mark A. Pavelchak, "Category-Based versus Piecemeal-Based Affective Responses: Developments in Schema-Triggered Affect," in Sorrentino and Higgins (1986), p. 170; Jones, p. 87; Khong, p. 28.

33. See Daniel Goleman, *Vital Lies, Simple Truths: The Psychology of Self-Deception* (New York: Simon & Schuster, 1985).

34. Dawes, pp. 69–70; Johnson and Sherman, p. 485; Weinberger and McClelland, p. 570; Taber, p. 35.

35. Conover and Feldman, p. 97; Fiske and Pavelchak, pp. 170 and 174–175; Mark L. Hoffman, "Affect, Cognition, and Motivation," in Sorrentino and Higgins (1986), pp. 244–80.

36. See Mortimer Mishkin and T. Appenzeller, "The Anatomy of Memory," *Scientific American,* 256, No. 6 (June 1987): pp. 80–89; Stuart M. Zola-Morgan and Larry R. Squire, "The Primate Hippocampal Formation: Evidence for a Time-Limited Role in Memory Storage," *Science* 250, No. 4978 (12 Oct. 90): pp. 288–90.

37. Conover and Feldman, pp. 98–100; Norman T. Feather, "Bridging the Gap between Values and Actions: Recent Applications of the Value-Expectancy Model," in Higgins and Sorrentino (1990), pp. 182–86.

38. Martha Cottam and Dorcas E. McCoy, "Image Change and Problem Representation after the Cold War," in Sylvan and Voss, pp. 117–18.

39. Knowing their procedures are unfamiliar to new customers, buffet operators often lay out their restaurants with partitioned walkways that channel customers from the entrance to the cash register and from there to the food before they can get to the tables. Having customers negotiate a sequence of physical structures is a remarkably effective way to create new scripts in their minds.

40. On changing knowledge structures, see Cottam and McCoy, p. 117; Sanjoy Banerjee, "Reproduction of Social Structures: An Artificial Intelligence Model," *Journal of Conflict Resolution* 30, No. 2 (June 1986): p. 225.

41. For just a few of the more notable examples, see Graham T. Allison and Philip Zelikow, *Essence of Decision: Explaining the Cuban Missile Crisis,* 2nd ed. (New York: Longman, 1999); John W. Kingdon, *Agendas, Alternatives, and Public Policies* (Boston: Little, Brown, and Co., 1984); James G. March, *A Primer on Decision Making: How Decisions Happen* (New York: The Free Press, 1994); Herbert A. Simon, *Administrative Behavior: A Study of Decision-Making Processes in Administrative Organizations,* 4th ed. (New York: The Free Press, 1997); Hedrick Smith, *The Power Game: How Washington Works* (New York: Ballantine Books, 1988); and James Q. Wilson, *Bureaucracy: What Government Agencies Do and Why They Do It* (New York: Basic Books, Inc., 1989).

42. This approach is consistent with Alexander George's method for developing theory by examining mechanisms that intervene between the independent and dependent variables in an apparent causal relationship. See Alexander George, "Case Studies and Theory Development: The Method of Structured, Focused, Comparison," in Paul G. Lauren (ed.), *Diplomacy: New Approaches in History, Theory, and Policy* (New York: The Free Press, 1979).

43. Perception is, in one sense, the product of a complex interplay between symbols and values and, in another, an ingredient with those elements in conceptions of "world view," the way one literally interprets the environment, and "ethos," the way one evaluates that environment in terms of tone, character, mood,

quality of life, morality, and aesthetics. See Geertz, "Ethos, World View, and the Analysis of Sacred Symbols," pp. 126–41.

44. See Kroeber and Kluckhohn, pp. 308–9.

45. See Wilson, pp. 90–110.

46. Sociologist Marion Levy took a similar stance when he wrote, "culture, in the sense used here, cannot 'cause' anything. However, it is true that, if one knows the culture of a given society, one can say a great deal about the limits of possible variation of action in the society and the possibilities or probabilities of social change." See Marion J. Levy, Jr., *The Structure of Society* (Princeton, N.J.: Princeton University Press, 1952), pp. 147–48.

47. For more on this theory, see Alexander L. George and William E. Simons, *The Limits of Coercive Diplomacy*, 2nd ed. (Boulder, Colo.: Westview Press, 1994), pp. 270–88.

CHAPTER 3

The Strategic Culture of Imperial Japan

Every nation's culture is driven by the forces of history and molded by the constraints of geography. In that regard, Japan is no different. Dwelling on a chain of islands off the coast of northeast Asia, the Japanese have been subject to cultural influxes from the Asian mainland, but have also enjoyed the security of isolation. This combination of influence and seclusion has produced a very homogeneous culture that reflects many of the same themes seen in other Asian societies, but interprets those themes in ways that are uniquely Japanese. To understand these interpretations, one must examine Japan's past.

This chapter describes some of the most prominent traits of Japanese culture and explains how they came to be. It begins with a brief historical survey examining the key social, political, and religious developments that influenced the formation of Japanese attitudes and behaviors. Building on this foundation, it then profiles the traits of Japanese culture most relevant to strategic decision making. It first describes the symbols and values that influence individual behavior, then broadens the analysis to determine how individuals interact in groups and make decisions. Afterward, it discusses several cultural traits that became particularly pronounced during the imperial era and explores how these attitudes, deeply rooted in Japan's national psyche, profoundly influenced governmental processes. Finally, this chapter summarizes these factors and develop 15 hypotheses for the comparative analysis across cases.

SOURCES OF JAPANESE CULTURE

The following survey is not a thorough treatment of the history of Japan in any sense, nor does it address all of the many elements that have worked together to define Japanese culture. Instead, it focuses on the events and themes in Japanese history that most prominently underpin the dominant traits of Japan's strategic culture in the imperial era.

Children of the Sun

The ancestors of the Japanese people were clans of nomadic warriors originating near the Altai Mountains in what is present-day Mongolia. Migrating east across Asia and down the Korean peninsula, these wandering groups began to cross the Tsushima Strait sometime before the third century A.D. The warrior-nomads easily dominated the small aboriginal groups and Malay-Polynesian settlers already occupying the region and thoroughly colonized the islands of Kyushu, Shikoku, and the southern portion of Honshu over a period of several hundred years. The society that emerged was a tribal, warrior culture comparable in some ways to those of early northwestern Europe.[1]

Sometime between the third and sixth centuries, a powerful warrior clan living in the Yamato basin, a fertile plain in southern Honshu, managed to gain supremacy over the other tribes in the area. According to the earliest written record, the Yamato chieftain won his right to rule in a series of bloody battles, but by the sixth century his successors had begun buttressing their claims to power with a myth of sacred legitimacy. Drawing on a mythology common to all the tribal groups, the Yamato chiefs claimed they had descended from the sun goddess, Amaterasu, the cardinal deity in the Shinto pantheon.[2]

Shinto, the "Way of the Gods," is the most distinctively Japanese of all religious belief systems and is still practiced today. However, it would be misleading to describe it as an organized religion. Shinto has "no founder, no inspired sacred book, no teachers, no martyrs, and no saints."[3] Nor does it embrace a theology or even a concept of ethics beyond an abhorrence of defilement and an emphasis on ritual purity. Rather, it is a collection of folk beliefs expressing animistic reverence for natural phenomena such as the sun, mountains, trees, water, rocks, and the process of fertility.[4] All these manifestations of nature are perceived as harboring a kind of divine presence, or *kami*, and worshipped accordingly. Ancestral spirits are also considered *kami*, and ancestor worship has been a central feature of Shinto throughout its history. Consequently, the Yamato chiefs drew from a great source of sociopolitical power when they claimed to have descended directly from Amaterasu, the mythological creator of Japan and her people.[5]

Standing on their claim of legitimacy through divine right and using other political stratagems, the Yamato clan gradually extended and solidified its control in southern central Japan. As a direct living descendant of the sun goddess, each Yamato chief enjoyed a position superior to other clan chieftains who had access only to lesser gods. To strengthen their hold on power, the Yamato family began installing kinsmen as local chieftains, loyal to the central family in policy and tribute, and they began appropriating fertile land and granaries in remoter areas of the domain. In the early years, their power was far from absolute, but the Yamato managed to establish the rudimentary framework of a centralized monarchy by the dawn of the seventh century.[6]

Influences from the "Middle Kingdom"

In the continuing effort to strengthen the power of the Yamato line, the Japanese began a mass importation of Chinese political ideas, administrative practices, and governmental institutions early in the seventh century. This influx coincided with China's reunification under the Sui and T'ang dynasties, following nearly four centuries of turmoil and war.[7] Key members of the Yamato family and their advisors were awed by the cultural sophistication of the great Middle Kingdom, and they were impressed with the Chinese emperor's ability to unify and rule such a vast land. So, like the early leaders of other Asian countries, the Japanese began to emulate Chinese ideas in the administration of their own domain. As a result, the Yamato kinsmen and their allies, now an emerging nobility, undertook a thorough study of the Chinese approach to governance and the philosophy on which it was based. That philosophy was Confucianism.[8]

Seventh-century Han Confucianism proposed that man and the natural world were mystically linked. Therefore, the behavior of men, particularly those in high places, could affect the natural order, which was sensitive to the ethical quality of their acts. If evil prevailed in human society, the natural world was similarly afflicted. Floods, earthquakes, and famines were not chance occurrences but the direct consequences of unjust rule or disharmony among men. According to Chinese Confucianists, in order to maintain an ethical balance in society, several conditions must be present. Governance must be trusted to the hands of a competent, deserving ruler who leads his or her people according to a system of just laws. Administrators must be impartial and fair, and they should be chosen on the basis of merit. In fact, the overriding virtue in Han Confucianism was *jin*, or benevolence, which stipulated that anyone in authority—emperors, bureaucrats, and even parents—must exercise good interpersonal relations lest their subjects rebel.[9] But just as importantly, subjects within the realm also had responsibilities. They were expected to conduct themselves according to an elaborate system of social ritual emphasizing filial piety, courtesy, and respect for the established social hierarchy. This body of formal and informal ceremony evolved in China over many generations and was called *li*, which translates loosely to propriety or the natural moral order.[10]

Confucian-based Chinese ideas had a significant impact on Japanese life and government in the seventh and eighth centuries. In 604 A.D., Yamato's Prince Shotoku Taishi promulgated a constitution that reflected a distinctly Confucian cosmology. The Shotoku Constitution enunciated a theory of social harmony stemming from the acceptance of the Yamato ruler's supreme authority as emperor. According to Shotoku, the emperor's influence was not just political; it was ethical and magical.[11] Subsequently, Japanese leaders enacted a written legal code based on Confucian principles, and by the middle of the eighth century nearly all literate Japanese had read Chinese philosopher Hsiao Ching's *Classic of Filial Piety*—Yamato Empress Koken (reigning 749–58 A.D.) required every home to have a copy.[12] In the words of historian Sir George Sansom, "it was thus impossible for the leaders of Japan, or for any persons of even modest education, to be free from the influence of Confucian ideas."[13]

Yet, ardent as Japanese leaders were in adopting Chinese ways, they never accepted Confucianism in total, and the early Japanese government never resembled the meritocracy so glorified in China. There was much in Confucianism that the Yamato nobility admired. The concept of a revered emperor with unquestioned authority advanced their desire to buoy the legitimacy of Yamato rule, and Confucianism's emphasis on law, ritual, and hierarchy all served to reinforce the existing social order. Moreover, China's obsession with filial piety fit well with early Japan's emphasis on loyalty to family and clan, and Confucian ancestor worship coincided with rituals long accepted in Shinto.[14] But the principle of selecting government officials on the basis of merit contradicted the Japanese nobility's practice of granting positions and titles to loyal clan members and making them hereditary. Consequently, the Yamato hierarchy rejected the notion of entrusting official appointments to the outcomes of a Confucian examination system such as the one that came to define civil service in China for more than a thousand years.[15] But most significantly, Japan never accepted Confucianism's concept of *jin*, that postulate of benevolence so central in the Chinese concept of government. Acquiescence to *jin* would have contradicted imperial sovereignty—it would have implied that Japanese subjects had the right to rebel in the face of unjust or incompetent rule.[16] Consequently, Japanese Confucianists emphasized each subject's duties to family, clan, and emperor, but they were largely silent on the rights of those ruled. They rejected *jin* while embracing *li*.[17]

While Confucianism's detached legalism influenced early Japanese values significantly, the religion that stirred Japanese passions was Buddhism. Buddhism began in India in the sixth century B.C. as an outgrowth of Brahmanism, a precursor to modern Hinduism. Buddhist practices revolved around achieving spiritual enlightenment and ending the cycle of reincarnation to which, according to Brahmanism, man was fated. The date Buddhism was introduced to Japan is uncertain, but many historians believe it reached the islands during the sixth century A.D., a period of increased economic, military, and cultural exchange with Korea.[18]

Having originated in India and spread across China, Buddhism developed a vast canon and embraced a comprehensive range of metaphysics. While Buddhism's complex theology was beyond the grasp of the typical seventh-century Japanese devotee, the faith spread rapidly among members of all classes in Yamato Japan. This was partly because it enjoyed enthusiastic support at court.[19] As a "Chinese" doctrine, it was considered culturally sophisticated and, like Confucianism, Buddhism's emphasis on peace and moral behavior was consistent with Yamato interests. In fact, Buddhism lacked serious opposition from any quarter, political or ecclesiastical. But the main reason for Buddhism's rapid growth in Japan was that it struck a resonant chord among the people. The Japanese were first attracted to this new religion by the magical power they saw in it and by its impressive ritual. But as they began to understand its doctrines, they were moved by the empathy and compassion they found there.[20] As Sansom explains:

In declaring that all earthly goods and pleasures are illusory and that all existence involves suffering, Buddhism was not stating a truth entirely repugnant to the minds of the Japanese, for what we know of their temperament from their earliest poetry leads to the belief that they were often depressed by a sense of the transitory nature of the very things that they most admired, beauty and splendor and power. Consequently the Buddhist concept of an interminable procession of change made a strong impression on their minds, while the doctrine of Karma was perhaps the strongest and most durable of all influences brought to bear upon Japanese life from abroad.[21]

Over the course of the seventh and eighth centuries Buddhism, Confucianism, and Shinto settled into a harmonious coexistence in Japan. All of these faiths made profound impressions on Japanese attitudes and behaviors, and each played a key role in solidifying the Yamato clan's hold on power. While Buddhism concerned itself with the spiritual needs of Yamato subjects, Confucianism focused on social, legal, and political issues. And, of course, there were the *kami*, Shinto's thousands of ever-present nature deities and ancestral spirits, of which the emperor was now chief.[22] But in the coming centuries, the imperial court would not maintain its hold on power and, ironically, religion would contribute to the erosion of the emperor's authority.

By the end of the eighth century, the Yamato court had become detached from the practical concerns of governing and, instead, was increasingly preoccupied with ritual and magic.[23] Government ministries and the bureaucracy had become fossilized with empty ceremonies that had little to do with the realities of administration. Secure in wealth and prestige, ninth- and tenth-century emperors frequently abdicated their thrones to escape the rigors of official ritual or pursue interests in the arts, leaving child successors to preside over public ceremonies and religious rituals.[24] In this environment of decadence and decay, advisors governed and opportunists prospered. More significantly, administrators and landowners in the rural provinces were left to manage local concerns without support or direction from Kyoto, the capital.[25] Eventually, a warrior aristocracy emerged among the provincial families, central authority broke down, and Japan returned to a clan-centered society similar to that seen before the emergence of the Yamato. In Kyoto, the emperor still held the throne, but by the eleventh century, the nation had devolved into feudalism and war.[26]

Early Feudalism—Japan's Dark Age

As authority from the imperial court disintegrated, hundreds of local conflicts erupted between various clans that jockeyed to fill the void. In time, alliances coalesced around two of the most powerful and influential families, the Taira and the Minamoto, and these groups began contesting for control of the imperial court at Kyoto. Over a 25-year period in the twelfth century, the Taira and Minamoto factions fought a series of wars that devastated Japan until the Taira were finally crushed in a great battle in 1185. The victor, Minamoto Yoritomo, then established himself as shogun (generalissimo) and ruled Japan from a military government headquartered in the coastal village of Kamakura.[27]

For most of the next 700 years, Japan saw various forms of military rule, punctuated by periods of shifting alliance and clan warfare. The early feudal period was one of turmoil and intrigue. However, despite the turmoil, one feature did remain constant—and that factor is particularly relevant to Japan's twentieth-century attitudes and behaviors—throughout the feudal period, Yamato emperors continued to hold court in Kyoto.[28]

Although provincial *daimyo* (warlords) battled among themselves for control of the countryside, not one of them, even when he managed to subdue the entire country and become shogun, ever removed the nominal ruler to declare himself emperor. Granted, the various shogun exercised sovereign authority in governing Japan—they made and enforced laws, taxed commercial activities, raised armies, and fought wars at home and abroad. Moreover, the imperial court eventually became a virtual hostage to the whims of the military overlords. Nonetheless, every warrior who won or inherited the title of shogun governed Japan in the emperor's name but not from his throne.[29]

There are several reasons the shogun all maintained this extended pretense. First, as military men, acculturated in a warrior society that esteemed courage, physical prowess, and personal honor, the early shogun were loath to take up the ritual posturing and ceremonial responsibilities that burdened whoever held the title of emperor. When Minimoto Yoritomo established his *bakufu* (literally, "tent government") in Kamakura, he had no intention of usurping the emperor's authority. He simply wanted to install a government that could enforce peace and administer the country efficiently. That required him to remain separate from the Confucian ritual and court intrigue that dominated Kyoto.[30] Later, as more power devolved from the capital and directly into the hands of provincial *daimyo* and the shogun, the title of emperor became increasingly irrelevant—Japan was becoming accustomed to government by vassalage.[31] But the most significant reason that no shogun ever aspired to be emperor might be rooted as much in culture as in power politics.

By the twelfth century Japan had been governed, nominally at least, by a single royal house for nearly 1000 years. Steeped in Shinto and Confucian tradition, medieval Japanese subjects saw the legal inheritors of the Yamato throne as direct descendants of Amaterasu, sun goddess and creator of Japan. Any general with dreams of claiming the throne for himself would have faced the unenviable task of deposing a living deity, then ruling an outraged populace as a mortal man. Far better to govern Japan as the emperor's representative, with one's position legitimized by the sovereign's official blessing, even if that blessing is coerced.

Another development in feudal society that had a profound impact on Japanese culture was the rise of the warrior class. Warriors were always an influential group in Japan. Even before the decay of imperial authority, clan affiliation and martial virtue largely defined life outside the capital. However, establishment of the Kamakura shogunate elevated the warrior class to a new station in society. As Sansom explains:

The Minamoto were not content with merely transferring the political control which had once been exercised as of right by the greatest noble houses to the victorious warrior class; they went on to mold this class into an independent, highly organized society with its own laws and its own standards of behavior. They were no longer the servants of aristocratic statesmen, but their masters.[32]

The code of behavior by which these new masters lived was both rigid and demanding. The quality valued most highly by members of the warrior class was loyalty. Building on Japan's traditional emphasis on fidelity to family and clan, as well as the now centuries-old inculcation in Confucian ethics, loyalty was elevated to a status that overshadowed every other virtue. Warriors were expected to be loyal to their parents and clan, but most of all they were expected to submit themselves, fully and without question, to the demands of their liege lords.[33]

In early feudal Japan, the relationship between lord and vassal was a lifetime commitment of personal loyalty. Every vassal was expected to put the life of his master above his own and, if need be, give his life freely in the service of his lord. Indeed, tales of old Japan abound with stories of warriors who deliberately fought to the death, or even killed themselves, after their masters fell in battle.[34] In fact, loyalty was so esteemed in this military society that warriors who gave advantage to enemies by betraying their own lords for personal gain were often apprehended and executed for treachery by the very enemies they had helped.[35]

In return for loyalty and service, lords looked after the needs of their retainers and often rewarded them with booty or lands confiscated from the enemy. But, in keeping with the Japanese interpretation of Confucian ethics, the moral bond of service was quite one-sided—warriors did not condition their loyalty on any expectation of reward. Rather, loyalty was considered both a natural duty and its own reward.[36] In fact, samurai, a word that eventually became synonymous with "warrior" and with "warrior class," literally means "one who serves."[37] The following passage, taken from a list of admonitions the warrior Hojo Shigetoki wrote for his son in 1247, reflects this spirit of selfless loyalty and service:

When one is serving officially or in the master's court, he should not think of a hundred or a thousand people, but should consider only the importance of the master. Nor should he draw the line at his own life or anything else he considers valuable. Even if the master is being phlegmatic and one goes unrecognized, he should know that he will surely have the divine protection of the gods and Buddhas.[38]

Another quality on which warriors placed a great deal of value was personal bravery. Warriors prided themselves on their courage, and they had nothing but contempt for those among them who showed cowardice. According to the code of military behavior that coalesced in the early feudal era, a warrior should never turn his back on the enemy or attempt escape, even when his cause is futile. Warriors were expected to die in battle, rather than retreat or suffer the shame of capture. This outlook typified the fatalistic view of life that developed in the warrior class during feudalism's extended period of civil strife, but it also reflected a keen recognition of class distinction, a belief that men of warrior heritage had a special calling both to serve and to lead those of other classes. This practical sense of mission was quite different from the mindset prevalent at the imperial court.[39]

The contrast in attitudes between Japan's nominal heads of state and those who actually governed was never more evident than in the way they handled the Mongol invasions during the thirteenth century. By 1264, Mongol leader Kublai Khan had conquered most of China and established the capital of his empire in present day Beijing. From his commanding position on the continent, the great khan soon brought Korea under his suzerainty through intimidation. Then he turned his eyes on Japan.[40]

At this point, the khan's Mongol and Chinese armies were exhausted from war, and the Mongolian occupation force had impoverished Korea, so he hoped to compel Japan to surrender without a fight as he had Korea. Therefore, between 1266 and 1272, he dispatched a series of envoys with letters addressed to the emperor demanding the island nation surrender or face a Mongol invasion. Whenever any of these delegations reached Kyushu, the military governor there promptly delivered the letters to the shogunal headquarters in Kamakura.[41]

Reading the khan's first communiqué, *bakufu* officials suspected the emperor would be unable to respond in a manner befitting the nation.[42] Yet, in keeping with the shogunate's role as imperial servants, they forwarded the letter to Kyoto where it caused near panic at court. Finally composing themselves, imperial officials answered the message with a stilted letter evading Mongol demands but hinting at possibilities of compromise, then they retreated into prayer for national deliverance. But before the emperor's letter could reach Mongol representatives, it had to pass through the hands of *bakufu* officials who found Kyoto's pretentious yet supplicating attitude unacceptable. Consequently, the shogunate withheld the letter and, instead, treated all of Kublai's repeated envoy missions with contemptuous silence. When it became evident that the khan would not let the matter rest, members of the imperial court retreated to a local shrine and cloistered themselves in religious ritual. Meanwhile, Kamakura began military preparations to meet the invasion.[43]

In 1274, resigned that Japan was not going surrender without a fight, Kublai Khan was finally able to assemble a force that he hoped would be adequate to take the islands. With a combined army of about 23,000 Mongol, Chinese, and Korean troops, transported by a fleet of 900 Korean ships, the khan's forces quickly overwhelmed and slaughtered two small Japanese garrisons on the islands of Tsushima and Ikishima, then headed for Kyushu.[44] Military officials on Kyushu got word of the imminent attack, and they quickly assembled a force to meet it while petitioning Kamakura for reinforcements.[45]

On November 19, the Mongols landed at Imazu, on Hakata Bay in northwest Kyushu, and they engaged the Japanese force the next morning while attacking the town of Hakata. Outnumbered by the battle-seasoned Mongols, the Japanese lost the town but fought stubbornly and managed to establish a defensive perimeter further inland by nightfall. There, they resolved to fight to the death in order to stall the Mongol advance long enough for reinforcements to arrive. But the fight was over. During the night the weather turned bad, and the Mongols put to sea to avoid being stranded in enemy territory should a typhoon destroy their naval support. The typhoon did strike, and the Mongol force was destroyed at sea at a cost of more than 13,000 lives.[46]

Convinced that the storm alone was responsible for the invasion's failure, Kublai Khan immediately sent a mission demanding that the emperor present himself at Beijing to pay homage. This time, the Khan's message never reached Kyoto. The shogunate was indignant that this barbarian would issue such orders to a living deity, so they simply ignored the Mongols and began military preparations to meet a second invasion. In 1275, the Khan sent another mission repeating his demand, but *bakufu* officials brought the Mongol emissaries to Kamakura and had them executed. In 1280, all members of a final Mongol delegation were beheaded where they landed on Japanese soil.[47]

Preparations to repel the second invasion mirrored those for the first, but on a higher level of intensity. The shogunate pushed its resources to the limit, financially and politically, employing every expedient the feudal system provided to build fortifications and raise an army of vassals. Meanwhile the emperor led a state procession to the Iwashimizu shrine to pray for the country's safety. The court also sent messengers to other great shrines imploring the gods to deliver the nation from the foreign enemy, and appeals were made to lesser national and local deities throughout Japan.[48]

The great invasion finally came in June 1281. A fleet of more than 1,200 ships, carrying 40,000 Mongol, Korean, and North Chinese troops were joined in an assault on the shores of northwest Kyushu by an even larger fleet ferrying 100,000 soldiers from southern China. This time the Japanese were prepared. Having fortified the island's most strategic points, the samurai were able to hold the massive attack force on the coast for more than seven weeks until, once again, a typhoon arose and helped the Japanese drive the invaders back into the sea. No precise record exists of how many of the khan's soldiers were lost in this adventure, but historians estimate that, perhaps, a third of the Korean fleet went down with its human cargo and well over half the southern Chinese were either cut down by samurai while trying to reach their ships or were lost later at sea.[49]

Although it took centuries to fully internalize the impact of these developments, the Mongol invasions ultimately made a dramatic impression on Japanese beliefs and attitudes. Already convinced they were children of the sun, the *kamikaze* (divine wind) that twice came to their rescue further confirmed to the Japanese of later eras that they were a chosen people led by an emperor who was surely a living god. Of course, military preparation and martial prowess played a crucial role in delivering the island nation from the Mongol threat, but the impression made most indelibly on the Japanese psyche was that when their survival was at stake, the gods had intervened—spiritual power had defeated physical power, and their emperor had been instrumental in making it happen.[50]

While the Mongol crisis was a seminal event in Japanese history, developments in the fourteenth century also left lasting imprints on the nation's culture. Over the first two decades of that century, internal dissention progressively weakened the Kamakura Shogunate until Emperor Go-Daigo, encouraged by Confucian scholars and the Buddhist clergy, gathered up the *bakufu*'s military opponents and challenged the shogun's authority. Forces still loyal to Kamakura defeated the imperial coalition early on, but though they captured the emperor and sent him into exile, Go-Daigo's supporters fought on. In 1333, the emperor escaped his confinement and rallied the nation to rise up against the *bakufu*, ultimately bringing down the shogunate. Emperor Go-Daigo then ruled the nation for three years until another military clique challenged his authority by supporting a rival claimant to the throne. Go-Daigo fled Kyoto and the country was torn by more than 50 years of civil war between supporters of the rival courts—a period known as the Southern-Northern Court era—until Shogun Ashikaga Yoshimitsu settled the dispute, firmly establishing the Ashikaga shogunate.[51]

Both Go-Daigo's short reign and the conflict that followed had a significant impact on the national consciousness. For the first time in centuries, an emperor ruled Japan in fact as well as in name, setting a precedent in Japanese minds that would exert a romantic appeal in later eras. More importantly, during the civil strife one of Go-Daigo's supporters, Confucian scholar Kitabatake Chikafusa, wrote *Jinno Shotoki* (On the Legitimacy of the Imperial Line), a history that passionately defended not only the legitimacy of the Southern Court, but the concept of imperial rule itself. As historian Delmer Brown explains:

[Kitabatake] wanted not merely to show that the Southern Court had legitimate claims to the throne, but also to emphasize the uniqueness, the greatness, and the divinity of the Japanese Imperial line, so that more people might feel impelled to give loyal and unselfish service to the rightful Emperor. He claimed that the uniqueness of the Imperial institution made Japan superior not only to China but also to India. But of greater significance was his emphasis on the idea that a special relationship existed between the Emperor and his people, to which he applied the word *kokutai* (national entity). From that time on, *kokutai* became a favorite subject of discussion for nationalist writers.[52]

The next significant turning point in Japan's cultural history occurred in the mid–sixteenth century as the Ashikaga shogunate disintegrated and, once again, provincial *daimyo* competed for control of the countryside and the title of shogun. Buddhism, long a political force in Japan, was a central factor in these struggles, as several of the most influential monasteries, besides incessantly fighting between themselves, openly sided with secular political factions and even supplied "warrior-priests" to augment the vassal forces of favored warlords.[53] Ultimately, these acts brought dire consequences on the heads of Buddhist clergy when Oda Nobunaga, a strongman they had once opposed, rose to power. Bitter over a previous defeat dealt him by Buddhist forces, Nobunaga systematically razed temples throughout Japan, including the vast monastery on Mount Hiei, overlooking Kyoto, which he burned to the ground along with its 3,000 inhabitants.[54] Nobunaga's pogrom dealt the faith a near fatal blow. Though Buddhism enjoyed a minor revival under the patronage of Nobunaga's successor, Toyotomi Hideyoshi, it ceased to be a significant force in Japanese life after the sixteenth century.[55]

Yet one sect of Buddhism had already made an indelible impression on the warrior class. Zen, an esoteric system of spiritual meditation, was especially attractive to the samurai. Unlike most other Buddhist doctrines, it did not rely on elaborate theoretical arguments, but upon a search for personal enlightenment through conviction and mental discipline. This concept found fertile soil among men who lived so close to death. For them, "there was an attraction, even a persuasion, in the belief that truth comes like the flash of a sword as it cuts through the problems of existence."[56] Much like early Shinto, feudal-era Zen was not institutional. It had no sacred buildings, no scriptures, and no rituals. Instead, it prescribed extended periods of seated meditation, a practice that nurtured in warriors the degree of stoic composure they needed to face death without fear. Ultimately, the stoicism Zen provided became a virtue in its own right, and its lasting character can be seen clearly in Japan's strategic culture in the twentieth century.[57]

Though Hideyoshi failed to return institutional Buddhism to its former luster, he too managed to contribute to Japan's evolving cultural milieu. Before Hideyoshi's reign as imperial regent, the samurai were largely an agrarian, warrior aristocracy.[58] Having risen as a class from the ranks of rural landowners, the warriors divided their time between warfare and farming, depending on the needs of their liege lords. But the violence that characterized the sixteenth century resulted in large numbers of men frequently moving to and from the fields, and this caused a considerable amount of economic disruption and social unrest.[59] Consequently, when Hideyoshi came to power in 1590, he issued a decree prohibiting farmers from owning weapons and restricting samurai involvement in agriculture, thus effectively separating warriors from the peasantry. This newly imposed limit on social mobility intensified the feelings of class distinction and hierarchy already strong in Japanese society. When Tokugawa Ieyasu became shogun, he segregated the social classes even more rigidly.[60]

Tokugawa Feudalism—A Culture Simmers

With Hideyoshi's death in 1598, feudal Japan endured one last period of civil war before Tokugawa Ieyasu reunified the country following his victory in the Battle of Sekigahara in 1600. Ieyasu's imperial confirmation as shogun in 1603 marked the beginning of the longest period of peace and central authority in Japan's history. The "Edo era" was characterized by urbanization, economic growth, the rise of a middle class, a flourish of education and artistic expression, and the development of government bureaucracy.[61] However, these many advances did not come without a price. The Tokugawa shogunate was a rigid police state, one almost completely cut off from the rest of the world for more than 200 years.[62]

Following Ieyasu's victory at Sekigahara, he took several strong steps to secure his hold on power. First, in keeping with feudal custom, he removed the most powerful *daimyo* who had opposed him and awarded their lands to loyal followers. Ieyasu and members of his family took the richest estates, and he placed his closest allies, his hereditary vassals, or *fudai,* in the country's most strategic locations. The allied *tozama,* warlords who were not hereditary vassals of the Tokugawa, were granted lesser domains. Those *tozama* who had sworn vassalage to Ieyasu only after defeat were placed on *han* (fiefs) in remote rural areas, isolated from centers of strategic, political, or economic importance. Next, the new shogun enacted a series of laws restricting travel, prohibiting work on fortifications, and even banning marriage between *daimyo* families without his permission—all to keep dissatisfied or ambitious vassals from forming alliances and conspiring against the shogunate.[63] To enforce these laws, Ieyasu placed spies in every *han,* reporting suspicious activities and disloyal words to the *bakufu.* But most significantly, the *shogun* instituted the practice of *sankin kotai,* or "alternate attendance," requiring all *daimyo* to spend every other year at the shogunal court in Edo and to leave their immediate families in the city as hostages while they were away.[64] But *bakufu* control was not a burden to be borne the *daimyo* alone.

Before long, Tokugawa law governed every aspect of society. Building on Hideyoshi's example, Ieyasu further restricted social mobility by defining a strict, hierarchical order of occupational class and social station, based on a Confucian model of society.[65] The samurai headed the Tokugawa hierarchy. Now a legally defined, hereditary caste, members of the warrior class were the only subjects allowed to carry weapons or hold public office. Already prohibited from farming or engaging in any mercantile occupation, the samurai became a privileged class, supported by stipends and taxes. Next came the peasants. Given Japan's limited acreage of productive land, Japanese leaders had always been concerned about food supplies, and those who produced food were long esteemed in Japanese society. Tokugawa decreed that only farmers could own arable land, and he made their class identity hereditary.[66]

Beneath the warriors and peasants were two lower classes, the artisans and the merchants. Confucianists considered these occupations socially inferior to farming because they did not produce anything. Artisans were held a grade above simple merchants because, at least, by crafting the materials they bought and sold, they added value to them. But merchants simply traded for profit, contributing nothing to society. In the eyes of seventeenth century Japanese, that was the lowest kind of socially acceptable occupation. With nearly all of Japanese society stratified into these four main classes, Tokugawa law proceeded to regulate every detail of social behavior, from the kind of house each caste could live in to the kinds of clothes they could wear and foods they could eat.[67]

Given Tokugawa Japan's extreme political and social rigidity, it is not surprising that the shogunate eventually felt compelled to close the islands to influences from the outside world. Beginning with the arrival of the Portuguese in 1542, Western ideas, particularly Christianity, had attracted a growing following among the Japanese. By the beginning of the Edo era, even a number of *daimyo* had become Christian. At first, Ieyasu was tolerant of Christian proselytization, and he encouraged foreign trade. However, as missionaries and their converts revealed their own intolerance, not only towards native faiths but even against rival Christian sects, the shogun came to see Western religion as a threat to civil order. Starting in 1613, Ieyasu took measures to counter Christian influence in Japan, but these first steps were not strongly enforced and missionaries continued to proselytize. However, as Christians expanded their intrigues against religious and political rivals to include the shogunate, *bakufu* officials persecuted them ever more vehemently until, in 1638, thousands of Japanese adherents rose up in revolt. Violently suppressing the insurrection, the shogunate put Japanese Christians to the sword and expelled all foreigners from Japan except for a small Dutch trade mission, which it confined to an island in Nagasaki harbor.[68]

Closed to influence from the outside world, Japan turned its eyes inward, and long-held ideas grew more refined and intense. Since their arrival in the seventh century, Confucian values had deeply penetrated the customs and consciousness of all Japanese. Now, with Christianity eradicated and Buddhism reduced to an empty shell, Confucian attitudes pervaded the nation.[69] But this was not the mystical, Han Confucianism that had come to the islands a millennium before; rather, the Confucianism of Tokugawa Japan was a rational philosophy concerned with how man could best fulfill his obligations in an increasingly complex society.[70] Filial piety, courtesy, and propriety were still central tenets, but owing to the powerful influence of Japan's feudal experience, loyalty, courage, and other martial virtues were even more highly esteemed.[71] In fact, despite the persistence of peace, the Tokugawa era heralded a renewed interest in the code of military conduct that had evolved since the days of Minamoto Yoritomo, a code that eventually came to be called *"bushido,"* the "way of the warrior."[72]

The most outspoken and influential evangelist in Japan's *bushido* movement was the samurai and Confucian scholar, Yamaga Soko (1622–85). Yamaga was deeply disturbed by the decadence he saw creeping into the warrior class during Tokugawa's extended peace. In a series of books and essays, he urged his fellow samurai to return to the austere life of self discipline more characteristic of warriors in earlier times. Yamaga stressed all the traditional martial virtues. Like the warriors of old, he said a samurai must make duty his highest devotion and place the needs of his lord above his own. But unlike his forebears, Yamaga insisted the arts of peace—especially letters and history—were also essential intellectual disciplines for warriors. According to Yamaga, the reason a samurai lived on a stipend was keep him "free to cultivate those arts and virtues which would enable him to serve as a model and leader for all others."[73]

This Confucian emphasis on education would have momentous impact on the samurai behind the restoration movement nearly two centuries later, as would Yamaga's insistence that a warrior's loyalty should be tendered to the emperor first and only to the shogun as the emperor's servant. Unfortunately for Yamaga, however, he was ahead of his time. Although some *bakufu* officials applauded his call for a return to martial virtue, most found his pleas for an acknowledgment of imperial authority politically dangerous. Consequently, the shogunate banished him to the remote, rural province of Ako, where he lived out the remaining years of his life.[74] But Yamaga's message did not go unheard, and as the Tokugawa era's extended peace and urbanization brought social change and eventually discord, later generations of samurai would remember his call for competent leadership and imperial veneration.[75]

Peace and prosperity brought decay to the socioeconomic structure of Tokugawa Japan. When first established, the Edo *bakufu* provided an effective framework for ending the violent turmoil of the sixteenth century. But the subsequent peace brought social changes that the Tokugawa system was ill-equipped to handle. With the threat of war nearly eliminated, most *daimyo* no longer needed a large number of retainers. And with the ever-growing burdens of shogunal taxation and *sankin kotai*, provincial lords could not afford to support more warriors than they absolutely needed. Consequently, thousands of samurai were turned out in the streets as *ronin* (literally, "wave men"), unable to find military work, yet prohibited by law from engaging in other occupations. Some of these *ronin* willingly gave up their samurai status and entered one of the lower classes, but many resorted to banditry or other illicit activities, further adding to the social strain.[76]

Meanwhile, the nation's economic foundation crumbled as the ruling class became progressively more indebted to society's lowest caste. Peace and urbanization were very good for commerce, and merchants prospered. But provincial lords and other upper-class samurai, facing a mounting financial burden, found themselves relying more and more on credit.[77] Occasionally, an impoverished aristocrat might bankroll his clan by marrying a daughter to the son of a wealthy merchant who was seeking to raise his family's social status, but these isolated cases did little to buoy the upper class as a whole.[78] Prohibited from owning land or engaging in commerce, the only source of revenue for most of the samurai elite was taxation, and the burden of these taxes fell on the peasants. Conditions grew steadily worse until, by the mid–nineteenth century, they approached a breaking point, as an effete caste of hereditary warriors struggled to remain solvent, while the masses beneath them chafed at having to support an unproductive aristocracy that had outlived its function.[79]

Moreover, sources of dissatisfaction were not confined to friction between castes; there was also a great deal of frustration within the samurai class itself. The Edo era's rigid stratification prescribed relationships within the four main castes, as well as between them, and Tokugawa law explicitly defined multiple layers of status and function among samurai. While the highest levels of the Edo aristocracy—the *daimyo*, ministers, advisors, and other direct vassals, or *hatamoto*, of the Tokugawa family— held the titular positions of power, a host of low-ranking samurai, working in the *bakufu* and the various *han*, carried out the actual task of administering the realm. As Tokugawa society became more complex and memories of war faded into the past, this group of nominal warriors evolved into a corps of bureaucrats with values and ideas that differed from those of their overlords. True to their warrior heritage, duty, service, and self-sacrifice still ranked as cardinal virtues among these men, but owing to both the growing complexity of their work and the strong Confucian influence in Edo society, education and competence came to be valued almost as highly. Ironically, these were the very qualities the *hatamoto* lacked. Relying on the expertise of low-level samurai, few overlords developed any administrative talent, yet they continued to fill key positions and receive large stipends based on their lineage. This led to a growing tendency of samurai-bureaucrats to find subtle ways (and ways not so subtle) to usurp the power of their superiors for the sake of administrative efficiency. In time, the willingness to risk one's career and usurp authority from incompetent aristocrats for the good of society came to be called *gekokujo* and was considered a form of moral courage.[80] Meanwhile, these men began to clamor for a system of appointment and promotion based on merit. And as economic conditions forced the *daimyo* to reduce expenses by cutting both stipends and employment within the ranks of warrior-bureaucrats, their frustration and bitterness swelled.[81]

Despite these strains, rank-and-file samurai still considered loyalty a supreme virtue, but social change during the Tokugawa period led them to interpret loyalty differently than in former eras. Japan entered the period as a collection of semi-autonomous fiefs, run by battle-hardened warriors. But just as the combined effects of pacification, urbanization, and education shifted samurai attention to issues beyond military prowess, they awakened in all Japanese a sense of nationhood or, as Kitabatake Chikafusa had expressed it five centuries earlier, *kokutai*.[82] As this new awareness developed, centuries-old beliefs that the Japanese were a chosen people led by a divine monarch resurfaced and intensified in Edo's fertile, Shinto-Confucian environment.[83] Consequently, by the nineteenth century, Japanese of all classes had begun to feel that the object of their loyalty should not be their local *daimyo* or even the shogun, but a source of authority much older and more deserving of their veneration—the emperor.[84]

Imperial Restoration—A Nation Awakens

When Matthew Perry's "black ships" entered Uraga Bay in 1853, Japan was ripe for social and political reform; pressure from the West provided the necessary catalyst. Ironically, Perry's first visit coincided with the death of Ieyoshi, the twelfth Tokugawa shogun. Faced at this difficult time with the disconcerting appearance of American naval force, *bakufu* officials turned to the *daimyo* for advice, thereby undermining shogunal control of foreign policy and raising the question of the Edo government's ability to handle the situation.[85] Debate over how to deal with the crisis spread, drawing in members of the imperial court and the powerful *tozama* houses on Kyushu, all hostile to Edo and alert for an opportunity to embarrass the shogunate. In 1858, the opportunity presented itself when Edo signed a series of unequal treaties opening Japanese ports to foreign trade and granting Westerners extraterritorial privileges. This development outraged many samurai and fed a growing "revere-the-emperor, expel-the-barbarians" movement, resulting in a wave of political violence against Westerners in Japan.[86] The West answered these attacks with a joint naval bombardment against coastal fortifications in Kyushu, to which Edo was powerless to respond. As a result, the Tokugawa shogunate was completely discredited, and in December 1867 a coalition of samurai and noblemen led by warriors from the powerful Satsuma and Choshu domains carried out a coup forcing the shogun to step down.[87] On January 1, 1868, 16-year-old Emperor Mutsuhito was renamed Meiji (Enlightened Government) and declared the de facto ruler of Japan. The Meiji Restoration was achieved.[88]

Japan's new leaders reorganized the nation's social and economic systems at an astonishing pace. Suddenly thrust into the role of ruler, the young emperor turned, most naturally, to the talented samurai from the *tozama* provinces in Kyushu who had united with him against the Tokugawa. Acting in the emperor's name, these warrior-bureaucrats promptly undertook a series of reforms ranging from eliminating class distinction to abolishing the feudal *han*.[89] The emperor's first advisors were three former samurai (Saigo Takamori, Okubo Toshimichi, and Kido Koin), often called the "triumverate," who guided the nation during the years immediately following the Restoration. But soon a second group emerged consisting of seven former, low-ranking samurai who hailed mainly from Choshu and Satsuma. Eventually known as *genro* (elder statesmen), these men orchestrated Japan's government for the rest of their lives, making decisions that the emperor unfailingly legitimized with his blessing.[90]

Over the next several decades, the *genro* coordinated one of the most remarkable modernization programs the world has ever seen, transforming a backward, feudal dominion, dependent on seventeenth-century technology, into a modern industrial nation.[91] The new leaders pensioned off the old feudal elite and converted Japan's society from an aristocracy, in which one's potential was determined by birth, to a meritocracy, in which one's success was the product of talent, education, and effort.[92] Although most *genro* had once been at the forefront of the "expel-the-barbarians" movement, the Western bombardment of Kyushu and subsequent travel abroad convinced them that Japan's only chance for survival lay in rapid modernization. Consequently, they embarked on a breakneck program to acquire Western knowledge and technology, a program that included both importing European experts and sending Japan's most promising youth abroad for education and training. This concerted effort put severe strains on the nation, both socially and financially, but the investment paid off. In a few short years, Japanese leaders managed to set up a national military establishment, institute compulsory education, and underwrite national banking, transportation, and industrial ventures.[93]

While these many advances impressed the Western nations, they soon became concerned about Japan's lack of political reform. Consequently, after considerable study and deliberation, *genro* Ito Hirobumi headed a commission that wrote a constitution defining Japan as a parliamentary monarchy, and Emperor Meiji signed it in 1889. Based on a German model, the Meiji Constitution was hailed by jurists at home and abroad as a sterling example of progressive government.[94] It legitimized the Privy Council of advisors on which the emperor relied so heavily. More importantly, it established a bicameral "diet," consisting of an upper house of noblemen and former Tokugawa elites and a lower house where seats were filled by popularly elected representatives. The constitution also established a judiciary, defined ministerial positions, and provided for a civil service.[95]

Yet, the Meiji Constitution was not a sound foundation for liberal democracy. Proclaiming that the emperor was sacred and inviolable, it vested in him all rights of law and sovereignty.[96] Consequently, the powers of the executive were so great that the diet could not originate any important legislation. Instead, the legislature functioned as a rubber stamp for measures submitted by the emperor's ministers and as a sounding board for public opinion. Likewise, the courts lacked independent authority. The judiciary was an arm of the Ministry of Justice and, therefore, subordinated to the executive branch of government. Conversely, the bureaucracy was extremely powerful. Mainly consisting of former low-level samurai, Meiji civil servants were, ostensibly, personal representatives of the emperor. This elite status, combined with the passivity conditioned into subjects by centuries of stern, feudal authority, tended to perpetuate the traditional attitude of *kanson minpi*, "official exalted—people despised."[97]

The most powerful individuals in the Meiji government were members of the Privy Council, cabinet-level ministers, and military chiefs. With direct access to the emperor, these men set domestic and foreign policy, used their influence in the diet to fashion policies into law, and put their decisions into effect through their control of the civil and military bureaucracies. They were commissioned by the emperor and were responsible only to him, which means, ultimately, they answered to the *genro* who counseled the emperor on all appointments. In fact, for almost two decades following promulgation of the Meiji Constitution, Privy Council seats and key ministerial positions were rotated among *genro* members themselves.[98]

Ultimately, the Meiji Constitution did little more than formalize the political status quo established by the *genro* and put a new face on a tradition with deep roots in Japanese history. Japan's new leaders eagerly molded their government into a form more comforting to Western observers, but the Meiji Constitution granted no more than token powers to any constituency that did not directly advise the emperor. And though the Restoration placed the emperor more prominently before the people and even granted him the legal and moral authority to govern, Meiji leaders wielded power in the same fashion as every other government had since the Heian era. The emperor legitimized the use of power, but he did little to exercise it himself. Instead, an oligarchy ruled in his name.[99] Interestingly, the selective nature of Japan's political reformation—donning the trappings of Western society while clinging to traditional values and customs—was indicative of the country's evolving approach to modernization in general.[100]

Japanese leaders reorganized the nation's social, economic, and political institutions to a remarkable extent, producing a society that, to all outward appearances, resembled those in the West. But the resemblance was only superficial. Although the *genro* first set out to westernize Japan in the fullest sense of the word, by the late 1880s they decided that not only was that goal impractical, it was undesirable. At first, Japan was enamored with Western science and customs, and some pro-Western liberals, such as Keio University founder Fukuzawa Yukichi, even suggested there might be political advantage in embracing Christianity as a national religion.[101] But Western customs lacked Japan's Confucian emphasis on courtesy and filial piety, making many Japanese uncomfortable, and Christianity contradicted the tradition of imperial divinity so central to Japan's national heritage. Ultimately, the discovery that Western religion and science were often in conflict led the Japanese to evaluate foreign ideas more critically. Westerners, in turn, contributed to Japanese disenchantment with their often condescending attitudes and their stubborn refusal to revise the unequal treaties obtained from the Tokugawa.[102]

With frustrations mounting, Confucianists and other intellectuals led a popular movement in the 1880s calling for a revival of pride in Japan's traditional culture and values. Writers in this movement lamented Japan's excessively Western orientation and insisted the native tradition ought not be abandoned so uncritically. Touching on themes reminiscent of Yamaga Soko, the cultural nationalists called attention to the dignity to be found in Japanese history and suggested that, with the leadership of Japan's divine emperor, their own nation was superior to all others in Asia and, perhaps, even to the West. The implications of this line of thought were not lost on the *genro*.[103]

Consequently, as Japan pressed ahead in its quest to match the West in technology and power, its leaders became much more selective when attempting to integrate new ideas into their society. They eagerly sought Western technical and managerial information in order to develop their industrial, commercial, and financial sectors, and they hired German and British military advisors to help them organize their armed forces. But, rather than attempt to assimilate ethical and philosophical concepts foreign to their heritage, Japanese leaders deliberately sought to preserve and even strengthen key elements of the native cultural tradition in order to magnify a popular sense of nationhood and motivate greater sacrifice from subjects in the modernization effort.[104] This campaign included a series of imperial rescripts—motivational messages written by *genro* members but promulgated under the emperor's signature—emphasizing Confucian ethics or martial virtues. These essays were aimed at people involved in critical functions in society, such as education, agriculture, and the armed forces. Schools became channels for indoctrination. Using standardized textbooks and compulsory bowing before the emperor's portrait, students were taught the importance of service and sacrifice in the name of *kokutai*.[105] In fact, the entire country was caught up in the *kokutai* movement as the government instituted a form of State Shinto in which the sun goddess mythology, ancestral veneration, the emperor, and nationhood became inseparably connected in a national theology.[106]

The implications of these developments are particularly relevant to this study. Japan coveted Western wealth and power, and its leaders first sought to build a Western empire in Asia.[107] But the Japanese were not Europeans—they did not think or behave like Westerners, either singly or in groups. So while the structure of Japanese society took on a Western facade, the symbols, values, and behavioral patterns behind that structure remained purely Japanese. Ultimately, those cultural elements colored the ways that Japanese leaders interpreted and responded to compellent threat, so we should examine them more carefully.

THE RELEVANT TRAITS OF JAPANESE CULTURE

Building on the historical foundation developed in the preceding section, I shall now profile those traits of Japanese culture most relevant to strategic behavior. This section begins by describing several important patterns of interpersonal behavior, and it examines the values that drive them. Then it explores how these individual patterns contribute to group dynamics and influence decision-making processes. Lastly, the profile focuses on the symbols and values behind several culture-related behaviors that were particularly pronounced during the imperial era.[108]

Obligation and the Ritual of Interpersonal Behavior

After centuries of Confucian influence, every Japanese is innately concerned about his or her responsibility to maintain order and harmony in society. As in China, Japanese interpersonal relations are governed by an elaborate maze of social ritual based on each individual's hierarchical relationship to others and the obligations one incurs in that relationship. Obligation is a powerful force in Japanese society. As anthropologist Ruth Benedict explained in her classic, *The Chrysanthemum and the Sword*, "Righteousness in Japan depends upon recognition of one's place in the great network of mutual indebtedness that embraces both one's forebears and one's contemporaries."[109] The Japanese word for all levels of obligation is *on*.[110]

Though Japanese customs resemble those in China, they differ significantly. Stemming from Japan's early rejection of *jin*, social obligations there take on a much more authoritarian character than do corresponding relationships in China. The Chinese consider benevolence the touchstone of all human relations. In China, a superior is expected to earn a subordinate's loyalty through the practice of good interpersonal relations, thereby cementing the obligation with a sense of justice and affection. But the Japanese have no such ethic. In Japan, obligation generally goes one way—*on* is *on*, and it must be repaid no matter how bitterly the obligator resents it.[111]

The Japanese recognize several levels of *on*, depending on the relation-

ships of those involved, and they classify the repayment of these obligations as either *giri* or *gimu*. Obligations that bind individuals in *giri* include
a variety of social debts ranging from the responsibility to repay a past
favor to the duty of revenge. The most traditional form of *giri* was the
feudal relationship between vassal and liege lord, frequently idealized in
modern fiction as a loving and unconditional exchange of loyalty and
protection. Today, *giri* relationships include those with employers, superiors, colleagues, friends, and even in-laws.[112]

It is important to understand that *giri* has nothing to do with justice or
"right and wrong." Rather, it is a strict system of accounting in which the
bearer of *on* is obliged to repay a benefactor in proportion to the original
favor. Modern *giri* rarely assumes the noble character that Japanese nos-
talgically associate with the past. In fact, one may call on *giri* to compel
another to do something distasteful, and repayment may even involve
something unjust or immoral, by non-Japanese standards. In any case,
being obligated in a *giri* relationship implies subordination, making one
feel inferior. Therefore, according to Benedict, Japanese strive to avoid
accepting favors from anyone not clearly defined as superior to them in
the social hierarchy. These factors help explain why the bonds of *giri* are
so often typified by resentment.[113]

Yet, not all *giri* relationships can be characterized as negative. Tokyo
University psychiatrist L. Takeo Doi points out that while Benedict's depiction of the *on-giri* framework is generally accurate, it overlooks some
of the more subtle nuances of Japanese emotion. Doi explains that *amae*,
the inward desire to be loved, is also a strong social motivator. *Amae* im-
pels individuals to engage in *giri* relationships with family, friends, and
even subordinates without the bitterness associated with *giri* between
strangers. Through *giri*, people satisfy feelings of *amae* by experiencing
ninjo, a mutual sensitivity to each party's emotional needs.[114]

The other major category of relationships under which the Japanese feel
obligated is *gimu*, which can be subdivided into *ko* and *chu*. *Ko* is the debt
an individual owes his or her parents and ancestors. Stemming from the
Confucian emphasis on filial piety, this debt is immeasurable. Once again,
however, Japanese tradition differs from the Chinese model. Filial piety
in China extends to all ancestors, no matter how long ago they lived.
Conversely, the Japanese only feel *gimu* for those ancestors they personally
knew—usually, grandparents and, occasionally, great-grandparents. Since
ko is immeasurable, it can never be fully repaid. Therefore, it outweighs
all debts of *giri*, even to the extent that a son will follow the demands of
his mother at the expense of the needs and feelings of his wife. And like
giri, *ko* is often a source of bitterness. Without the softening influence of
jin, it adds an autocratic quality to one-on-one relationships that tends to
arouse antagonisms between parents and children.[115] Ironically, the only
form of *gimu* that is not frequently associated with resentment is also the

one obligation that, in the imperial era, was greater than *ko*. That obligation is *chu*, one's debt to the nation and the emperor.[116]

Now that we understand how the Japanese conceive the repayment of *on*, let us examine what Benedict calls "*giri* outside the circle of *on*" or "*giri* to one's name."[117] Unlike the forms of *giri* and *gimu* discussed above, *giri* to one's name does not stem from obligations to any specific persons or entities. Rather, it is a general code of behavior, evolved largely from Confucian etiquette and *bushido*, that serves to guide individuals through the complexities of social interaction without causing shame to themselves or others. Avoiding shame, or maintaining "face," is a strong motivator in Japanese society.[118] So much so, that one of the most important duties in this category of *giri* is the responsibility to maintain self-control. In Japan, stoicism is a virtue, and emotional outbursts, regardless of the provocation, bring loss of face. Likewise, living according to one's station is also important, owing to the strong hierarchical orientation in Japanese society. But whatever one's social standing is, competence is highly admired. So all Japanese feel they must meet their professional commitments, or appear to, even if it means not admitting to personal error or ignorance. Because they find loss of face so demeaning, they take great pleasure in the *giri* of personal revenge for any perceived slight or insult.[119]

Owing to the extreme emphasis their society places on social ritual and face, the Japanese are courteous to a fault. They make every possible effort to avoid open confrontation. In group endeavors, when they have to resolve an important issue, each speaker cautiously lays out his or her view while closely watching the reactions of other participants. As open confrontation is acutely embarrassing, they try to avoid outlining their positions precisely or focusing on the differences between them. Instead, communicators try to get their points across by implication. Consequently, a speaker's body language and a receiver's intuition are almost as important as verbal ability.[120] This nervous caution pervades nearly all social environments. In the office, Japanese workers avoid asking questions that may embarrass colleagues, and in most social settings subordinates defer conversation to superiors who carry on bland monologues, carefully evading potentially contentious topics. Most of all, the Japanese go to great pains to avoid direct competition with others within their group, in order to lessen the chance of giving or taking offense.[121]

Along with its emphasis on obligation and duty, Japanese culture is distinctive in that values tend to be more particular than universal. That is, the Japanese tend to define morality by context.[122] Sociologist Robert Bellah attributes this condition to the long feudal experience in which loyalty to a particular family, lord, or *han* took precedence over any commitment to universal values such as truth or justice.[123] Whatever the cause, Japanese tend to define right and wrong in terms of what kind of obligation a particular situation places them in—in other words, whether the case requires a fulfillment of *chu*, *ko*, or *giri*—and what rules apply to that repayment of *on*.[124] This explains why a woman may lie when asked to do so by someone for whom she carries *on*, or why a happily married man might seek the company of a barmaid without feeling guilt, as physical pleasures are considered outside the "circle of *on*."[125]

Given this context-dependent moral framework and the overriding need to avoid open confrontation, Japanese often behave in ways that seem duplicitous to people outside their culture. They may say one thing in public and something completely different behind closed doors. The source of this contradictory behavior lies in two related concepts—*tatemae-honne* and *omote-ura*. *Tatemae* (principle) refers to the standard of behavior one is expected to exhibit in any particular public situation. It is that to which one must outwardly agree in order to get along.[126] Conversely, *honne* (reality) is what one really believes to be true. Likewise, *omote* (front) refers to what one actually says or does in public settings, while *ura* (back) is what one keeps private or hidden away from the sight of others. Working within this ambiguous moral orientation, Japanese political leaders may publicly declare one position to satisfy a sense of obligation to their constituents (*omote* expressing *tatemae*) while negotiating a completely different policy in private meetings *(ura)*. All the while, he or she may secretly believe neither policy will work and something entirely different is needed *(honne)*.[127] But whatever the source of a Japanese leader's paradoxical behavior, one thing is consistent: the values he or she uses to determine what stance is appropriate are, invariably, extensions of a core value in Japanese society—preservation of the group.[128]

Group Dynamics and Decision Processes

Life in Japan, perhaps more than in any other society, is group oriented. From early childhood to death, Japanese see themselves not as individuals but as members of families, schools, companies, political associations, clubs, and cliques. Indeed, the "homogeneous, conformist in-group [is] the basic unit of society."[129] Consequently, Japanese tend to interpret everything in terms of affiliation and feel lost when not connected with some group.[130]

According to social anthropologist Nakane Chie, principles of the Japanese social group clearly mirror those of the traditional household institution, or *ie*. The traditional household was made up of a lord and his immediate family, their retainers, and the wives and children of those retainers, all forming an integrated, corporate group. Emotional bonding was very strong within these groups, more so even than between the lord and his adult siblings who were members of other households.[131]

In modern Japan, the *ie* framework can be seen in every group, and it pervades larger organizations as well. Every private company and public agency functions as an *ie*, with the employer as its head. Employees and their families are all considered members of this notional household, and the employer takes responsibility for their well-being. In return, employee families make the company their central focus, placing its interests above those of non-immediate family members living apart and not connected with the company. Taken as a whole, the establishment embodies a large, corporate family, but it can also be divided into smaller households.[132]

Every organization in Japan, public or private, consists of a network of functional groups. Though institutions may differ in form and function, the groups within them share many of the same characteristics. Functional groups tend to be small, around 10 members, even in large organizations. Each arranges itself hierarchically, according to seniority. Members of the group with greater seniority bond with newer members forming *sempai-kohai*, or senior-junior, relationships, and emotional ties become very strong. Private and public employment may last a lifetime, but the emotional security that functional groups provide is not unconditional. Members are expected to support the norms and goals of the group, whether they believe in them or not, and peers apply a gentle but unrelenting pressure towards conformity.[133] To illustrate, let us examine the way functional groups handle decision making.

The Confucian emphasis on harmony requires that members reach consensus on all important issues with which the group is concerned. Given the subtleties of Japanese social ritual, making important decisions can be a lengthy undertaking. A typical meeting to decide a critical policy or procedure might begin with key *sempai* cautiously laying out alternative viewpoints, always taking care to protect the feelings of others in the group. He or she will make an effort to include everyone's input, and all members participate in the discussion to some extent, so a majority position soon emerges. However, a decision cannot be made, nor can work commence, until everyone in the group expresses support. Assertiveness is considered rude, and members avoid directly saying no.[134] On particularly difficult issues, the meeting may have to break for lunch or even adjourn for the night, but eventually the majority position gains strength. Sociological studies have found that when it includes about 70 percent of participants, minority advocates generally concede for the sake of harmony.[135] Occasionally, mavericks do attempt to hold out. This rogue behavior draws pressure from peers, which increases sharply over time. The ultimate penalty is ostracism, but rarely are extreme measures necessary. Each individual's emotional dependence on group membership tends to reinforce the desire for consensus so deeply conditioned in Japanese society.[136]

Given Japan's strong focus on group loyalty and rigid hierarchy, vertical rather than horizontal bonds predominate in Japanese society. Once again, this reflects patterns seen in the traditional *ie*, as each samurai felt more strongly connected to his parents and members of his own household than to his siblings. As Nakane points out, it may also stem from the fact that loyalties among those in lower classes focused on the village, rather than on caste affiliation as in some cultures.[137] In any case, the Japanese tendency to define correct behavior in terms of context and obligation serves both to strengthen vertical bonds and weaken horizontal links, as circles of obligation are defined largely by group membership. Japanese feel strong obligations to members of their own group, and the *on-giri* interaction also links group members to those above and below them in the social or organizational hierarchy. Frequently, individuals at different levels in the same line of authority form *oyabun-kobun* (patron-client) relationships that last a lifetime.[138] But this kinship does not extend to anyone outside the same vertical chain of authority, and behavior toward outgroup persons is not constrained by the bonds of obligation.[139]

Consequently, Japanese tendencies toward competition or cooperation are determined largely by the frame of reference in which the participants find themselves. Companies may compete viciously with one another until a "parent" organization—such as the pre-war *zaibatsu* (financial cliques) or today's Ministry of Economy, Trade, and Industry (METI)—brings them into the same *ie* where they can develop common interests and goals. In similar fashion, every agency or company leader strives to bolster an organization-wide sense of *ie*, thereby enhancing cooperation between departments. Even so, the tendency for Japanese workers to focus on their own functional group is strong, and when that happens they can become uncommunicative, competitive, or even hostile to collateral groups.

However, that does not imply the Japanese need a strong, assertive leader before they will cooperate with one another—quite the contrary. Despite the autocratic nature of certain personal relationships, group leaders are expected to do little more than serve as figureheads, symbols of solidarity.[140] Consequently, Japanese workers distrust and resent managers who attempt to strongly influence the decision-making process. In Japanese society, "the first and usually the all-consuming obligation of leadership is to maintain group morale and above all not to impose an independent will or even to determine policy directions."[141] The essence of Japanese leadership lies in consensus building. Managers, chiefs, directors, and ministers are expected not to lead their respective organizations, but to provide a warm, paternalistic environment in which subordinates can reach decisions through consensus. Leaders are expected to foster a sense of *ie* so that those beneath them will cooperate with one another.[142]

The combined effects of unassertive leadership and consensus decision making have resulted in a tradition of *ringisei*, or "decision making from below," in Japan's government agencies and ministries.[143] In *ringisei*, administrative decisions are made through the circulation of a document called a *ringisho*. The process begins when a low-ranking administrator drafts a *ringisho* proposing a new idea or, perhaps, a solution to some existing problem. The document then circulates among other officials in the organization who affix their seals to certify their agreement with the policy proposed. Following a sometimes complex and circuitous route, the document reaches higher and higher levels in the organization until it finally arrives on the chief executive's desk. When he approves the *ringisho*, the decision is made.[144]

Ringisei epitomizes the Japanese decision-making process. In giving all offices the opportunity to approve a *ringisho*, the document represents a consensus decision. If some department does not accept it, little face is lost as the originator was a low-ranking administrator and his or her department can attribute the blunder to inexperience. But if the *ringisho* successfully makes its way through the system, everyone gets some credit. The leader, far from asserting his authority, simply endorses the unanimous will of his subordinates; the decision he approves is the product of the paternalistic environment he created in his *ie*. As every official had a say on the *ringisho* and the chief did not impose his own will, everyone in the organization feels obligated to support the decision.[145]

Yet, there is more to *ringisei* than meets the eye. Rarely will an administrator draft a *ringisho* if he or she suspects a substantial chance exists that someone will reject it—to do so would cause a personal loss of face. Consequently, Japanese bureaucrats invest considerable effort in *nemawashi* (literally, "root binding"), a series of informal consultations with members of other work groups, departments, and even outside agencies—anyone who might have a veto on the formal *ringisho* when it comes around—until unofficial understanding and agreement is reached.[146] If the originator cannot persuade everyone concerned to support the proposal, the *ringisho* is usually withheld or, if it was put in circulation before a conflict was discovered, withdrawn. Ultimately, *nemawashi* is a central feature of Japanese decision making in all its manifestations, whether *ringisei* is involved or not. The Japanese go to great lengths to prepare the ground for whatever plan they intend to initiate. To move precipitously would invite confrontation and loss of face.[147]

As the following chapters will illustrate, the peculiarities of Japanese decision making significantly impacted the way Japan responded to compellence. But before I proceed to that portion of the study, I must complete one last segment of the strategic culture profile. I must explain how Japanese leaders distorted traditional values and symbols in the imperial era.

Values and Symbols in Imperial Japan

The historical survey described how Meiji leaders attempted to strengthen public empathy with certain traditional values in order to motivate greater sacrifice from subjects in the modernization effort. That program came to fruition in the imperial era with profound effects on Japanese attitudes. This section analyzes the impact of Japanese ultra-nationalism on the popular interpretation of traditional values, and it examines symbols the Japanese came to associate with certain nationalist themes.

In his book, *Japanese Political Culture: Change and Continuity*, political scientist Ishida Takeshi proposes that not only was group cohesiveness a core value in Meiji Japan, but "to catch up with and surpass the Western powers" was a national goal that eventually achieved core-value status as well.[148] As Ishida explains:

Generally speaking, it may be better to deal with a national goal as a matter of policy rather than of value; but in the case of Japan, because of the immanent nature of value orientation and the strong tradition of group cohesiveness, once the national goal is decided, the goal becomes internalized in [the] popular mind to form a part of the value itself. Since the goal to catch up with and surpass the Western powers was considered imperative for the maintenance of national independence, this goal occupied a major role in the national value system.[149]

But as this profile has illustrated, the strong tradition of group cohesiveness to which Ishida refers was not focused at the national level, but at the level of household, *han*, and village, instead. Therefore, in order to internalize this national goal in the minds of Japanese subjects and thereby elevate it to value status, Meiji leaders had to redirect popular loyalties from local entities to the nation. To that end, they employed a technique with deep roots in tradition—one used persistently by Japanese public and private leaders thereafter—they enlarged the public conception of *ie*.[150]

Using a wide variety of propaganda vehicles, imperial leaders persistently emphasized that the Japanese people were a single family, the children of their divine emperor. But the emperor was more than a simple father figure representing corporate harmony and national solidarity. As heir to an imperial line, unbroken for ages eternal, he was the ultimate object of filial piety. Moreover, as the repository of both spiritual authority and political legitimacy, the emperor was also the embodiment of absolute value.[151] Building on these themes, Japanese leaders sought to modernize their country and, eventually, match the national power of Western nations by constantly striving for greatness and perfection according to the principles of *bushido*.[152]

Formerly a list of rules for samurai conduct, Meiji leaders transformed the Code of *Bushido* into a national ethos that blended personal sacrifice and martial values with state Shinto. The qualities of loyalty, obedience, diligence, frugality, and filial piety had long been cornerstones of

Confucian-martial ethics. Meiji leaders redirected these virtues from local authorities to the emperor, giving them a sacred quality. As a result, the bounded, contractual nature of *giri* was replaced by the unlimited obligation of *gimu*, and every deed of service rendered the state became a loving act of *chu*, a payment on the debt than can never be fully repaid.[153]

Furthermore, if the obligations of *bushido* were limitless, so were the powers it promised. Building on historical themes such as the sun-goddess legend and the myth of divine intervention during the Mongol invasions, imperial leaders exploited the traditional belief that the Japanese were a chosen people. The emperor was sacred, inviolable, and infallible. If Japan served the emperor to the fullest expectations of *bushido*, she would realize her destiny despite the West's material and financial advantages. Western nations based their power on military force, and Japan struggled to catch up. But inwardly the Japanese placed their greatest faith in "spirit over matter." Though they raced to match the West in armament, ships and guns were considered merely the outward manifestations of the Japanese spirit, just as the sword had symbolized that spirit in the past.[154]

Ultimately, as the traditional *ie* grew to engulf all of Japan in a single corporate family, *bushido*, Shinto, the emperor, and *kokutai* all became inseparably linked. *Bushido* came to symbolize all that was virtuous and patriotic, and Japan became a nation of samurai doing *chu* for a sacred father according to its precepts. The concept of *kokutai*, the national entity of Japan, broadened to engulf all the primary national goals—first, restoration; then, building a strong country; and finally, establishing a continental empire—and internalized those goals as a single core value.[155] The emperor became the consummate symbol of *kokutai*. Deified by Shinto mythology and venerated as the heir in an unbroken line of imperial authority, the emperor not only legitimized the power of government, he headed the national family. Consequently, as *kokutai* grew to represent all that Japan was as a nation, so did the emperor.[156]

WHAT THIS SUGGESTS ABOUT IMPERIAL JAPAN'S STRATEGIC BEHAVIOR

This book has reached a crucial juncture. Earlier, I modeled a conceptual linkage between culture and strategic decision making and thereby derived a theory about how strategic culture affects compellence outcomes. I have now profiled those aspects of Japanese culture this theory suggests conditioned Tokyo's responses to coercive threat during Japan's imperial era. What remains to be done before I can test this theory against the historical record is to hypothesize just how the factors identified in the Japanese culture profile affected the behavior of Japanese leaders in the three compellence cases selected. Of course, the study's principal

Table 3.1
Japanese Cultural Traits Relevant to Strategic Decision Making

TABLE OF RELEVANT CULTURAL TRAITS

Symbols	Values	Social Behaviors
	Core Values—	Harmony-Seeking Behaviors—
Emperor	- *Kokutai*	- Consensus Decision Making
Amaterasu	- Harmony—Group Preservation	- Non-Assertive Leadership
Yamato	- Surpass the West, Colonize	- Bottom-Up Policy Making
		- Pressure to Conform
	Warrior Virtues—	- Confrontation Avoidance
Bushido	- Courage	- Elaborate Social Ritual
Samurai	- Loyalty, Service	- Indirect Communication
47 Ronin	- Diligence	- Exaggerated Courtesy
Kamikaze	- Stoicism	- Competition Avoidance
	- Face, Avoiding Shame	
	- Fatalism	Group Identification Dominance—
		- *Ie* Frame of Reference
	Confucian Virtues—	- In/Out-Group Discrimination
Kanson	- Hierarchy	- Factionalism
Minpi	- Order, Regulation, Law	
	- Debt Repayment	Hierarchy-Based Behaviors—
	- Contextual Morality	- Patron-Client Relationships
	- Filial Piety	- Hierarchy-Based Discrimination
Gekokujo	- Competence	- Vertical Bonding
	- Propriety	

hypothesis is my thesis—that culture conditioned the perceptions, strategic preferences, and decision-making processes of Imperial Japan's leaders, causing them to respond to coercive threat in ways that cannot be fully explained by cost-benefit analysis or balance of interest theories. But to test this hypothesis in a falsifiable manner, I must develop a series of supporting hypotheses linking specific cultural traits to predicted behaviors. Table 3.1 facilitates developing those hypotheses.

Table 3.1 depicts the specific symbols, values, and social behaviors I propose are relevant to strategic decision making.[157] Related factors are loosely grouped together, both within and across categories. I must emphasize, however, that the complex nature of culture cannot be accurately depicted in such a two-dimensional arrangement; factors widely separated on the table may be, and often are, closely interrelated. Yet organizing the elements into loose groupings of associated factors simplifies the task of applying them to the strategic culture theory. By linking them to their respective perceptions, strategic preferences, and decision-making processes within the imperial Japanese government, I derive the following hypotheses:[158]

Hypothesis 1. Japanese leaders will comply with the coercer's demands if they are convinced that further resistance will jeopardize one or more of Japan's core values. Conversely, Japanese leaders will resist the coercer's demands if they believe that compliance will jeopardize one or more of those core values. Evocation of symbols associated with these values will intensify the responses.

Hypothesis 2. The acculturation of warrior virtues throughout Japanese society will strengthen Japanese resolve to resist compellence. The glorification of courage, loyalty, service, and diligence will make compliance with an adversary's demands seem dishonorable. Evocation of symbols associated with these values will intensify Japan's will to resist.

Hypothesis 3. Tendencies toward stoicism will increase Japanese abilities to resist compellence. Japanese leaders will be slow to acknowledge that they have been denied the benefits of further resistance, and Japanese at all levels of society will be less responsive to the pain of punishment.

Hypothesis 4. The need to maintain face and avoid shame will increase Japanese tendencies to resist compellence. Compliance with an adversary's demands will seem shameful.

Hypothesis 5. The Japanese regard for hierarchy will make Japanese leaders more compliant with a coercer's demands if they believe the coercer represents a source of authority superior to themselves. Conversely, if the coercer represents a source of authority they perceive as subordinate or inferior to themselves, Japanese leaders will resist the compellence attempt more stridently.

Hypothesis 6. The Japanese regard for order, regulation, law, and debt repayment will make Japanese leaders more compliant with compellence if they perceive the coercer's demands are justifiable according to some code of law. Conversely, Japanese leaders will resist compellence more aggressively if they believe they have legal justification for doing so. However, Japanese tendencies toward contextual morality may mitigate their sensitivities to legal authority, as they may be inclined to challenge the coercer's justification on the grounds of lack of jurisdiction or outmoded standards.

Hypothesis 7. Japanese tendencies toward contextual morality will complicate efforts to satisfy a coercer's demands, as leaders will find themselves in moral dilemmas when trying to serve competing internal constituencies. Their words and actions will seem duplicitous to external audiences.

Hypothesis 8. Japan's devotion to filial piety will make Japanese leaders more resistant to compellence if they perceive such resistance is in the best interests of their national father, the emperor. However, if they become convinced that further resistance is contrary to the emperor's interests, they will become compliant.

Hypothesis 9. Japan's admiration for competence and propriety will make Japanese leaders more resistant to compellence, as compliance with an adversary's demands would suggest military and civilian leaders are less than competent in defending the nation's interests.

Hypothesis 10. The tradition of *gekokujo,* usurping governmental authority when subordinates believe policy makers are acting incompetently or inappropriately, will inhibit the Japanese government's ability to deal with coercive threats in a timely and effective manner. When subordinate groups are dissatisfied with national policies, they will act independently, confounding the government's attempts to effectively deal with external challenges. Alternatively, national decision makers will be deterred from taking necessary courses of action when they fear that such steps will antagonize subordinate groups and risk *gekokujo.*

Hypothesis 11. Japan's bottom-up, consensus-driven, decision-making process will make it difficult for Japanese leaders to respond quickly and effectively to coercive threat.[159] The bottom-up nature of the Japanese policy-making process will tend to make responses to external threats proposed by individual agencies parochial and self serving. Efforts to reach internal consensus will result in bloated, unreasonable counteroffers to coercers' demands. Pressures on advocates of unpopular alternatives to conform to majority positions will perpetuate bureaucratic inertia and frustrate the development of innovative approaches to resolving national crises.

Hypothesis 12. Due to the dynamics entailed in Japan's consensus decision-making process, the policies the Japanese government develops in response to coercive threats will vacillate from time to time with changes in makeup of the functional, decision-making group. This will complicate efforts to respond quickly and effectively to compellent threats and confound efforts to communicate effectively with coercers.

Hypothesis 13. The Japanese dichotomy between *tatemae* (principle) and *honne* (reality), combined with tendencies toward non-assertive leadership, will result in Japanese leaders publicly professing policies contrary to their personal preferences, thereby confusing communications with coercers and complicating efforts to reach accommodation with them.

Hypothesis 14. Japanese abhorrence to personal confrontation will result in bureaucratic inertia, complicating efforts to respond quickly and effectively to coercive threat. Leaders opposed to established positions will avoid directly communicating their dissatisfaction to political opponents, delaying and confounding the reevaluation of existing policies.

Hypothesis 15. Japan's ability to respond quickly and effectively to coercive threats will largely depend on its leaders' perceptions of the scope and breadth of the *ie* (households) to which they belong. When Japanese leaders set their frames of reference on a national-level *ie,* they will respond to external threats in a timely, unified manner. However, when frames of reference devolve to agency- or service-level *ie,* Japanese leaders will become parochial and decision making will be hindered by factionalism.

FINAL THOUGHTS

This chapter examined the symbols, values, and patterns of social interaction relevant to Japan's strategic behavior during the imperial era, and it explored the sources of those traits. However, the process of profiling Japan's strategic culture also revealed that the Japanese government mounted an intense propaganda program during the late nineteenth and early twentieth centuries. Designed to motivate extraordinary sacrifice from Japanese subjects, that program focused on and magnified certain traditional values and symbols. In fact, they were the very values and symbols relevant to this study.

This discovery shows no original insight as many historians have made the same observation. Yet, it does raise some important questions that must be considered in addition to those implied in the foregoing hypotheses. Were Japanese leaders conscious of the distortions they introduced into their own culture, or were they oblivious to the way their interpretations differed from historical renderings? Either way, did the cultural interpretations they created influence their own strategic behavior? Were they pure puppet masters, or were they entangled in the very strings they used to manipulate their subjects. Of course, these issues comprise only a portion of the larger question—whether Imperial Japan's strategic culture influenced the ways that Japanese leaders responded to compellence. That is the central question of this study. To answer any of these questions, we must turn to the case studies in the chapters that follow.

NOTES

1. Delmer M. Brown, *Nationalism in Japan: An Introductory Historical Analysis* (Berkeley, Calif.: University of California Press, 1955), pp. 7–11; Lawrence E. Grinter, "Cultural and Historical Influences in Sinic Asia: China, Japan, and Vietnam" in Stephen J. Bank, Lawrence E. Grinter, Karl P. Magyar, Lewis B. Ware, Bynum E. Weathers, *Conflict, Culture, and History: Regional Dimensions* (Maxwell AFB, AL: Air University Press, 1993), p. 149; H. Byron Earhart, *Religions of Japan* (San Francisco: Harper & Row, Publishers, 1984), p. 10.

2. Brown, pp. 7 and 11; Peter Duus, *Feudalism in Japan* (New York: Alfred A. Knopf, 1969), pp. 19–20; Peter R. Moody, Jr., *Tradition and Modernization in China and Japan* (Belmont, Calif.: Wadsworth Publishing Company, 1995), p. 92.

3. George B. Sansom, *A History of Japan to 1334* (Stanford, Calif.: Stanford University Press, 1958), p. 25.

4. Edwin O. Reischauer and Marius B. Jansen, *The Japanese Today: Change and Continuity* (Cambridge, Mass.: The Belnap Press, 1995), pp. 200–209.

5. Moody, pp. 68–70; Sansom, pp. 24–28.

6. Duus, pp. 20–22.

7. The Sui Dynasty began with the accession of Yan Ch'ien in 581 A.D. and stood until 618 when replaced by the T'ang Dynasty (618–907).

8. Brown, pp. 11–13; Duus, p. 22.

9. Ruth C. Benedict, *The Chrysanthemum and the Sword* (Boston: Houghton Mifflin, 1946), p. 117. Chinese Confucianists described an emperor's right to rule as the "Mandate of Heaven." If an emperor did not rule competently and justly, he could lose that mandate in the eyes of his subjects and they would be morally entitled to rebel. See Tekeshi Ishida and Ellis S. Krauss, *Democracy in Japan* (Pittsburgh: University of Pittsburgh Press, 1989), p. 4.

10. Duus, p. 23; Moody, pp. 59–60; Sansom, p. 71.

11. Robert N. Bellah, *Tokugawa Religion: The Values of Pre-Industrial Japan* (Boston: Beacon Press, 1957), p. 87.

12. Bellah, p. 89; Duus, p. 24.

13. Sansom, p. 70.

14. Ibid., p. 97.

15. During one period in the seventh century, the Japanese did employ an elaborate system of schools and examinations in an effort to emulate Chinese methods. However, this scheme was merely perfunctory in terms of selection for office. Only court officials were allowed to enter the schools, and examination outcomes had little bearing on later appointments. See Duus, p. 27–28.

16. Benedict, p. 117; Ishida and Krauss, p. 5.

17. Earhart, p. 31.

18. Brown, p. 13; Earhart, p. 29; Sansom, p. 25. See also Richard Cavendish, *The Eastern Religions* (New York: Arco Publications, 1980) and L. M. Hopfe, *Religions of the World* (Encino, Calif.: Glencoe Publishing Co., 1976).

19. Brown, p. 13; Earhart, 32–33. Prince Shotoku, author of the Confucian-based constitution mentioned earlier, was also one of Buddhism's most ardent champions in early Japan.

20. Earhart, p. 30; Sansom, pp. 61–63.

21. Sansom, pp. 61–62.

22. Earhart, p. 30. As Shinto had no complex theology or ethical system, its main contribution to Japanese values stemmed from the belief in the emperor's divinity and that the Japanese were a chosen people.

23. Bellah, p. 88.

24. Duus, p. 29; Sansom, pp. 195–200.

25. The Yamato established their first capital at Nara in 710 A.D. In 794, they moved it to Heian, the early name of the city of Kyoto.

26. Brown, pp. 21–22; Duus, pp. 27–36.

27. Lawrence E. Grinter, "Cultural and Historical Influences in Sinic Asia: China, Japan, and Vietnam," in Stephen J. Blank, et al. *Conflict, Culture, and History: Regional Dimensions* (Maxwell AFB, Ala.: Air University Press, 1993), pp. 151–52. Throughout the text of this book, I cite Japanese names in the form commonly used in Asia—surname, followed by given name. When referring to any individual by a single name, I use the one most commonly referenced in academic literature. Members of prominent families, such as the Minamoto, are often referred to by their given names, though historically significant individuals who lack famous lineage are usually mentioned by surname. When citing Asian names in notes and the bibliography, I use standard reference methods: given name first in notes, surname first in the bibliography.

28. The Japanese are immensely proud that a single dynasty has held the imperial throne throughout Japan's history. However, that is not to say that emperors in the twentieth century are the biological descendants of the Yamato rulers of old. Japanese customs of adoption and inheritance differ from western conventions in that function and qualification take precedence over blood in issues of succession. Consequently, it was not uncommon for the throne to shift from one family branch to another or even be conferred to an adopted son when politically expedient. See Harumi Befu, "Corporate Empasis and Patterns of Descent in the Japanese Fam-

ily," in Robert J. Smith and Richard K. Beardsley (eds.), *Japanese Culture: Its Development and Characteristics* (Chicago: Aldine Publishing Co., 1962), pp. 34–42.

29. Grinter, p. 152.

30. Duus, pp. 50–51.

31. Duus, p. 56; Moody, p. 92.

32. Sansom, p. 311.

33. Grinter, pp. 150–155; Sansom, p. 359.

34. Duus, p. 42.

35. Sansom, p. 361.

36. Duus, p. 42; Ishida and Krauss, p. 5; and Sansom, p. 360.

37. The Japanese word for warrior is *bushi*. The warrior class was the *buke*.

38. Hojo Shigetoki, "The Message of Master Gokurakuji," in William Scot Wilson, trans., *Ideals of the Samurai: Writings of Japanese Warriors* (Burbank, Calif.: Ohara, 1982), p. 38.

39. Duus, pp. 42–43.

40. James Murdoch, *A History of Japan*, Vol. 1: *From the Origins to the arrival of the Portuguese in 1542* A.D. (New York: Frederick Ungar Publishing Co., 1964), p. 498; Sansom, p. 439.

41. Kozo Yamamura, ed., *The Cambridge History of Japan*, Vol. 3, *Medieval Japan* (Cambridge: Cambridge University Press, 1990), pp. 131–32 and 135–37. Also see Brown, pp. 25–26; Sansom, pp. 439–40.

42. Sansom, p. 440.

43. Ibid., pp. 439–41.

44. Murdoch, p. 507; Yamamura, p. 138.

45. Sansom, p. 442.

46. Brown, p. 26; Murdoch, pp. 508–13; Sansom, pp. 443–44; Yamamura, pp. 139–42.

47. F. Brinkley, *A History of the Japanese People: From the Earliest Times to the End of the Meiji Era* (New York: The Encyclopedia Britannica Co., 1914), pp. 361–62; Brown, p. 26; Sansom, pp. 444–45.

48. Sansom, pp. 445–47; Yamamura, p. 146.

49. Brinkley, p. 363; Sansom, pp. 448–50.

50. Brown, pp. 26–27; Grinter, p. 152.

51. Brown, pp. 30–32.

52. Brown, p. 32. On reading this passage, political scientist Yoichiro Sato pointed out that, while Kitabatake may have coined the term "kokutai" during this period, the idea did not consolidate within the national consciousness until a much later era.

53. Brinkley, pp. 462–64.

54. Ibid., p. 485.

55. Buddhism claims millions of adherents in modern Japan, but its numerical strength is largely the residual effect of a Tokugawa-era edict requiring subjects to declare some religious affiliation other than Christianity. Buddhism's influence on Japanese values waned sharply after the Nobunaga persecution, and Tokugawa-era declarations were more a product of political obligation than religious conviction. See Bellah, p. 51; Reischauer and Jansen, pp. 206–207; and Ryusaku Tsunoda, William T. de Bary, and Donald Keene, *Sources of Japanese Tradition* (New York: Columbia University Press, 1958), p. 331.

56. Sansom, p. 429.

57. Benedict, p. 242; Earhart, pp. 36–37; Moody, p. 62; Edwin O. Reischauer, *The Japanese* (Cambridge, Mass.: The Belnap Press, 1977), p. 60; Sansom, pp. 429–31; Alan Watts, *The Way of Zen* (New York: Vintage Books, 1985), p. 107.

58. Though Hideyoshi ruled Japan as surely as any of his predecessors, not having descended from the Minamoto, he was ineligible for the title of shogun. Therefore, he was granted the title of "Imperial Regent" and governed in the name of the emperor. This arrangement had precedent in both the Heian and Kamakura eras.

59. Grinter, p. 153.

60. Duus, p. 90.

61. The period of the Tokugawa shogunate is often called the Edo era because Tokugawa Ieyasu established the headquarters for his *bakufu* in Edo, present-day Tokyo.

62. Grinter, pp. 154–55.

63. See "Laws Governing the Military Houses," in Tsunoda, et al., 1958.

64. Brown, pp. 49–50; Duus, pp. 91–96; Moody, pp. 98 and 100; and E. Herbert Norman, *Japan's Emergence as a Modern State: Political and Economic Problems of the Meiji Period* (Westport, Conn.: Greenwood Press, 1940), pp. 14–15.

65. Duus, p. 105; Earhart, pp. 30 and 40.

66. Benedict, pp. 61–68; Moody, 95–96.

67. Benedict, pp. 61–68; Moody, pp. 96–97. In addition to these four main social classes, there were also the nobility and the *eta*. The nobility, members of branch houses of the imperial family, held samurai status, but were considered a cut above other warriors in social distinction. The *eta* were a caste of untouchables who disposed of the dead, handled sanitation projects, and performed other services considered "unclean," such as butchering meat and tanning leather.

68. Brinkley, pp. 546–55; Brown, pp. 42–47; Earhart, p. 39; Moody, pp. 98–99.

69. Shinto also enjoyed a revival in this period. However, as Shinto lacks a system of ethics, Tokugawa values and attitudes stemmed from Confucianism almost exclusively. See Brown, pp. 51–54; Earhart, p. 19; Reischauer and Jansen, p. 204.

70. Brown, pp. 51–52; Tsunoda, et al., p. 311.

71. Given the rigid stratification of Tokugawa society, each class, with its separate problems and social orientation, had a unique ethical focus. Emphasis on martial virtue was most representative of the samurai, of course, while the other classes placed more importance on diligence, frugality, and obligation to family. However, as the Edo era progressed, the strongest attributes of each class tended to influence the ideas of the others until, by the mid–nineteenth century, Japan was nearly homogeneous in attitude and value orientation. See Bellah, pp. 83, 121–22, and 124–31.

72. As Ruth Benedict points out, the term *bushido* is a fairly recent one. Though used earlier, the term did not become common until the early twentieth century when it was popularized by Inazo Nitobe in his 1899 classic, *Bushido: The Soul of Japan*. Nevertheless, the conception that Nitobe romanticized was essentially the notional warrior code as it had evolved in the late Edo era. See Benedict, p. 175; Inazo Nitobe, *Bushido: The Soul of Japan* (Tokyo: Charles E. Tuttle Co., 1941).

73. Brown, pp. 53–54; Tsunoda, et al., p. 395.

74. Tsunoda, et al., pp. 396–97. Yamaga's exile in Ako is also significant in terms of Japan's cultural history. In 1703, 47 *ronin* (masterless samurai) assassinated a close confidant of the shogun to avenge the death of their lord, Asano Naganori, two years earlier. Having violated Tokugawa law, the *ronin* later committed suicide to preserve their honor and Asano's. But, as vengeance and willingness to die for one's lord were both highly esteemed in Japan's Confucian-martial culture, the 47 *ronin* were hailed as tragic heroes, and the entire episode was celebrated throughout Japan as a sterling example of martial virtue. The Yamaga connection is direct—Asano and the 47 *ronin* were from Ako, where Yamaga spent his exile. Before his death, Yamaga had educated the Ako samurai in Confucian ethics and *bushido*. See Brinkley, pp. 606–08.

75. Moody, p. 101; Tsunoda, et al., p. 397.

76. Moody, pp. 96–97; Norman, p. 17.

77. Brown, p. 58.

78. Moody, p. 97; Norman, pp. 19 and 55.

79. Moody, p. 97; Norman, pp. 19–25.

80. Sidney Giffard, *Japan Among the Powers, 1890–1990* (New Haven, Conn: Yale University Press, 1994), p. 88.

81. See Thomas C. Smith, "'Merit' as Ideology in the Tokugawa Period," in R. P. Dore (ed.), *Aspects of Social Change in Modern Japan* (Princeton, N.J.: Princeton University Press, 1967), pp. 71–90.

82. John Whitney Hall, "A Monarch for Modern Japan," in Robert E. Ward (ed.), *Political Development in Modern Japan* (Princeton, N.J.: Princeton University Press, 1968), p. 36.

83. Yamaga was one of the first Edo-era writers to focus on this theme when he asserted that Japanese culture and traditions were superior to those of China because a single, divine line had occupied Japan's imperial house, while China had seen numerous dynasties rise and fall. See Tsunoda, et al., pp. 396–97.

84. Brown, pp. 58–61; Takeshi Ishida, *Japanese Political Culture: Change and Continuity* (New Brunswick, Conn.: Transaction Books, 1983), pp. 5–6.

85. Brown, p. 74; Moody, pp. 119–20.

86. Brown, pp. 76–80; Moody, p. 120.

87. Although the shogun willingly stepped down, subsequent mistreatment by the imperial court at the behest of Choshu and Satsusma agitators provoked him and several loyal retainers to attempt counter coups. These insurrections were all put down in short order. See Brinkley, p. 678.

88. Brinkley, pp. 664–78; Brown, pp. 80–90; Duus, pp. 108–9; Moody, p. 120.

89. Hall, p. 44.

90. Because the *genro* worked behind the scenes, there is relatively little written about them in Western scholarship beyond the biographies of leading individuals. Records were not kept of their meetings, and there is not complete agreement, even among Japanese scholars, on who the *genro* were. Most sources list Matsukata Masayoshi (1835–1924), Inoue Kaoru (1836–1915), Yamagata Aritomo (1838–1922), Kuroda Kiyotaka (1840–1900), Ito Hirobumi (1841–1909), Oyama Iwao (1842–1916), and Saigo Tsugumichi (1843–1902). Some sources also include Katsura Taro (1848–1913) and Saionji Kimmochi (1849–1940) who the Emperor apparently added to the roll early in the twentieth century. Henceforth, when I use the terms *genro* or "elder statesmen," I am referring to one or more of these nine individuals.

See Moody, pp. 124–25; Roger F. Hackett, "Political Modernization and the Meiji *Genro*," in Ward, pp. 65–97.

91. Do not confuse the *genro* with the *genro-in*, or "Council of Elders." The *genro-in* was a senate established in 1875 charged with enacting laws for the Empire. It never achieved any real legislative power and was abolished in 1890 following promulgation of the Meiji Constitution. See Hackett, p. 68.

92. Nobutaka Ike, *Japanese Politics: Patron-Client Democracy* (New York: Alfred A. Knopf, 1957), 67.

93. Brown, pp. 91–100; Grinter, pp. 155–56.

94. Hall, p. 57.

95. See the Meiji Constitution in its entirety in Brinkley, Appendix 1, pp. 732–40.

96. Brown, p. 115; Dan Fenno Henderson, "Law and Political Modernization in Japan" in Ward, p. 421; and Masao Maruyama, "Politics as a Science in Japan: Retrospect and Prospects," Arthur Tiedemann, trans., in Masao Maruyama, *Thought and Behavior in Modern Japanese Politics* (London: Oxford University Press, 1963), p. 229.

97. Ike, pp. 27–30 and 68; Ishida and Krauss, pp. 6–7; Robert M. March, *Reading the Japanese Mind: The Realities Behind Their Thoughts and Actions* (Tokyo: Kodansha International, 1996), p. 121; Moody, pp. 122–23.

98. Henderson, pp. 419–26. Between 1885 and 1900, the seven main *genro* held a total of 40 ministerial positions between them. See the table in Hackett, p. 72.

99. Curtis H. Martin and Bruce Stronach, *Politics East and West: A Comparison of Japanese and British Political Culture* (Armonk, N.Y.: M.E. Sharpe, 1992), p. 16.

100. John M. Maki, "Expansion by Force and Diplomacy: Traditional Militarism" in Marlene Mayo (ed.), *The Emergence of Imperial Japan: Self Defense or Calculated Aggression?* (Lexington, Mass.: D.C. Heath and Co., 1970), p. 31.

101. Marius B. Jansen, "Changing Japanese Attitudes Toward Modernization" in Marius B. Jansen, ed., *Changing Japanese Attitudes Toward Modernization* (Princeton, N.J.: Princeton University Press, 1965), p. 69.

102. Ibid., pp. 70–71. Also see Brown, pp. 125–26; George B. Sansom, *The Western World and Japan: A Study in the Interaction of European and Asiatic Cultures* (New York: Alfred A. Knopf, 1950), pp. 367–73.

103. Brown, pp. 112–20; Jansen, p. 70.

104. Reinhard Bendix, "Preconditions of Development: A Comparison of Japan and Germany" in Dore, p. 67; Sheldon Garon, *Molding Japanese Minds: The State in Everyday Life* (Princeton, N.J.: Princeton University Press, 1997), p. 8; Ishida, *Japanese Political Culture*, p. 5.

105. Bendix, p. 82.

106. Brown, pp. 101–3; Earhart, p. 43; Hall, pp. 25–28; Moody, p. 73.

107. Marius B. Jansen, "Modernization and Foreign Policy in Meiji Japan" in Ward, p. 175.

108. Because cultural change is a slowly evolving process, one can still see today most of the traits I describe in this section. With this in mind, and to avoid cumbersome, past-tense sentence constructions, I discuss most elements of Japanese culture using present-tense expressions. However, whenever I describe symbols, values, or behaviors exaggerated in, or unique to, the imperial era, I point that fact out and discuss them in the past tense.

109. Benedict, 98.

110. Karel van Wolferen, *The Enigma of Japanese Power: People and Politics in a Stateless Nation* (New York: Alfred A. Knopf, 1989), p. 193.

111. Benedict, p. 117. Also see Martin and Stronach, p. 13.

112. Benedict, pp. 133, 136–37, and 139–41; Martin and Stronarch, p. 13.

113. Benedict, pp. 140–42.

114. See L. Takeo Doi, "Amae: A Key Concept for Understanding Japanese Personality Structure" in Smith and Beardsley, pp. 132–39; Doi, "Giri-Ninjo: An Interpretation" in Dore, pp. 327–34; Martin and Stronach, p. 13; Wolferen, p. 257.

115. Benedict says relationships between father and son and mother-in-law and wife are particularly prone to this friction.

116. Benedict, pp. 121–25; Moody, p. 70.

117. Benedict, pp. 145.

118. March, pp. 28–29.

119. Benedict, pp. 145–64.

120. Japanese refer to intuitive communication—that is, sensing what someone really means to communicate even though they are outwardly saying something different—as *haragei*, or "belly art." For more on *haragei*, see Quansheng Zhao, *Japanese Policymaking—The Politics Behind Politics: Informal Mechanisms and the Making of China Policy* (Westport, Conn.: Praeger, 1993), p. 138.

121. Reischauer and Jansen, p. 136. I am indebted to Yoichiro Sato for explaining that face saving and confrontation avoidance often takes place at a surface level while participants manipulate one another in subtle blame games and ostracization. Consequently, group solidarity is maintained symbolically, while group composition may change. For more details on the elaborate social rituals to which Japanese resort in order to avoid confrontation, see March, pp. 19–40; Chie Nakane, *Japanese Society* (Berkeley, Calif.: University of California Press, 1972), pp. 35 and 123–24; Frederick S. Hulse, "Convention and Reality in Japanese Culture," in Bernard S. Silberman (ed.), *Japanese Character and Culture: A Book of Selected Readings* (Tucson, Ariz.: The University of Arizona Press, 1962), pp. 298–99 and 303–4.

122. Martin and Stronach, pp. 28–29.

123. Bellah, p. 13.

124. Benedict, p. 195.

125. Ibid., p. 177.

126. See March, pp. 19–31.

127. Martin and Stronach, pp. 30–31; Wolferen, pp. 235–36; Zhao, pp. 6 and 137–38.

128. Ishida, *Japanese Political Culture*, p. 4. By "core value" I mean one that takes precedence over most other values. Core values usually have deep historical roots, and other values are often derived from them.

129. Ishida, *Japanese Political Culture*, p. 7. Also see Martin and Stronach, p. 15.

130. Earhart, p. 11; Reischauer and Jansen, p. 128.

131. Nakane, p. 7; Wolferen, pp. 51–52 and pp. 165–66.

132. Nakane, pp. 7–8. Also see Ishida, *Japanese Political Culture*, p. 115; Martin and Stronach, p. 13; and Wolferen, pp. 16–17. Yoichiro Sato disagrees with Nakane's use of the *ie* anology. He maintains that the higher one moves on the ladder of social and administrative units, the more likely the family-like unity becomes more symbolic than tangible and less relevant to policy making.

133. Ike, p. 10; Moody, pp. 93–94; Martin and Stronach, pp. 21–23; Nakane, p. 7; Wolferen, pp. 340–46.

134. Political scientist Peter Moody writes, "American presidents complain that when the Japanese say yes they really mean no; they are irked when they explain their troubles to visiting Japanese prime ministers and foreign ministers, and the Japanese statesmen say: 'I understand; I will do my best'—and then nothing happens. For one thing, 'I will do my best' may be a polite way of saying no—as any Japanese in that circumstance would understand." See Moody, pp. 312–13.

135. Nakane, pp. 144–45.

136. Ibid. Also see Martin and Stronach, p. 22; Lucian W. Pye, *Asian Power and Politics: The Cultural Dimensions of Authority* (Cambridge, Mass.: The Belnap Press, 1985), pp. 168–70 and 176–78. Karel van Wolferen argues that true consensus in Japan is mythical because complete agreement is never reached without resorting to subtle forms of coercion through social intimidation. See Wolferen, pp. 337–39 and especially 340–46.

137. Nakane, pp. 23–25.

138. Moody, pp. 93–95, 286, and 288–89.

139. Ishida, *Japanese Political Culture*, pp. 108–9; Moody, pp. 94–95; Nakane, pp. 23–63.

140. Relationships between father and son and mother-in-law and wife tend to be autocratic; yet, family groups as a whole are governed by consensus. See Hall, p. 27.

141. Pye, p. 171.

142. Martin and Stronach, pp. 16 and 21–23; Moody, p. 289; Pye, pp. 171–74.

143. Martin and Stonach, p. 244. The literal translation of *ringisei* is "a system of reverential inquiry about a superior's intentions."

144. Mohamad Ala and William P. Cordeiro, "Can We Learn Management Techniques from the Japanese Ringi Process?" *Business Forum* 24, Nos. 1, 2: pp. 22–23; Kiyoaki Tsuji, "Decision-Making in the Japanese Government: A Study of Ringisei" in Ward, pp. 457–58; Zhao, pp. 121–22.

145. Ala and Cordeiro, pp. 22–23; Martin and Stronach, p. 22; Pye, pp. 171–72; Wolferen, p. 339.

146. Ala and Cordeiro, p. 23; Moody, p. 312; Zhao, pp. 201–2.

147. Martin and Stronach, p. 238; Moody, p. 312; Wolferen, p. 338.

148. Ishida, *Japanese Political Culture*, p. 4.

149. Ibid., p. 5.

150. For a thorough examination of the traditional way that Japanese avoid conflict by enlarging the in-group unit to absorb the conflicting parties, see Takeshi Ishida, "Conflict and Conflict Accommodation in Japan: Viewed in Terms of *Omote-Ura* and *Uchi-Soto* Relations," in Ellis Krauss, Thomas P. Rohlen, Patrica G. Steinhoff, *Conflict in Japan* (Berkeley, Calif.: University of California Press, 1984). Also see Pye, p. 163; Wolferen, pp. 165–66 and 259–62.

151. Maruyama, "The Theory and Psychology of Ultra-Nationalism" in Maruyama, p. 8. Also see Brown, p. 98; Wolferen, p. 251.

152. Pye, p. 163.

153. Bellah, pp. 91–93; Doi, "Giri-Ninjo: An Interpretation," pp. 331–32; Pye, p. 166.

154. Benedict, pp. 22–23.

155. Bellah, p. 105.

156. Brown, pp. 152–56; Hall, pp. 51–59; Martin and Stronach, p. 16.

157. Readers will note that this table lists very few symbols. I found it impossible to analyze Japan's history and national psyche in sufficient depth to identify all possible schemas that events might trigger in the minds of Japanese leaders. Therefore, I provide a sampling just large enough to generate hypotheses. As the cases will reveal, Japanese leaders called up these schemata and a surprising number of others with dramatic results.

158. All these supporting hypotheses presuppose that the effects of culture will manifest themselves in ways that cannot be fully explained by cost-benefit analysis or balance of interest theories. I omit stating that in every hypothesis to avoid repetition.

159. In the context of these hypotheses, an "effective" response to coercive threat is one that maximizes Japan's interests, whether by resisting or complying with the coercer's demands.

CHAPTER 4

The Triple Intervention

The Sino-Japanese War of 1894–95 marked the dawn of Japan's modern, imperial era. In its first employment outside the home islands, the Japanese military—newly reorganized, trained, and equipped along Western lines—astounded the world with a series of decisive victories against Chinese land and naval forces. Japan seized a remarkable amount of territory within the first six months of war, and the tide of Japanese conquest soon began to threaten Western interests in China. Consequently, as the belligerents moved toward peace in early 1895, representatives from several nations warned the Japanese that if they chose to retain territory on the Asian mainland, certain Western Powers would intervene. Nonetheless, Tokyo was not deterred. In the Treaty of Shimonoseki, Japan forced China to cede not only the islands of Formosa and the Pescadores, but also the Liaotung Peninsula in Manchuria.

Japan would not enjoy the fruits of victory unspoiled. Soon after the treaty terms became known, Russia, France, and Germany jointly "advised" the victors to return Liaotung to China. Although this timely intervention was not completely unexpected, Japanese leaders were stunned. They recognized this advice to be nothing less than a thinly veiled threat, one they felt compelled to heed unless they could persuade at least one other Western nation to champion their cause. But all efforts to gather support came to naught, and after a few days the proud victors of the Sino-Japanese War humbly agreed to return the most valuable parcel of their conquered territory to China. Surprising as this turn of events may seem, it is even more puzzling when examined in light of the dynamics normally associated with compellence and deterrence.

Although compellence and deterrence are theoretically similar, states-men and scholars generally agree that the former is inherently more dif-ficult than the latter. Both functions involve a coercer attempting to manipulate an adversary's calculation of costs and benefits. But while the only goal of deterrence is restraint, compellence requires the adversary to change its current behavior or perform some overt act that it would not otherwise choose to do. A deterred nation may have little or nothing in-vested in an action not yet begun, but a nation yielding to compellence must give up the benefits of its current endeavor and write off any sunk costs as well. In addition, deterrence is less provocative than compellence. Deterrence places the privilege of choice on the adversary, giving him the "last clear chance" to avoid conflict.[1] But compellence throws down the proverbial gauntlet, and this overt challenge demands humiliation. Though a nation deterred from some action can usually save face by de-nying its intention to take the prohibited step in the first place, a nation compelled is exposed as such before its own public and the world.

These considerations raise interesting questions for the case at hand. If compellence is indeed a more difficult strategy to effect than deterrence, why did the Western Powers fail to deter Japan from claiming the Liao-tung Peninsula, yet so easily compel her to return that territory? Why would Japan fight a costly war and defiantly claim its prize—a territory then occupied by 100,000 Japanese troops—only to return that prize at the request of three nations that lacked any comparable force in Asia? In sum, why did the triple intervention succeed so easily?

To answer these questions, I examine not only the triple intervention itself, but the diplomatic and military maneuvers that preceded it. Then, I evaluate these events from several perspectives. Punishment- and denial-based compellence theories go a long way toward solving the triple in-tervention mystery, and a balance of interests analysis also provides some of the missing pieces. But before we can fully understand why Japanese leaders responded to the triple intervention in the way they did, we must evaluate their actions in terms of a rationality defined not by our symbols and values, but by those of Imperial Japan.

FROM TRIUMPH TO HUMILIATION

War between Japan and China erupted in July, 1894 after more than 20 years of bitter contention over which nation should control Korea.[2] The Tonghak Tong, a radical Korean nationalist group, sparked the conflict when its followers revolted earlier that year. The king of Korea answered the uprising with force, but his troops were defeated in their first skirmish with the rebels. On May 31, 1894, he asked China to help him put down the rebellion, and Chinese troops deployed to the "hermit kingdom" al-most immediately. In keeping with the Tientsin Treaty, the Chinese government notified Japan that it was dispatching troops to restore order in its "tributary state."[3] Both the tone and substance of this note antagonized Tokyo, as Japan had long rejected the notion of Korea's tributary relationship to China. Therefore, Japanese leaders decided to counter the Chinese expeditionary force with one of their own. They deployed a brigade to Korea in the first week of June.[4]

Suspicion, tension, and frustration characterized the month of June, 1894. With the sudden arrival of foreign military force, the Tonghak Rebellion dissolved without further violence, and Korea asked both China and Japan to withdraw their troops. However, Peking and Tokyo, each wary of the other's designs, ignored Seoul's request. Tensions rose quickly, as Koreans and foreigners alike expected fighting to break out if Chinese and Japanese troops inadvertently met. To avoid a confrontation, Peking proposed they effect a simultaneous withdrawal, and Chinese leaders asked Britain and Russia to mediate a settlement to defuse the crisis.[5] However, having deployed a brigade to Korea, Japanese leaders decided to use the opportunity to press Peking on the suzerainty issue.[6] Therefore, Tokyo refused mediation, asserting the insurrection had not been fully suppressed. Furthermore, Japanese leaders charged that the rebellion had occurred because the Korean government was corrupt and inefficient, so Prime Minister Ito Hirobumi proposed they resolve the crisis by sending a joint Sino-Japanese Commission to reform the Korean state. But as the Tonghak uprising had already been put down, China rejected the idea. Peking pointed out that Japan had insisted that Korea was independent, so any domestic reform should be left to the Koreans. Dissatisfied with that response, the Japanese decided to deal directly with Seoul with the aim of getting Korean authorities to affirm their independence from China. To that end, they proposed an extensive reorganization of the Korean government. The king ignored this overture. Frustrated with the standoff, Japan began to mobilize for war.[7]

A One-Sided War

On July 11, 1894, the Imperial Cabinet decided that Japan must solve the Korea problem even if it meant going to war with China. That day Japanese leaders notified Peking that deploying more troops to Korea would be considered a hostile act. The following day, Japanese Foreign Minister Mutsu Munemitsu cabled his minister to Korea, Otori Keisuke, informing him that the time had come to take decisive steps, and "any pretext for beginning an active movement quickly would be satisfactory, so long as it did not provoke any concerted international criticism."[8] In essence, Mutsu gave Otori permission to start a war.[9]

It did not take much to set off the tinderbox that Korea had become. On July 19, Otori delivered an ultimatum to the Korean government di-

recting them to expel all Chinese troops and implement the reforms requested earlier, and he gave the Koreans three days to respond. The Seoul
government met this deadline, but the Japanese declared their answer
"vague and incomprehensible."[10] Using Korean intransigence as their pretext, the Japanese seized the royal palace on July 23 and compelled the
king to sign an agreement calling for the expulsion of Chinese troops. Two
days later, three Japanese warships encountered three Chinese men-of-
war, and a battle ensued in which the Japanese captured one Chinese
vessel and damaged the others. The Japanese squadron then sighted a
Chinese troopship en route to Korea and sank it along with 1,100 soldiers.[11] Finally, on July 29, ostensibly acting on the Korean king's request
to expel the Chinese, the Japanese brigade engaged and defeated the Chinese expeditionary force in Korea.[12]

To the world's astonishment, Japan proved more than a match for
China's backward, disorganized military establishment.[13] Peking and To-
kyo exchanged formal declarations of war on August 1, 1894, and in mid-
September, Emperor Meiji established his Imperial Headquarters in
Hiroshima. On September 17, the Japanese navy decisively defeated the
Chinese fleet in the Battle of the Yalu, giving Japan command of the waters
around Korea and northern China. Meanwhile, China deployed more
troops to Korea from the north and, linking with remnants of the first
expeditionary force, they established a stronghold at Pyongyang. But the
Japanese brigade at Seoul, now heavily reinforced, marched north and
defeated this force on September 16. Continuing their northern advance,
the Japanese crossed the Yalu River and marched into Manchuria on October 24. That same day, a second Japanese force landed at Pitzewo, on
the Liaotung Peninsula, capturing Talienwan on November 6 and Port
Arthur on November 21. The Japanese landed a third force on Shantung
Peninsula in late January, 1895, and the Chinese port city of Weihaiwei
fell to a combined attack from land and sea on February 12.[14]

By March, 1895, the two prongs of the Japanese advance in Manchuria
were linked and poised to descend on Peking from the northeast, while
the Shantung force was prepared to converge on the Chinese capital from
the southeast. By this time, however, both belligerents were negotiating
earnestly to end the war. Beaten and humiliated time and again, Peking
had been working feverishly to stop the conflict since early October. But
instead of negotiating bilaterally with Japan, the Chinese first tried to
persuade the Western Powers to mediate a settlement favorable to China
and, later, to intervene and reverse some of Japan's gains. Chinese leaders
knew the Japanese advance threatened Western interests, and they hoped
to use that knowledge to their advantage.[15]

Western Interests and Diplomatic Intrigue

Western interests in Asia revolved around colonization, trade, religious
missions, and the security of occidentals involved in those pursuits. Russia

was the Power most interested in the region and, therefore, most concerned about developments in the Sino-Japanese War. With territory spanning the Eurasian landmass, Russia was finally in reach of achieving her "manifest destiny" of becoming a transcontinental empire. Completion of a railroad line across the continent would be the final step in that grand project. Then Vladivostok, her "jewel in the East," would be linked to western Russia and European commerce. But Russian leaders had an interest in Asia they felt was even more important than completion of the Trans-Siberian railway. St. Petersburg's first priority was the procurement of an ice-free port.[16]

For centuries, Russian rulers had been acutely aware of the economic, political, and military limitations of an empire denied access to the sea by ice several months a year. By the late nineteenth century, the tsars had fought several wars in efforts to obtain a warm-water harbor. Now, as Russian power expanded eastward, ports in Korea and Manchuria offered the possibility of providing the year-round access the Russians so desired, and on completion of the Trans-Siberian railway, those ports could be linked with the western half of the nation. But all of Russia's dreams depended on St. Petersburg's ability to blunt the efforts of other powerful nations to get territorial concessions in the region Russian leaders coveted. Therefore, in 1894 it was vitally important to them that the status quo in Asia be maintained. Failing that, they had to contain Japan's continental expansion as much as possible.[17]

With those hopes in mind, Russian leaders responded warmly when, in June, 1894, China's foremost statesman, Viceroy Li Hung-chang, asked them to mediate a settlement to forestall the war. On Li's behest, Russia's minister to Tokyo, Mikhail Hitrovo, met with Japanese Foreign Minister Mutsu and expressed St. Petersburg's desire to see a restoration of peaceful relations between Japan and China. He further asked if Japan would be willing to withdraw her forces from Korea in the event that China withdrew her troops. As mentioned earlier, Mutsu resisted the Russian mediation bid, just as he had the British, asserting Japan's desire to reform the Korean government. He did, however, assure Hitrovo that Japan's only interest in Korea was to secure that state's independence; if war did occur with China, Japan intended to remain on the defensive.[18] But St. Petersburg suspected the Japanese were being less than candid about their intentions on the continent, so on June 30, Hitrovo formally presented Mutsu the following note:

The Korean government has officially informed representatives of all foreign powers in Korea that the domestic rebellion has been quelled. It has also requested the assistance of those representatives in having both China and Japan withdraw their troops from Korean soil. The Russian government therefore advises the government of Japan to comply with the Korean request and reminds Japan that if she refuses to recall her troops simultaneously with the Chinese withdrawal, she will be obliged to bear serious responsibility for the consequences.[19]

Despite the ominous tone of this communiqué, Japanese leaders refused to be intimidated. Immediately after Hitrovo left, Mutsu delivered the note to Prime Minister Ito. According to Mutsu, "Ito read the message and remained deep in thought for some time. Then, quietly but deliberately, he declared that there was no longer any way Japan could withdraw [its] forces from Korea."[20] The following day, Mutsu drafted a firm response detailing Japan's position and declining Russia's advice. After obtaining imperial sanction, Mutsu delivered the reply to Hitrovo on July 2.

Even before hearing from Mutsu, Hitrovo observed that Japan continued to mobilize for war and that Japanese public opinion had been whipped into a jingoistic fervor. Consequently, he informed St. Petersburg on July 1 that it was unlikely that the Japanese government would or could back down, even it wanted to. Unconvinced, Russian Foreign Minister Nikolai Karlovich Giers urged Hitrovo to continue pressing the Japanese to withdraw, asserting that "Japan's proposal for Korean administrative reforms is merely an excuse for her intervention."[21] But, after reading Japan's formal reply for himself on July 6, Giers finally accepted Japan's resolve and directed Hitrovo to thank the Japanese government for assuring Russia they had no aggressive intentions regarding Korea.[22] On July 15, the Russian consul in Tientsin informed Li Hung-chang that Russia had decided not to intervene in the Sino-Japanese dispute for the following reasons:

1. The Russian army and navy in the Far East are not strong enough.
2. If the Russian Government accepted the Chinese view and demanded the withdrawal of Japanese troops, there is a possibility that Japan would not agree to it and that Russia and China would have to unite and enter into war against Japan. Russia does not want to go to war, and she does not want to "vanquish Japan speedily only to increase the power of China."
3. If Russia avoids taking positive action unilaterally towards the present problem, but unites with a third country to withdraw her troops at a more favorable opportunity, Russia could escape the charge of harboring designs on Korea and thus prove her fairness accordingly.[23]

Russia was not the only Power anxious about developments in northeast Asia. When events in Korea began to suggest that conflict was unavoidable, Britain became concerned about the safety of its trade establishment in Shanghai. Consequently, after failing to mediate a settlement to forestall the war, British diplomats turned their attention more directly to the safety issue and managed, in July, 1894, to get Mutsu to assure them Shanghai would not be made into a war zone.[24]

When war broke out, Britain promptly declared neutrality along with the other Powers, but London remained involved behind the scenes throughout the conflict.[25] In October, after the tide of war turned clearly against the Chinese, Li Hung-chang convinced the British to try to bring some combination of Western Powers together to check Japan's expansion on the continent. Subsequently, Britain approached the United States, Russia, France, and Germany, proposing they jointly intervene to end the war on terms guaranteeing Korea's independence and with China paying Japan an indemnity.[26] But, once again, the British effort failed. While the United States was concerned about trade and the safety of missionaries in northeast Asia, America's nineteenth-century policy of avoiding foreign entanglements led President Grover Cleveland to reject all overtures to work with the European Powers.[27] Russia, France, and Germany also objected to intervening at that point, but for different reasons.[28]

Considering Russia's failed attempt at coercive diplomacy in June, it is not surprising that St. Petersburg declined to support Britain's bid to intervene in October. Despite her special interest in northeast Asia, Russia was no stronger then than she had been earlier. Conversely, Japan had not only grown considerably stronger on the continent, but she had also demonstrated a level of military prowess totally unexpected before the war. Moreover, Russian leaders realized that if they joined Britain in an attempt to compel Japan and failed—a likely scenario in their eyes, considering Japan's early show of resolve and subsequent battlefield success—they would probably have to choose between fighting the Japanese alone or backing down in disgrace. The United States had flatly rejected London's proposal for joint intervention. Germany and France, though they would find reasons to join Russia in the triple intervention months later, had no significant interests in northeast Asia. Even though Britain was making an effort to bring the Powers together to intervene on China's behalf, London made it clear that diplomacy was the limit to which Britain would carry the issue. Under these conditions, St. Petersburg saw little chance of success, and Britain's October intervention proposal became a dead letter.[29]

Nonetheless, the Powers remained anxious about developments in the war, and Mutsu became increasingly concerned about whether they might soon intervene to impose peace on terms favorable to China. Even as Britain was making its failed bid for joint intervention, Her Majesty's government approached Japan directly in an effort to mediate a settlement. On October 8, Britain's minister to Japan, P. Le Pour Trench, met with Mutsu to officially ask if the Japanese government would accept, as terms of peace, the independence of Korea, guaranteed by the Powers, and an indemnity to Japan for the expenses of the war. When Mutsu replied that his government would have to consider Britain's question carefully and answer at a later date, Trench added that Britain had consulted other European Powers on this subject and that Russia would soon make a similar recommendation.[30] The next day Mutsu received a telegram from Japan's minister in Italy, Takahira Kogoro, concerning rumors of a European intervention. Takahira reported that the Italian foreign minister had told him that "so far, the understanding between Great Powers is confined to mutual protection of their subjects, but the intervention is not unlikely if future circumstances necessitate."[31] The Italian minister added that the dismemberment of China would be dangerous to peace. Then he handed Takahira a note offering the good offices of Italy to broker a settlement on terms matching those suggested by the British. While Mutsu considered these developments, a telegram arrived on October 12 from Japan's minister to Russia, Nishi Tokujiro, warning that Britain was trying to enlist Russia's support in the joint intervention previously discussed.[32]

But despite Mutsu's apprehensions, he was not about to yield to Western pressure prematurely, especially considering Japan's steady advance on the battlefield. While the rumors troubled him and he could not ignore Trench's implications that Britain was in the process of organizing a joint intervention, Mutsu suspected the British threat was more bluff than substance. Throughout the period, he frequently met with the Russian, German, French, and American ministers, and none of them acted in ways that suggested their governments might be conspiring to move against Japan. In fact, when Mutsu told Hitrovo about the terms Trench had suggested, the Russian minister "explicitly declared that the Japanese government could not reasonably accede to any proposal so vague as that forwarded by Britain."[33]

Considering Japan's success on the battlefield, Mutsu felt he could not possibly accept the meager terms Britain was proposing. Nonetheless, the British were waiting for an answer, and Mutsu decided the time had come to consider the terms Japan would offer, should an opportunity for peace present itself.[34] Consequently, on October 12, Mutsu informed Takahira that he was going to delay answering the British as long as possible, and he directed him to stall the Italians as well.[35] He drafted three alternative replies to the British proposal and sent them to Hiroshima for Prime Minister Ito to discuss at the Imperial Headquarters. In Plan A, Japan would require China to recognize Korea's independence, cede Port Arthur and Talien Bay to Japan, conclude new commercial and navigational treaties with Japan (based on those China had with the West), and indemnify Japan for the military expenses incurred in the war. Plan B included all the terms of Plan A but added the cession of Formosa and had Korea's independence guaranteed by the Powers. But in Plan C, the Japanese government would insist on learning China's intentions before deciding what terms Japan would require for terminating hostilities.[36]

Along with the draft responses, Mutsu sent Ito a letter in which he explained his reasoning behind each of the three alternatives, and he expressed his own apprehensions about the situation. While Plan A stated clearly what Mutsu thought Japan should expect to gain from its victory in the war, his provision for "Great Power" oversight in Plan B was based on the thought that Western involvement in Korea might ensure a more durable peace.[37] But Mutsu was more than a little concerned about Britain's motives. He pointed out that Trench had asked him directly, at one point, what Japan's peace terms would be. Mutsu wondered if the real purpose in Britain's overture might have been to lure Japan into declaring its aspirations on the continent so that British leaders, and perhaps others, could weigh those costs against the risks of intervention.[38] Consequently, Plan C was designed to withhold Japan's terms from the intervention-prone Powers and force China to negotiate directly with Japan.

Although Ito liked Plan A, Mutsu's rationale for Plan C struck a resonant chord. Therefore, after corresponding with the prime minister several more times, Mutsu sent the following note to the British on October 23:

The imperial government fully appreciates the friendly motives which prompted the inquiry of Her Britannic Majesty's government. Thus far, Japan's arms have been attended with complete success; nevertheless, the imperial government is inclined to think that, in the present stage of the war, affairs have not made sufficient progress to insure a satisfactory outcome of negotiations. The imperial government cannot but refrain from expressing, at this time, its views as to the terms upon which the war could be terminated.[39]

Faltering Steps Toward Peace

As the Japanese army crossed into Manchuria in late October and won the dramatic battles of November, China's pleas for intervention became shrill. On October 31, China's Council of Ministers, the *Tsungli Yamen*, asked the United States to mediate an end to the war, and American Minister to China Charles Denby forwarded their request to Washington.[40] But before Denby could get an answer, China also approached Secretary of State Gresham and the foreign ministers of Britain, Russia, Germany, and France and asked them to intervene as well.[41] Despite the embarrassment this episode caused, President Cleveland still agreed to try and mediate a settlement, and he directed American Minister to Japan Edwin Dun to determine if Tokyo would accept the good offices of the United States in the interests of securing an honorable peace.[42] Meanwhile, Denby stressed to the *Tsungli Yamen* that American involvement would only be possible if the United States was the sole mediator.[43] The Chinese were inclined to agree to this condition. In fact, they told Denby that if Japanese leaders were to accept American mediation, China also would instantly. But the *Tsungli Yamen* still chose to withhold its final decision about the role it wanted America to play in securing peace until they determined whether the European Powers intended to intervene.[44]

To China's misfortune, European intervention did not materialize in

November, and Japan also refused American mediation. As the Chinese were still unwilling to approach Japan directly on the issue of peace, Mutsu felt they were not yet sufficiently "repentant." Furthermore, with Japanese forces advancing steadily in Manchuria, "war fever in Japan continued to be rampant," so Japanese leaders "concluded that any commencement of peace talks at that moment would be premature."[45] Consequently, on November 17, Mustsu sent Dun a memorandum that officially thanked the United States government and went on to say:

The universal success which has thus far during the conflict attended the arms of Japan would seem to relieve the imperial government of the necessity of invoking the cooperation of friendly powers to bring about a cessation of hostilities. [Nevertheless,] the imperial government has no wish to press its victories beyond the limits which will guarantee to Japan the just and reasonable fruits of the war. Those limits cannot, however, be said to have been reached until China finds herself in a position to approach Japan directly on the subject of peace.[46]

Throughout the remainder of November and all through December, 1894, China and Japan continued to fence over the issue of negotiations, using the American ministers in Peking and Tokyo as conduits. On November 22, having been rebuffed by the Japanese for going through Washington, the *Tsungli Yamen* sent Mutsu a message through Denby and Dun requesting peace talks and stating China's terms—recognition of Korea's independence and payment of a reasonable indemnity to Japan.[47] In response, the Japanese government declined to discuss terms and, instead, said that if China was really interested in making peace, she should appoint properly qualified plenipotentiaries to represent her in formal talks.[48] On November 30, Peking said that in order to appoint emissaries qualified to negotiate the question of peace, China would need to know, in a general way, what Japan's terms would be.[49] But Japan held firm. On December 2, Mutsu reiterated that until the accredited representatives of both sides were convened in conference, Japan would not divulge its peace terms.[50] Defeated on this point, Peking said they would appoint plenipotentiaries as Japan desired and suggested they meet at Shanghai on a date of Japan's choosing.[51] Once again, however, Mutsu decided to blunt the Chinese initiative, and he directed Dun and Denby to tell Peking that before the Japanese government would appoint its representatives, China must inform them of the names and ranks of the Chinese plenipotentiaries. Furthermore, the meeting place would have to be in Japan.[52]

Finally, beaten in diplomacy as well as in battle, Peking conceded every detail of the upcoming peace talks. Chinese leaders named their representatives, suggested they conduct the negotiations in Nagasaki, and asked Tokyo to tell them the names and ranks of the plenipotentiaries Japan intended to appoint. Triumphantly, Mutsu informed China that the talks would take place in Hiroshima, and Tokyo would appoint its own representatives only after the Chinese delegates arrived.[53] But the Japanese still worried about the prospects of Western intervention.

Although the Powers failed to find common ground in late 1894, they remained deeply concerned about Japan's continental advance and its potential impacts on their interests. In November, several European nations expressed anxiety about the possibility that Japan's actions in Manchuria could cause the Ch'ing Dynasty to fall, resulting in the dismemberment of China. Having first raised the issue in October, Italy's foreign minister met with Minister Takahira on November 11 and, once again, urged Japan to keep its "actions and conditions within [the] proper sphere, first, to avoid [the] dismemberment of China or [the] fall of her Government, [and] secondly, to limit [the] disturbance of general order [to] the small[est] degree possible."[54] The Italian minister went on to say, "this does not necessarily mean to withhold Japan from territorial acquisition, but cession of territory by China may cause third Power[s] to demand [their] share."[55] That same day, Mutsu also received a telegram from Minister Nishi in St. Petersburg warning that Britain had just approached Russia with fears that Japan's unhindered success might soon result in China's dismemberment.[56] On November 12, Minister Aoki wired Mutsu from Berlin reporting that the German foreign minister had "expressed a hope that Japan should not press the present affairs to extreme consequences such as destruction of the present dynasty."[57]

With these reports reaching Tokyo, Japanese leaders remained apprehensive and alert for any comment from European diplomats that might suggest what terms the West considered appropriate for Japan to demand in settlement. In November, Russia and Germany informed Japanese officials that the Chinese had again asked them to mediate an end to the war. Both assured Japan that they had refused Peking's request and, instead, advised the Chinese to approach Tokyo directly about negotiating peace.[58] As Germany's interests in northeast Asia were relatively minor, the Japanese had no reason to doubt Berlin's friendly intentions; but Russia was another matter. Therefore, on November 28, when Giers brought up the Chinese mediation request, Nishi took the opportunity to ask whether Russia might soon cooperate with Britain or some other Power to intervene in the war. Giers said Russia did not think the time had come to act, but, as Japan did not appear to be satisfied with Korean independence and the payment of an indemnity, the Powers would "cooperate to see their mutual interests not injured on the conclusion of the war."[59]

Although Giers's statement seemed straightforward, the Russians continued to cloud the water in regard to their intentions. On December 22, Hitrovo called on Mutsu to inform him the tsar was pleased to hear that negotiations between Japan and China were about to begin. The minister assured Mutsu that "the Russian government will make no interference regarding the demands of Japan advanced by her as condition for speedy termination of hostilities so far as they do not injure the Korean independence as promised at first by Japan."[60] Hitrovo added that "peace between Japan and China should be concluded by the two governments without permitting the interference of any Great Powers," and that "consequently, in order to prevent interference of any Great Power, it would be profitable to exchange ideas between Japan and Russia, and in that object the Russian government would not be unwilling to exert their efforts."[61] Finally, Hitrovo offered his personal opinion that Russia would have no objection to Japan occupying Formosa.

In these remarks, Mutsu suspected Hitrovo was hinting that Russia wanted to reach some secret understanding with Japan about the peace terms without involving the other European Powers. But as Mutsu "did not consider it prudent to seize the initiative on a question which might well have profound implications in the future," he did not follow up on the Russian's lead.[62]

As it turns out, Russia and the other Powers were growing impatient to know Japan's peace terms—so impatient, in fact, that in January, 1895, Russia and France finally agreed to act with Britain to try and pressure Japan into revealing them. On January 25, Britain's foreign minister, the Earl of Kimberly, directed his minister in Tokyo, Mr. Trench, to tell the Japanese government that, even if China's upcoming peace overtures are not acceptable to Japan, Britain hopes Japan will, at least, "declare what are the terms which they demand . . . [so] that peace may be speedily concluded."[63] Kimberly added that the Russian minister had been given the same instructions and Trench should consult with him, but that they should act separately. In keeping with these directions, Trench met that week with Hitrovo and French Minister to Japan Jules Harmond. After comparing instructions from their respective governments, all of them passed the same message to Japanese Vice Foreign Minister Hayashi Tadasu in separate meetings on January 31 and February 1.[64]

Hayashi was not moved. He told Trench that "any overtures the Chinese may make . . . would certainly not be acceptable to the Japanese government."[65] He went on to say that if the Chinese plenipotentiaries were found to be vested with full powers, the Japanese government would be quite willing to communicate to them the conditions of peace; but if not, Hayashi thought his government would refuse to state its demands. Hayashi closed the meeting by telling Trench he did not believe the Chinese were really sincere in their desire for peace, but were sending their envoys, instead, to get an armistice and to "spy out the land."[66]

A False Start at Hiroshima

Both China and Japan approached the Hiroshima talks with a sense of bitterness. Chinese leaders resented the way Mutsu had dominated every point of the meeting arrangements, and they felt particularly humiliated at having been compelled to meet outside China.[67] But Mutsu and Ito were also angry. The Chinese plenipotentiaries, Chang Yin-huan and Shao Yu-lien, though lauded by Peking as men of rank and distinction, were not, in the eyes of Japanese leaders, of sufficient standing to merit their negotiating an international agreement of this importance. Furthermore, Shao was infamous in Japan for having put a price on Japanese heads when he served as governor of Formosa early in the war. The Japanese believed Peking's choice of Chang and Shao was a deliberate affront to Japan's dignity and an effort by the Chinese to save face.[68]

The Japanese had other misgivings regarding the upcoming negotiation. A few days before the conference was to begin, Ito confided to Mutsu his concerns about divulging Japan's terms too early in the meeting. He asserted that, in the past, China had been known to deliberately fail to invest its representatives with the full authority that international law customarily stipulates for making agreements. In this case, Peking's appointment of low-ranking men like Chang and Shao made Chinese motives doubly suspect. Therefore, Ito and Mutsu resolved to insist on a thorough examination of the Chinese envoys' certificate of investiture before opening the meeting. Should Chang and Shao lack the full authority to negotiate an agreement, the Japanese would break off the talks before they began and, thereby, avoid tipping their hand regarding Japan's peace terms.[69]

The conference went as Ito predicted. On February 1, 1895, the plenipotentiary delegations from China and Japan met at the Hiroshima prefectural office and exchanged credentials. Ito and Mutsu were Japan's representatives, and they presented a letter from the Emperor investing them with full power to commit the Japanese government to an agreement. Chang and Shao presented two documents, but neither paper authorized the Chinese representatives to make an agreement without first wiring the *Tsungli Yamen* for approval.[70] Consequently, Ito and Mutsu refused to open negotiations, despite pleas from Chang and Shao, and later from Peking, to allow them to rectify the situation by sending amended authorizations by wire or courier.[71]

But Ito and Mutsu were not satisfied simply to send the Chinese home empty handed. Before they sent Chang and Shao away, they "thought it necessary to have them openly acknowledge that their investiture of full powers was inadequate."[72] Therefore, upon receipt of the documents from the Chinese representatives, Mutsu produced a memorandum he had prepared for the occasion in advance and read it to the Chinese. It said, in part:

In order to avoid, as far as possible, any future misunderstanding, the Japanese plenipotentiaries desire reciprocally to be categorically informed in writing, whether the full powers which have been communicated to them by the Chinese plenipotentiaries, but which they have not as yet examined, embody all the authority confided by His Majesty the Emperor of China to the Chinese plenipotentiaries in connection with the negotiation and conclusion of peace.[73]

Chang and Shao retired to their quarters to compose their response. The next day, they sent Mutsu and Ito an official note which read, in part:

We beg to state in reply that our commissions handed to you at the same time in exchange, embody full powers given by our Imperial Majesty for the negotiation and conclusion of peace, with authority to conclude articles to that end and to sign them. In order to insure the more prompt execution of the treaty we may agree upon, we shall wire the terms for Imperial sanction, and fix the date for signature; after which the same shall be taken to China for examination by His Imperial Chinese Majesty, and being found proper and in good and due form, will be ratified.[74]

The Japanese took this response to be an admission that Chang and Shao lacked credentials matching those of Ito and Mutsu. Therefore, they summoned the Chinese plenipotentiaries for one final meeting. When everyone was assembled, Ito and Mutsu each read an official declaration breaking off negotiations. But as the Chinese were leaving, Ito pulled aside Wu T'ing-fang, a man who had served Li Hung-chang during the Tientsin Treaty negotiations in 1885 and with whom Ito was personally acquainted. Ito told Wu:

As soon as you return home, convey to Viceroy Li this message, which I send along with the utmost feelings of sincerity. Let the viceroy fully understand that our refusal to continue negotiations with these particular Chinese envoys is not prompted by any love of war or distaste for peace. We consider the earliest possible restoration of peace to be important for both of our countries, and especially for China, and we are therefore fully prepared to resume negotiations whenever China becomes sincerely desirous of peace and appoints properly qualified plenipotentiaries. China remains the repository of many old customs and traditions, and the Peking government frequently seems unable to observe the universal practices of international intercourse. Nevertheless, on this particular matter we insist that China act in accordance with the prevailing rules of international law. I make these remarks to you privately on the strength of our long-standing acquaintanceship, which dates back to our meeting in Tientsin. My comments are made merely in a personal capacity and should not be construed as comprising any formal statement to the Chinese plenipotentiaries.[75]

Wu thanked the prime minister and asked him if the rank and reputation of the departing envoys had been an obstacle to the talks. Ito said they had not, but added:

Of course, the higher the rank and prestige of the plenipotentiary selected, the smoother the talks will proceed. . . . The appointment of someone like Prince Kung or Viceroy Li, for example, would be most convenient, for it will take someone with great power to carry out whatever agreements are reached and prevent the agreements from becoming meaningless scraps of paper.[76]

With that, Wu joined the rest of the Chinese delegation. Several days later, the plenipotentiaries Peking had sent to Hiroshima to negotiate peace left Japan without having had any opportunity to discuss terms.

Western reaction was muted, but deliberate. The Powers conceded that Japan was within her rights in refusing to negotiate with envoys who lacked proper accreditation, so there was no official protest from any Western capital. Nevertheless, European leaders were disappointed that the conference had fallen through, and they were particularly annoyed that Japan still chose to withhold her conditions of peace. Consequently, when Mutsu again held silent on peace terms in a meeting with Trench on February 14, the British minister reminded him that:

Japan had gone to war for the avowed purpose of restoring peace and order in Korea, and of freeing it from the yoke of China. The Chinese were now driven out of that country. Japan had, therefore, no excuse for prolonging the war. If Japan was really sincere in her desire for peace she should now conclude it, but, if she hoped to be successful, she must be moderate in her demands. She could scarcely expect Chinese plenipotentiaries, whatever their rank and influence, to sign away any portion of mainland China.[77]

In response, Mutsu insisted Japan had no desire to dismember China, but he remained evasive when questioned further about specific peace terms.

Two days later, Hitrovo also visited the foreign minister. Once again, Hitrovo emphasized Russia's friendship to Japan and argued that it would be to the mutual advantage of both countries to have an exchange of views on the terms of peace. Given this opening, Mutsu informed Hitrovo that Japan felt obliged to require some territorial concessions from China as the fruits of victory, and Japan wished to know whether such a demand might affect the interests of Russia or other Powers. Hitrovo replied that it would be quite natural for Japan to expect territorial concessions from China, and that it had long been Russia's desire to have an ice-free port in Korea. He went on to say, as he had in December, that he believed Russia would have no objection to Japan taking Formosa, but added that he felt it would be unwise for Japan to abandon her insular position and seek expansion on the continent. He also said, "certain Powers were bound to protest the cession of any mainland territory to Japan."[78] But when Mutsu pressed him on whether Russia, in particular, had any interests in the settlement other than the independence of Korea, he simply said there was none worth noting, but he hoped Japan would do nothing to hurt the Russo-Chinese tea trade.[79]

The Peace of Shimonoseki

After the first delegation returned to China, Peking and Tokyo both began working to get another round of peace talks underway. By February, 1895, China was losing ground to the Japanese army almost daily and desperate to end the war. The Japanese were also eager to reach a settlement, as Tokyo believed that if they lost much more time, some combination of Powers would intervene. With that consideration in mind, Mutsu and Ito decided to depart from their earlier tactic of keeping Japan's peace terms secret. According to Mutsu, he and Ito hoped that by forewarning Peking that Japan intended to acquire territory in the settlement, the next Chinese negotiators could come to the talks prepared to reach an agreement more quickly. Therefore, on February 17 Mutsu notified China, through the American intermediaries, that any future Chinese peace envoys must be invested with full powers to negotiate, among other issues, "the cession of territories as a consequence of war."[80] Almost simultaneously, Peking notified Tokyo that Li Hung-chang had been appointed minister plenipotentiary and would come to Japan invested with full powers to negotiate a settlement. After the exchange of several more messages, China and Japan agreed to hold the next round of peace talks in Shimonoseki and the conference was scheduled to begin on March 20, 1895.[81]

Mutsu's February 17 message regarding territorial concession triggered a curious response from St. Petersburg. On February 24 Hitrovo called on Mutsu and read an official telegram from Russia's new foreign minister, Prince Aleksei B. Lobanov-Rostovskii, that said:

It appears . . . that the Japanese government desires the dispatch of Chinese plenipotentiaries invested with full powers to conclude a treaty involving the independence of Korea, payment of an indemnity, cession of territory, and the conclusion of a new Sino-Japanese treaty of commercial relations. . . . If the Japanese government declares that it will recognize Korea's independence in both name and fact, our government can advise the Chinese government to invest their plenipotentiaries with full powers in conformity with the above-mentioned conditions and can even advise the other Great Powers to act in the same vein as our government on this matter.[82]

This note left Mutsu somewhat puzzled concerning St. Petersburg's true intentions. Nevertheless, he decided to take the Russian message at face value and, on February 27, sent Hitrovo a memorandum saying:

The imperial government was gratified to learn from Your Excellency's verbal communication of the 24th instant that the basis of peace laid down in our telegram . . . will receive support from the Russian government . . . The imperial government does not hesitate to declare with regard to the statement of Your Excellency that Japan's policy toward Korea has undergone no change and that the imperial government recognizes in fact as well as in name the independence of Korea.[83]

But, surprisingly, Mutsu was not particularly alarmed when the German minister to Tokyo called upon Vice Minister Hayashi on March 8, nor did he take Berlin's message at face value when he read the following note:

The government of His Majesty the Kaiser advises the Japanese government to hasten the conclusion of peace with China and to moderate her terms. China has invited the great European Powers to intervene. Several are now willing in principle to do so and have agreed to act together. The more these Powers demand of China as the price of their intervention, the less will remain for Japan. It is to Japan's advantage, therefore, to conclude an equitable peace before intervention occurs. According to reports reaching the German government, Japanese demands for cessions of continental territory would be certain to provoke intervention.[84]

According to Mutsu, the Japanese had frequently felt that Germany's attitude toward them regarding the war was not entirely dependable. Consequently, as Japan's decision regarding her peace terms had already been made, Mutsu directed Hayashi to thank the German minister for the information but elected not to take any action.[85]

The Shimonoseki Peace Conference began on schedule, and the Japanese wasted no time in gaining the upper hand. After exchanging credentials, Li opened the talks with a memorandum requesting that both sides call an immediate armistice before the plenipotentiaries begin negotiating the terms of settlement. Ito and Mutsu objected to a cease-fire, as the constant Japanese advance in Manchuria strengthened their negotiating posture; but as Mutsu had alluded to the possibility of an armistice in one of his early messages to Peking, he and Ito agreed to formally consider the issue. The next day, Mutsu presented a memorandum granting the armistice provided the Chinese agree to the following conditions: the Japanese would occupy the Chinese cities, fortresses, and fortifications at Taku, Tientsin, and Shanhaikuan; the Chinese forces in those locations would surrender all their arms and supplies; Japan would take control of the rail line between Tientsin and Shanhaikuan; and China would pay Japan for all military expenditures incurred during the cease-fire.[86] Realizing the Japanese were asking for terms they knew the Chinese could not accept, Li objected strenuously and a long discussion ensued. Ultimately, Li withdrew his request for an armistice, and the plenipotentiaries agreed to begin discussing the actual peace terms the next morning.[87]

However, that evening an incident occurred that changed the complexion of the negotiation, if not the outcome. A Japanese extremist shot Li Hung-chang in ambush as he returned to his lodging. The elderly statesman survived the attack, but was seriously wounded. Suddenly anxious about appearing to have committed a serious breach of faith and international law, all of Japan responded to the incident with a profuse outpouring of sympathy and public indignation. Emperor Meiji issued an imperial rescript expressing his regret, and he sent his personal physicians to Li's bedside. The empress sent along bandages that she made for him herself. As news of the attack spread, Shimonoseki filled with throngs of people eager to pay their respects at Li's quarters, and thousands of letters, telegrams, and gifts arrived from all over Japan. Faced with this unfortunate turn of events, Mutsu and Ito felt compelled to demonstrate Japan's good faith and granted China the unconditional cease-fire Li had requested earlier.[88]

Despite the attack on Li Hung-chang, the Shimonoseki Peace Conference resumed a few days later. With the elder Li bedridden for the duration of the talks, Peking appointed his adopted son, Li Ching-fong, as China's plenipotentiary and transferred to him the full powers to negotiate a settlement.[89] Even so, Li Hung-chang continued to orchestrate China's participation in the negotiations, as his son brought all the Japanese proposals to his bedside and elder Li drafted the notes and memoranda expressing Peking's official position.[90]

On April 1, 1895, Mutsu finally delivered Japan's peace terms to the Chinese delegation, and the talks began in earnest. In order to end the war, Japan expected China to recognize Korea's independence; cede the Liaotung Peninsula, Formosa, and the Pescadores to Japan; pay an indemnity of 300,000,000 Kuping taels;[91] sign new commercial and navigation treaties with Japan comparable to those China had with the West; open seven new ports to Japanese trade; and reduce or eliminate a list of taxes, duties, and trade restrictions on Japanese commercial enterprises in China. Additionally, Japan intended to occupy Weihaiwei and Mukden until the indemnity was fully paid.[92] Li Hung-chang answered this proposal with a lengthy memorandum protesting the cession of Liaotung because it was part of the Ch'ing Dynasty's home province, and he objected to ceding Formosa on the grounds that Japan had not taken that territory during the war. Furthermore, Li said China could not pay such a high indemnity, especially if Japan insisted on taking the rich territory it was demanding in Liaotung.[93]

During the next week, Li Hung-chang sent the Japanese several more notes and memoranda, trying to convince Mutsu and Ito to reduce their demands for territory and money. Throughout the negotiation, he kept the *Tsungli Yamen* informed of his progress, and they repeatedly urged him to hold out for every possible concession. But knowing that China was desperate to end the war, the Japanese held firm on the issue of territorial cession. On April 10, Ito presented a revised draft of Japan's terms, lowering the indemnity by a third and reducing the number of Chinese ports to be opened from seven to four.[94] Li attempted to haggle further. But on April 14, when Ito informed him that this would be Japan's final offer, Li wired the *Tsungli Yamen* and said, "If we agree to the current Japanese terms, we can save Peking; but otherwise, it is difficult to predict what will happen. I am therefore compelled to conclude the treaty without awaiting further instructions."[95] On reading this telegram, the *Tsungli Yamen* told Li that if all avenues of negotiation appeared closed, he could go ahead and sign an agreement.[96]

The Chinese and Japanese plenipotentiaries signed the Treaty of Shimonoseki on April 17, 1895. Then, they extended the armistice for 21 days to give both emperors time to ratify the agreement. The Sino-Japanese War was officially over.[97]

The Powers Intervene

News of the Treaty of Shimonoseki was received with jubilation by a Japanese public already drunk on victory. But the celebration did not last long. On April 23, 1895, the ministers of Russia, France, and Germany called on Vice Foreign Minister Hayashi to officially protest the article of the treaty concerning China's cession of the Liaotung Peninsula to Japan. Hitrovo delivered a memorandum declaring:

The government of His Majesty the Emperor of All the Russias, in examining the conditions of peace which Japan has imposed on China, finds that the possession of the peninsula of Liaotung, claimed by Japan, would be a constant menace to the capital of China, would at the same time render illusory the independence of Korea, and would henceforth be a perpetual obstacle to the peace of the Far East. Consequently, the government of His Majesty the Tsar would give a new proof of its sincere friendship for the government of His Majesty the Emperor of Japan by advising it to renounce the definitive possession of the peninsula of Liaotung.[98]

The French and German ministers also delivered memoranda. The text of Harmond's message was nearly identical to the Russian communiqué, but German Minister Felix Frieher von Gutschmid's note called on Japan to "accept the advice of the *Dreibund* [three-federation] as she could hardly hope for victory in a war against the three Powers."[99] Surprised by the threatening tone of this message, Hayashi remarked:

Although both the Russian and French Ministers have advised Japan in a friendly manner, contending that the advice was given in the interest of peace in the Far East, and urging mature deliberation on the part of Japan, your memorandum could be construed as a warning to Japan to obey the overture or risk a clash of arms. If that is the case, Japan's national honor and the feelings of its people must be taken fully into account. As the German memorandum is written in Japanese, Japan desires to be informed whether or not there has been a mistranslation.[100]

At this point, Gutschmid became perplexed and, in an attempt to disguise his embarrassment, replied:

The memorandum of the German Government had no intention of implying the application of any pressure against Japan. Should there be any words that give such an impression, that is due to faulty diction. I wish to state that the purport of the German memorandum is no different from those of the Russian and French ministers.[101]

The day the three ministers delivered their memoranda, Ito was in Hiroshima and Mutsu was at his home in Maiko, recuperating from illness. Therefore, Hayashi sent both of them telegrams explaining what had transpired and asking for instructions. Coincidentally, Mutsu had anticipated the intervention from having followed reports from Japan's ministers in St. Petersburg and Berlin, and he had just wired Ito saying:

According to cables received from Ministers Aoki and Nishi, it would appear that a coercive intervention by the European Powers is inescapable. They will have the opportunity to object to the settlement, for we did not initially reveal to them what we were demanding of China, and they are only now in a position to be officially cognizant of the peace terms. One must therefore conclude that if our government had indicated its demands and conditions to the powers at the start, the very problems which are now approaching would in fact have confronted us from a much earlier point. But as we have long since opted for a bold policy, our best course in the face of any threats is to show ourselves fully determined to hold tenaciously to our current position. Once one decides to "ride the tiger," he is well advised to hang on tightly when the ride begins. Pray inform me in all frankness of your own views on this matter.[102]

The following morning, after having read Hayashi's telegram, Ito cabled Mustu informing him that they were about to convene an imperial conference on the triple intervention, and he wanted Mutsu's views. Mutsu responded saying his views had not changed since the day before—Japan should hold firmly to its position without giving an inch. He added that after they had had an opportunity to evaluate the subsequent actions of the Powers, they could deliberate the matter further. But in the meantime, he urged the government to make no final decisions. Unfortunately, there was no time for Ito to wait for Mutsu's response before going into the conference.[103]

On April 24, 1895, Ito Hirobumi met with War Minister Yamagata Aritomo, Navy Minister Saigo Tsugumichi, and several top military staff

officers before Emperor Meiji at the Hiroshima Imperial General Headquarters.[104] After outlining the situation, Ito proposed that the council
choose one from three alternative plans:

1. Definitely reject the advice of the three Powers, even if Japan makes more enemies in doing so.
2. Hold an international conference with the Powers to settle the issue.
3. Accept the recommendation of the Powers, and return the Liaotung Peninsula
   to China as a favor.[105]

After considering the alternatives carefully, the military officers argued
convincingly against plan number one. Russia had been concentrating its
fleet in northeast Asian waters since the previous autumn. The latest intelligence reports had indicated that military authorities in Vladivostok
had called up the reserves, canceled leaves, and ordered Russian ships to
prepare for sailing on a 24-hour notice. Meanwhile, Japan had just finished
a taxing war. Financial resources were stretched, supplies were low, and
the troops were weary. More importantly, Japanese forces were in poor
positions to defend the home islands, as the cream of the army was in
Manchuria and the fleet was deployed in the Pescadores. According to
Mutsu, "In this situation, it would prove to be quite hopeless a task to
take on even the Russian fleet, let alone the combined naval forces of the
three intervening Powers."[106]

On the other hand, the conferees could not see acquiescing as called for
in plan number three. While it might save Japan from an attack by the
Powers, the army and navy would be dangerously antagonized, and the
Japanese people, who had supported the war so ardently, would be in-
furiated. Consequently, the leaders at Hiroshima decided to seek an international conference to settle the issue.[107]

That evening, Ito left for Maiko and met with Mutsu at his home the
following morning. They were joined there by Finance Minister Matsukata
Masayoshi and Home Minister Nomura Yasushi.[108] When Ito explained
the decision reached the day before, Mutsu objected strongly, insisting the
Japanese government should hold firm to determine the Powers' true intention while searching for some diplomatic breakthrough. Ito, however,
felt that it was hardly necessary to inquire further into the motives of the
three Powers. Russia, in particular, had made its intentions clear since the
previous year. Therefore, rejecting the Powers' recommendation would be
dangerous. Moreover, he feared there was no room for the diplomatic
maneuvering that Mutsu envisioned as the crisis was about to blow up.
Mutsu continued to argue, but Matsukata and Nomura sided with Ito,
and eventually the foreign minister adopted a more conciliatory tone.[109]

Even so, Mutsu still vehemently opposed the idea of submitting the
issue to an international conference. First, he was concerned that if they

invited the three intervening Powers to such a meeting, they would also have to invite at least two or three other Powers, and he doubted whether they could get five or more Powers to sit down at the same table. Furthermore, arranging a conference of that magnitude would take time, but the exchange of ratification instruments for the Sino-Japanese treaty was due in just a few days; failure to ratify the treaty as scheduled might imperil the settlement with China. But most importantly, Mutsu feared that submitting the Liaotung Peninsula question to an international conference would open the field to other claims by the Great Powers, resulting in a multitude of demands that could completely undermine the Treaty of Shimonoseki.[110]

Though fearful of confronting the *Dreibund*, Ito, Matsukata, and Nomura conceded that Mutsu's apprehensions about the conference plan were valid. But if Japan could not oppose the Powers, yet dared not open the issue to international debate, what could Tokyo do? Discussing the matter further, the four ministers decided that they should, at all costs, strive to keep the intervention issue separate from the treaty ratification problem. Ultimately, if the three Powers were firmly resolved, the Japanese would have no choice but to accept their advice, at least, in part. But Japan must not appear to give in to China, and Tokyo must not let Peking seize on the intervention as an opportunity to refuse to ratify the Treaty of Shimonoseki. As the exchange of ratification instruments was scheduled for May 8, still 10 days away, the ministers decided to see if they could persuade the Powers to withdraw or modify their advice, all the while, weighing their responses carefully to discern what their future actions might be. Also, Mutsu would use the time to seek the support of other Powers in an attempt the counter the threat of the *Dreibund*.[111]

Finally resolved on a plan, Nomura took the new decision to Hiroshima for imperial sanction. Meanwhile, Mutsu set out to map and, if possible, exploit the newly emerging diplomatic terrain.

No Help and No Reprieve

Mutsu went to work immediately. On April 25, he cabled Nishi, directing him to ask Foreign Minister Lobanov to reconsider the advice given two days earlier. He told Nishi to explain that returning the Liaotung Peninsula would be extremely difficult because Emperor Meiji had already ratified the Treaty of Shimonoseki. Nishi was to emphasize further that Japan and Russia shared a long and unbroken friendship that neither should jeopardize and that, in keeping Liaotung, Japan would do nothing to endanger Korean independence or otherwise menace Russian interests in the Far East.[112] On the same day, Mutsu sent two telegrams to Kato Takaaki, Japan's minister to London. The first directed Kato to inform the

British foreign minister that Japan intended to reassure the intervening Powers regarding Tokyo's stance on Korean independence and offer, in compromise, to "make Yinkoh and one port on the peninsula free ports."[113] But the second telegram to Kato said:

You will also say, if you think it wise to do so, that the sinister designs of Russia against northeastern Manchuria and [the] northern portion of Korea are but poorly veiled under her present demands. You will then say that [the] situation is somewhat critical and ask [the] minister of foreign affairs how far Japan may count on [the] support of Great Britain if she replies to the three Powers in the sense indicated. You are to take [the] most prompt action on this situation and telegraph the result at once.[114]

The following day, Mutsu also directed Japan's ministers to seek support in the United States and Italy; but all these efforts came to naught. Britain's Lord Kimberly informed Kato that "while entertaining [the] most friendly feeling to Japan," Britain also must maintain friendly relations with the other Powers. Moreover, the British doubted whether the Powers would accept Japan's offer of compromise. Therefore, Britain had decided to stand neutral on the issue.[115] Likewise, while Secretary of State Gresham offered America's help in urging China to ratify the treaty, he could pledge nothing that would violate the United States' policy of neutrality.[116] Only Italy expressed an interest in standing with Japan against the *Dreibund*, but even Rome would not speak out unless joined by London and Washington.[117] Meanwhile, Nishi's efforts to get St. Petersburg to withdraw its advice were fruitless. Lobanov told him the tsar had denied the request because Japan had not given Russia sufficient reason to do otherwise.[118]

Given Japan's failure to raise international support or get Russia to alter its stance, Ito and Mutsu concluded it was time to seek a compromise. Consequently, on April 30, Hayashi instructed Japan's ministers in St. Petersburg, Paris, and Berlin to inform the Powers that, "after the honor and dignity of Japan shall have been satisfied by due exchange of ratifications of the Treaty of Shimonoseki," Japan would be willing to introduce a supplementary act modifying the treaty to renounce its possession of the Liaotung Peninsula except for the region of Port Arthur.[119] Still, they were unsuccessful. Though Nishi argued passionately for St. Petersburg to accept the compromise, Foreign Minister Lobanov told him the Imperial Cabinet had met the day before and decided unanimously that Japan's possession of Port Arthur was unacceptable. Nishi also informed Tokyo that there were rumors in Europe that Russian, French, and German fleets would soon rendezvous at Kiel, Germany, and proceed from there to the Far East.[120] Japan's ministers in Paris and Berlin also reported firm rejections to Tokyo's offer of compromise. The Powers were insisting Japan accept the original recommendation without change.

Japan Capitulates

When Mutsu received Nishi's disheartening cable on May 3, he realized he had run out of options. Worse, he was running out of time. The day before, China had formally requested a postponement of the exchange of treaty ratifications on grounds that the outcome of the triple intervention would bear on provisions of the settlement. Realizing the treaty was about to become unhinged, Mutsu decided the time had come to concede completely to the Powers, but, in keeping with the original plan, continue standing firm against the Chinese.[121]

Subsequently, on May 4, Ito convened a meeting of all available cabinet ministers and members of the Supreme Command in Mutsu's hotel room in Kyoto. There, Mutsu presented his case for retroceding the Liaotung Peninsula, as the Powers had advised, but pressing the Chinese relentlessly to exchange treaty ratification instruments. Given the preceding week's diplomatic failures, the conferees quickly agreed with the general thrust of the foreign minister's proposal. However, debate ensued on whether Japan should demand additional compensation for returning Liaotung or simply give it back as a magnanimous gesture. On this issue, Mutsu asserted that if they claimed to accede wholly to the Powers' advice, yet sought to put conditions on that gesture, Russia would become suspicious of Japan's intentions. Furthermore, if they were to seek Russia's approval for compensation only to be refused, Japan would have no recourse but to accept further embarrassment. Discussion of these issues lasted nearly the entire day, but as Ito firmly supported Mutsu's position, the other cabinet members eventually concurred as well.[122]

With consensus finally at hand, Mutsu drafted a memorandum saying simply: "The imperial government of Japan, acting in accordance with the advice of the Russian, German, and French governments, hereby agrees to renounce its claim for permanent possession of the Liaotung Peninsula."[123] Later that evening, after Ito returned from the Kyoto Imperial Palace with the emperor's sanction, Mutsu wired the memorandum to the Japanese ministers in St. Petersburg, Berlin, and Paris with instructions for them to present it to their host governments immediately.[124]

The remaining events are almost anticlimactic. On the last day of the armistice, China and Japan exchanged instruments ratifying the Treaty of Shimonoseki. Acting on China's May 2 request, the Japanese government first consented to a five-day postponement of the exchange. However, Russia and Germany urged Peking to ratify the treaty as soon as possible, once they had Japan's assurance concerning the return of Liaotung, and with the help of the good offices of Britain, the United States, and Germany, Li Hung-chang was persuaded to withdraw the Chinese request. At the eleventh hour, China tried once more to alter the terms by inserting an article in the treaty concerning the Liaotung retrocession and by objecting to the annexation of Formosa. But the Japanese adamantly refused to consider changing the treaty in any way. The ratifications were finally exchanged late on the night of May 8, 1895.[125]

The following day, Minister Hitrovo called at the Japanese Foreign Ministry and read an official note from the government of Russia. Later that day, the French and German ministers appeared and read nearly identical notes. Hitrovo's note said:

The government of His Imperial Majesty the Tsar is informed that Japan has renounced her right to take permanent possession of the Liaotung Peninsula and hastens to acknowledge that the government of His Majesty the Emperor of Japan has given by this decision new proofs of its great wisdom. We hereby extend our congratulations to you in the interests of universal peace.[126]

On May 10, 1895, Emperor Meiji issued an imperial rescript, countersigned by all cabinet ministers, announcing the retrocession of the Liaotung Peninsula to China. The emperor declared that, in winning independence for Korea, Japan's object in the war had been achieved; therefore, the retrocession in no way reflected upon the dignity and honor of Japan. Emperor Meiji then called upon the Japanese people to restrain themselves in their actions.[127]

That event concludes the case of the triple intervention. With these facts on the table, one can clearly see how Japanese leaders arrived at the decisions they made; but it still is not clear *why* they behaved the way they did during the crisis and the events leading to it. To understand those details, one must analyze the triple intervention in terms of what we know about compellence and the strategic culture of Imperial Japan.

ANALYSIS OF THE TRIPLE INTERVENTION

The triple intervention offers a multitude of variables to sort and weigh as I analyze the dynamics of compellence. The case includes elements of both punishment and denial. It also juxtaposes a series of definitive strategic developments in Asia against a complicated backdrop of European balance-of-power diplomacy. But most importantly, the triple intervention provides a showcase in which to examine the subtle ways that culture conditioned Japan's strategic decision-making processes as that country's leaders anticipated and responded to coercive threat. In this section, I examine these many variables in terms of the compellence theories addressed in this study. The analysis begins with the most basic classes of compellence thought, punishment and denial, and concludes with the most complex, a culture-based appraisal.

Punishment and Denial—An Analysis of Costs and Benefits

To examine the triple intervention in terms of punishment and denial, I must determine how effectively the coercers convinced Japanese leaders that the *Dreibund* could raise the cost of defying its demands (punishment) or deny Japan the benefits of its preferred course of action (denial). That presents a challenge in this case. The triple intervention is unusual among examples of successful compellence in that the *Dreibund* did not explicitly threaten the government of Japan. That is, in offering their "friendly advice," Russia, France, and Germany never made it clear what consequences awaited Japan had its leaders elected to ignore that advice. Therefore, it is uncertain whether their implied threat was oriented more toward punishment or denial. Nevertheless, the coercers' intentions and, more importantly, the way Japanese leaders interpreted those intentions, are discernible from case events.

The historical record suggests the Powers probably intended to deny Japan the benefits of occupying Liaotung by seizing control of the seas around northern China and isolating Japanese forces on the continent from the home islands. Although France and Germany had no significant military force in the region, Russia had both navy and army units based at Vladivostok. Moreover, St. Petersburg had begun augmenting its Asian fleet in late 1894, and by May, 1895, its naval strength at least matched that of Japan. During this period, Russia also reinforced its army contingent in northeast Asia, but with a strength of only 30,000 troops in March, 1895, this force was a poor match for Japan's 100,000 soldiers in Manchuria.[128] Therefore, one might reasonably conclude that the Powers, if put to the test, would mainly rely on their combined naval superiority to quarantine Japan, thus denying her the fruits of her recent victory.

On the other hand, at least one Russian leader considered the possibility of punishing Japan by attacking the home islands. Recalling the meeting in which he had first proposed compelling Japan to return Liaotung, Russian finance minister, Count Serge Witte, later wrote in his memoirs:

I proposed that we present an ultimatum to Japan, giving her a choice between giving up the claim to the Liaotung Peninsula in return for a sizable indemnity that would compensate her, as victor, for her expenditures in the war, or being subject to military action on our part. Of course, this was not the time to decide what action to take, but it might extend as far as the bombardment of several Japanese ports.[129]

However, most important is not what Russia and the other Powers actually intended to do, but what Japanese leaders thought the *Dreibund* would do if they ignored their advice. On this question, Mutsu's account of the decision conferences at Hiroshima and Maiko on April 24 and 25 suggests the Japanese considered elements of both punishment and denial in their interpretation of the Powers' implied threat. Japanese decision makers were particularly concerned about the Russian fleet that had recently reinforced in northeast Asian waters and the possibility that French and German fleets might soon augment it. This combined armada could cut Japan off from her forces on the mainland, jeopardizing all the gains achieved in the war. But Japanese leaders were at least as concerned that, with their own army and navy deployed away from the home islands, Japan would be helpless, and the *Dreibund* could use its naval superiority to punish her at will.

Ultimately, theoretical comparisons of punishment and denial are less important in this case than simply understanding that, by not issuing a specific threat, the *Dreibund* effectively manipulated both costs and benefits in Japan's decision calculus.

A more interesting question might be how, by offering nothing more than "friendly advice," the Powers could deliver a threat so credible that Tokyo interpreted it as an ultimatum. Once again, the strategic situation speaks for itself. Though the Japanese military had recently proven its metal in a dramatic series of victories, it was exhausted and Japan was financially overextended by the strains of war. The Russian fleet seemed more than a match for the Japanese navy and was perfectly positioned to interdict the sea lanes between Japan and the continent. In these circumstances, Russia's sudden mobilization at Vladivostok, combined with rumors in Europe that a joint Russian, French, and German Fleet was en route, was more than enough to convince the Japanese that the Powers intended to back their advice with force.

This simple, balance-of-forces argument also largely explains why the Powers, though successful in compelling the Japanese to abandon the Liaotung Peninsula in 1895, were unable to deter Japan from taking that territory in 1894 or from going to war in the first place. As Russia could not challenge Japan's naval superiority until late in the war, Tokyo felt free in June, 1894, to reject St. Petersburg's advice to withdraw from Korea and could also ignore Western mediation efforts later that fall. The Powers were simply unable to raise the costs of defying their will, or to deny Japan the benefits of her continental aggression, until Russia had sufficient force in theater to do so.

But though this analysis of costs and benefits explains a great deal, it still leaves a number of questions unanswered. For instance, how was Russia able to convince France and Germany, traditional enemies with little or no interest in northeast Asia, to join her in a venture that brought them to the brink of war with Japan? How strongly bonded was the three-Power coalition, and how willing were the individual members to use force, had Japan rejected their advice? Furthermore, given that British diplomats had spent the better part of the war trying to convince other Powers to join London in an intervention, why did Britain not join the

Dreibund when it finally came about? Lastly, was there anything Japan could have done to forestall or defeat the triple intervention?

To answer these questions, I must broaden the analysis to look beyond a simple, linear calculation of costs and benefits. I must weigh the interests of the parties involved and determine how Japanese leaders perceived those interests.

The Balance of Interests in the Triple Intervention

A broader analysis of this case suggests the outcome of the triple intervention was rooted as much in European, balance-of-power diplomacy as it was in the strategic situation in Asia. The Sino-Japanese War substantially threatened the interests of both Britain and Russia. Yet, except in early 1895, when they coordinated their diplomatic overtures in an effort to convince the Japanese government to reveal its peace terms, these two Great Powers were unable to find enough common ground to work together. In 1894, St. Petersburg repeatedly declined London's proposals to join forces. But later, when Russia urged the Powers to take a united stand against Japan's continental gains in the Treaty of Shimonoseki, only France and Germany saw it in their interests to take up the Russian cause. By then British leaders had reevaluated the balance of power and adjusted their policy accordingly.

Throughout the war, British policy was driven not only by London's concerns about trade and the balance of power, but by public opinion as well. Early in the conflict, as London worried about economic interests and the safety of its subjects in Shanghai, the British press railed at Japanese aggression and urged the government to intervene. But as the war progressed, Japan kept her word in respecting Shanghai's neutrality, despite Tokyo's belief that China was storing arms there.[130] This, along with Japan's careful treatment of Westerners in Korea and other occupied areas, eventually served to allay Britain's most immediate fears. But in late 1894, as the Japanese army pressed its advantage in Manchuria, a new concern came to London's attention.

Britain, along with Italy and Germany, began to worry that Japan's dramatic advance in northern China might soon cause the Ch'ing Dynasty to fall. This concern, however, was not based on any sentimental attachment to the Manchu royal house. Rather, they feared that a collapse of the Peking government would trigger a scramble for Chinese territory among the Western Powers, and Russia, Britain's rival in Asia, was best positioned to profit from such a melee. During this period, Italy often found common interest with Britain, explaining why Rome's overtures to Japan in October and November, 1894, were but echoes of London's.[131] Conversely, Germany was not yet ready to take sides in the Sino-Japanese dispute, but Berlin could see no advantage in allowing Russia, one of Germany's traditional enemies, to gain the upper hand in Asia.

So, as China and Japan moved unsteadily toward peace in early 1895, Britain and Russia were both interested in knowing Japan's peace terms, but for different reasons. Russia, of course, worried that Japan intended to keep the territory and ports that St. Petersburg coveted in Manchuria. Britain, on the other hand, feared that if Japan's terms were too severe, Russia would intervene or China would fall, working to Russia's advantage either way. Meanwhile, British public opinion shifted dramatically as the Japanese continued to demonstrate their military dominance in northern China.[132]

As the war approached an end, the British press began to argue for allowing Japan to keep the fruits of her victory. Impressed with Japanese military prowess, the British public was increasingly convinced that Japan was a rising power in Asia, and a growing number of political columnists felt London should align itself with Tokyo to counterbalance St. Petersburg's growing influence in Peking. This analysis likely coincided with conclusions already reached in the British Foreign Office. Consequently, though Russia repeatedly urged Britain to join the intervening Powers, London refused.[133]

But, ironically, British leaders also declined to oppose the *Dreibund,* even though Italy was willing to stand beside them. This may seem surprising, given London's concern that a conflict between the Powers and Japan would ultimately work to Russia's advantage, for London was all but certain that Japan would refuse the advice of the *Dreibund*.[134] But there are several possible reasons for Britain's decision. Perhaps she feared that openly siding with an Asian nation against three European Powers was too risky a position to take, particularly considering how avidly London had lobbied for joint action against Japan early in the war. Or, perhaps Britain felt that returning the Liaotung Peninsula to China was a reasonable solution to the current crisis, so long as Russia did not take any additional territory in the process. But it could be that London appraised the composition of the *Dreibund* and concluded it would fracture on its own, once the Japanese resisted as British leaders expected. Indeed, Russia, France, and Germany were strange bedfellows.

Given Russia's obvious interests in northeast Asia, it is not surprising that St. Petersburg moved to intervene, once Russian leaders finally learned the details of Japan's peace terms. In fact, Mutsu and other observers have postulated that the Russians began planning an intervention months earlier, but deliberately misled Tokyo by saying they had no interest in the settlement other than Korean independence, all the while letting Japan commit herself to an irreversible course.[135] However, more recent scholarship suggests that, despite Russia's interests in Asia, St. Petersburg lacked a well defined Far East policy until late in the war.[136]

Indeed, when Russian Finance Minister Witte first proposed the intervention in the April conference mentioned earlier, the only support he received was from the army minister. Lobanov reacted with cold silence, and most of the others were indecisive.[137] With this level of ambivalence, St. Petersburg surely would not have intervened alone. In fact, without the support of a third Power, Russia probably would not have ventured this course even with the French by her side, for they too were uncertain and reluctant.

France's main interest in the triple intervention lay in maintaining its newly formed alliance with Russia. Relations between the two countries had grown increasingly close since 1890, when Paris financed St. Petersburg's venture in the Trans-Siberian railway. Then, in January 1894, after Germany inadvertently let Bismarck's 1887 treaty with Russia lapse, Paris successfully negotiated the Franco-Russian alliance, effectively squeezing out its traditional enemy. This was an unexpected coup for the French. According to Mutsu, France's need to use Russia to counter Germany had been "a matter of life or death" for some time.[138] Though Mutsu may have overstated his case, French leaders clearly felt it important to stand by their new-found Russian allies, despite the fact that St. Petersburg was willing to let Japan have Formosa and the Pescadores, territories that France coveted.

Even so, France was not eager to antagonize Japan. Throughout the war, Paris had maintained friendly relations with Tokyo. Like the British, France recognized that Japan was a rising power in Asia, and on several occasions, French diplomats even hinted that Paris was interested in forming an alliance with Japan.[139] Moreover, French leaders generally felt the time for a successful intervention had past. As France was then bogged down in Africa, Paris could ill afford a risky military confrontation elsewhere on the globe.[140] Therefore, when Europe first learned of Japan's peace terms and Russia began to lobby the Powers to join forces against Tokyo, France hesitated. However, when French leaders discovered Germany had already approached St. Petersburg offering to support Russia in a joint action, they felt bound to throw in as well.

Germany's motives in the triple intervention were rooted more in the European balance of power than in any commercial or strategic interest in Asia. Stinging from their diplomatic blunder in letting the Russian treaty slip from Berlin to Paris, German leaders were alert for any opportunity to drive a wedge into the Franco-Russian alliance. Russian frustration concerning Japan's gains in Manchuria presented that opportunity, and in late March, 1895—even before Japan divulged her peace terms and before St. Petersburg approached the Powers requesting a joint intervention—Berlin told Russian leaders that Germany would be willing to join them in any action they might choose to pursue against Japan.[141] In this move, Germany sought to prove its friendship to Russia and embarrass France in a single stroke.

So Germany was the linchpin in the triple intervention. The Russians were both surprised and elated by Berlin's unsolicited offer. All but resigned that Japan's territorial accession in Manchuria had become a fait accompli, Germany's unexpected bid gave Witte the leverage he needed to convince the tsar that the Asian situation might be salvageable.[142] Conversely, Germany's offer stunned French leaders, just as Berlin had intended, as they suddenly realized their despised enemy was ingratiating itself with France's most important ally. This placed the French in a quandary. Paris had little interest in northeast Asia and did not want to antagonize the Japanese over an issue they thought was already a lost cause. Furthermore, French leaders detested the notion of engaging in any kind of joint action with Berlin.[143] But France could not allow Germany to appear to be Russia's only supporter, especially with the ink still wet on the yet untested Franco-Russian alliance. Consequently, Paris reluctantly joined the *Dreibund*.[144]

Yet, ironically, Berlin may not have even wanted the triple intervention to succeed. Despite their need to pry Russia apart from France, German leaders had no love for St. Petersburg, nor had they any desire to advance Russian interests in Asia. In fact, when the Italian foreign minister offered to oppose the *Dreibund*, he confided to Minister Takahira that Berlin had privately informed Rome that, "The whole thing is dramatic [in other words, Germany's participation in the intervention is a sham], and therefore, Germany and Italy can act on opposite sides without separating [the] Triple Alliance . . . "[145] According to the Italian minister:

The truth of the German scheme is simply to break [the] Franco-Russian understanding in continental politics, thus placing France finally in an isolated position. But Germany knows Russia must be checked somewhere. Under these circumstances, if England, Italy, and the United States of America can be united on Japan's side, the question may be settled without very serious consequences . . . [146]

All of this suggests the *Dreibund* was cobbled together on a very shaky foundation, and its ability to stand in the face of resistance was anything but sure. France had little interest in northeast Asia, chafed at the idea of working with Germany, dreaded offending Japan, and could not afford another military entanglement. Germany's interests in Asia were even less than France's, and Berlin probably wanted the enterprise to fail or, at least, to stalemate. Only Russia had a tangible interest in the affair. But despite Ito's assertion that St. Petersburg's intentions had been clear since the year before, Russia's intentions had been anything but clear. Russian leaders had straddled the fence for months, urging Tokyo to moderate its claims against Peking, but promising their friendship and support all the while.

That is because, despite Russia's obvious concern that Japanese gains would damage their interests, St. Petersburg doubted that it could impose its will on Japan. Even after Berlin offered its support, only Witte and the army minister were confident in Russia's ability to prevail.

Given the *Dreibund's* instability, one must wonder why Japan did not stand against it more strongly. Granted, the ominous strategic situation fostered a fear of escalation among Japanese leaders, and the impending deadline for exchanging the ratified treaty heightened their sense of urgency. Moreover, with the United States, Britain, and, ultimately, Italy standing neutral, Tokyo found itself completely cut off from Great Power support. Even so, given the constant flow of diplomatic intelligence from Japan's ministers abroad, Mutsu and Ito clearly had more than enough information to recognize the glaring cracks in the Powers' facade.[147] So why didn't they, at least, apply some stress to the *Dreibund* to see if it would rupture?

There are several measures Japanese leaders might have taken to resist the Powers, short of blatantly refusing their advice. For instance, Tokyo might have instructed all its diplomats in third-party countries to unofficially inform their host governments that, while Japan still hoped to find a peaceful solution to the Powers' concerns, Tokyo could not accept the advice as tendered.[148] Meanwhile, the Japanese should have begun redeploying their fleet to home waters. Assuming a speed of 10 knots, it would have taken approximately three days to move the fleet from the Pescadores to the Tsushima Straits. This move would have raised the level of tension between *Dreibund* members, while leaving ample time for other diplomatic approaches before the scheduled treaty ratification. While putting up this initial show of resolve, they could have also taken a more aggressive stance to bring London and, subsequently, Rome over to their side.[149] Although British leaders sought to avoid involvement in the affair, they did not want to see a larger war in Asia, nor did Britain want to see Russia get a stronger foothold in northern China. If Tokyo's firmness failed to sway London, the Japanese might have frankly suggested that, though they felt Britain's interests in Asia were more compatible with Japan's than were Russia's, without London's active support, Tokyo might eventually be forced to accommodate St. Petersburg at Britain's expense. That is, Japan might cede some amount of Chinese or Korean territory to Russia rather than return the Liaotung Peninsula to China. Finally, if all else failed, Tokyo might have approached St. Petersburg directly, offering to cede a port in Korea to Russia and force China to grant the Russians a railroad clearance across Manchuria—all on the condition that the *Dreibund* withdraw its advice.

These are but a few of the many options Japanese leaders might have considered. Granted, these kinds of maneuvers would have been riskier than the course Japan actually chose, and there is no guarantee they would have succeeded. But without first putting up a strong front, Tokyo could not gauge whether Russia, France, and Germany would have really stood together in the face of a possible war. These alternatives would have had at least as good a chance of succeeding as the feeble pleading to which Tokyo ultimately resorted. But if Japan's sudden timidity seems curious, a more fundamental question might be, why would Tokyo allow the triple intervention to occur in the first place?

Japan had ample warning that the West would intervene should Tokyo retain territory on the Chinese mainland, yet Japanese leaders did nothing to forestall that eventuality, despite obvious opportunities to do so. On at least two occasions Hitrovo told Mutsu that Russia was interested in reaching a private agreement with Japan concerning the peace terms. Evidently, St. Petersburg was opening the door to a compromise in which Russia and Japan could share the spoils of war to the advantage of both. On either of those occasions (and, for that matter, at any other time up to the intervention), Mutsu might well have bought the Russians off with the port-and-access offer mentioned earlier. Yet, he chose to remain silent.

While this may be puzzling, the greater mystery is why Tokyo, after hearing time and again that the Powers would not stand for a cession of mainland territory, would have even demanded such exorbitant terms at Shimonoseki. Granted, the Powers' failure to deter Japan from going to war in 1894 and success in compelling her to return Liaotung in 1895 may both be explained by Russia's interim naval deployment to Asia. But if Japan's behavior can be explained simply on the basis of a shifting balance of forces, why was Tokyo not deterred from trying to keep Liaotung after the Russian fleet was fully deployed?

Clearly, the puzzle is not yet finished. While a rational analysis encompassing the theoretical principles of punishment, denial, and the balance of interests may go a long way toward explaining the outcome of the triple intervention, it still leaves many questions unanswered. To explore these remaining issues, we must examine Japan's behavior in terms of the perceptions, preferences, and processes that constituted her strategic culture.

Strategic Culture and the Triple Intervention

The Japanese government's strategic preferences, once fully understood, should explain a great deal about Japan's responses to compellent threat. Yet, before one can truly comprehend Tokyo's preferences as they related to the Sino-Japanese War and the triple intervention, one must appreciate the way Japanese leaders perceived the world in the late nineteenth century. For perception is the lens through which decision makers interpret the strategic environment, and culture gives that lens its tint.

In many respects, Japan was a captive of her Confucian world view. After more than 1,000 years of social conditioning, every person, group, and institution in Japan was ranked, relative to those around it, and each knew its station. So it should be no surprise that when the Japanese finally looked beyond their shores, they saw the world in terms of order and hierarchy. Western governments believed the world condition to be anarchic, its true nature only partly concealed by a thin veneer of legal custom; but Japan surveyed the international community and saw a hierarchy of nations, ordered by degrees of industrial development and military might, and governed by international law.[150]

It was in this conception of the world that the Meiji government developed its strategic preferences. Having seen their nation humiliated in being forced to accept a series of unequal treaties with the West, the young samurai who led the restoration movement concluded that Japan's station in the international order must be quite humble, and they vowed to rectify that situation. But the only way they could see to do that was through emulation, so they made westernization a national crusade.

Over the next 30 years, the Japanese did everything in their power to raise Japan's standing in the world. To this end, they made immense sacrifices to industrialize and reorganize their society; but the westernization campaign had external components as well. In 1876, the Japanese government began to emulate the international behavior of their Western oppressors, compelling Korea to open its doors and sign a treaty patterned after the unequal treaties forced upon Tokyo only 20 years earlier. Likewise, promulgation of the 1889 constitution was more an international statement than a domestic one, as Japanese leaders hoped they could earn the Powers' respect by donning the trappings of a Western constitutional monarchy. To a large extent, it worked. In 1894, despite tensions brought on by the Sino-Japanese War, Tokyo finally persuaded London and Washington to sign new treaties recognizing Japan as an equal participant in the community of nations, and Japan revised her treaties with the other Powers in 1895 and 1896.[151]

By the mid-1890s, Meiji leaders believed Japan had risen from the lowly position she formerly held in the international hierarchy. In fact, the Japanese were convinced that theirs had become the foremost nation in Asia. Now, as superiors in the Asian community, the Japanese looked with disdain on China and Korea who, with their traditional institutions and undeveloped economies, were still helpless before the West. As an emerging power, Tokyo believed Japan was entitled to colonize the lesser developed portions of Asia, just as the Western nations had done. Moreover, in keeping with Confucian tradition, the Japanese felt they had a right—indeed, a paternal obligation—to compel their backward neighbors, particularly Korea, to embrace reform in the same spirit as did Japan. Nevermind that Korea did not want Japan's fatherly guidance—the Japanese would put Seoul's house in order whether the Koreans liked it or not. After all, Japan's responsibilities as "elder uncle" did not include benevolence or

good interpersonal relations.[152] Consequently, Japan's strategic preferences on the eve of the Sino-Japanese War were rooted as much in Tokyo's
desire to redress Japan's standing in Asia, vis-à-vis China and Korea, as
in a desire to acquire territory.

Japan's behavior before, during, and after the war consistently reflected
Tokyo's obsession with convincing Peking and Seoul that Japan was the
new head of the Asian family of nations. The crisis began when China
called Korea its "tributary state" and turned to war when the Koreans
tried to ignore Tokyo's insistence that Seoul affirm its independence from
Peking. Once the fighting erupted, Japanese leaders would not be satisfied
with simply defeating China; they had to humiliate Peking at every opportunity to demonstrate Japan's superiority to the old Middle Kingdom.
As China became desperate for peace, Tokyo refused to discuss ending
the war until Peking was "repentant" enough to approach Japan directly.
Later, once a dialog had begun, the Japanese used every means available
to take face from the Chinese, from dictating details of the conference
arrangements to sending Peking's first plenipotentiaries home in disgrace.[153] Even at Shimonoseki, with peace at hand, Mutsu and Ito were
determined to deny China an armistice and make the negotiation as coercive as possible, before they were frustrated in that scheme by the attack
on Li.

Confident as they were in Japan's superiority over its Asian neighbors,
the Japanese still considered themselves inferior to the Western Powers.[154]
Throughout the Sino-Japanese conflict, Mutsu and Ito were preoccupied
with what the Powers thought of their actions and whether they might
eventually intervene. Consequently, Mutsu listened intently to the Western ministers in Tokyo and carefully weighed every scrap of information
from abroad to keep abreast of the Powers' policies and intentions. Finally,
after Mutsu and Ito decided to let the West know that Japan would demand territory in settlement with China, the Japanese urged both Hitrovo
and Lobanov to tell them if Russia's interests would be injured when
Japan made its claims on the continent.

All of this is hierarchically oriented behavior. Tokyo was determined to
confirm Japan's dominance in Asia and establish an *oyabun-kobun* (patron-
client) relationship with Korea. Yet, while striving to bring subordinate
nations in line, the Japanese carefully avoided provoking those governments they considered superior to Japan. Granted, Tokyo maintained a
degree of passive resistance to the West throughout the conflict, rejecting
advice and mediation offers from Russia, Britain, and others. But that is
not inconsistent with subordinate behavior in Japanese groups, as juniors
often subtly test the boundaries set by their elders. What is important to
note is that Japanese leaders were always concerned about Western interests and tried to harmonize Japan's objectives—in form, if not always in
substance—with those interests. This effort can be seen throughout the

war, but is most evident at the end when Mutsu and Nishi went so far as to discuss Russian concerns in the settlement with Hitrovo and Lobanov. In essence, the Japanese were asking for permission to take territory on the continent, while promising to safeguard a superior's interests.

In some respects, this explains why Japan was not deterred from claiming the Liaotung Peninsula at Shimonoseki, yet capitulated to the triple intervention so quickly. Whether St. Petersburg deliberately misled Japan regarding Russia's interests in the settlement, Mutsu and Ito seemed to interpret Russian ambivalence as tacit approval for taking territory on the mainland. Then, when the intervention finally did materialize, the shock Japanese leaders felt at having misinterpreted Russia's intentions, along with their surprise at Germany's involvement, undoubtedly contributed to the paralysis the Japanese exhibited in trying to deal with the crisis. In fact, if the Japanese believed, as Mutsu insists, the Russians had deliberately misled them, their sense of shock would have been compounded. They would have felt betrayed by a superior nation that had repeatedly assured them of its friendship and good will. But Japan's claims at Shimonoseki were driven by far more than Japanese misperception of Russian interests.

Japan's exorbitant peace terms were determined months before the settlement and were products of that country's consensus decision-making process. Anticipating the Hiroshima Conference, Japanese leaders began discussing terms in late December, 1894, using the alternative plans Mutsu had sent Ito in October as a basis. As might be expected, every constituency in the Japanese government argued for terms that best served its own interests. The navy considered the Liaotung Peninsula important, but insisted the annexation of Formosa was essential. Should Japan be unable to retain Liaotung, naval leaders suggested they cede it to Korea. Tokyo could then compel Seoul to lease it back. Army officials argued there was no comparison between territory in Manchuria, where Japanese troops had bled and died, and Formosa, where Japan had not yet set foot. Furthermore, the Manchurian territory was strategically situated between Korea and China and therefore important to Japan's long-range strategic objectives. Meanwhile, the officials charged with managing Japan's economic policies lobbied for demanding as large an indemnity as possible to defray the costs of the war. Submit these varied interests to a consensus decision in an environment of unqualified military success, and the result was inevitable—Japanese leaders included the desires of virtually every constituency in the peace terms. Simple as this solution was, the outcome proved to be unfortunate for Japan.[155]

The sense of shared investment in the bloated terms served to unify Japanese leaders in their mission, but it also denied them the flexibility needed to achieve a durable peace. Clearly, Mutsu and Ito could not waiver from their territorial demands at Shimonoseki and risk the censure of military leaders. More importantly, once the Japanese government reached a consensus decision on the peace terms in January 1895, Mutsu could negotiate nothing with Russia or any other government that might compromise those terms. Therefore, though Mutsu may have been disinclined to respond to Hitrovo's November, 1894, flirtation for a "secret understanding" because Russian strength was not yet a threat, by February he could not possibly act on Hitrovo's second overture, even though the Russian fleet had, by then, begun to menace Japan's security. Nor could the Japanese change course in the last days before Shimonoseki when several governments warned them that any cession of continental territory would cause "certain Powers" to intervene. They simply lacked the maneuverability to forestall the inevitable—they were lashed to the mast by their own consensus decision. Japan's position was made all the more inflexible by the jingoism so rampant in Japanese public opinion.

Nineteenth-century Japan was a nation of samurai in spirit, if not in fact. During the country's long Edo-era isolation, the martial virtues that were previously the exclusive domain of the warrior class gradually permeated every level of Japanese society. Following the restoration, Meiji leaders exploited public identification with these values to foster nationalism and inspire greater levels of sacrifice in the modernization effort.

By the 1890s, the public had been subjected to two decades of nationalist indoctrination, and the effects of this extended, deliberate manipulation of cultural symbols were profound. The Japanese people, though generally courteous and mild as individuals, had become militant and aggressive as a group. Conditioned to believe that Japan was a chosen land led by a divine emperor, they were impatient to throw off the last vestiges of Western oppression—the humiliating unequal treaties—and push forward to find Japan's place in the sun. Moreover, as most Japanese were poorly informed about world affairs and had never had direct contact with the West, they lacked the cautious attitudes their leaders exhibited regarding policies that might affect the Powers. In essence, though the Ito government still placed itself somewhere below the Powers in the hierarchy of nations, much of the Japanese public was convinced that their country was at least equal to those in the West.

Consequently, public opinion both empowered and constrained Tokyo throughout the Sino-Japanese War. When Mutsu and Ito first decided to sent troops to Korea in 1894, Japan's state-controlled newspapers began agitating in support of the government's expressed goals—Korean reform, expulsion of the Chinese, and ultimately, war with China. The public responded immediately with a wave of militant patriotism, enabling Tokyo to prosecute the war aggressively without fear of domestic censure. But Japanese leaders soon discovered that inspiring militarism was much easier than controlling it. With Japan's military forces victorious at every turn, the public did not want to hear about compromise, Western interests, or even ending the war. Each time the Ito government suggested it might consider any kind of restraint, political opponents provoked public condemnation by accusing the government of being soft on China. Ultimately, Mutsu and Ito discovered that the national unity that had first enabled them to prosecute the war so effectively later served to deny them the flexibility needed to end it on terms acceptable to the West.[156]

With all these dominos in place, the outcome of the triple intervention was almost inescapable. When the *Dreibund* delivered its advice, Japanese leaders suddenly realized that Russia did, indeed, have interests worth defending in Manchuria and the Treaty of Shimonoseki would not deter them from acting. Moreover, the Japanese discovered that other Powers would move against them, even if they had little interest in the situation at hand, and even if they were nominally hostile to one another. The combined impact of these revelations shattered Tokyo's conception of the strategic situation and stunned Japanese leaders into near paralysis. Consequently, when the first decision conference met at Hiroshima—without Mutsu and other cabinet members, Ito was the only civilian present—military leaders drove a quick consensus against challenging the West in any way. But with the domestic perils of conceding to the Powers' equally daunting, the conferees could think of nothing more resourceful than submitting the issue to an international conference—in essence, they decided to plead their case before a jury of Japan's superiors.

The civilian conferees at Maiko showed little more strategic initiative than had their colleagues the day before. Of course, Mutsu had the presence of mind to thwart the decision to seek an international conference; but after the consensus between Ito, Nomura, and Matsukata overwhelmed his proposal to resist the *Dreibund*, Mutsu's subsequent ideas were timid and unimaginative. Requests for support from neutral Powers and pleas for the *Dreibund* to withdraw its advice would be followed by offers of compromise and, finally, capitulation.

The epilogue of the triple intervention was but a final testament to Japan's deep cultural conditioning. Awed by the combined censure of three superior nations, Japan's fate was sealed. Nevertheless, in keeping with their Confucian nature, the Japanese refused to let Peking alter the Treaty of Shimonoseki in any way. Even when rebuked from above, one cannot permit an insolent inferior to go unpunished. In a civilized society, order and face must be maintained.

CONCLUSION

There may be nothing the Japanese could have done to resist the triple intervention. Even alone, the Russian fleet may have been more than the war-weary Japanese navy could handle; augmented by French and German vessels, it would have been overwhelming. Clearly, Britain was the key to Japan's salvation. But London was so determined to remain on the sidelines that it would have been difficult for the Japanese to promise or threaten anything of sufficient magnitude to persuade the British to act. Without Britain, Italy was lost; and without either of them, Japan would have been hard pressed to rupture the *Dreibund*, despite its tenuous foundation. Consequently, the triple intervention may have succeeded no matter how Japan's strategic culture manifested itself, or whether it even existed.

Nevertheless, without carefully analyzing how culture conditioned Japan's perceptions, strategic preferences, and governmental processes, one cannot quite understand Tokyo's behavior before or after the intervention. An assessment of each country's interests in the affair may reveal how the crisis came about, but it does not explain *why* Japan let it happen. Likewise, an examination of how Japanese leaders calculated their costs and benefits in response to the *Dreibund*'s implied threat may reveal why Japan ultimately capitulated, but it fails to explain why Japanese leaders behaved so meekly throughout the crisis or why they viewed their strategic options so narrowly. In conclusion, one cannot fully comprehend the outcome of the triple intervention without understanding how culture conditioned Japan's strategic behavior in the late nineteenth century.

Yet, analysis of the triple intervention does not confirm that strategic culture can affect compellence outcomes. In this case, the operative variable from a cultural perspective—Japan's hierarchically rooted awe of the Western Powers—argues for the same outcome as the operative variable in a cost-benefit analysis—the *Dreibund*'s naval supremacy. Therefore, the results are inconclusive. Fortunately, the analysis of Tokyo's response to Washington's compellence attempt in the oil embargo tells quite a different story.

NOTES

1. See Thomas C. Schelling, *Arms and Influence* (New Haven, Conn.: Yale University Press, 1966), pp. 69–78.

2. For background on Sino-Japanese relations regarding Korea see Hugh Borton, *Japan's Modern Century: From Perry to 1970* (New York: The Ronald Press Co., 1970), pp. 187–92; Ian Nish, *Japanese Foreign Policy 1869–1942: Kasumigaseki to Miyakezaka* (London: Routledge & Kegan Paul, 1977), pp. 21–24. For an articulate presentation of Japan's rationale (pre–World War II account of nineteenth-century Korea issues), see Roy Hidemichi Akagi, *Japan's Foreign Relations 1542–1936: A Short History* (Tokyo: The Kokuseido Press, 1936), pp. 113–35.

3. The Tientsin Treaty (also called the Sino-Japanese Treaty of 1885 and the Li-Ito Convention) was negotiated between Japanese *genro* Ito Hirobumi and Chinese Viceroy Li Hung-chang to defuse a near confrontation in Korea in 1885. In it, China and Japan agreed to three points: 1) both would withdraw troops from

Korea within four months; 2) each would notify the other before deploying troops to Korea in the future; and 3) neither China nor Japan would take part in training the Korean army. See Akagi, p. 131.

4. Borton, p. 233.

5. See the 3 July 1894 telegram from U.S. Minister to China Charles Denby to U.S. Secretary of State Walter Q. Gresham in *American Diplomatic and Public Papers: The United States and China*, Series III, *The Sino-Japanese War to the Russo-Japanese War 1894–1905, The Sino-Japanese War I* (hereafter referred to as ADPP) (Wilmington, Del.: Scholarly Research, Inc., 1981), p. 1:147.

6. Japan's motives in Korea are clearly revealed in Mutsu Munemitsu's personal memoir, *Kenkenroku*. Mutsu was Tokyo's foreign minister during the Sino-Japanese War and the triple intervention. Writing in December, 1895, shortly before dying of tuberculosis, Mutsu provides a vivid account of Japan's perceptions, objectives, and analyses throughout the period. Indeed, Mutsu was so frank that on his death the Japanese government seized his manuscript and suppressed it for 34 years. This work is a particularly important source for my study. Though clearly biased and self-serving—the memoir is, in part, Mutsu's effort to defend himself against charges that he and Ito won the war but lost the peace—it offers a superb, first-hand account of case events. More importantly, Mutsu reveals how Japanese decision makers perceived themselves and the world around them in 1895. For Japan's motives in Korea in 1894, see Munemitsu Mutsu, *Kenkenroku: A Diplomatic Record of the Sino-Japanese War, 1894–5*, edited and translated with historical notes by Gordon Mark Berger (Tokyo: University of Tokyo Press, 1982), pp. 11–39.

7. Borton, pp. 233–34.

8. Mutsu, p. 37.

9. Borton, p. 234; Mutsu, p. 37.

10. Mutsu, p. 37.

11. The troopship was the *Kowshing*, a transport vessel under British registry and flag. Britain filed an official protest for the sinking, but withdrew it after investigation revealed that the Japanese had opened fire only after the Chinese troops had fired upon them. Diplomatic traffic, eyewitness depositions, and press extracts concerning this case are available in *British Documents on Foreign Affairs: Reports and Papers From the Foreign Office Confidential Print*, Part I, Series E (hereafter referred to as BDFA), edited by Ian Nish (New York: University Publications of America, 1989).

12. F. Brinkley, *A History of the Japanese People: From the Earliest Times to the End of the Meiji Era* (New York: The Encyclopedia Britannica Co., 1914), pp. 700–701; Chitoshi Yanaga, *Japan Since Perry* (Westport, Conn.: Greenwood Press, 1949), p. 244.

13. Before the war, Peking and the West seemed certain that Japan could not stand against China's military might. For a typical prewar assessment of the relative strengths of China and Japan, see the 25 June 1894 editorial in Shanghai's English-speaking *North-China Daily News*, in which the editor praises China's modern fleet, fortifications, and army and refers to Japan as "an insignificant enemy." The clipping was enclosed in a dispatch from the U.S. Minister in Peking, Charles Denby, to Secretary of State Walter Gresham and is provided in ADPP, p. 1:107.

14. Akagi, p. 149; Yanaga, p. 245.

15. Akagi, pp. 150–52.

16. Morinosuke Kajima, *The Emergence of Japan as a World Power, 1895–1925* (Rutland, Vt.: Charles E. Tuttle Co., 1968), p. 24; Yanaga, p. 248.

17. Kajima, p. 24; Yanaga, p. 248.

18. Mutsu, p. 41. A Japanese foreign ministry summary of this meeting is provided in Morinosuke Kajima, *The Diplomacy of Japan 1894–1922*, Volume 1, *Sino-Japanese War and Triple Intervention* (Tokyo: The Kajima Institute of International Peace, 1976), pp. 85–88.

19. Mutsu, p. 42. The text of this note is provided in its original French in Kajima, *The Diplomacy of Japan*, p. 77.

20. Mutsu, p. 42; Kajima, *The Diplomacy of Japan*, p. 89.

21. Giers's 3 July 1894 telegram to Hitrovo in Kajima, *The Diplomacy of Japan*, p. 91.

22. Kajima, *The Diplomacy of Japan*, p. 91.

23. Ibid., pp. 93–94.

24. See the 23 July 1894 telegram from British Minister to Japan R. S. Paget to British Foreign Minister the Earl of Kimberly in BDFA, p. 4:69.

25. Mutsu, p. 55.

26. See the 6 October 1894 dispatch from U.S. Minister to Britain W. E. Goschen to U.S. Secretary of State Walter Gresham in ADPP, p. 1:252.

27. For the American response to the British overture in October, see Secretary Gresham's 6 October 1894 dispatch to Minister Goschen in ADPP, p. 1:252. For a full explanation of the American position, see Secretary Gresham's 24 November 1894 telegram to Minister Denby in ADPP, pp. 1:318–19.

28. Akagi, pp. 150–52; Yanaga, p. 248.

29. Akagi, p. 150.

30. Kajima, *The Diplomacy of Japan*, p. 135.

31. Takahira's 9 October 1894 telegram was not Mutsu's first warning of intervention rumors in Europe. On September 24, Japan's Minister to Germany, Viscount Aoki Shuzo, wired Mutsu with concerns about "something going on . . . among the Western Powers . . . [regarding] an exchange of views over intervening with armed force." But Aoki said he was certain Germany and Great Britain were not the originators of these discussions. See Aoki's telegram to Mutsu and Takahira's 9 October 1894 telegram to Mutsu in Kajima, *The Diplomacy of Japan*, pp. 132–33 and 136–37.

32. See this telegram in Kajima, *The Diplomacy of Japan*, p. 136.

33. Mutsu, p. 130.

34. Ibid., pp. 130–31.

35. Mutsu's 12 October 1894 telegram to Takahira in Kajima, *The Diplomacy of Japan*, p. 136.

36. Kajima, *The Diplomacy of Japan*, pp. 137–38; Mutsu, p. 131.

37. Mutsu's letter did not address why he added the cession of Formosa to Plan B. Perhaps he felt Japan was entitled to some additional compensation in return for the surrender of control of Korea to the Powers.

38. See Mutsu's letter in Kajima, *The Diplomacy of Japan*, p. 138.

39. Mutsu, p. 132.

40. Charles Denby's 31 October 1894 dispatch to Secretary of State Gresham in ADPP, pp. 1:274–82.

41. Akagi, p. 150.

42. Gresham's 6 November 1894 dispatch to Dun in ADPP, p. 1:299.

43. Denby's 10 November 1894 dispatch to Gresham in ADPP, pp. 1:300–303.

44. Denby's 10 November 1894 telegram to Gresham in ADPP, p. 1:299.

45. Mutsu, p. 139.

46. Ibid.

47. Mutsu, p. 140.

48. Denby's 30 November 1894 dispatch to Gresham in ADPP, pp. 1:345–47.

49. Ibid. Also see the *Tsungli Yamen*'s 29 November 1894 note to Denby, in ADPP, pp. 1:343–44.

50. Mutsu's 2 December 1894 note *verbale* in Kajima, *The Diplomacy of Japan*, p. 179.

51. Denby's 12 December 1894 telegram to Dun in Kajima, *The Diplomacy of Japan*, p. 179.

52. Denby's 19 December 1894 telegram to Gresham in ADPP, p. 2:25.

53. See Denby's telegrams to Dun on 20 and 29 December 1894 and 5 January 1895, and Mutsu's notes *verbale* for transmission to Denby on 26 and 31 December 1894 and 7 January 1895 in Kajima, *The Diplomacy of Japan*, pp. 180–82.

54. Takahira's 11 November 1894 telegram to Mutsu, in Kajima, *The Diplomacy of Japan*, p. 140.

55. Ibid.

56. Nishi's 10 November 1894 telegram to Mutsu in Kajima, *The Diplomacy of Japan*, pp. 139–40.

57. Aoki's 12 November 1894 telegram to Mutsu in Kajima, *The Diplomacy of Japan*, p. 141.

58. Aoki's 14 November 1894 telegram to Mutsu and Nishi's 1 December 1894 telegram and dispatch to Mutsu in Kajima, *The Diplomacy of Japan*, pp. 141 and 146–50.

59. Nishi's 1 December 1894 telegram to Mutsu in Kajima, *The Diplomacy of Japan*, pp. 146–47.

60. Kajima, *The Diplomacy of Japan*, p. 150.

61. Ibid.

62. Mutsu, pp. 225–26.

63. Kimberly's 25 January 1895 telegram to Trench in BDFA, p. 5:39.

64. The ministers met with Hayashi because Mutsu was already in Hiroshima for the conference. See Trench's 31 January 1895 very confidential dispatch to Kimberly in BDFA, p. 5:98.

65. Ibid.

66. Ibid.

67. Denby's 20 December 1894 dispatch to Gresham in ADPP, 2:27–39.

68. Mutsu, p. 279 (Chp. XVI, n. 1).

69. Ibid., 153. No doubt, following this discussion, Mutsu communicated these concerns to Hayashi, resulting in the remarks the vice foreign minister made to Trench on 31 January 1895.

70. These documents are provided in Kajima, *The Diplomacy of Japan*, pp. 186–87.

71. Mutsu, pp. 153–62.

72. Ibid., p. 154.

73. Provided in Kajima, *The Dipomacy of Japan*, p. 188.

74. Ibid., p. 189.

75. Mutsu, pp. 159–60.

76. Ibid., p. 160.

77. Trench's very confidential 15 February 1895 dispatch to Kimberly in BDFA, pp. 5:141–42.

78. Mutsu, p. 227.

79. Ibid., pp. 226–27.

80. Mutsu's note *verbale* in Kajima, *The Diplomacy of Japan*, pp. 195–96.

81. Mutsu, pp. 164–66.

82. Ibid., p. 228.

83. Ibid., pp. 228–29.

84. Mutsu, p. 237.

85. Ibid., p. 238.

86. Provided in Kajima, *The Diplomacy of Japan*, p. 204.

87. Mutsu, pp. 167–71. Transcripts of this and the other discussions conducted at Shimonoseki are provided in Kajima, *The Diplomacy of Japan*, pp. 195–280.

88. Mutsu, pp. 174–79.

89. Li Ching-fong had accompanied his father on the trip and served as his assistant before the attack.

90. Akagi, p. 158.

91. A Kuping tael was a Chinese gold coin minted during the reign of Emperor Guangxu (1875–1908). Each weighed 575.64 grains (troy).

92. Provided in Kajima, *The Diplomacy of Japan*, pp. 220–22.

93. Provided in Kajima, *The Diplomacy of Japan*, pp. 223–31.

94. Ito presented the revised terms because Mutsu was absent due to illness. The revised terms are provided in Kajima, *The Diplomacy of Japan*, pp. 234–35.

95. Mutsu, p. 198.

96. Ibid.

97. Ibid., p. 201.

98. Ibid., p. 203. The original French text is provided in Kajima, *The Diplomacy of Japan*, p. 196.

99. Kajima, *The Emergence of Japan as a World Power*, p. 16.

100. Ibid.

101. Ibid. Also see Kajima, *The Diplomacy of Japan*, pp. 294–95; Mutsu, p. 203; Trench's confidential 30 April 1895 dispatch to Kimberly in BDFA, 5:361.

102. Mutsu, p. 205.

103. Ibid., pp. 206–7.

104. Ito, Yamagata, and Saigo were all *genro*.

105. Kajima, *The Diplomacy of Japan*, p. 298.

106. Mutsu, p. 207.

107. Kajima, *The Diplomacy of Japan*, p. 299.

108. Of this group, Ito and Matsukata were *genro*.

109. Tatsui Takeuchi, *War and Diplomacy in the Japanese Empire* (New York: Russell & Russell, 1967), p. 117. Also Kajima, *The Diplomacy of Japan*, p. 299; Kajima, *The Emergence of Japan as a World Power*, p. 19; Mutsu, p. 208.

110. Mutsu, p. 208.

111. Ibid., pp. 208–9.

112. Mutsu's 25 April 1895 telegram to Nishi in Kajima, *The Diplomacy of Japan*, p. 302.

113. Mutsu's 25 April 1895 telegram to Kato in Kajima, *The Diplomacy of Japan*, p. 303. Presumably, Mutsu is referring to the port city of Yingkow, on the Liaotung Peninsula, and an additional port on the Korean peninsula.

114. Ibid.

115. Kato's telegrams to Mutsu on 28 and 29 April 1895 in Kajima, *The Diplomacy of Japan*, pp. 304–5.

116. Kurino's 29 April 1895 telegram to Mutsu in Kajima, *The Diplomacy of Japan*, p. 306.

117. Mutsu, p. 241.

118. Nishi's 27 April 1895 telegram to Mutsu in Kajima, *The Diplomacy of Japan*, p. 304.

119. The text of the messages to all three ministers is typified by Mutsu's 30 April 1895 telegram to Hayashi in Kajima, *The Diplomacy of Japan*, p. 308.

120. Nishi's 3 May 1895 telegram to Mutsu in Kajima, *The Diplomacy of Japan*, p. 309.

121. Kajima, *The Diplomacy of Japan*, p. 310; Mutsu, p. 217.

122. Mutsu, p. 218.

123. Ibid.

124. Kajima, *The Emergence of Japan as a World Power*, p. 23.

125. Kajima, *The Diplomacy of Japan*, p. 312.

126. Ibid., pp. 218–19. The text of this note is provided in its original French in Kajima, *The Diplomacy of Japan*, p. 311.

127. Takeuchi, pp. 118–19.

128. Yanaga, p. 249.

129. Serge Witte, *The Memoirs of Count Witte*, translated and edited by Sidney Harcave (Armonk, N.Y.: M. E. Sharpe, Inc., 1990), p. 228.

130. See the numerous diplomatic communications on this issue in BDFA, pp. 5:335–39.

131. Actually, Italy was a member of the Triple Alliance formed in 1882 with Germany and Austria-Hungary. These countries were traditional rivals with Russia, further explaining Italy's concern about St. Petersburg's potential gains in Asia.

132. This shift can be tracked in Mutsu, pp. 88–89, 107, and 135 and in the various press extracts provided in BDFA and ADPP.

133. On 10 April 1895, Kimberly informed Russian Minister de Staal that, "In the opinion of Her Majesty's government, considering the absolute and unbroken success of the Japanese arms, those terms [keeping Liaotung] were not unreasonable; and although they might be inconvenient in certain respects to the Western Powers, they did not appear to us to be so vitally injurious as to justify war with all its incalculable consequences. Moreover, public opinion in this country would not tolerate recourse to force." See Kimberly's 10 April 1895 telegram to Lascelles in BDFA, p. 5:183.

134. According to the American Minister in Tokyo, Edwin Dun, the consensus opinion of the foreign diplomatic community there was that Japan would reject the Powers' advice. Furthermore Lord Kimberly, the British foreign minister, was repeatedly given the same assessment by British diplomats abroad and by Japa-

nese Minister Kato. On April 25, two days after the advice had been tendered to Japan, Kimberly described a recent meeting in which he told Russian Minister de Staal, once again, that Britain would not join the Dreibund, saying, "Her Majesty's Government's view as to the whole policy of the communication which it is proposed to make to Japan is that it is one in which they cannot join even on the understanding suggested, as they could not risk the eventuality which, under present circumstances, they consider extremely probable, if not certain, of the communication being ignored by Japan." See Dun's 9 May 1895 dispatch to Gresham in ADPP, pp. 2:362–68; Trench's 21 April 1895 and 9 May 1895 telegrams to Kimberly and Kimberly's 24 April 1895 telegram to Trench in BDFA. Also see Kimberly's 25 April 1895 telegram to Lascelles, pp. 5:229–30.

135. American Minister to Japan Edwin Dun also believed this, and interwar Japanese historian Roy Hidemichi Akagi echoes this theme. See Mutsu, pp. 230–37; Dun's 5 June 1895 dispatch to interim Secretary of State Edwin F. Uhl in ADPP, 2:380–93; Akagi, p. 164.

136. Kajima, *The Emergence of Japan as a World Power*, p. 25.

137. Kajima, *The Diplomacy of Japan*, p. 314; Witte, p. 228; Yanaga, pp. 249–50.

138. Mutsu, p. 243.

139. Mutsu, pp. 107 and 243.

140. On May 2, Britain's minister to Paris, Henry Howard, reported, "France has the Madagascar expedition on her hands, she is in great want of money, and a loan for a large amount will, it is said, be rendered imperative within the very near future. A fresh military expedition in the Far East, under these circumstances is not, therefore, likely to be popular in France, and unless the Japanese difficulty is not amicably settled before the Chambers meet, it is thought not improbable that the Ministry may fall." See Howard's 2 May 1895 telegram to Kimberly in BDFA, p. 5:274.

141. See Lascelles's 28 March 1895 telegram to Kimberly in BDFA, p. 5:150.

142. Remember, Germany's offer came in late March, so Witte knew he had German support when he first proposed the intervention at the conference in early April.

143. The French minister to Peking expressed this sentiment in a conversation with British Minister O'Conor on May 1, 1895. See O'Conor's 1 May 1895 telegram to Kimberly in BDFA, p. 5:701.

144. This analysis is consistent with Mutsu's conclusions. It also explains why, as Hayashi later related to Trench, Harmond's demeanor was notably milder than Hitrovo's or Gutschmid's when they delivered their "friendly-advice" memoranda. Mutsu, pp. 243–44.

145. This quote is excerpted from Takahira's 27 April 1895 telegram to Mutsu, provided in Kajima, *The Diplomacy of Japan*, p. 351.

146. Ibid.

147. Ironically, on May 8, after the crisis, the Japanese seemed to recover from their mental paralysis and Nishi sent Mutsu a lucid analysis of the triple intervention. In this lengthy dispatch, Nishi correctly assessed French and German motives and even discussed the doubts Russian leaders had harbored during the affair. See Nishi's 8 May 1895 telegram to Mutsu in Kajima, *The Diplomacy of Japan*, pp. 315–16.

148. This actually happened to a certain extent, as Kato and Kurino told London

and Washington that they believed Japan would probably refuse the advice. I maintain that the message should have been firmer and more consistent, to raise the Powers' apprehensions, yet delivered in the form of personal opinions in order to avoid provoking the *Dreibund* prematurely.

149. Even after the Americans insisted on remaining neutral, the Italian foreign minister reassured Takahira that Italy would take up Japan's cause if London would speak up first. See Takahira's 27 April 1895 telegram to Mutsu in Kajima, *The Diplomacy of Japan*, pp. 352–53.

150. Many aspects of Japanese behavior during the conflict suggest that Meiji leaders, in conceiving a Confucian model of the world, may have interpreted the framework of international law as a kind of modern ritual for regulating the behavior of states. That is not to suggest that Japanese leaders faithfully abided by the spirit of that law, but they did seem preoccupied with its form. For instance, Tokyo carefully legitimated all of Japan's actions in Korea with forced treaties and other written agreements, even to the extent of coercing the king to sign an order expelling the Chinese. Also, throughout *Kenkenroku*, Mutsu ridicules the Chinese for their apparent lack of facility in modern legal procedures, just as he and Ito do personally at Hiroshima. Finally, Mutsu's early strategy of keeping the peace terms secret until after a treaty is signed was in the apparent expectation that with a signed treaty in hand, Japan's gains would be a fait accompli, as the Powers would be less likely to countermand a legal agreement between nations.

151. Akagi, p. 111.

152. Recall that, unlike China, Japan's brand of Confucianism did not embrace *jin*.

153. Asian face-saving rituals are subtle and complex. The Chinese were, indeed, trying to save face and insult the Japanese by sending Chang and Shao to Hiroshima. But for Mutsu or Ito to admit they had been insulted would have entailed a further loss of face; thus, when talking to Wu, Ito denied the Chinese appointments had been a problem. Nevertheless, the Japanese returned the insult with interest—not only by sending the Chinese home empty handed, but by first forcing them to write a memorandum declaring their inadequacy and then lecturing them about it in official declarations at the close of the conference. All of this humiliated the Chinese deeply.

154. Mutsu is very revealing when he writes, "The Japanese people can be justly proud of the fact that our armies not only demonstrated their great military prowess but also proved Japan's ability to adopt and utilize the civilization of Europe. But frankly speaking, while the Japanese are not as incapable of adopting European civilization as our European detractors once believed, we have not yet really advanced to the sublime position assigned us by our more enthusiastic European admirers." Mutsu, pp. 108–9.

155. Mutsu, pp. 143–45.

156. The day Japan received the Powers' advice, Tokyo shut down all the country's major newspapers for the duration of the crisis.

CHAPTER 5

The Oil Embargo

In 1940, Japan was firmly committed to creating a new order in East Asia. During the previous decade, the Japanese army had expanded its hold in China, first occupying and creating a puppet regime in Manchuria, then driving Chiang Kai-shek's nationalist government from its capital in Nanking. Now, with the European democracies locked in a life-and-death struggle with Nazi Germany, Tokyo believed the time was ripe for a major realignment in the hierarchy of nations. No longer would the Western democracies determine the economic and political destinies of other countries in Europe and Asia. A new sphere of influence was emerging in the West with Berlin at its center. With Britain, France, and the Netherlands distracted and weakened, Tokyo would soon guide its Asian brothers into a new era of prosperity based on Confucian principle and the might of Imperial Japan.

But Japan's ascent was not yet clear of obstacles. Once again, expansion on the continent threatened the interests of Russia, her traditional enemy. As the struggle against the Chinese nationalists grew ever more bitter, the Japanese found themselves increasingly at odds with another major Power in the Pacific, the United States. Despite two bloody clashes with Soviet troops in the late 1930s, Tokyo managed to negotiate a neutrality pact with Moscow in 1940, convincing most Japanese leaders that they had solved the Russian problem, at least for the time being. But the difficulties with Washington were much more complex. The United States was more than Japan's rival in the western Pacific; it was also her principal source of strategic materials. Therefore, in order to subdue China and realize their new order, the Japanese would have to either placate Washington or seize alternative sources of the materials their war machine needed.

Ultimately, they tried both options, but succeeded at neither. Far from being placated, the Americans stiffened their resolve and attempted to discourage Japan from pursuing its aspirations in China by withholding the very resources the Japanese military needed. Turning then to the second alternative, Japanese leaders set themselves on a collision course with Washington and, eventually, their own destruction.

While the broad brush of these events is well known, there are several aspects of Japanese behavior leading to the Second World War that are puzzling when considered on purely objective grounds. For instance, given Tokyo's cautious nature in previous eras, why was Japanese behavior so recklessly provocative in the decade just before the war? And considering Japan's military and diplomatic successes during that period, why was the Japanese government so unstable? Indeed, Tokyo saw the passing of 13 cabinets between 1931 and the attack on Pearl Harbor in 1941. During the same period, the Japanese government was rocked by three coup attempts, and two prime ministers fell to assassins' bullets. How might these developments have affected the way Japanese leaders responded to compellent threat in 1940 and 1941?

Most importantly, why would Japan choose to go to war against the United States? Studies commissioned by Japanese leaders in 1941 revealed that Japan could not defeat an adversary so rich in resources and industrial capacity. In fact, only weeks before Pearl Harbor, one of Japan's most aggressive militarists, General Tojo Hideki, openly conceded that a war with America would be a fight for survival with the odds stacked against Japan. Given those stakes and dismal prospects for success, why could not Tokyo accommodate Washington's demands and wait for a more favorable time to pursue Japan's dream of Asian hegemony? In sum, why did the Japanese refuse to yield to American compellence?

In this chapter, I examine the way Japanese leaders responded to American efforts to compel them to stop aggressing on the Asian continent and I review the events that led to that confrontation. I first explore Japan's behavior in the 1930s, highlighting actions that set the stage for conflict with the United States. Then I examine the way Japanese leaders responded to American compellence efforts, focusing closely on the chain of events beginning in 1940 and culminating with the attack on Pearl Harbor on December 7, 1941.

In the analysis that follows, I suggest we cannot fully understand why Japanese leaders chose war over compliance to American demands without appreciating how culture colored their worldview and conditioned their strategic preferences and governmental processes. Punishment and denial theories standing alone fail to explain why Tokyo did not consider

quite the opposite occurred. Army officials maintained it was they who saved the emperor and his government from insurrection, and in April, 1936, when the *jushin* (senior statesmen) selected Hirota Koki to be prime minister, his war minister, General Terauchi Hisaichi, refused to serve unless he and the army had direct approval over all other cabinet selections.[27] Consequently, the Hirota government was composed mainly of senior army officers and civilians who shared the army's views on foreign and domestic policy. Now, with the army in control of the government and the *Tosei ha* steering the army, Japan's decades-old dream of subduing and exploiting China was reaffirmed and strengthened.[28]

The new cabinet soon embarked on a coordinated effort to better prepare Japan for war. The military's share of the national budget quickly rose to nearly 50 percent as a wave of munitions orders flooded Japan's industrial sector. In December, 1936, Tokyo signed the Anti-Comintern Pact with Berlin in order to deter a Soviet advance on Japan's northwestern flank should the Kwangtung Army find it necessary to move southward into China. The Ministry of Education published the nationalist treatise, *Fundamentals of Our National Polity*, and made it required study in all schools and colleges.[29] In sum, the government set out to marshal every resource in Japanese society—military and diplomatic, public and private, spiritual and material—to support the nation's strategic requirements.[30]

But even military control of the cabinet failed to bring stability to the government. In early 1937, a political firebrand in the Diet verbally attacked War Minister Terauchi, and the general resigned in protest, bringing down the Hirota government. The *jushin* then chose General Ugaki Kazushige to form the next government, but the army vetoed the appointment by refusing to nominate a war minister. Consequently, General Hayashi Senjuro assumed the mantle of leadership. However, his domineering tactics soon united the Diet against him, and though he dissolved the lower house in a counter attack, subsequent elections returned an even stronger opposing coalition, forcing him to resign.

At this point, all eyes turned to Prince Konoe Fumimaro. Descended from one of the oldest noble families in Japan, Konoe enjoyed strong support from all sides: the militarists, the bureaucrats, the financiers, the industrialists, and political leaders in the Diet. He was Saionji's protégé, and though the aged *genro* had lost most of his effective power, he retained unequaled personal prestige. Konoe was acceptable to both extremists and moderates in the army—the extremists believed they could persuade him to follow their policies, and the moderates expected him to bridle the extremists. Ironically, when the new prime minister assumed office in June, 1937, he barely had time to settle into the job when a crisis arose to test his metal. The moderates would be disappointed in the outcome.

From War in China to a New Order in East Asia

While the factional conflicts were unfolding in Tokyo, the Kwangtung Army worked energetically, not only to consolidate its control in Manchukuo but to extend its hold into northern China as well. The truce that ended the fighting after the Manchurian conquest required the Japanese army to remain north of the Great Wall in Manchuria. But the agreement also specified that Chinese forces must remain south of Peking, and the 5,000 square miles between them was made a demilitarized zone patrolled by a police force friendly to Japan. Consequently, the Kwangtung Army now had a presence in North China, and they proceeded to gain an ever growing degree of administrative control in the region using their proven technique of local settlement followed by the formation of autonomous governing councils. In time, Kwangtung Army patrols began providing "security" in the demilitarized zone. Moreover, stemming from the 1901 Boxer Protocol, Japan also maintained a sizable garrison in Peking. By 1937, incidents arising from accidental contacts with Chinese forces were frequent.[31]

One such incident occurred near midnight on July 7, 1937, when a Japanese patrol on night maneuvers clashed with Chinese troops at Marco Polo Bridge outside Peking. Unlike the Manchurian Incident five years earlier, the "China Incident" was a spontaneous, unplanned event, and neither the Konoe government nor the army was certain how to handle it. At first, the case seemed insignificant—just one more in a series of disputes to be settled by local commanders. But a locally brokered cease-fire soon broke down, and the skirmish developed into full scale fighting between Chinese and Japanese forces. These developments sparked a debate between hard-line and moderate factions on the Japanese General Staff. While the hard-liners wanted to use the incident to strike a blow against the Kuomintang and to secure their hold in North China, the moderates feared the conflict would drag Japan into a protracted war. Konoe and the cabinet were pulled one way, then another, and the decision to mobilize the Japanese army was made and canceled four times in the first three weeks of the crisis. Finally, when word arrived on July 26 that Chiang Kai-shek was moving his main army into the theater, the hard-line argument won the day, and Tokyo sent three fresh divisions to North China.[32] Soon, fighting broke out in Shanghai, and Japan sent reinforcements to that front as well. Though neither planned it, China and Japan were at war.[33]

As the conflict spread, Western leaders became concerned about the growing instability in the Far East and, in particular, Japan's aggressive behavior. On October 5, President Roosevelt delivered his famous "Quarantine Speech" in which he declared that "the existing reign of terror and international lawlessness" had reached the stage at which "the very foundations of civilization" were seriously threatened.[34] He called for a concerted effort by all peace-loving nations to oppose the actions that were creating this state of international anarchy and instability. The following day, both the League of Nations and the U.S. Department of State declared that Japan's actions in China were violations of her treaty obligations. In November, delegates from 19 nations met in Brussels to consider peaceful means for resolving the conflict between China and Japan. Although the Brussels Conference was held in accordance with a provision of the Nine-Power Treaty of 1922, Japan refused to participate, maintaining that its dispute with China was outside the purview of that agreement. Consequently, the conferees could do little more than strongly urge China and Japan to suspend hostilities and accept third-party mediation to help resolve their differences.[35]

Meanwhile, the Konoe Cabinet was having more and more difficulty controlling the army, and the General Staff was even less successful in controlling its commanders in the field. As the war spread, the United States began evacuating the 10,000-odd Americans living in China, many of them traveling by river on, or escorted by, the nine gunboats the U.S. Navy had on station in the country. On December 12, one of those gunboats, the U.S.S. *Panay*, was evacuating Americans from Nanking when it was sunk, along with two other American vessels, in a bombing attack by Japanese aircraft.[36] The subsequent American protest brought an immediate apology from Tokyo and an offer to pay reparations, easing tensions for the moment. However, when Nanking fell on December 17, the successive days of wanton looting, rape, and murder perpetrated by Japanese troops made an indelible impression on the Western Powers and further convinced the Chinese that they must resist Japan at all costs.[37]

With the capture of Nanking, the more moderate among Japan's military leaders began to urge the government to find an end to the fighting. Most Japanese believed that once Chiang Kai-shek had lost his capital, he would be defeated. But, far from beaten, the generalissimo extracted his army intact and withdrew upriver to Chungking, where he established a provisional capital and emerged more popular than ever. With fears of protracted war rising once more, a growing chorus of officers called for Japan to open negotiations while it held a position of strength. Ironically, by this time, the Konoe Cabinet had stiffened and was indignant that the Chinese had proven so intransigent.[38] Moreover, with the unbroken string of Japanese victories, public support for the war was riding high. Consequently, on January 16, 1938, the prime minister announced that Japan would "stop dealing with the Kuomintang government and await the establishment of a new Chinese administration, with which she would cooperate wholeheartedly in adjusting Sino-Japanese relations and building a new China."[39] Meanwhile, Japan's army air forces began bombing Chungking.[40]

America's sense of moral outrage intensified during the next few months as the Japanese army repeatedly bombed Chinese cities in efforts to break the Kuomintang's will to resist. Consequently, on June 11, 1938, Secretary of State Cordell Hull publicly condemned the practice of bombing civilians and its "material encouragement." Then, on July 1, the State Department sent a letter to 148 companies involved in the manufacture of aircraft parts informing them that the U.S. government strongly opposed the sale of airplanes or aeronautical equipment that would materially aid or encourage the bombing of civilians in any part of the world. In 1939, the government extended this "moral embargo" to materials essential to airplane manufacture and to materials and information required to produce high-quality aviation gasoline.[41]

Finally resigned to a long war in China, the Konoe government set out to complete the national mobilization that had begun under the Hirota Cabinet. Passage of the National Mobilization Law in March, 1938, gave them the power to put the nation on a wartime footing. They used it liberally. In little more than a year, all male subjects between the ages of 16 and 50 were required to register for the draft, and the Ministry of Finance was authorized to control prices and wages, appropriate private property, and force mediation in all labor disputes. In the meantime, the prime minister streamlined his cabinet, referring all vital issues to a five-minister conference consisting of himself and the ministers of war, navy, foreign affairs, and finance. But most significantly, Konoe's intellectual advisors decided Japan needed an ideology to rationalize its desire to link the recently conquered territories of Manchukuo, Inner Mongolia, and North, Central, and South China with Japan in a unified economic and strategic block.[42] They christened the ideology the "New Order in East Asia."[43]

For Konoe and his advisers, it was important to provide moral justification for Japanese imperialism, while differentiating it from Western colonialism. They believed Japan needed a rationale that was more positive than the simple rejection of Western liberalism, individualism, and communism so prevalent in Japan's contemporary propaganda. Therefore, they turned to a traditionalist critique of modern society that had become an important element in Japanese nationalism. As historian W. G. Beasley explains:

Western imperialism, they said, because it was self-seeking, was tyranny (hado). By contrast, Japanese expansion, which sought to free Asia from the West, was just. Its object was a partnership. For practical reasons, this must be a partnership in which Japan led, resting on an ethic in Japanese form: on Japan's 'national polity' (kokutai), manifested in Japan's 'imperial way' (kodo). That is to say, the Confucian concept of what was just must be combined with a Japanese idea of how to achieve it (implying that Japan must take over China's historical role in Asia, as well as that of the West).[44]

Konoe believed this ideology provided ample justification for continuing the war against the Kuomintang. Drawing from the writings of ultranationalist Miyazaki Masayoshi, he argued that Chaing Kai-shek was morally unqualified to govern China because he embodied the unification of British, French, and Soviet imperialism. Only after Chiang was eliminated could China join Japan and Manchukuo in a "free union of liberated East Asian nations," living under "the rule of righteousness." Then Japan would assume its rightful place in guiding Asia, and "the Western concept of freedom" would be replaced by "the Eastern concept of morality."[45]

Amidst a rising tide of protests over Japanese infringements on the rights of Americans in China, Konoe found an opportunity to proclaim the new ideology when the Imperial Army captured Canton in late 1938. On November 3, the prime minister declared that Japan would seek to ensure the permanent stability of East Asia through the establishment of a New Order.[46] With the Kuomintang government reduced to the status of "a mere local regime," Konoe called on the people of China to join Japan and Manchukuo in a tripartite relationship of mutual aid and coordination to secure international justice, defend against communism, and foster economic cohesion throughout East Asia.[47] The United States strongly objected to the New Order policy and informed Japan that it considered it, and Japan's growing disregard for American rights in China, to be violations of the Open Door and the Washington System of treaties. In a series of communications culminating in an official note to Foreign Minister Arita Hachiro on December 30, the Americans asserted that the principles of equal opportunity, as embodied in the Open Door, "have long been regarded as inherently wise and just" and "are general in their application and not subject to nullification by a unilateral affirmation."[48] Nonetheless, Tokyo continued to extol its New Order ideology and, in 1940, wrote it into a formal treaty signed by Japan, Manchukuo, and the puppet government of occupied China.[49]

Meanwhile, the Japanese army began a deliberate campaign to drive Western commercial and political interests off the Asian continent. As their forces spread southward, Japanese commanders used the guise of military necessity to constantly interfere with foreign firms trying to do business in China. They restricted river travel to Japanese boats; they made the Japanese-sponsored currency the only legal tender in occupied China; and they repeatedly disrupted shipping facilities servicing the Western Powers. In June, 1939, the antagonism turned bitter when the Japanese commander at Tientsin blockaded the British and French concessions there and ordered his troops to humiliate Westerners with abusive treatment and public strip searches.[50]

As evidence accumulated that Japanese authorities were going beyond simply violating American rights to the point of destroying property and even endangering lives, the Roosevelt Administration began to consider possible means of commercial retaliation against Japan. In July, 1939, the U.S. government notified the government of Japan that it planned to terminate the 1911 Treaty of Commerce and Navigation between the two nations at the end of the six-month period prescribed by the agreement.[51] This action removed a legal obstacle to any embargo the United States might choose to impose on Japan in the future. By terminating the commercial treaty, Washington signaled Tokyo that the United States was finally preparing to do more than talk to defend its interests—American leaders would try to compel the Japanese to change their behavior.[52]

War in Europe—Lines Drawn in Asia

While losing the commercial treaty disturbed Japanese leaders, they had far more serious problems to deal with in the summer of 1939. In May, the Kwangtung Army overreacted to skirmishes with Soviet troops at Nomonhan on the Mongolian frontier, escalating a border dispute into an undeclared war that raged all through the summer.[53] Although local Japanese commanders had provoked two previous skirmishes with the Russians in as many years—shelling Soviet gunboats on the Amur River in 1937 and fighting a bloody battle for Changkufeng Hill at the intersecting borders of Korea, Manchuria, and Siberia in 1938—neither were as costly or embarrassing for Japan as the Nomonhan conflict. Both sides threw aircraft, armor, and artillery into the fight, and though Japanese soldiers impressed the Russians with their courage, the Kwangtung Army was severely outclassed by Soviet material and operational superiority. Before the conflict ended, Japan lost more than 18,000 men. But Nomonhan was only the military side of a much larger problem.[54]

On August 23, while Russian soldiers were killing Japanese, Tokyo was stunned when Germany signed a nonaggression pact with the Soviet Union. This development nullified the deterrent effect of the Anti-Comintern Pact, exposing Japan to the threat of being caught between China and Russia in a two-front war. Moreover, Berlin's actions violated its anti-comintern commitment to seek Tokyo's consent before entering into an accord with Russia.[55] This raised a great deal of public indignation in Japan, bringing down the government of ultranationalist Hiranuma Kiichiro and causing, at least temporarily, a strong anti-German sentiment throughout the country.[56] Therefore, when Hitler invaded Poland, starting the Second World War on September 1, 1939, Tokyo declared it would not become involved and would, instead, concentrate on settling the China Incident. At the same time, the Foreign Ministry began working feverishly to resolve the Nomonhan conflict and to end Japan's sudden diplomatic isolation, achieving the former in mid-September.[57]

But Japan watched with great interest when the German blitzkrieg rolled across Western Europe. The fall of the Netherlands and France raised anxieties in Tokyo about whether Japan's access to raw materials in the Netherlands East Indies and French Indochina might be jeopardized, either by German annexation or an Allied countermove. In April, Foreign Minister Arita publicly expressed his government's concern for the maintenance of the status quo in the Indies. Meanwhile, Japanese newspapers began asserting that Japan had special economic interests in the Indies and certain rights in Asia comparable to those claimed by the United States in its Monroe Doctrine. These developments alarmed Washington, prompting Secretary Hull to officially state that any non-peaceful alteration of the status quo would be "prejudicial to the cause of stability, peace, and security not only in the region of the Netherlands Indies but in the entire Pacific area."[58] In conversations with Ambassador Horinouchi Kensuke on April 20 and May 16, Hull firmly told the ambassador that Japan's policies bore no resemblance to the Monroe Doctrine.[59] Hull further said that not only did he endorse maintaining the status quo in the Indies, he "placed the matter on a far broader ground," reminding the ambassador that the United States disapproved of Japan's overall policy in Asia. In both meetings, Horinouchi repeatedly assured Hull that Japan also had no desire to alter the status quo in the Indies. Yet, when Ambassador Joseph C. Grew approached Foreign Minister Arita suggesting the United States and Japan formalize their understanding on that issue, Arita deferred on grounds that such an arrangement might violate Japan's policy of noninvolvement in the European conflict.[60] Finally, on June 28 the Japanese Foreign Ministry announced that the governments of the Netherlands and the Netherlands East Indies had assured Tokyo that they would take no measures to prevent the export of the materials Japan desired. Confrontation was averted for the moment, but American leaders knew the Japanese were pressing Dutch colonial authorities for greater economic concessions.[61]

Japanese leaders believed the key to solving their diplomatic crisis and to easing the economic threat from the United States was to bring the China conflict to a close. To that end, they formally inaugurated the Chinese puppet regime of Wang Ching-wei at Nanking in March, 1940, in hopes that it would help bring the demise of the Kuomintang by winning popular support away from Chiang Kai-shek. But Chiang was unaffected by this ploy and continued to fight from his stronghold in western China. Frustration grew in Tokyo, and the more stubbornly Chiang held on, the more bitter Japanese leaders became that Western support was making his resistance possible. Consequently, in July, 1940, Japan demanded that Britain close Hong Kong and the Burma Road in order to prevent military supplies from reaching Chungking. With France having fallen the month before and the Battle of Britain now being fought to determine England's fate, London could not afford to risk an attack in Asia. Therefore, the British reluctantly compromised with Japan, keeping Hong Kong open, but closing the Burma Road on July 15 for three months. During that time, Britain turned back the blitz and Chiang Kai-shek endured against the Japanese. But by then, much had changed in Japan.[62]

Germany's startling success in the spring of 1940 had made a dramatic impact on Japanese public opinion. The rapid collapse of Belgium, the Netherlands, and France, along with the British flight from Dunkirk, made the German army seem invincible, rekindling enthusiasm throughout Japan for seeking a closer relationship with the Nazis. This, in turn, strengthened the position of those on the Army General Staff who advocated joining an Axis alliance. However, most navy leaders opposed such a move, fearing it would antagonize the United States and jeopardize Japan's access to American oil. The emperor and his advisors also favored a conciliatory policy with the Anglo-Americans. So when the army presented Prime Minister Yonai Mitsumasa a memorandum recommending that Japan join the Axis, he rejected it. Consequently, the war minister resigned, bringing down the Yonai government in July, 1940.[63]

This convinced Tokyo that the time had come for strong measures. With Japan facing political and economic pressures at home, a diplomatic crisis abroad, and, of course, the interminable war in China, national leaders and the *jushin* agreed once more that only Prince Konoe had the charisma to pull the country together. Konoe accepted the appointment as prime minister and set out to assemble his second cabinet.[64] But before he inaugurated his government, he met with his three most important cabinet members—War Minister General Tojo Hideki, Navy Minister Admiral Yoshida Zengo, and Foreign Minister Matsuoka Yosuke—to hammer out an agreement on how to handle the national emergency facing the new government.[65]

The "Outline of a Basic National Policy" they developed reflected the convictions of all four ministers in this inner circle.[66] With Konoe's return to power, the policy reaffirmed Japan's commitment to a planned national economy and building a strong economic bloc with Manchukuo and China. But with *Tosei* leader General Tojo in the cabinet, it focused more squarely on southern expansion as a remedy to Japan's dependence on foreign resources. Matsuoka, who was both pro-army and pro-expansion, coined a new phrase, the "Greater East Asia Co-prosperity Sphere," to reflect Japan's desire to add French Indochina and the Netherlands East Indies to Konoe's New Order in East Asia. The foreign minister also favored Japan joining the Axis alliance, but Admiral Yoshida once more expressed the navy's concern about doing anything that would seriously antagonize Britain or the United States. Therefore, for the time being, Japan's national policy focused on achieving two main goals: "(a) to hasten the end of the conflict in China; (b) to solve the problem of the south within such scope as would not lead to war with other Powers."[67] Simply stated, Japan would seek to penetrate the southern regions through peaceful means in order to avoid further alienating Washington. But as they would soon discover, that task would be impossible.[68]

Japanese-American relations were severely strained already, and Tokyo's actions in 1940 only strengthened the convictions of those American leaders who felt the United States should take stronger measures to curb Japan's aggressive behavior. When Germany invaded Western Europe, the United States Pacific Fleet was conducting exercises off Hawaii. Japan's sudden interest in the Indies prompted American authorities to leave the fleet on deployment at Pearl Harbor rather than return the ships to their home ports on the West Coast.[69] On July 2, Congress passed the Export Control Act, authorizing the president to prohibit the export of basic war materials in the interest of national defense. In August, following Britain's forced closure of the Burma Road, the president used the new law to curtail the export of aviation gasoline and most types of machine tools to Japan.[70] But even as American leaders were taking this step, Japan was secretly pressing French authorities for rights to base aircraft in Indochina and move troops through the region for military operations against the Kuomintang. French colonial leaders held out as long as they could, but with France in German hands and the allies not yet prepared to come to their aid in Southeast Asia, they soon yielded to the inevitable. The Japanese Imperial Army moved into northern Indochina on September 22, 1940.[71]

This development roused Washington to apply stronger economic measures against Japan. On September 26, President Roosevelt restricted American iron and steel scrap exports, permitting shipments only to countries in the western hemisphere and to Britain.[72] Though American leaders insisted the restrictions were motivated by a need to conserve materials for the United States defense program, the Japanese were convinced they were aimed at Japan. Consequently, Tokyo protested the action strongly in notes on October 7 and 8 and in a meeting between Ambassador Horinouchi and Secretary Hull.[73] But Hull had no sympathy for Japan, and he sternly informed the Ambassador that . . .

It was unheard of for one country engaged in aggression and seizure of another country, contrary to all law and treaty provisions, to turn to a third peacefully disposed nation and seriously insist that it would be guilty of an unfriendly act if it should not cheerfully provide some of the necessary implements of war to aid the aggressor nation in carrying out its policy of invasion.[74]

While Japan's move into French Indochina angered the Roosevelt Administration, the Americans were even more disturbed five days later when Tokyo signed a treaty with Germany and Italy forming an Axis military alliance. Though Admiral Yoshida and the navy had opposed such a move, Foreign Minister Matsuoka believed an alliance with Germany was crucial to deterring the United States from moving against Japan. Therefore, he made casting Japan's lot with the Axis Powers a personal crusade. Matsuoka courted the Germans throughout the summer, holding initial discussions with Ambassador Eugen Ott and later with Heinrich Stahmer whom Berlin had sent to negotiate a treaty. The Foreign Minister's campaign gained momentum on September 6 when he convinced the four-minister conference to talk to Germany, at least, about forming a closer relationship. Navy leaders still hesitated, but with Germany apparently winning the war in Europe, more and more young officers were eager for Japan to share in the victor's spoils.[75] The turning point came when heart problems forced Admiral Yoshida to resign his post as navy minister. Yoshida's replacement, Admiral Oikawa Koshiro, was less intractable than his predecessor, and on September 14 he finally withdrew the navy's objections to a treaty provided Japan retained the right to determine the circumstances in which she would offer military assistance to the Axis Powers. Japan signed the Tripartite Pact on September 27, 1940.[76]

The Tripartite Pact would prove to be one of the largest obstacles to repairing Japanese-American relations before the Second World War. American leaders found its provisions particularly offensive. In this agreement, the Axis Powers declared their intention to divide Europe and Asia into spheres of interest with Germany and Italy controlling the West and Japan heading its New Order in East Asia. Beyond that, the signatories agreed to "assist one another with all political, economic, and military means" should one of the three contracting Powers be attacked by a Power not yet involved in the European war or in the Chinese-Japanese conflict.[77] This provision was clearly aimed at the United States.[78] The Axis Powers in Europe were threatening to intervene should America move against Japanese aggression in Asia. More seriously, with Washington now openly committed to a policy of supporting the British in their war against Germany, Japan had obligated itself to declaring war on the United States should America enter that conflict. The battle lines were drawn.

Washington Defines the Issues—Matsuoka Weaves a Web

Throughout the remainder of 1940 and the first months of 1941, Japan's relationship with the United States and its allies continued to deteriorate. Tokyo increased its pressure on Dutch colonial authorities by presenting Batavia a list of 22 demands for trade and immigration concessions reminiscent of those issued China during the First World War.[79] The Dutch continued to resist. Meanwhile, on December 10 President Roosevelt extended export controls to iron ore, pig iron, ferro alloys, and other iron and steel products, permitting shipments only to the western hemisphere and Britain.[80] Once again, Tokyo protested the restriction and, once more, Washington justified its action in the name of national defense.[81]

By 1941 American leaders were all but resolved to the inevitability of war with Germany and Japan; it was mainly a question of how much time the nation would have to complete its preparations. On January 6, President Roosevelt told the congress that never before had American security been so threatened. He declared that direct assaults were persistently being made on the democratic way of life, both by arms and by deadly propaganda.[82] A week later, Secretary Hull was more specific in his testimony before the House Foreign Affairs Committee concerning the Lend-Lease bill. Hull said it was clear that:

Japan has been actuated from the start by broad and ambitious plans for establishing herself in a dominant position in the entire region of the Western Pacific. Her leaders have openly declared their determination to achieve and maintain that position by force of arms and thus to make themselves masters of an area containing almost one half of the entire population of the world.[83]

Across the Pacific, Foreign Minister Matsuoka had begun taking a tougher line as well. On January 21 he told the Diet that the Netherlands East Indies lay within the Greater East Asia Co-prosperity Sphere, and there was no other course open to Japan but to secure economic self-sufficiency in Asia. The following month he told the Diet Budget Committee that "ultimately, diplomacy is force, and it goes without saying that diplomacy not backed by strength can accomplish nothing."[84] Nevertheless, the foreign minister still hoped he could achieve Japan's objectives without provoking war with the United States.

Matsuoka staked his foreign policy on the belief that the United States would be deterred from interfering in Asia if faced with a grand coalition of totalitarian Powers. But the coalition he envisioned embraced more than just Germany and Italy; it included the Soviet Union as well. Therefore, while the foreign minister courted Berlin in the summer of 1940, he also began wooing Moscow, telling the Soviet ambassador that he had long wanted to see a Russo-Japanese rapprochement. Once the Tripartite Pact was signed, Matsuoka enlisted Germany's help in trying to persuade the Russians to sign a nonaggression treaty with Tokyo. As this issue coincided with a German desire to see Moscow recognize the spheres of interest laid out in the Axis alliance—and, in return, to offer Soviet Russia Southwest Asia, stretching from India to the Bosphorus—Hitler and his foreign minister, Joachim von Ribbentrop, championed the Japanese cause to Soviet Foreign Commissar Vyacheslav Molotov when he visited Berlin in November, 1940. But Molotov was suspicious of Axis intentions, and the Russians expected more economic concessions in return for their cooperation than Tokyo was willing to give.[85] Therefore, Matsuoka's effort to assemble a united front against the United States stalled for the time being.[86]

As a result, Matsuoka decided the time had come to take matters into his own hands. On February 3, 1941, he explained his plan for "adjusting" Japanese-Soviet relations to the liaison conference, a body of key civilian and military leaders who met regularly to coordinate governmental policy. After getting their approval, the foreign minister set out on a whirlwind diplomatic tour, leaving Tokyo in late March to visit Moscow and Berlin twice and Rome once in a span of three weeks. While in Berlin, Matsuoka met with Ribbentrop, who attempted to discourage him from pursuing a treaty in Moscow.[87] But Ribbentrop did not say why he felt Japan should distance itself from Russia—he did not tell Matsuoka that Germany was about to betray its Soviet ally. Consequently, the headstrong Japanese foreign minister disregarded his colleague's advice and proceeded to Moscow where Josef Stalin greeted him warmly on April 12. They signed a five-year neutrality pact the following day.[88]

On April 21, Matsuoka returned to Tokyo at the pinnacle of his career. When he assumed office nine months earlier, Japan was politically divided and diplomatically isolated. Now, thanks to his aggressive diplomacy, the Japanese Empire was allied with the most powerful nations in Europe, and though the Russo-Japanese Neutrality Pact fell somewhat short of the grand coalition the foreign minister had envisioned or even the non-aggression treaty he had first sought, it at least secured Japan's rear, freeing the army to move south. The only obstacle that remained was the United States, and even that problem seemed to be moving toward a diplomatic breakthrough.

When Matsuoka arrived in Tokyo, he found government leaders remarkably optimistic about the prospects of a settlement with Washington. Nomura Kichisaburo, Japan's newly appointed ambassador to the United States, had just sent them a "Draft Understanding" that did not seem to violate the spirit of the Tripartite Pact. Nomura insisted Secretary Hull had no objection to the agreement, and he urged the government to accept it at once.[89] However, Nomura neglected to tell his superiors that Hull had accepted the Draft Understanding only as a starting point for further discussions. On the other hand, Nomura did forward a note Hull had given him just before he cabled the text to Tokyo. Hull's note stated that before the United States and Japan could begin any formal negotiation leading to a general settlement, as a "paramount preliminary," they would have to agree on the following four points:

1. Respect for the territorial integrity and the sovereignty of each and all nations.
2. Support of the principle of non-interference in the internal affairs of other countries.

3. Support of the principle of equality, including equality of commercial opportunity.

4. Non-disturbance of the status quo in the Pacific except as the status quo may be altered by peaceful means.[90]

Ironically, though most Japanese leaders believed they were close to getting what they wanted in the Draft Understanding, Matsuoka strongly objected to Japan responding to the document without further consideration. Unlike his colleagues, he feared the agreement would, indeed, violate Japan's commitment to the Axis Powers. In fact, he argued that if the United States was to enter the war in Europe, the Tripartite Pact would obligate Japan to fight on Germany's side, making a Japanese-American rapprochement pointless. Consequently, Matsuoka insisted on taking at least two weeks to consider the document, and, though Konoe objected, he also informed his Axis partners of the "American" proposal.[91] As a result, Japan did not respond to the Draft Understanding until mid-May.[92]

In the meantime, Matsuoka sent Nomura an unofficial, interim reply, informing Hull that Japan would do nothing to jeopardize the Axis alliance and suggesting the United States join Japan in a neutrality pact. He added that German and Italian leaders considered the war as good as won and asserted that America's intervention would only prolong the conflict and cause untold human suffering. Nomura realized it would be unwise to hand Hull such an inflammatory note, so he read it to him instead, focusing on excerpts and skipping over the most provocative passages. Hull quickly brushed off any suggestion of a neutrality pact and urged Japan to begin talks on the basis of the Draft Understanding.[93] A few days later, Hull clarified Washington's position vis-à-vis the Axis. He warned Nomura that "Hitlerism" would prove not only a scourge to other parts of the world, but that it would eventually be applied to Japan just as it had to friendly countries in Europe. He further emphasized that the United States was determined that Hitler would not get control of the seas—America would resist the German advance whether it took one, five, or ten years. The ambassador only bowed and smiled.[94]

On May 12, Tokyo finally sent Washington a counterproposal to the Draft Understanding, along with an oral explanation of its provisions. Opening with the hope that the two nations might "establish a just peace in the Pacific," the memorandum proceeded to defend Japan's role in the Tripartite Pact and specified that America's attitude towards the European war should be "directed by no aggressive measures as to assist any one nation against another." Regarding the "China Affair," Japan proposed that the United States acknowledge the "three principles as enunciated in the Konoe Statement," urge Chiang Kai-shek to negotiate with Tokyo, and cut off aid to the Kuomintang should Chiang refuse.[95] The memorandum went on to assert that the Japanese expansion in the southwest Pacific was of a peaceful nature, so the United States should resume normal trade with Japan and cooperate in the procurement of natural resources for her. Finally, Tokyo proposed that the United States and Japan jointly guarantee the independence of the Philippine Islands and establish that territory as a neutral entity.[96]

Over the next several weeks, while American leaders considered the Japanese proposal, Hull met with Nomura frequently in attempts to clarify several key issues. First, it was important to Washington that Tokyo agree that the United States was acting only in self-defense in aiding Britain and, therefore, promise not to enter the war on Berlin's side should the United States declare war on Germany. Also, American leaders wanted the Japanese to give them a straightforward commitment to withdraw troops from China and a promise not to use force in Southeast Asia.[97] Unfortunately, those were the very issues that Nomura could not concede, as the central pillar of Matsuoka's diplomatic program was to deter American intervention in Asia so Japan would be free to create its co-prosperity sphere. To do that, Japan needed the threat of Axis intervention and, therefore, was compelled to remain faithful to the Tripartite Pact.[98]

On June 21, Hull handed Nomura the official American response to Japan's May 12 proposal in the form of a revised draft accompanied by an explanatory annex and letters to be exchanged between the governments.[99] The wording of the revised draft was similar to Japan's proposal with several notable differences. Regarding the European war and the Tripartite Pact, Washington proposed the two governments exchange letters confirming that Japan would not be obligated to disrupt peace in the Pacific should the United States have to defend itself pursuant to hostilities in Europe. The draft also stipulated that, once Japan presented terms for settlement with China that were in harmony with the Konoe principles, the president would suggest to the government of China that it enter into negotiations with Japan. However, the American proposal said nothing about terminating aid to Chungking. The Americans set aside for future discussion the issue of Japanese troops in China, but the proposal stipulated that neither country had territorial designs in the Pacific area. Finally, instead of agreeing to co-administer Philippine independence and neutrality, the American draft simply acknowledged Japan's willingness to enter into such negotiations if and when the United States chose to do so. The gist of the American position was clear: before the United States was willing to restore normal trade with Japan, Tokyo would have to abandon the Tripartite Pact and give up its dream of creating a Greater East Asia Co-prosperity Sphere.[100]

Washington's proposal made Matsuoka angry, but he had to push negotiations with the United States aside; he had more immediate problems to deal with in June and July, 1941. While Tokyo was waiting for the American response, negotiations in Batavia had broken down. It had finally become clear that Dutch colonial authorities were not going to grant Japan unlimited access to oil and other resources in the Netherlands East Indies, so Tokyo recalled its mission on June 17. At that point, the army and navy chiefs of staff began arguing for a full military occupation of French Indochina and Thailand as a prelude to moving against the Indies. Matsuoka objected, fearing such a move would provoke a British and American intervention. Debate on this issue held the attention of several liaison conferences until June 22, when an even more dramatic development occurred—Germany invaded the Soviet Union.[101]

The German advance into Russia put Japan in a dilemma and signaled the end of the foreign minister's political career. Having negotiated both the Tripartite Pact and the Russo-Japanese Neutrality Pact, Matsuoka found himself in an untenable position. As soon as Germany declared war on Russia, Berlin began pressing Tokyo to attack the Soviets in the Far East. Matsuoka considered the Axis alliance to be critically important, so he argued passionately for Japan to answer the German call to arms. But army leaders were ambivalent about moving north. Though army sentiment tended to be pro-German, the general staff had hoped to avoid a two-front war, and the Nomonhan debacle was still fresh in their memory. Meanwhile, navy leaders fought harder than ever for a southern advance, and with the foreign minister in growing disfavor, Prime Minister Konoe eventually sided with the joint military consensus. Japan would move south.[102]

The Southern Advance Provokes an Oil Embargo

On July 2, 1941, Emperor Hirohito held an imperial conference where he sanctioned the momentous document, "An Outline of National Policies in View of the Changing Situation." This article formalized decisions reached in several prior liaison conferences—decisions that would eventually prove crucial to the destiny of Japan. First, Japan would settle the war in China as quickly as possible by increasing pressure on the Kuomintang and seizing the foreign settlements. Second, the Japanese would invade French Indochina immediately, even if it risked war with Britain and the United States. Third, Japan would continue to honor its neutrality pact with the Soviet Union until Germany was on the verge of defeating Russia, then Japan would seize Soviet possessions in the Far East. Finally, Japan would continue its diplomatic efforts to keep the United States from entering the European war. But should the Americans go to war in Europe, Japan would honor its obligations under the Tripartite Pact.[103]

Tokyo took immediate steps to implement the new policies. The government ordered a general mobilization, and all Japanese merchant ships were called home from the Atlantic Ocean. On July 16, Konoe resigned his cabinet, and the emperor immediately reappointed him prime minister and ordered him to form a new government. This calculated gesture enabled Konoe to remove anyone in his cabinet who did not enthusiastically support the new policy direction—the only minister not invited to return was Matsuoka, who was replaced by Admiral Toyoda Teiijiro.[104] In the meantime, the Japanese ambassador to France handed the Vichy government an ultimatum: grant Japan the rights to build naval bases at Saigon and Camranh Bay and give Japan eight airfields in Indochina. They were to respond by July 20, or Japan would take the colony by force. The French yielded, and by the end of the month, there were nearly 50,000 Japanese troops in southern Indochina.[105]

This move caused a great deal of concern in Washington, as it placed Japanese forces astride the southeast Asian shipping lanes and within striking range of the Philippines. On July 23, after hearing that France had granted Japan basing rights in southern Indochina, acting Secretary of State Sumner Welles informed Ambassador Nomura that the United States believed the French had been coerced into the agreement and, if so, Tokyo's behavior violated the spirit of the ongoing Japanese-American discussions.[106] Nomura replied that Japan must be assured of an uninterrupted source of rice and raw materials and that Chinese and de Gaullist agitators were stirring up trouble, threatening the flow of those supplies. According to Welles, Nomura further rationalized the occupation in terms of Japan's security, saying "Japan believed that certain foreign powers were bent upon a policy of encirclement of Japan and that the step taken was purely a precautionary measure in the nature of a safeguard."[107]

But the Americans refused to accept Nomura's explanations, and the following day President Roosevelt, for the first time, openly threatened to cut off the supply of oil to Japan. Meeting with Nomura, Welles, and Chief of Naval Operations Admiral Harold Stark, Roosevelt said that for two years the United States had permitted American oil to be exported to Japan because, had it not done so, Japan would have been furnished with an incentive or a pretext for attacking the Netherlands East Indies. The president explained that many Americans were now asking why, while they were being asked to conserve gasoline, the United States should be exporting oil to Japan, a country that "had given every indication of pursuing a policy of force and conquest in conjunction with the policy of world conquest and domination which Hitler was carrying on." Roosevelt dismissed Nomura's explanations for the occupation and said the United States could only assume that Japan was occupying Indochina for the purpose of further aggression. He said that Japan's actions created in America "the most serious disquiet."[108]

The president then proposed that if Japan would refrain from occupying Indochina, he would do everything in his power to obtain binding declarations from Britain, China, the Netherlands, and, of course, the United States, neutralizing the colony and thereby ensuring that none of those countries would undertake any military actions from, in, or against the region. He further said he would urge the British to refrain from supporting de Gaullist activities in the territory and would try to ensure Japan was afforded market access to food supplies and raw materials there. According to Secretary Welles, Nomura said he would immediately report the offer to Tokyo, but he did not seem optimistic as to the result.[109]

Nomura's doubts were well placed. Japan continued to move troops into southern Indochina, and within a couple of days, American leaders decided the threat of a Japanese attack in the southwest Pacific had become so great that they must no longer concern themselves with avoiding the risk of war, but deal instead with the problem of preventing a complete undermining of American security. At this point Washington decided "that discontinuance of trade with Japan had become an appropriate, warranted, and necessary step—as a warning to Japan and as a measure of self defense."[110] On July 26, 1941, President Roosevelt issued Executive Order Number 8832 freezing Japanese assets in the United States. This action soon brought trade between the two countries to a virtual standstill.[111] The flow of oil stopped.[112]

The mood in Tokyo turned grim, as Japanese leaders now faced a crisis and few apparent options. In an imperial conference on July 31, Emperor Hirohito asked his chief of the navy general staff, Admiral Nagano Osami, what course he thought Japan should pursue concerning the United States. Nagano, who had been one of the most strident advocates for the southern advance, said that Japan should try hard to avoid war and even withdraw from the Tripartite Pact, if it came to that. But if negotiations failed, Japan would have no alternative but to seize the initiative, for under the embargo her oil reserves would last for only two years. Planning Board President Suzuki Teiichi confirmed Nagano's assessment about the oil supply. The emperor then asked if Japan could win a sweeping victory if it undertook an aggressive campaign. Nagano said he doubted that Japan could win at all. Consequently, the choice seemed clear: either reach an agreement with the United States or fight a war with doubtful prospects of victory. But War Minister Tojo refused to consider any settlement that would limit Japan's freedom to move either north or south, and Lord Keeper of the Privy Seal Marquis Kido Koichi asserted that betraying the Axis allies would only earn America's contempt.[113]

With these constraints, Konoe and Toyoda were hard pressed to find some middle ground for a settlement. Over the next several days the two ministers worked with army and navy leaders to hammer out a response to Washington's latest proposal. But the prime minister was not sanguine about prospects of being able to satisfy the Americans. Konoe was coming to the conclusion that, perhaps, the only way to head off a war between

Japan and the United States was for him to meet with President Roosevelt personally and work out an agreement face to face.[114]

On August 6, Tokyo responded to President Roosevelt's offer to neutralize French Indochina with a counteroffer. In this communication, Japan proposed that the United States "suspend its military measures in the southwestern Pacific area" and advise Britain and the Netherlands to do so as well, restore normal trade with Japan, and get Chiang Kai-shek to negotiate "a speedy settlement of the China Incident." In return, Japan promised to refrain from stationing its troops in the southwestern Pacific area *except* French Indochina and to withdraw those troops when the China Incident was settled. Additionally, Tokyo offered to guarantee the neutrality of the Philippines. When delivering this proposal, Nomura read an oral statement that, once again, defended Japan's actions on the grounds of self-defense and said they were "absolutely necessary in order to prevent from getting beyond control the Japanese public opinion which had been dangerously aroused because of the successive measures taken by the United States, Great Britain, and Netherlands East Indies against Japan and, consequently, in order to preserve peace in the Pacific."[115]

The American response came quickly. As the Japanese counterproposal disregarded Roosevelt's suggestion that Indochina be neutralized, Washington concluded that Tokyo was "attempting to take full advantage— military, political, and economic—of the Japanese fait accompli in occupying southern Indochina."[116] Consequently, on August 8 Hull informed Ambassador Nomura that he considered the Japanese reply "lacking in responsiveness" to the president's offer. Hull further said that Tokyo's recent actions had removed the basis for understanding with the United States; he thereby ended their series of informal conversations. Nomura then asked Hull whether he thought it would be possible for Roosevelt and Konoe to meet in order to discuss adjusting relations between the two countries. Hull replied that "it remained with the Japanese government to decide whether it could find means of shaping its policies accordingly and then endeavor to evolve some satisfactory plan."[117]

Throughout the remainder of August, 1941, the movement toward war began to accelerate on both sides of the Pacific. On August 14, President Roosevelt met with British Prime Minister Winston Churchill at Argentia Bay, Newfoundland, where they jointly declared their commitment to the Atlantic Charter, a set of "common principles in the national policies of their respective countries on which they based their hopes for a better future for the world."[118] Pursuant to this covenant, Roosevelt and Churchill agreed to act in parallel in resisting any new acts of Japanese aggression. Meanwhile, as Japan's oil stocks declined with each passing day, Japanese military leaders became increasingly impatient with their government's inability to solve the American problem through negotiation. On August 16, the navy general staff presented the first draft of a policy document entitled, "The Essentials for Carrying Out the Empire's Policies," at a joint conference of army and navy section chiefs. When approved, this document would formalize the decision to prepare for war while the civilian government proceeded with negotiations.[119]

With pressure mounting on Konoe and Toyoda to either find a diplomatic solution to the embargo or clear the way for military action, Ambassador Nomura met with President Roosevelt and Secretary Hull on August 17 and asked them to resume the informal conversations previously suspended. The Ambassador also urged the president to meet with Prime Minister Konoe to discuss adjusting Japanese-American relations. In response, Roosevelt read Nomura a statement recounting Japan's recent actions and warning that if Tokyo chose to continue its program of military domination, the United States would be compelled to take immediate steps to ensure its security and safeguard its interests. The president then told Nomura that before the United States could consider resuming informal discussions, the Japanese government would have to furnish a clearer statement of its attitudes and plans. However, Roosevelt was somewhat open to the idea of meeting with Konoe.[120]

Grasping at what appeared to be an opening, Prime Minister Konoe personally wrote President Roosevelt on August 27, urging that they meet to exchange views. Konoe said that, while the informal discussions conducted earlier had been appropriate in spirit and content, resuming them would not meet current needs because the situation was "developing swiftly and might produce unforeseen contingencies." Therefore, it was an "urgent necessity" that they meet as soon as possible.[121] Roosevelt and Hull were encouraged by the cordial tone of the prime minister's letter. However, recalling that Konoe had been head of government when Japan invaded China in 1937, and remembering the many instances of Japanese aggression since that time, the Americans suspected that Japan might later twist any settlement based on general principles to their own ends. Moreover, if Roosevelt and Konoe failed to reach an agreement, Japanese propaganda might then blame the Americans for that failure. Consequently, in his September 3 reply to Konoe's letter, President Roosevelt said he was very interested in collaborating with the prime minister, but they should take precautions to ensure the proposed meeting is successful. Before they could meet, Roosevelt said that Japan and the United States must agree on the practical application of four principles that the American government regarded to be the foundation upon which relations between nations should rest. In a statement accompanying his letter to Konoe, the president cited the four points that Secretary Hull had given Nomura in April 1941.[122]

The same day that President Roosevelt handed his letter to Nomura, the liaison conference met in Tokyo and approved "The Essentials for Carrying Out the Empire's Policies." Having thus agreed to conduct negotiations and war preparations simultaneously, Japanese leaders set the first 10 days of October as the deadline for reaching a settlement with the United States—failing that, Japan would go to war.[123] But when Konoe presented the document to Hirohito on September 5, the emperor became concerned, as it seemed to emphasize military confrontation instead of diplomacy. Summoning the military chiefs to the palace, he admonished them to make every possible effort to negotiate a settlement before resorting to war.[124] The Supreme Command assured him that negotiation would be the first priority. Nevertheless, with the military services preparing for battle and a deadline for ending negotiations moving closer each day, thoughts of war soon took center stage in the minds of Japanese leaders.[125]

Over the next month, Japanese and American diplomats struggled to reach an understanding on the principles that Washington had made prerequisite to a meeting between Roosevelt and Konoe. On the evening of September 6, while dining with U.S. Ambassador Grew, the prime minister maintained that he subscribed to Hull's four points and urged, once again, that an early meeting with President Roosevelt be arranged. But the many memoranda and statements exchanged in the following weeks revealed that neither side was willing to give ground on its fundamental position; and the fundamental positions of Washington and Tokyo were diametrically opposed. The Japanese refused to abandon their holdings in China—having invested billions of yen, 100,000 casualties, and their national honor—but the Americans insisted on terms that not only guaranteed the sovereignty of China, but prohibited Japan from expanding elsewhere in the Far East as well. Japan wanted trade restored immediately and promised to withdraw from Indochina after "settling the China Incident"; but the United States insisted that Japan withdraw from Southeast Asia immediately, and Washington was willing to restore trade only after Tokyo demonstrated its commitment to the four points. Finally, there was the Tripartite Pact. The American government wanted a firm commitment that Japan would not declare war on the United States should America's ever-growing assistance to Britain draw it into war with Germany. Konoe and Toyoda tried desperately to convince Washington that rapprochement would lead to a reliable friendship; but ultimately they could not give the commitment that American leaders demanded.[126]

Time was running out. On September 29, Ambassador Nomura warned Secretary Hull that if the proposed meeting did not take place soon, the Konoe Ministry might be replaced with a less moderate government. Nonetheless, Washington's statement on October 2 took exception to certain qualifications the Japanese had put on their last interpretation of the four points, and American leaders insisted on a clarification before agreeing to arrange the summit. This note triggered a series of meetings in Tokyo. Army leaders were convinced the negotiations had reached a dead end and Japan should proceed to war. Navy leaders were still doubtful of Japan's ability to defeat the United States, and some wanted to continue the talks, but they were afraid to oppose the army directly.[127]

Konoe and Toyoda also wanted to continue the negotiations. Alarmed by the way military leaders were becoming resolved for war, Konoe called a meeting at his home on October 12 to try to persuade War Minister Tojo that there was still hope for a settlement with the United States. He failed. At a cabinet meeting the following day, Tojo reminded everyone of the operational considerations that had led to the decision of September 6. He said that if that policy was to be repudiated, all who had taken part in making it should resign, having failed in their obligation to the emperor. After the meeting, Konoe tried one last time to resolve issues with his war minister, but Tojo refused to meet with him. Consequently, on October 16, Konoe resigned.[128]

Tojo Takes the Helm—Japan Marches to War

Two days later, the emperor appointed General Tojo to be prime minister and ordered him to form a government. Tojo made Admiral Shimada Shigetaro his navy minister and appointed Togo Shigenori as foreign minister. He retained the war minister's portfolio for himself, serving in both capacities simultaneously. Aware of the recent dissension between the army and the navy, Emperor Hirohito summoned Tojo and Shimada to the palace and told them, "we believe that an exceedingly grave situation confronts the nation. Bear in mind, at this time, that cooperation between the army and the navy should be closer than ever before."[129] Afterward, the emperor ordered Marquis Kido to tell the two ministers that they should study the current situation carefully, without being bound by the imperial conference decision of September 6. In other words, the October deadline for going to war was rescinded.[130]

With the emperor's concerns in mind, the liaison conference met almost daily throughout the remainder of October, 1941, reexamining whether Japan should go to war against the United States. Experts from the army, the navy, the Finance Ministry, and the Planning Board all presented statistics comparing rates of resource supply and consumption in various scenarios: not going to war (but resisting American demands); war in November, 1941; and war in March, 1942. The figures painted a gloomy picture. Without access to strategic materials, the Japanese Navy would have fuel for only about 18 months; aviation fuel was in even shorter supply. Seizing the Indies would extend the nation's oil stocks, but, even then, supplies of other strategic materials, particularly steel, would limit Japan's war-making potential to two or three years at most. The forecasts were even darker if war was put off until the following spring. Meanwhile, Japan's steel-making capacity was only one-thirteenth that of the

United States, and the American defense buildup was escalating with every passing month.[131]

Given these projections, army and navy leaders argued for an immediate decision for war, but Foreign Minister Togo and Finance Minister Kaya Okinori held out for continuing the negotiations. Discussions between the opposing camps turned bitter, and Tojo struggled to moderate their angry exchanges and foster consensus. On October 30, he defined the decision in terms of three alternatives: 1) avoid war and undergo great hardships; 2) settle matters with immediate war; and 3) set a deadline for war, but continue to negotiate until that date arrives. The prime minister insisted that conferees reach a decision on November 1, even if they had to meet all night.[132]

On the day of Tojo's deadline, after 17 hours of debate, the liaison conference finally agreed on option three and chose November 30 as the last day of negotiation. In the meantime, the Foreign Ministry prepared two proposals for Washington. Proposal A was a slightly softened version of Tokyo's past overtures—Japan would withdraw some troops from China after the conflict there was settled, then remove the rest in about 25 years. If American leaders did not accept this formula, Tokyo would offer Proposal B, a modus vivendi, restoring conditions to those before July, 1941. That is, Japan would offer to withdraw its troops from southern Indochina on condition that the United States remove the freeze on Japanese assets and restore the flow of oil. Tojo, Admiral Nagano, and General Sugiyama Gen briefed the emperor on the liaison conference outcome the following day, and on November 5 the imperial conference met and Hirohito sanctioned the plan without comment.[133]

Over the next few weeks, the Japanese made their final offers for settlement and completed their preparations for war. On November 7, Ambassador Nomura presented Proposal A to Secretary Hull and urged him to reply quickly. Hull brushed the offer aside by suggesting that Japan demonstrate some moral leadership and launch a real "new order in East Asia" by mending its ways. Frustrated, Nomura asked to see the president and was received on November 10. Roosevelt dismissed the proposal just as quickly, saying that if Tokyo wanted to prove its sincerity, it should begin moving its troops out of China and Indochina. Thus, Proposal A died on delivery. Foreign Minister Togo was not surprised, but he wanted his last hope for negotiation to succeed. Therefore, he sent a professional diplomat, Kurusu Saburo, to Washington to help Ambassador Nomura bargain with the Americans. On November 20, Nomura and Kurusu presented Japan's final offer, its modus vivendi.[134]

The Americans were well aware that rejecting this proposal would mean war. Ambassador Grew had observed the darkening mood in Tokyo. On November 3, he reported that Japanese leaders were close to making "an all-out, do-or-die attempt, actually risking national *hara kiri*, to make Japan impervious to economic embargoes abroad rather than to yield to foreign pressure."[135] Two weeks later, he urged Washington to "guard against sudden Japanese naval or military actions in such areas as are not now involved in the Chinese theater of operations," and he noted the "probability of the Japanese exploiting every possible tactical advantage, such as surprise and initiative."[136] But Hull and Roosevelt did not need Grew's worried reports to grasp the gravity of the situation. American intelligence had long since broken Japan's diplomatic codes using their decryption machine code-named "MAGIC." Consequently, throughout the many months of discussion, Hull and Roosevelt had read the diplomatic traffic between Japanese leaders and their representatives in Washington, and they usually knew what Tokyo's proposals would be, even before its ambassadors came to call. This time, they knew Japan's modus vivendi would be its final offer. If it failed, Japan would attack.[137]

But as much as American leaders wanted to avoid or, at least, delay war with Japan, they could not accept Proposal B for several reasons. First, it made no mention of Japan's role in the Tripartite Pact, leaving Tokyo free to honor its pledge to support Berlin in a war against the United States. Second, it prohibited the United States from further augmenting its forces in the southwest Pacific, a crucial requirement for ensuring American security against future Japanese expansion. Most importantly, the proposed agreement stipulated that the United States would "refrain from such measures and actions as would be prejudicial to the endeavors for the restoration of general peace between Japan and China." According to the oral statement that accompanied the proposal, that meant the United States would have to stop sending aid to Chiang Kai-shek. In sum, Tokyo was asking Washington to surrender its most important issues in return for a promise that Japan would merely move its troops from southern Indochina to the northern part of the colony.[138]

Knowing that Japan was about to end negotiations, Hull decided it was important to close the talks with a firm and clear statement of the American position. Consequently, on November 26 he countered Japan's final offer with his sweeping "Outline of Proposed Basis for Agreement between the United States and Japan." This document called for Japan to completely withdraw from China and Indochina, abandon its extraterritorial rights in China, and sign a nonaggression pact with all countries concerned in the Far East. When Hull handed the document to the Japanese diplomats, Kurusu said his government would likely interpret it as tantamount to a termination of negotiations. In fact, Tojo and other Japanese leaders considered it an ultimatum.[139] The time for talk was over.[140]

Tokyo immediately set the machinery of war in motion. At 6:00 P.M. on November 26, the task force whose mission was to attack Pearl Harbor set sail from Hitokappu Bay in the Kurile Islands. When Prime Minister Tojo informed the emperor of the Hull note, Hirohito said he wanted to consult the *jushin* before sanctioning a final decision for war. Once assembled and appraised of the situation, some of the former prime ministers expressed concern about the prospects of a war against the Anglo-Americans, and Konoe wondered if it still might be possible to wait a while longer. But none of them suggested that Japan accept Hull's proposal.[141] Ambassador Nomura also urged Tokyo to allow him to continue negotiations, but Foreign Minister Togo and Finance Minister Kaya were now finally convinced that Tojo and the Supreme Command were right—war was unavoidable.[142]

The final strokes were put in place over the next week. On December 1, the imperial conference convened and Emperor Hirohito sanctioned the liaison conference's decision to begin the war.[143] The following day the Foreign Ministry directed Japan's embassies and consulates in American and British territories to destroy their cipher equipment and burn their classified files. Meanwhile, the Supreme Command informed navy and army field commanders that war with the United States would commence on December 8 (Tokyo time). On December 3, Togo notified Italy and Germany that war between Japan and the United States was finally at hand, and he asked them to confirm that they too would declare war on Washington once hostilities began. Mussolini responded immediately; Hitler agreed two days later.[144]

On December 6, with reports of suspicious Japanese movements in Southeast Asia and MAGIC intercepts indicating war was imminent, President Roosevelt telegraphed a personal message to Emperor Hirohito. After reminding the emperor of the long years of friendship between the two countries, the president cited American concerns about the Japanese troops in Southeast Asia and urged him to "give thought in this definite emergency to ways of dispelling the dark clouds" that were rising over the Far East.[145] It was too late. The Imperial Army delayed delivering the note to the palace for 10 hours. But Japan's declaration of war was also late. Togo sent the rambling, 14-part message to the Japanese Embassy on December 6, with instructions for Nomura and Kurusu to deliver it at precisely 1:00 P.M. (Washington time) the following day. However, due to delays in decoding and typing the document, the diplomats were unable to hand it to Secretary Hull until 2:20 P.M.—after the attack had already begun.[146]

In the meantime, at 7:49 A.M. (Honolulu time) Imperial Navy Commander Fuchida Mitsuo, leader of the first wave of aircraft in the raid on Pearl Harbor, radioed his superiors the code phrase *"Tora! Tora! Tora!"* ("Tiger! Tiger! Tiger!"), informing them the attack had achieved the element of surprise for which they had hoped. Compellence had failed—Japan and the United States were at war.[147]

ANALYSIS OF THE OIL EMBARGO

The oil embargo is a complex case requiring several layers of analysis to be fully understood. I begin by weighing the costs and benefits Japanese leaders considered when deciding whether to resist Washington's attempts to compel them; however, in this case, a linear, punishment-and-denial-based evaluation raises more questions than it answers. Some of these problems can be resolved by broadening the investigation to consider the relative interests of the nations involved, but the most serious ones cannot. Only when we appreciate the way culture colored the worldview of Japan's leaders, biased their strategic preferences, and conditioned their decision-making processes can we fully understand why Tokyo chose to defy the American compellent threat.

Punishment and Denial—The Costs and Benefits of Resistance

To evaluate this case in terms of punishment and denial, I must first determine which strategy American leaders were trying to apply and how those efforts were interpreted in Tokyo. A punishment strategy would have involved trying to dissuade Japan from aggressing in Asia by raising the costs of that aggression until, in Tokyo's decision calculus, those costs outweighed the benefits of their conquests. Conversely, a denial strategy would have worked on the other side of the equation. In that approach, American leaders would have tried to deny Japan the benefits of their aggression so that no amount of cost was worth the effort.

In this case, Washington's economic sanctions incorporated elements of both punishment and denial. From the onset, American leaders used sanctions to punish Tokyo for its continental aggression. However, as the confrontation intensified, the progressive nature of the embargoes focused ever more squarely on reducing Japan's ability to carry out its expeditionary operations. Japanese leaders clearly interpreted American actions in that light. Each sanction was chosen to send a message to Tokyo while, simultaneously, reducing Japan's capacity for aggression: restrictions on aviation equipment and gasoline followed Japanese air attacks on civilians; iron and steel export prohibitions were aimed at Japan's armament industry; and the oil embargo was intended to deny Japan fuel for further expansion in the southwest Pacific. Japanese leaders had no misgivings about the consistent theme in these actions. Discussions in meetings and conferences from the first humanitarian embargo to the decision for war focused on how much each sanction might impair Japan's military machine.

Yet, the slow, progressive nature of this "graduated embargo" approach may have contributed to the failure of Washington's compellence efforts.

As Thomas Schelling explains in *Arms and Influence,* a crucial factor in any compellent strategy is the coercer's ability to establish a credible commitment to achieving his objective.[148] The gradual way Hull and Roosevelt escalated American sanctions may have convinced Japanese leaders, early on, that the United States lacked the commitment to seriously interfere with Japan's plans to dominate Asia. Hull may have inadvertently reinforced this impression with his repeated denials, in 1939 and 1940, that the export restrictions were aimed at Japan.

Moreover, throughout the 1930s, the Japanese used "salami tactics" to successfully circumvent Western commitments in Asia.[149] Starting with the Mukden Incident in 1931, they occupied more and more Chinese territory, snatching a piece at a time, and they progressively infringed on Western rights there. Although Washington protested these actions vehemently, until the end of the decade the United States did not consider any one case of aggression serious enough to resist with force, or even with economic sanctions; nor did any other Western nation. Consequently, by 1940 the eastern coastal region of China was in Japanese hands, and Western commercial interests had been nearly pushed off the continent.[150] All of this may have suggested to Japanese leaders that Washington lacked the resolve to make a serious effort to resist Japan's advance.

But I can carry this argument only so far. By the end of 1940, Hull and Roosevelt had established a pattern of meeting each new aggression with a further restriction on the export of strategic materials, and Japanese leaders, particularly those in the navy, were increasingly fearful that the United States might soon resort to an oil embargo. Of course, the April 1941 Draft Understanding momentarily convinced some officials that they could placate Washington without surrendering any substantive issues. But over the next two months, Hull made the American position perfectly clear: he wanted Japan to abandon its Axis commitments, end the war in China, and stop advancing into southeast Asia. And though the Americans avoided making overt threats and explicit demands, by answering each of Japan's misdeeds with an increasingly severe embargo, Washington sought to deter further aggression by fostering in Tokyo the expectation of undesirable consequences for those actions. Meanwhile, the ever-tightening squeeze of the sanctions created an automatic mechanism that would have eventually forced Japan to yield to Washington's implicit demands. As records throughout 1941 confirm, the Japanese clearly understood all of this. Yet, for some reason, neither deterrence nor compellence worked.

Given that Washington demonstrated a credible commitment to achieving its coercive objectives, we are left with assessing how the Japanese weighed the various costs, benefits, and risks when deciding whether to resist or comply with American demands. At this point, we should remember that after the Americans cut off the flow of oil, the liaison conference carried out extensive studies to determine the short- and long-term impacts of the embargo and what chances Japan might have in winning a war against the United States. Historians have frequently derided these studies as superficial and overly optimistic, but it is important to note that, even given these liberal estimates, no one in Tokyo believed Japan stood much of a chance of victory. Moreover, data presented in the studies suggested that Japan's prospects were growing dimmer with each passing day—the navy was consuming 400 tons of oil an hour, and the United States was accelerating its already immense industrial output and steadily reinforcing its installations in the southwest Pacific.[151]

These circumstances imbued Japan's military leaders with a sense of desperation. If Japan was to have any chance at all, the Supreme Command maintained in the fall of 1941, she would have to attack by early December. Once the winter monsoon season set in, large-scale naval operations would be out of the question until March, 1942. By then, the United States would be considerably stronger and Japan's oil stocks would be depleted even further. But how might Japan win? No one in Tokyo believed Japan could militarily defeat the United States. But if Japan should seize the initiative and achieve a limited victory with a surprise attack, she might be able to establish a defensive perimeter strong enough to endure until the United States lost the will to fight. Notes prepared for the September 6 imperial conference observed:

A war with the United States and Great Britain will be long, and will become a war of endurance. It is very difficult to predict the termination of war, and it would be well nigh impossible to expect the surrender of the United States. However, we cannot exclude the possibility that the war may end because of a great change in American public opinion, which may result from such factors as the remarkable success of our military operations in the south or the surrender of Great Britain.[152]

With these thoughts in mind, Tojo and the military chiefs framed the decision as a choice between war with a slim chance of victory on the one hand, and a certain, slow death by strangulation under the heel of American sanctions on the other. Consequently, the alternatives Japanese leaders saw before them were extremely limited: Japan could resist the sanctions passively or actively; she could prepare for an immediate war, or negotiate for American concessions while making additional preparations; she could go to war in March, 1942, or attack as soon as preparations were completed. In a September, 1941, meeting with the emperor, Admiral Nagano compared Japan to a desperately ill man in need of a life-giving transfusion. Denied that lifeblood, only a risky operation might save his life. The operation could kill him, but without it, the patient would surely die of gradual exhaustion.[153] Later, when Tojo was trying to convince Konoe that the time for negotiation had run out, he said, "it is sometimes necessary for a man to jump from the Kiyomizu Temple into the ravine below."[154]

Thus, Japan's leaders transformed a decision about whether to comply with American demands into a choice between a narrow chance for survival and no chance at all. No one weighed the costs of compliance against the possible benefits of that alternative, or against the costs, benefits, and risks of war. The possibility of conceding to American demands simply never made it to the decision agenda. And though Foreign Minister Togo tried to bring those calculations to the table, he was soundly overruled. In the October 30 Liaison conference, when he asked, "what would happen to Japan if the American proposals were accepted in their entirety," everyone present responded with shock and unanimously asserted that the "empire would become a third-rate country."[155] According to an army observer, the foreign minister's thoughts "gave everyone a strange feeling."[156]

Consequently, given a choice between certain strangulation and fighting for a small chance of survival, Japan's leaders made a rational decision—they chose to fight. But why did they frame the decision in those terms? Why, if they believed national survival was at stake, would nearly everyone in the Liaison conference, doves as well as hawks, refuse to even consider agreeing to American demands. Was fighting a war against vastly superior odds preferable to becoming "a third-rate country"? Why didn't anyone in Tokyo consider what might happen to Japan should it lose this war? And why would withdrawing from China make Japan a third-rate country? These are all difficult questions to answer in terms of cost-benefit analysis, but they are not the only riddles this case brings to mind.

After reviewing the historical record, a non-Japanese observer might conclude that the Japanese placed themselves in a dilemma of their own creation. After all, they could have reached an agreement with Washington earlier in 1941 at terms far less costly than the total withdrawal from China. One would wonder why they did not do so. But that also raises a question about Washington's behavior. Why would Hull and Roosevelt increase their demands over the course of the negotiation rather that stating their maximum terms up front, then working toward compromise? This question, at least, can be answered with an assessment of the relative interests of the countries involved in this case.

The Balance of Interests in the Oil Embargo

A narrow analysis of the balance of interests in this case might suggest that Tokyo decided to resist Washington's demands because Japan had greater interests on the Asian continent than did the United States. Both nations held territory in Asia—the United States had the Philippines; Japan had Korea, Formosa, Manchukuo, and occupied China—and both countries had substantial commercial interests in China and Indochina. But one could argue that Japan's proximity in Asia and her greater dependence on external sources of raw materials would tend to make Tokyo more motivated than Washington in any test of resolve. Indeed, the Japanese frequently referred to the special economic interests they believed proximity and their urgent needs entitled them, and as late as 1940 American leaders seemed willing to concede Japan some special position in Asia, provided American interests there were secure. However, any analysis that focuses exclusively on these issues would miss the broader significance of events leading to the war.

American interests in China were both commercial and sentimental. China was a land in chaos. Since the mid–nineteenth century, the European Powers and Japan had competed for control of the Chinese countryside, its people, and their resources. After the fall of the Ch'ing Dynasty in 1912, China suffered even greater turmoil as regional warlords joined in the struggle for power. The United States had no territorial ambitions in China, but Americans hoped to tap the vast potential market promised in China's immense population. Therefore, from 1899 onward, the United States tried to mediate fair and equal access to commercial opportunities in China and preserve the country's administrative and territorial integrity by getting the Powers to agree to what Secretary of State John Hay first called the "Open Door Policy." Beyond that, many Americans dreamed that China would eventually emerge as a new democracy and set an example for the rest of Asia to follow. Japan's advance in the 1930s not only encroached upon the Open Door, it threatened that dream.

But despite the depth and breadth of American interests in Asia, developments in Europe eventually overshadowed everything Japan was doing in China. America's cultural, political, and economic ties with Europe were far stronger than those with Asia. The United States shared a common heritage with the European community of nations. Americans spoke the same language as Britain and her commonwealth, and they were more heavily invested in those countries than in other regions of the world. Most importantly, the United States shared a sense of political destiny with other Western democracies, a feeling that a threat to one of them was, somehow, a threat to all. Therefore, when Nazi Germany swept across Western Europe in the spring of 1940, Washington responded with alarm. Japan's advance in China had threatened American interests and American dreams—Hitler's advance in Europe threatened American survival.

Consequently, Japan's alliance with the Axis Powers forced Washington to reappraise American interests in Asia and change its conception of the

Japanese threat. It was bad enough that Japan had abrogated its commitment to the Open Door and abused American dreams of democracy in China. But when Japan signed the Tripartite Pact, Tokyo's behavior and rhetoric took on a new and sinister quality in Washington's eyes. Japan's expansion in China became linked to Nazi Germany's conquest in Europe, and Konoe's New Order in East Asia became a part of Hitler's crusade to dominate the world. Ultimately, Matsuoka's proclamation of a co-prosperity sphere was seen as a declaration that Japan intended to conquer all of Asia. Where Japan's behavior before the Axis alliance threatened America's interests and trampled its ideals, Tokyo's marriage with Hitler convinced Washington that Japanese expansion was now a threat to the survival of the United States.

Even so, America was not yet prepared to respond to this threat. By the time Japan resumed its active aggression in the late 1930s, the United States had largely recovered from the Great Depression. However, by then isolationism had been codified in a series of neutrality laws, and the combined impact of years of economic, political, and legal constraints on projecting American power had left the nation's military capabilities withered. Nonetheless, Hull and Roosevelt bore no illusions concerning the threat Germany presented, and if the Tripartite Pact was ever invoked as written, Japan would have to be stopped as well. Therefore, as the decade drew to a close, Roosevelt set out to overcome the isolationism and lack of military preparedness that stood in the way of a direct American confrontation with the Axis Powers.

These factors help explain why Hull and the president progressively stiffened American demands on Japan instead of working toward a compromise. Before the Tripartite Pact, Tokyo might have accommodated Washington by guaranteeing China's sovereignty and reviving Japan's commitment to the Open Door. But the alliance with Germany made that kind of settlement impossible. Yet, the United States was ill-prepared for war in 1940 or early 1941, so the Americans agreed to negotiate with Tokyo, hoping to separate Japan from the Axis Powers and avoid war in the Pacific, or at least to delay the conflict long enough to reinforce its position in Asia. Meanwhile, the Roosevelt Administration launched a concerted campaign to educate the American public on the need to confront the Axis threat. As the Nazi menace became more apparent, Washington drew ever closer to London. Congress repealed the neutrality laws, equipped the British, and eagerly funded America's rearmament. Ultimately, as negotiations with Tokyo revealed that Japanese leaders intended to honor their Axis commitments, and as the Imperial Army continued its expansion into Southeast Asia, Hull and Roosevelt concluded that war with Japan was inevitable. When MAGIC intercepts informed American leaders that Japan would soon break off negotiations and attack, Hull decided to state Washington's conditions in the firmest and clearest terms possible. If the United States was to be forced to fight for survival, she would settle for nothing less than Japan's complete withdrawal from continental Asia.

Britain's interest in the American confrontation with Japan reflected the pivotal role London anticipated the United States might play in any war with the Axis Powers. As the China conflict deepened, the British grew increasingly fearful that Japanese attacks on Hong Kong and Singapore were imminent. They were well aware that Japan resented Britain's power and coveted her possessions in Asia. Moreover, Tokyo had already expressed its resentment for Britain's support of Chiang Kai-shek and pressed London to close Hong Kong. It should be no surprise that, shortly after Tokyo signed the Tripartite Pact, British leaders complained to Washington that they believed the Japanese were about to attack the crown colonies in Asia. Still struggling for survival at home, Britain desperately wanted to bring the United States into the war, and London began pressing Washington for a commitment to fight should Japan attack British possessions but not those of the United States. Despite British concerns, American leaders feared being drawn into war before having adequately rearmed and, therefore, resisted making such a promise.[157]

Germany also recognized America's potential importance in a global conflict, so Hitler and Ribbentrop did their best to keep the United States out of the European war. The main purpose of bringing Japan into the Axis alliance was to deter Washington from entering the war or supporting Britain too aggressively. Beyond that, the Germans hoped to weaken their enemies in Europe by having Japan attack them in Asia. As soon as Tokyo was a bona fide ally, Berlin began urging the Japanese to attack Singapore. After Hitler turned on Stalin, he urged them to drive north into Siberia. But Tokyo resisted both proposals. An isolated assault on Singapore would have exposed Japan's flank to an American counterstrike from the Philippines, and despite all of Matsuoka's pleading that Japan must support its ally in a war against Soviet Russia, the supply of oil lay south, not north.

Moscow's interests, like London's, revolved mainly around protecting its homeland from the threat of Nazi Germany. Though Stalin had signed a nonaggression pact with Hitler and accepted a share in the partition of Poland, he bore no illusions that Germany was the Soviet Union's ally. The Russian leader expected a German invasion and had signed the nonaggression pact to buy time for his own military preparations. Ironically, the Soviets were almost as suspicious of Japan as they were of Germany, which explains why they blunted all overtures for a Russo-Japanese nonaggression treaty in late 1940 with unreasonable demands for economic and territorial concessions. But a few months later, with the German army massing on the Polish frontier, Stalin warmly embraced Matsuoka and signed a neutrality pact with almost no negotiation. Stalin knew the Germans would soon attack, and he sought to secure his rear and, possibly, cleave the Tripartite Pact by befriending its Asian member.

Clearly, governments on both sides of the Atlantic subordinated their interests in Asia to concerns about developments in Europe. Japanese leaders understood this fact and tried to use it to their advantage. Although the China war had begun as a spontaneous escalation of the Marco Polo Bridge incident, the war in Europe that soon followed seemed to offer Tokyo the opportunity to "settle" the affair and expand the Empire while the Western Powers were distracted and weakened. Japan was pleased to see Germany leap to an early advantage. Berlin had few interests in Asia while its enemies were Tokyo's long-time competitors in China and the southwest Pacific. Events unfolding during the first months of the conflict seemed to suggest that a new sphere of influence was emerging in Europe around Germany. More and more Japanese became convinced that if Tokyo aligned itself with Berlin, Japan might be able to establish a similar sphere of influence in East Asia. It was an opportunity to build Konoe's New Order, an opportunity many Japanese did not want to miss.

Consequently, Japan's interests in this confrontation were straightforward—her leaders sought to break their dependence on foreign imports and to expand the Empire. As noted earlier, somehow the Japanese turned their conception of these issues into a question of survival. As American leaders had come to associate Japan's behavior with that of Nazi Germany, *stopping* Japanese expansion had become an issue of survival in their minds. With leaders on both sides of the Pacific having decided that the security of their nations would ultimately turn on Japan's destiny in Asia, war was inevitable.

But records of the meetings in which Japanese leaders sealed their decision for war suggest there was more at stake in Japan's decision calculus than factors of survival or defeat, expansion or strangulation. Speaking for the emperor near the end of the December 1 imperial conference, Privy Council President Hara Yoshimichi said:

In negotiating with the United States, our Empire hoped to maintain peace by making one concession after another. But to our surprise, the American position from beginning to end was to say what Chiang Kai-shek wanted her to say and to emphasize those ideals that she had stated in the past. The United States is being utterly conceited, obstinate, and disrespectful. It is regrettable indeed. We simply cannot tolerate such an attitude.[158]

Such a statement might seem bizarre when considered from a non-Japanese perspective. What concessions had Japan made? Though it may be no surprise that Tokyo chose to cast Washington as Chiang's political servant, why would the Japanese characterize the United States—a country they clearly acknowledged as more powerful than their own—as "utterly conceited, obstinate, and disrespectful" simply because its leaders seemed committed to a consistent set of ideals? Wouldn't those terms better describe Hitler and Ribbentrop, who had recently caused two political crises in Tokyo by changing policies toward Soviet Russia without consulting their Japanese allies?

Perhaps, some clues to the answers of these questions lay in Prime Minister Tojo's closing remarks at the same conference when he said:

At the moment, our Empire stands at the threshold of glory or oblivion. We tremble with fear in the presence of His Majesty. We subjects are keenly aware of the great responsibility we must assume from this point on. Once His Majesty reaches a decision to commence hostilities, we will all strive to repay our obligations to him . . . and set His Majesty's mind at ease.[159]

Indeed, the foregoing pronouncement is laden with symbols that provide insight into the thinking of Japanese leaders in 1941, but we can only comprehend these symbols when we see them in terms of the strategic culture of Imperial Japan.

Strategic Culture and the Oil Embargo

Many scholars have attempted to explain Japan's behavior in the decade leading to the Second World War in terms of her descent into fascism. Observing the similarities in Japan's behavior with the actions of those fascist countries in Europe that ultimately became her allies, historians have often concluded that Tokyo abandoned its caution in the 1930s at a rate proportionate to Japan's conversion to that ideology. Indeed, the decade of the 1930s was a seminal period in Japan's political evolution, and fascism in Japan bore striking similarities to its counterparts in Europe. But a closer examination reveals that Japanese fascism exhibited singular traits stemming from Japan's unique cultural heritage, and though the fascist movement may have catalyzed Japan's expansionist tendencies, the movement itself was more a product of the Japanese cultural experience than it was an engine of destiny. Ultimately, Japan's behavior leading to the war reflected the strategic preferences of her leaders, choices made after weighing their conception of the strategic environment in terms of Japanese values. Nevertheless, in order to understand how strategic culture affected the decisions Japanese leaders made in responding to the American compellent threat, we must briefly examine Japanese fascism and determine the role it may have played, along with culture, in conditioning Japanese behavior.

In many ways, fascism in Japan resembled its counterparts in Germany and Italy. Fascists in all three countries rejected the idea that individuals were entitled to basic liberties, and they opposed any expression of liberal democracy through party politics. Fascists on both continents advocated foreign expansion and, therefore, tended to glorify military power and war. They all rejected the notion of class warfare. In fact, members of all three movements saw themselves as national guardians in the struggle against Marxism. Most notably, all three brands of fascism tended to foster racial myths and emphasize exaggerated conceptions of national essence.[160]

Although Japanese fascism shared a great deal of common ground with its European cousins, it is important to note how compatible these traits were with Japan's cultural orientation. Fascism's rejection of personal liberty fared well in a land where the individual's needs were routinely subordinated to those of the group. Its obsession with foreign conquest coincided with Japan's long-cherished dream of expanding on the Asian mainland, and its exaltation of military power found fertile soil in a society that glorified the ideals of warrior virtue. Most importantly, fascism's tendencies to foster racial myths and exaggerate the concept of national essence were accepted without question by a people who believed they were governed by a living deity, an emperor with whom they were related by blood.

But despite the similarities, fascism in Japan exhibited three prominent traits that separated it from ideologies originating in Europe. First, all fascist groups in Japan emphasized the family system as a basic characteristic in the structure of the Japanese state. Like all Japanese of the period, the fascists saw Japan as a nation of interrelated families with the Imperial House as the main family and the emperor's subjects as members of branch houses. This was no abstract conception—while fascists in Germany may have euphemistically referred to a fatherland and a German national family, the Japanese maintained that all their countrymen were factually and historically related by blood. Second, while fascism by its very nature tended to emphasize a centralization of power in the state and a strengthening of that power through the control and encouragement of industrial development, Japanese fascism was notably agrarian in character. Stemming largely from the feudal experience, the Japanese tended to distrust strong expressions of central authority and resented the growth of urban power when achieved at the expense of village autonomy. But, ironically, the same individuals who railed at the growing centralization of power in the Imperial Government, invariably supported the notion of a strengthened state sovereignty centered on the emperor. This internal contradiction contributed to an irrational quality that tended to characterize the fascist ideologies originating in Japan.[161] Finally, fascism in Japan was notable for its emphasis on the "greater Asia principle," a belief that Japan bore an obligation to emancipate other Asian countries from European colonialism and bring them into a family of nations headed by Japan.[162]

Clearly, the traits of Japanese fascism that separated it from similar ideologies from Europe are completely consistent with the culture profile I presented in chapter 4 of this book. Emphasis on a family-system state reflects the focus on the *ie*, or traditional household, so prevalent in Japanese society. The agrarian flavor that seemed to permeate Japanese political ideologies reflects the competitive, in-group/out-group perspectives that tend to characterize societies ordered on vertical bonds. Japan's preoccupation with a "greater Asia principle" suggests that Japanese fascists, like their forebears in the first Sino-Japanese War, tended to perceive the international political environment in terms of their own conceptions of Confucian hierarchy.

All of this suggests that although the rise of fascism may have created conditions conducive to Japan's expansionist tendencies in the 1930s, it was more a vehicle for the expression of those aspirations than a source of them. Therefore, in order to interpret Japan's behavior in 1941, we must examine circumstances that facilitated the rise of fascism in terms of Japanese perceptions and values, then determine how those ideational factors conditioned the strategic preferences and governmental processes in which Japan's fascist leaders operated when answering the American compellent threat.

The rise of fascism can be traced to several interrelated phenomena that began following the First World War, and all of them were firmly rooted in Japanese culture. First, the gradual passing of the *genro,* those elder statesmen who had engineered the Meiji Restoration and steered Japan's government for decades afterward, had a subtle but profound effect on governmental cohesion and political coherence. Second, the rise and rapid proliferation of ultranationalist groups laid the foundation for a fascist movement to form and gain a following among military officers. Finally, the growing tendency of lower-echelon military leaders to make and carry out their own policies, independent of the civilian government, resulted in a diffusion of authority setting the stage for power to re-crystallize in the form of a fascist state.

After personally administering the nation throughout the last decades of the nineteenth century, the aging *genro* stepped out of the public eye in 1901 and allowed a second generation of statesmen to take the reigns of government.[163] For the next dozen years, the role of prime minister alternated between Katsura Taro and Saionji Kimmochi, protégés of the two most influential *genro,* Yamagata Aritomo and Ito Hirobumi. Katsura, like his mentor, was a conservative army man from Choshu. Though Ito had also come from Choshu, his protégé, Saionji, was a former samurai from Satsuma. Thus, by turning repeatedly to these two statesmen, the *genro* preserved the Meiji tradition of alternating the helm of government between former samurai from the two most powerful houses that had brought down the Tokugawa shogunate. After stepping down, the *genro* continued to orchestrate domestic and foreign affairs, acting through their juniors and through the de facto veto they possessed in being the emperors' personal counselors, but as the years passed, their ranks grew thin. With Saigo Tsugumichi's death in 1902, five of the original seven remained. Though the emperor eventually added Prime Ministers Katsura and Saionji to the club, only three *genro* lived to see the end of the First World War. With the passing of Matsukata in 1924, Saionji Kimmochi was the only living *genro* until his death in 1940.[164]

As the *genro* became fewer, their ability to coordinate the affairs of state waned. Nearly all the elder statesmen had protégés firmly entrenched in the highest levels of the government's key ministries and in the military services. But where the old guard had sustained a national outlook on governance, their juniors tended to be more parochial. Consequently, as each *genro* died, his protégé became notably less inclined to coordinate his ministry's activities with those of the other sectors of government. Instead, second-generation leaders tended to focus on their own organizations' interests, sometimes at the expense of other agencies and the nation as a whole.[165] The rise in parochialism that accompanied the passing of the *genro* dramatically illustrates the tendency in Japanese society for large organizations to break down into competing factions when members experience a change in their frames of reference. While the *genro* lived, they constituted a governing *ie*, a household of retainers who shared a common experience in restoring the emperor to power. As the emperor's personal retainers, the *genro* were committed to making his government function smoothly. National policies were decided by consensus, and though *genro* members often bitterly disagreed with one another, once a consensus was reached, each *genro* returned to his respective ministry—or, if retired, passed the decision to his protégé—and the will of the *ie* was faithfully carried out. But as the *genro* died, the sense of family that made policy making in the Meiji government so coherent began to evaporate. Second-generation leaders found themselves heads of their own *ie*, and without coordination from above or strong lateral bonds with other ministries, they began to compete viciously for resources and policy advantage. Of course, each leader still felt a strong vertical bond to the emperor, but without a governing family to coordinate national decision making, each of the ministry- and service-level *ie* had their own ideas about how the emperor could best be served.

Just after the First World War, as the passing of the *genro* began to take its fullest effect on governmental cohesion, ultranationalist societies began forming. Over the next decade, they proliferated rapidly. These organizations began as reactions to bolshevism, which most Japanese saw as a threat to imperial sovereignty, but there were other factors that stimulated their growth. The rapid industrialization carried out during the Meiji era had put considerable strain on the rural population, exacerbating the agrarian sentiments noted earlier. Moreover, in the 1920s the Japanese economy suffered a number of dramatic downturns, making conditions even worse. At first, the ultranationalist groups were simply reactionary bodies with no positive plan for national reconstruction; but as it became increasingly evident that the government lacked the cohesiveness to deal effectively with Japan's problems, several key ultranationalist leaders began to advocate changing the structure of government so that the imperial will might be carried out more effectively.[166]

With the onset of the Great Depression, conditions grew even worse, and the ultranationalists soon developed an eager following among junior officers in the Japanese military. These men were drawn largely from rural stock, and they had become increasingly disaffected with the civilian government's inability to deal with the growing economic hardships facing their families back home. Inspired by the writings of ultranationalists such as Kita Ikki, the young officers hoped to bring about what they called the "Showa Restoration," a revolution to create a totalitarian state administered by a military dictatorship.[167] According to Kita, Japan's current political and economic plight was the result of the selfishness of political parties and the *zaibatsu* (financial cliques). Only the military had remained loyal to the traditional belief that the Japanese race was really one large family under the paternalistic protection of the emperor and his government. Therefore, argued Kita, the military should restore the emperor to his rightful place, redistribute the nation's wealth on a more equitable basis, and then conquer Manchuria and Siberia for their raw materials.[168]

By the early 1930s, numerous ultranationalist secret societies had formed in the Imperial Army and Navy, and Japanese leaders were forced to deal with a series of assassinations, coup attempts, and plots to instigate war in Manchuria. As this case reveals, the government and the general staff were hard-pressed to restrain the radical activities of young officers, and neither sources of authority seemed willing to discipline them strongly. Countless conspiracies were uncovered with the only result being reassignment for the individuals involved. Even assassinations yielded only light sentences and verdicts glorifying the perpetrators as tragic heroes. This penchant for low-level military leaders to take "direct action," and the tendency of their superiors to tolerate such behavior, also had firm roots in Japanese culture. During the Edo period the expression *gekokujo* was used to describe situations in which low-ranking samurai usurped authority from incompetent aristocrats for the good of society.[169] Assassination for a noble cause had been a romantic ideal even before the 47 *ronin* were lionized for murdering everyone in the household of Lord Kita in 1701. Consequently, as Japanese of all strata became increasingly disillusioned with the government's inability to handle the nation's mounting problems, the notion of direct action assumed a respectable, even heroic, persona.

But much of this changed following the February Incident in 1936. This insurrection of nearly 1,500 *Kodo ha* sympathizers convinced army officials that they could no longer tolerate direct action and factional violence in the military or government. Therefore, they promptly convicted and executed 17 key conspirators, then purged the army of any remaining *Kodo* officers in positions of power. Yet, Japanese leaders did not disavow the spiritual principles of *Kodo,* the "Imperial Way." In fact, they later made *Kodo ha* leader General Araki Sadao inspector general of military education, the army's chief propagandist. The *Tosei ha* and other factions did not object to the *Kodo* faction's extreme emphasis on service, sacrifice, and military virtue, provided these qualities were not stressed at the exclusion of more tangible sources of power, such as armament. Instead, it was the group's tendency to resort to radical violence, rather than its spiritual philosophy, that made its continued existence incompatible with the objectives of senior army officers. Consequently, the era of direct action had largely come to an end.

Paradoxically, the military extremists no longer needed low-level direct action after 1936. When War Minister General Terauchi forced Prime Minister Hirota to submit all cabinet selections to the army for approval, he finally achieved what the young officers had always hoped for—the army had gotten control of the government. Japan had become a fascist state. Ironically, even fascism failed to bring real cohesiveness to the Japanese government—ministries still competed for policy advantage, the army quarreled with the navy, and factions within the military services continued to struggle for influence. Nevertheless, fascism's triumph did remove from the foreign policy debate such liberal notions as disarmament, and it served to reaffirm Japan's commitment to several long-held, culturally rooted, convictions and objectives. In *Fundamentals of Our National Polity,* published in late 1936, Japanese leaders reminded the nation they were one family, headed by the Son of Heaven. As such, loyalty to the emperor was equivalent to filial piety, and serving him defined ultimate morality. The manifesto proceeded to declare that "war is not destruction or the subjugation of others, but instead is the creation of harmony and peace which results from bringing others to the Imperial Way."[170]

This clearly illustrates how fascism served to catalyze the expansionist tendencies already present in Imperial Japan by manipulating and intensifying the symbols and values deeply embedded in Japanese culture. But it still does not explain the behavior of Japan's leaders in 1940 and 1941. Granted, there may have been strong motivations for Japan to expand on the Asian mainland, but that does not explain why Tokyo would not, or could not, yield to the American compellent threat. To come to grips with that question, we must examine Japanese values more deeply and better determine how they came to influence Tokyo's strategic preferences.

According to Japanese political scientist Maruyama Masao, the principal feature that differentiates Japanese ultranationalism from ideologies originating elsewhere is the relationship between morality and the state.

In concepts of European nationalism, the state is a value-neutral, political entity. Although the state makes laws enforcing commonly accepted norms of behavior, it leaves the determination of those norms to specially designated social groups, such as the church, and it leaves interpretations of personal morality to individual conscience. However, stemming from Japan's traditional values and the political changes wrought in the Meiji Restoration, the ultranationalist doctrines that evolved in early twentieth-century Japan conceived a very different role for the state in terms of morality.[171]

The Meiji Restoration combined two principal sources of authority in Japanese society, thereby setting in motion a growing conception of moral legitimacy that eventually denied Japanese leaders the political flexibility they needed to respond to the world around them. In pre-Meiji Japan, spiritual sovereignty resided in the emperor while all political power and authority was vested in the shogun and his *bakufu*. But the Restoration combined those sources of authority in the person of the emperor and, in doing so, made the determination of social values a domain of the state. As a result, the ultranationalists tended to base their control over Japanese society on internal values instead of external laws. All definitions of truth, morality, and beauty were derived from national values, and neither scholarship nor art could exist apart from *kokutai* (national entity).[172] More importantly, this fusion of civil and spiritual authority eventually made the Japanese government's domestic and international conduct a self-legitimizing function.

As Japanese sovereignty incorporated both spiritual authority and political power, the emperor myth grew until by the 1930s he was regarded as "the eternal culmination of the true, the good, and the beautiful throughout the ages and in all places."[173] According to this point of view, anything the government of Japan chose to do, provided the act was sanctioned by the Son of Heaven, was politically and morally correct. Apply this standard of morality in the context of Japan's conception of her Confucian obligation to liberate Asia, and it becomes clear that the only way the Japanese government could achieve virtue was to ensure that *kokutai* spread out from the central household until the "four corners of Asia [were] under one roof." In this conception, Japan was an elder brother guiding its younger brothers to the beautiful truth radiated by a divine father, and the advance of the Imperial Army was "nothing other than the life-giving sword that destroys evil and makes justice manifest."[174]

Combine this mindset with the contextual nature in which Japanese leaders viewed truth and morality, and it becomes clear how Tokyo could so casually disregard the treaties that American leaders believed they were honor-bound to observe. The Japanese were genuinely puzzled when Washington, in response to Konoe's proclamation of a New Order in East Asia, insisted the Open Door was based on universal principles of equal opportunity and "not subject to nullification by unilateral affirmation." Certainly, Japan had signed treaties agreeing to the Open Door during the Washington Conference in 1922, but that had been 16 years earlier. Since that time the Imperial Army had conquered the eastern half of China and extended the emperor's divine righteousness throughout the region. Japan had not signed the treaties in bad faith—they earnestly believed the Open Door was appropriate in 1922—nor did they see any duplicity in their behavior in 1938. But the context had changed. China was now part of the New Order and the Open Door Policy was simply obsolete.

Ultimately, as virtue and Japanese national conduct had become one in the same, Tokyo found it impossible to negotiate with Washington regarding Japan's behavior in Asia. The emperor had blessed all of Japan's advances, so they were, by definition, righteous. Therefore, territorial concession was inconceivable—not only would it have caused Japan an enormous loss of face, but it would have suggested the emperor was wrong in sanctioning the acquisition in the first place. That would have brought the emperor's divinity into question and threatened the survival of kokutai. Consequently, all Japan could offer in the negotiation was to forestall further advances on the continent, operations that Japanese leaders had planned but not yet submitted to the throne for approval. In this light, while Roosevelt and Hull felt Tokyo was trying to legitimize a fait accompli when they ignored the president's plea that they neutralize Indochina, Japanese leaders believed they were making a major concession in offering to refrain from taking the rest of Southeast Asia.

The political inflexibility that resulted from this fusion of spiritual authority and national power explains why Japan could not yield to Washington's coercive pressure in 1941, but it does not explain other peculiarities in Tokyo's behavior in the months leading to the war. In examining case events, one gets the impression that almost no one in Japan wanted war with the United States. Clearly, Prime Minister Konoe and Emperor Hirohito hoped to avoid a confrontation, and they were two of the most influential men in Japan. Yet at each turn in the negotiation, Japanese leaders not only blunted American offers but countered with proposals that raised the level of tension by asking for concessions that were obviously unacceptable to Washington. To understand how they could act in such a self-defeating manner, one must consider how Japanese patterns of interpersonal behavior conditioned the governmental process in which decisions were made in prewar Tokyo.

Historians have frequently criticized Prince Konoe for his weakness in being unable to control Japan's aggressive military leaders and avoid the catastrophic war with the United States. He has been described as indecisive and frail in body and spirit. As Prime Minister, Konoe is said to have "lacked commanding purpose and energy," and he has been accused of pursuing a policy of "government by acquiescence."[175] Indeed, there was much in the prince's character to support such condemnation. He was known to feign illness and hide in his villa when it appeared that decisions were not about to go his way, and contemporaries said he frequently whined about the pressures of office and wanted to quit. But much of the criticism of Konoe has been made without considering the role of leadership in the Japanese decision-making process.

As explained in the culture profile, a leader in Japan does not lead in the Western sense of the word; instead, he creates an environment that brings parties together and fosters consensus. When considered in that light, Konoe's behavior was archetypally Japanese. He was chosen to be prime minister in 1937 and again in 1940 because he was the one man Japanese leaders believed could work with the many hostile factions that comprised their fragmented government. All the power brokers in Tokyo liked Prince Konoe. He had an engaging demeanor and was a good listener. Most importantly, he had the ability to address issues in such a way that suggested to those on every side of an argument that he understood their concerns and was open to persuasion. Though Western critics have often interpreted this trait as weakness or indecisiveness, in Japan, where decisions are made by consensus and direct confrontation causes a loss of face, empathy is the essence of good leadership.

Unfortunately, charismatic as he was, even Konoe was unable to overcome the undertow of Japan's bottom-up decision-making process. Frequently during his second and third terms in office, the prime minister tried to mediate the demands of key ministers, generals, and admirals in such a way that they could reach a consensus on terms that Washington would accept; but the leaders with whom Konoe had to deal had relatively little flexibility with which to compromise.[176] Each was head of an *ie* and brought the consensus-driven demands of his own fiefdom to cabinet meetings and liaison conferences. Originating from junior and intermediate-level officers in their respective organizations, these positions tended to be rigid and self-serving. The army wanted to subdue China, and they also wanted to move south. Yet, they would not be denied the freedom to move north, should an opportunity present itself. Navy officers wanted oil—if not from the United States, then from the oil-rich Indies, which meant they would also have to take Singapore and the Philippines. The Foreign Ministry wanted to continue negotiating and insisted until the end that it could get concessions from Washington through diplomacy. Combine these unbending demands in a series of consensus-driven decisions on how to deal with the United States, and the results were predictable: Japanese leaders answered every American proposal with a counterproposal asking for more concessions. As Washington then snubbed each Japanese offer, the tide in Tokyo shifted inexorably toward war.

The emperor faced similar constraints on his ability to shape Japanese policy. As records of the 1941 imperial conferences indicate, Emperor Hirohito was not sanguine about prospects of war with the United States. Moreover, those close to the monarch later testified that thoughts of declaring war against Britain, a country for which he held strong affection, troubled him deeply. Yet, even as spiritual and political father of the national polity, he was limited in his ability to determine the content of policies brought before him for sanction. Each proposal was born in the bowels of a ministry or service staff and worked its way up the organizational ladder, getting consensus approval at each level. Next, ministers or general staff chiefs hammered out the details until reaching unanimous agreement. The document then went to the liaison conference where key cabinet members and the service chiefs developed a consensus on what the final policy would be. Ultimately, the emperor received the proposal as a carefully choreographed, scripted briefing in which conferees feigned to discuss all sides of the issue, but always concluded with a unanimous, preordained decision.[177] This does not suggest that the emperor did not participate in the policy-making process. On the contrary, records indicate that Hirohito was intimately involved in *nemawashi* (informal consensus building) at several levels, perhaps even guiding that effort. Military and civilian leaders briefed him on policy developments almost daily, and he thoroughly questioned these officials, sometimes expressing terse dissatisfaction with their answers. Moreover, he regularly provided his input to political policies and military plans as they were being formulated, going so far as editing draft documents in red ink.[178] Yet, ultimately, the emperor had but one voice in a pluralistic decision-making system that required consensus to function. His voice was undeniably influential, but it was one voice, nonetheless.[179] Once a policy reached the imperial conference, the emperor faced a unified, consensus decision from the entire government and combined general staff. Withholding his sanction in that situation was out of the question. Granted, the Meiji Constitution gave him the authority to do so, but social custom prohibited it.

In sum, though a number of Japan's key leaders wanted to avoid war with the United States, they were powerless to overcome the tide of demands rising from the various constituencies within the government and, particularly, from the army. Konoe struggled desperately to head off a stalemate with Washington, finally resorting to pleas for a face-to-face meeting with President Roosevelt.[180] But by mid-September, with War Minister Tojo pressing the army's position that war was unavoidable, the prime minister could no longer build a consensus. Therefore, he did the only thing left to do for a Japanese leader in that circumstance—he resigned.

When Tojo became prime minister while retaining the post of war minister, his leadership responsibilities expanded. In addition to being a champion of the army's position, as prime minister the general became responsible for building a national-level consensus. This new obligation weighed on him heavily. The navy still wanted to avoid war with the United States, and the emperor had personally admonished Tojo and Navy Minister Admiral Shimada to work together more closely. But when the October studies revealed how desperate the situation facing Japan really was, navy leaders agreed that war was the only reasonable alternative.

Ironically, that decision too was an expression of Japan's culturally biased view of the world. While Tojo and the army had long been willing to "jump from the Kiyomizu Temple" or, as Ambassador Grew had said, "make an all-out, do-or-die attempt, risking national *hara kiri*" in a war against the United States, many navy leaders had wanted to avoid such a catastrophic confrontation. Yet, when internal studies informed the liaison conference that Japan's chances of victory were even more remote than they had imagined, the navy promptly joined the chorus for war. This dramatically illustrates the vein of fatalism that ran so strongly in the psyche of Japan's prewar military leaders. Stemming largely from mythic interpretations of the nation's thirteenth-century salvation from two Mongol invasions, Japanese leaders believed that when all seemed hopeless, the sacred virtue of the emperor would carry the day. After all, as a direct descendant of the sun goddess, the emperor was inviolable and infallible. If they served him to the fullest expectations of *bushido,* Japan would triumph despite the West's material and financial superiority. Ultimately, Japan's decision for war reflected the faith its leaders maintained in the concept of "spirit over matter."

CONCLUSION

This case offers strong testimony regarding the way culture conditions a nation's response to coercive threat. Washington's compellence strategy focused first on punishing Tokyo for aggressing on the Asian continent and later on denying Japan the ability to continue its conquests. American leaders imposed increasingly severe restrictions on the export of strategic materials, culminating in a total embargo on the one resource Japan needed most—oil. Though the early sanctions had no effect, the oil embargo created an automatic mechanism that should have eventually forced Japan's compliance with American demands. Passive resistance would have meant certain strangulation, war against the United States was probable suicide, and nothing on the Asian continent was worth risking national survival. Yet no Japanese leader even considered complying with Washington. Clearly, cost-benefit analysis, standing alone, does not adequately explain why Tokyo refused to yield to American compellence.

An analysis of the balance of interests in this case only partially explains Japan's behavior. Tokyo's foreign policy was driven by a need to free

Japan from its dependence on foreign imports and an unswerving desire to expand on the Asian continent. As Japanese leaders believed Germany was emerging as the dominant nation in Europe, they joined the Axis alliance in hopes of deterring the United States from interfering with their Asian conquests. Later, Tokyo also signed a neutrality pact with Moscow to secure the Imperial Army's rear, freeing it to settle the China Incident and advance into Southeast Asia. All of this makes perfect sense, but an explanation based on the balance of interests fails to explain the most crucial issue in this case—why Japanese leaders would consider continental expansion so important that they would risk national survival rather than give up that dream.

Japan's obsessive drive to expand on the Asian continent can only be understood when seen in light of her strategic culture. Since the early years of the Meiji Restoration, Japanese at all levels of society had been fascinated with the notion, based on their conception of Confucian hierarchy, that Japan's military and technological superiority in Asia not only entitled her to expand on the continent, but obligated her to reform her backward Asian brothers. This popular dogma gained strength as the imperial era progressed. Over time, the fusion of spiritual authority and political power in the person of the emperor fostered a conception of political righteousness, making Japanese national conduct a self-legitimizing function. Moreover, these culturally rooted perceptions and values both facilitated the rise of fascism in Japan and found violent expression in that movement.

Most importantly, Japan's conviction that its conquests were righteous denied Tokyo the political flexibility to deal effectively with the American coercive threat, and that led to a catastrophic war. The emperor was sacred and infallible, so Japanese leaders could not concede any imperially sanctioned territorial gains without questioning Hirohito's divinity. Japan's bottom-up, consensus-driven governmental process complicated matters, resulting in unrealistic proposals emanating from Tokyo. As the emperor was the embodiment of *kokutai* and *kokutai* had come to represent all that was Japan, any threat to the emperor myth was perceived as a threat to national survival. Consequently, Japanese leaders could not acquiesce to American demands under any circumstances. In the end, the threat of war with a nation possessing immense industrial and military potential triggered a deep-seated, culturally-conditioned response from Japan's leaders, a fatalistic trust in the spiritual power of *bushido* to deliver the nation from crisis.

Japan's response to the oil embargo offers telling evidence that strategic culture can effect compellence outcomes. While analyses using non–culture-based approaches suggest that Japanese leaders should have eventually complied with Washington's demands, the strategic culture model helps explain why they could not do so. The following chapter will examine Tokyo's responses to American attempts to compel surrender at the end of the Second World War and will offer evidence strengthening the strategic culture thesis even further.

NOTES

1. Richard Storry, *A History of Modern Japan* (London: Cassell & Co., Ltd., 1960), p. 182.

2. See more about the conspiracy and the Japanese government's attempts to bring the Kwangtung Army staff under control in Herbert P. Bix, *Hirohito and the Making of Modern Japan* (New York: Perennial, 2000), pp. 230–35.

3. W. G. Beasley, *Japanese Imperialism, 1894–1945* (Oxford: Clarendon Press, 1987), pp. 191–92; Hugh Borton, *Japan's Modern Century: From Perry to 1970* (New York: The Ronald Press Co., 1970), p. 372.

4. Bix, p. 235.

5. Beasley, pp. 192–93; Bix, pp. 236 and 239; Borton, pp. 372–73; Ikuhiko Hata, "Continental Expansion, 1905–1941" in *The Cambridge History of Japan*, Volume 6, *The Twentieth Century*, trans. Alvin Coox (Cambridge: Cambridge University Press, 1988), pp. 194–95.

6. The Meiji Constitution designated the emperor as supreme commander of all military forces; therefore, the operational chain of command ran from the emperor to the general staff, bypassing the cabinet and the war minister. The army and the navy answered directly to the emperor.

7. Beasley, p. 193; Bix, pp. 241–43; Borton, pp. 375–78; Ian Nish, *Japanese Foreign Policy, 1869–1942: Kasumigaseki to Miyakezaka* (London: Routledge & Kegan Paul, 1977), pp. 179–80; Storry, pp. 188–90; Chitoshi Yanaga, *Japan Since Perry* (Westport, Conn.: Greenwood Press, 1949), pp. 553–56.

8. See Stimson's 20 October 1931 telegram to American Charge d'Affairs Neville in United States Department of State, *Papers Relating to the Foreign Relations of the United States: Japan, 1931–1941* (hereafter referred to as PRFRUSJ) (Washington, D.C.: U.S. Government Printing Office, 1943), pp. 1:27–28. Also see Borton, p. 374; Nish, p. 181.

9. In the 1928 Paris Peace Pact, 63 countries, including all the Great Powers except the Soviet Union, renounced war as an instrument of national policy and pledged to settle all disputes between them by peaceful means. For Stimson's entire statement to Japan, see his 7 January 1932 telegram to the United States Ambassador to Japan Forbes in PRFRUSJ, p. 1:76.

10. Bix, p. 250.

11. Ibid., p. 247.

12. Beasely, pp. 194–97; Borton, p. 379; Nish, pp. 183–87; Yanaga, pp. 560–62.

13. Nish, pp. 188–91.

14. Ibid. Also see Storry, p. 193; Yanaga, pp. 162–65.

15. Borton, p. 380.

16. Bix, pp. 254–56; Borton, pp. 380–81; Giffard, p. 87; Storry, p. 192; Yanaga, pp. 502–4. The Saito government also marked the end of an era in another respect:

Saito was the last prime minister chosen by the aged *genro*, Saionji. The emperor trusted subsequent prime-ministerial selections to a group of former prime ministers, the *jushin* (senior statesmen).

17. James B. Crowley, *Japan's Quest for Autonomy: National Security and Foreign Policy, 1930–1938* (Princeton, N.J.: Princeton University Press, 1966), p. 202.

18. Borton, p. 382; Crowley, pp. 202–6; Storry, p. 193; Yanaga, p. 510.

19. Borton, p. 382.

20. Crowley, pp. 203–4; Yanaga, p. 510.

21. Beasley, p. 181; Sidney Giffard, *Japan Among the Powers, 1890–1990* (New Haven, Conn.: Yale University Press, 1994), p. 87; Storry, p. 193.

22. Bix, p. 297; Borton, pp. 386–87; Giffard, p. 99.

23. Borton, pp. 378 and 396 n. 20; Storry, pp. 198–99; Yanaga, pp. 516–17.

24. Bix, pp. 299–300.

25. Borton, p. 388; Storry, p. 199; Yanaga, p. 517.

26. Bix, p. 301.

27. The military services had been able to tyrannize the Cabinet since 1900 when *genro* Yamagata Aritomo convinced the emperor to decree that the positions of war minister and navy minister could only be filled by active-duty flag officers in the two highest grades. Subsequently, whenever the military ministers found themselves in serious disagreement with their colleagues on the cabinet, they could bring down the government by resigning; for then, none of their uniformed peers would accept an appointment to replace them and the cabinet would have to resign as well. See Borton, p. 285.

28. Borton, p. 389; Storry, pp. 199–200; Yanaga, p. 518.

29. Bix, pp. 313–14.

30. Borton, p. 391; Storry, p. 200.

31. Beasley, pp. 201–3; Borton, p. 381; Yanaga, pp. 568 and 571.

32. Bix, p. 321.

33. Beasley, p. 203; Borton, pp. 401–2; Giffard, p. 105; Hata, pp. 303–5; Nish, p. 222; Yanaga, pp. 572–73.

34. The text of Roosevelt's speech is provided in United States Department of State, *Peace and War: United States Foreign Policy, 1931–1941* (hereafter referred to as PWUSFP) (Washington, D.C.: U.S. Government Printing Office, 1943), pp. 383–87.

35. Ibid., pp. 50–52.

36. That same day the Japanese also sank British gunboat H.M.S. Ladybird by artillery fire.

37. Borton, p. 403; Ralph E. Shaffer (ed.), *Toward Pearl Harbor: The Diplomatic Exchange Between Japan and the United States, 1899–1941* (New York: Markus Wiener Publishing, 1991), pp. 56–61; Storry, 203–4; Yanaga, 574–75. For the diplomatic exchanges concerning the Panay incident, see PWUSFP, pp. 395–98.

38. Bix, pp. 343–44.

39. Nish, p. 224.

40. Borton, p. 404; Hata, p. 307; Nish, p. 224.

41. PWUSFP, pp. 89 and 421–22.

42. Konoe pioneered the use of think tanks in Japan. In this case, his advisers were a group of ultranationalist intellectuals belonging to the *Showa Kenkyukai* (Showa Study Association), formed in 1936.

43. Beasley, p. 204; Gordon M. Berger, "Politics and Mobilization in Japan, 1931–1945" in *The Cambridge History of Japan*, p. 134; Bix, p. 347; Borton, pp. 405–8; Yanaga, pp. 521–22.

44. Beasley, pp. 204–5.

45. Ibid., p. 205.

46. Bix, p. 349.

47. The full text of Konoe's statement is provided in PRFRUSJ, 1:477–78.

48. U.S. Ambassador Joseph C. Grew's 30 December 1938 note to Arita in PRFRUSJ, p. 823.

49. See Arita's 18 November 1937 note to Grew; Embassy Counselor Eugene Dooman's 19 November 1937 record of a conversation with Arita; and Grew's 30 December 1938 note to Arita in PRFRUSJ, pp. 1:797–800, 801–6, and 820–26.

50. Bix, p. 352; Borton, pp. 409–10; Yanaga, p. 581.

51. Bix, p. 353.

52. See Hull's 10 July 1939 memorandum of a conversation with Japanese Ambassador Horinouchi; Hull's 26 July 1939 note to Horinouchi; and Hull's 26 August 1939 memorandum of a conversation with Horinouchi in PWUSFP, pp. 465–67, 475, and 480–82.

53. Bix, p. 351.

54. Bix; p. 351; Borton, p. 410; Alvin Coox, "The Pacific War" in *The Cambridge History of Japan*, pp. 321–22; Yanaga, p. 577.

55. Bix, p. 352.

56. Borton, p. 426 n. 9; Nish, pp. 232–34.

57. Borton, p. 410; Coox, p. 322; Nish, p. 231–32; Storry, p. 207.

58. Hull's 17 April 1940 statement in Department of State Bulletin, p. 2:411, provided in PWUSFP, pp. 515–16.

59. Hull's memorandums of meetings with Horinouchi on 20 April and 16 May 1940 in PWUSFP, pp. 517–19 and 532–36.

60. Yanaga, p. 585.

61. Beasley, pp. 229–30.

62. Beasley, p. 208; Borton, p. 411; Herbert Feis, *The Road to Pearl Harbor: The Coming of the War between the United States and Japan* (Princeton, N.J.: Princeton University Press, 1950), pp. 69–71; Nish, p. 234; Yanaga, p. 584.

63. Borton, p. 411; Feis, pp. 49–55 and 76–83; Nish, p. 234.

64. Bix, p. 367.

65. Borton, pp. 411–12; Giffard, pp. 110–11; Saiichi Imai, "Cabinet, Emperor, and Senior Statesmen" in *Pearl Harbor as History: Japanese-American Relations 1931–1941*, trans. H. Paul Varley, ed. Dorothy Borg, and Shumpei Okamoto with the assistance of Dale K. A. Finlayson (New York: Columbia University Press, 1973), pp. 73–74.

66. Throughout Konoe's second ministry, he tended to rely on this "four-minister conference" in much the same way that he had used the five-minister conference in his first government.

67. Bix, pp. 367–68; Feis, p. 85.

68. Bix, pp. 367–68; Beasley, pp. 226–27; Borton, pp. 411–12; Feis, pp. 84–87; Nish, p. 236.

69. James H. Herzog, *Closing the Open Door: American-Japanese Diplomatic Negotiations, 1936–1941* (Annapolis, Md.: Naval Institute Press, 1973), pp. 54–63.

70. PWUSFP, p. 97.

71. Bix, pp. 375–76; Beasley, p. 230; Yanaga, p. 586.

72. PWUSFP, p. 97.

73. Notes from the Japanese Embassy to the Department of State on 7 and 8 October 1941 and the memorandum concerning Hull's meeting with Horinouchi PRFRUSJ), 2:223–28.

74. Ibid., pp. 2:225–28.

75. See Ambassador Grew's prescient assessment of these dynamics in his 12 September 1940 telegram to Hull in PWUSFP, pp. 569–72.

76. Bix, pp. 375–80; Borton, pp. 410–12; Feis, pp. 110–21; Giffard, p. 212; Nish, pp. 237–40; Yanaga, pp. 587–88.

77. *The Tripartite Pact* in PRFRUSJ, pp. 2:165–66.

78. Bix, p. 380.

79. In 1915, while the West was preoccupied with the war in Europe, Tokyo presented Peking a list of "Twenty-One Demands" designed to extend and solidify Japan's hold on Manchurian territory, resources, and commerce and to acquire vast territorial holdings on the Shantung Peninsula. The 22 demands issued to Batavia in 1940 did not include territorial concessions; however, the annual import-export quotas Tokyo specified would have made the Indies a captive market. Moreover, the Japanese also demanded increased immigration quotas, mining concessions, and other privileges that would have made the territory a virtual economic colony—in essence, a part of the Greater East Asia Co-prosperity Sphere. For more on the demands issued to Dutch colonial authorities, see Yanaga, pp. 587–88.

80. Department of State 10 December 1940 press release in PRFRUSJ, p. 2:232.

81. Japan's 21 December 1940 note to the Department of State and the Department of State's 7 January 1941 note to the Japanese Embassy in PRFRUSJ, pp. 2:237–38.

82. Yanaga, p. 589.

83. Hull's 15 January 1941 statement before the Committee on Foreign Affairs, House of Representatives in PWUSFP, pp. 612–18.

84. Yanaga, pp. 589–90.

85. Feis, pp. 145 and 147.

86. Ibid., pp. 145–49.

87. Yanaga, p. 591.

88. Bix, pp. 393–94; Borton, pp. 418–19; Fies, pp. 180–87; Giffard, p. 113; Nish, pp. 241–43; Yanaga, pp. 591–93.

89. The Draft Understanding was the product of efforts from several individuals, inside and outside the two governments, to salvage Japanese-American relations. Nomura had met with Hull repeatedly since early March, trying to explain the "true" nature of Japanese policy in a way that would be acceptable to the Americans. Meanwhile, two American clergymen who had lived in Japan, Catholic Bishop James Walsh and Father James Drought, responding to pleas from contacts in Japanese government and business circles, approached President Roosevelt and offered to draft a comprehensive settlement of the problems between the two governments. Roosevelt and Hull were skeptical, but willing to give even this fleeting hope of peace a chance. See Feis, pp. 174–77.

90. Borton, p. 419; Feis, pp. 177–78; Herzog, p. 155.

91. It is ironic that the Japanese considered the Draft Understanding an American proposal, as it was a product of the joint efforts of Walsh, Drought, Japanese financier Ikawa Sadao, and Colonel Iwakuro Hideo, assistant chief of the military affairs section of the Japanese War Ministry.

92. See notes of the 20th and 21st liaison conferences on 22 April and 3 May 1941 in Nobutaka Ike (trans. and ed.), *Japan's Decision for War: Records of the 1941 Policy Conferences* (Stanford, Calif: Stanford University Press, 1967), pp. 19–27. Also see Feis, pp. 193–95; Giffard, p. 113; Nish, pp. 243–44; Yanaga, p. 593.

93. Feis, p. 194; Ike, pp. 27–28.

94. See Hull's memorandum of the 11 May 1941 meeting with Nomura in PWUSFP, pp. 653–56.

95. In the oral explanation, Tokyo specified Konoe's three principles to be: 1) neighborly friendship; 2) joint defense against communism; and 3) economic cooperation. It further stated that these principles imply a mutual respect for sovereign territories without annexation or indemnities; but it also referred to "the inherent characteristics of each nation for cooperation as good neighbors and forming a Far Eastern nucleus contributing to world peace."

96. See the draft proposal Nomura delivered to Hull on 13 May 1941 in PWUSFP, pp. 656–59.

97. Ike, p. 43.

98. See Ike, p. 34.

99. Between May 12 and June 21, the United States and Japan also exchanged unofficial draft proposals as they worked at clarifying the issues between them.

100. Draft proposal Hull handed to Nomura on 21 June 1941 in PWUSFP, pp. 677–83.

101. See notes of the 29th, 30th, and 31st liaison conferences held on 11, 12, and 16 June 1941 in Ike, pp. 47–56. Also see Bix, pp. 394–95; Borton, p. 420; Feis, p. 207.

102. See Bix, pp. 399–400; and notes of the 32nd, 33rd, 34th, 35th, 36th, and 37th liaison conferences held on 25, 26, 27, and 28 June and 1 July 1941 in Ike, pp. 56–77.

103. See notes of the imperial conference of 2 July 1941 in Ike, pp. 77–90.

104. Bix, p. 400.

105. Bix, p. 400; Borton, p. 421; Coox, p. 328; Feis, pp. 224–25; Giffard, p. 114; Nish, pp. 244–45; Storry, pp. 209–10; Yanaga, p. 595.

106. Cordell Hull was ill and recuperating at a health resort in White Sulphur Springs, West Virginia.

107. Welles's 23 July 1941 memorandum of conversation with Nomura in PWUSFP, pp. 693–97.

108. See Welles's 24 July 1941 memorandum of a meeting between Roosevelt and Nomura in the Oval Office in PWUSFP, pp. 699–703.

109. Ibid. Welles said that after hearing Roosevelt's offer, Nomura " . . . made some statement which was not quite clear to the effect that such a step would be very difficult at this time on account of the face-saving element involved on the part of Japan and that only a very great statesman would reverse a policy at this time."

110. PWUSFP, p. 127.

111. Within a week, Britain, the Dominions, India, Burma, and the Colonies issued orders parallel to the American freeze. See Bix, pp. 401–3; Feis, pp. 236–50; PWUSFP, pp. 126–27.

112. Ironically, Hull and Roosevelt did not intend to stop oil exports to Japan completely—they meant to use licensing to regulate the flow, only prohibiting the shipment of certain grades of fuel. However, for nearly a month, while Hull was recuperating in White Sulphur Springs, hard-liners in the State Department sat on Tokyo's license requests. When Hull and Roosevelt discovered what had happened, they decided they could not then resume any amount of oil exports without appearing to concede to Japanese demands. See Feis, pp. 242–50.

113. Bix pp. 401–2; Feis, pp. 251–52; Herzog, p. 174.

114. Bix, pp. 403–4; Feis, 252–53.

115. See the oral statement and proposal Nomura handed to Welles on 6 August 1941 in PWUSFP, pp. 705–7.

116. PWUSFP, p. 128.

117. See the 8 August 1941 memorandum of a conversation between Hull and Nomura and the 8 August 1941 American response to Japan's 6 August 1941 proposal in PWUSFP, pp. 707–10.

118. PWUSFP, p. 111.

119. Ike, p. 129.

120. See Hull's memorandum of the 17 August 1941 meeting with Roosevelt and Nomura, including the texts of two statements by Roosevelt to Japan, in PWUSFP, pp. 712–17.

121. Konoe's 27 August 1941 letter to Roosevelt in PWUSFP, pp. 721–22.

122. Roosevelt's 3 September 1941 oral statement to Nomura and the accompanying letter from Roosevelt to Konoe in PWUSFP, pp. 729–32.

123. Bix, p. 409.

124. Feis, pp. 266–67; Ike, p. 133. Bix argues that Hirohito was mainly concerned that military leaders were rushing to war before adequate preparations were in place. He further asserts that the emperor could have avoided war at this point, but chose not to. See Bix, pp. 409–12.

125. Borton, pp. 421–22; Feis, pp. 266–67; Ike, pp. 133–34; Yanaga p. 597.

126. Feis, pp. 271–81; Ike, pp. 167–76.

127. Borton, p. 422; Feis, p. 277; Ike, p. 181; Storry p. 212.

128. Bix, p. 417; Borton, p. 422; Ike, p. 184; Yanaga, p. 598.

129. Ike, p. 185.

130. Ibid., pp. 184–85.

131. See notes of the 59th, 60th, 61st, 62nd, and 63rd liaison conferences held on 23, 24, 25, 27, and 28 October 1941 in Ike, pp. 184–96.

132. See notes of the 65th liaison conference held on 30 October 1941 in Ike, pp. 196–99.

133. See notes of the 66th liaison conference and the imperial conferences held on 1 and 5 November 1941 in Ike, pp. 199–239. Also see Bix, p. 421.

134. Bix, p. 224–25; Coox, p. 337; Feis, p. 303–9; Herzog, pp. 198–202.

135. Grew's 3 November 1941 telegram to Hull in PWUSFP, pp. 772–75.

136. Grew's 17 November 1941 telegram to Hull in PWUSFP, pp. 788–89.

137. Unfortunately, Tokyo never transmitted the date and location of the attack to its diplomats abroad, as that was such a closely guarded secret that even cabinet ministers were not told. See notes of the 29 November 1941 liaison conference in Ike, pp. 260–62. Also see pp. Bix, 427–28; Borton, p. 428 n. 17; Feis, pp. 308–9; Herzog, pp. 202–4.

138. Coox, pp. 337–38; Feis; pp. 309–10.

139. Though some historians point out that Hull submitted this note as a "strictly confidential, tentative, and uncommitted" proposal, Japanese leaders interpreted it for what it was, a de facto termination of negotiations. See Coox, p. 338.

140. Bix, pp. 428–29; Borton, p. 424; Coox, p. 338; Giffard, pp. 118–19; Herzog, pp. 207–10; PWUSFP, pp. 142–44; Yanaga, p. 601.

141. Bix, p. 430.

142. Coox, pp. 338–39; Ike, p. 257.

143. Bix, pp. 431–33.

144. Notes of the imperial conference of 1 December 1941 in Ike, pp. 262–83. Also see Feis, pp. 230–31.

145. See Roosevelt's 6 December 1941 telegram to Hirohito in PWUSFP, pp. 829–31.

146. Coox, p. 340; Feis, pp. 337 and 341; Herzog, pp. 222–26.

147. Coox, pp. 341–42.

148. Thomas C. Schelling, *Arms and Influence* (New Haven, Conn.: Yale University Press, 1966), pp. 36–55.

149. For a thorough discussion on salami tactics, see Schelling, pp. 66–69.

150. Ironically, instances of Japanese aggression during the first half of the decade were, in fact, examples of the Kwangtung Army using salami tactics against its own civilian government and even against the Army General Staff in Tokyo. Only after the army's *Tosei* faction got control of the government was this stratagem sanctioned and codified as part of a deliberate expansion strategy.

151. See notes of the 59th liaison conference held on 24 October 1941, in Ike, p. 186.

152. Notes of the 6 September 1941 imperial conference in Ike, p. 153.

153. Bix, pp. 411–12.

154. Robert J. C. Butow, *Tojo and the Coming of the War* (Princeton, N.J.: Princeton University Press, 1961), pp. 267 and 267 n. 6 and n. 7.

155. Notes of the 65th liaison conference held on 30 October 1941, in Ike, pp. 196–99.

156. Ibid., p. 199.

157. Batavia sought a similar commitment from Washington and was also unsuccessful.

158. Notes of the 1 December 1941 imperial conference in Ike, pp. 281–82.

159. Ibid., p. 283.

160. Masao Maruyama, "The Ideology and Dynamics of Japanese Fascism," in Masao Maruyama, *Thought and Behavior in Modern Japanese Politics*, translated and edited by Ivan Morris (Oxford: Oxford University Press, 1963), p. 34.

161. This confusion of attitudes was largely the result of the fusion of spiritual and political authority in the person of the emperor that occurred in the Meiji Restoration. In previous times, political power rested in the *bakufu* (the shogun's administrative government) while spiritual sovereignty resided in the emperor. Subjects living in the feudal *han* (fiefs) came to distrust and resent *bakufu* authorities, but they unfailingly revered the emperor. When the Restoration united the two sources of authority, many Japanese transferred their feelings of resentment to the Imperial bureaucracy and to the "cities" in general, but continued to endorse the notion of centralizing more and more power in the person of the emperor.

162. Maruyama, pp. 36–51.

163. See Roger F. Hackett, "Political Modernization and the Meiji *Genro*" in Robert E. Ward (ed.), *Political Development in Modern Japan* (Princeton, N.J.: Princeton University Press, 1968), pp. 72 and 91.

164. Hackett, pp. 65–98; Nish, pp. 62–64.

165. For more on parochialism in Imperial Japanese agencies, see Masao Maruyama, "The Theory and Psychology of Ultra-Nationalism" and "Thought and Behavior Patterns of Japan's Wartime Leaders," in *Thought and Behavior in Modern Japanese Politics*, translated by Ivan Morris, pp. 14–16 and 123–24.

166. Maruyama, "The Ideology and Dynamics of Japanese Fascism," pp. 27–28.

167. Borton, p. 370. Kita's *General Outline for the Reconstruction of Japan*, published in 1924, is often called the *Mein Kampf* of Japanese fascism. Over the next dozen years, Kita was involved, directly or indirectly, in a number of plots and coup attempts. He was finally executed in 1936 for his involvement in the February Incident, the revolt of *Kodo ha* sympathizers in the army.

168. Borton, pp. 369–71; Crowley, p. 94; Yanaga, p. 492.

169. Giffard, p. 88.

170. See "Fundamentals of Our National Polity," in Bernard S. Silberman (ed.), *Japanese Character and Culture: A Book of Selected Readings* (Tucson, Ariz.: The University of Arizona Press, 1962).

171. Maruyama, "Theory and Psychology of Ultranationalism," p. 3.

172. Ibid., pp. 3–6.

173. This is an excerpt from General Araki Sadao's *The Spirit of Soldiers in the Emperor's Land*, cited in Maruyama, "Theory and Psychology of Ultra-nationalism," p. 8.

174. Excerpted from Foreign Minister Arita Hachiro's 29 June 1940 radio broadcast, cited in Feis, p. 64. Also see Takeshi Ishida, *Japanese Political Culture: Change and Continuity* (New Brunswick, N.J.: Transaction Books, 1983), pp. 93 and 98; Maruyama, "Theory and Psychology of Ultra-nationalism," pp. 8–9; Yanaga, p. 541.

175. For instance, see Beasley, p. 204; Feis, p. 282.

176. An exception, of course, is when Konoe sided with military leaders, over the objections of Foreign Minister Matsuoka, in support of the push into southern Indochina. But, once again, this illustrates the Japanese leader's role as consensus builder, even if he personally disagrees with the decision. Matsuoka's removal also demonstrates the fate of Japanese decision makers who persist in bucking the tide of consensus.

177. This description of policy development and functions of the liaison conference and imperial conference is drawn largely from the introduction in Ike, pp. xiii–xxvi.

178. Pulitzer Prize winning historian Herbert Bix has unearthed numerous records documenting Hirohito's intimate involvement in the policy making process, deflating arguments from other historians that the emperor was merely a figurehead or was unaware of policy developments before the final products were presented to him in imperial conferences. See this material in Bix, *Hirohito and the Making of Modern Japan*.

179. For a thorough, balanced assessment of Hirohito's role in decision making during the interwar years, see Peter Weltzer, *Hirohito and War: Imperial Tradition and Military Decision Making in Prewar Japan* (Honolulu: University of Hawaii Press, 1998).

180. Konoe had concluded that the difficulty in reaching an understanding with Roosevelt was due to their inability to communicate effectively from a distance. In Japan, communication between individuals is much more than a verbal articulation of ideas. It is an elaborate ritual in which nuances are expressed through subtle gestures and facial expressions. Konoe believed that if he could just talk with the president face to face, he could communicate effectively enough to settle the most crucial differences between the two countries.

CHAPTER 6

The Surrender of Japan

By almost every measure, Japan was militarily defeated by the end of 1944. Following an impressive series of victories in early 1942, the imperial advance ground to a halt as America's military and industrial might came to bear. With victory in the Battle of Midway, the initiative in the Pacific war passed to the United States. Japan's military forces continued to fight courageously, but, forced to defend a far-flung island empire, they were beaten in one encounter after another. In the June, 1944, Battle of the Philippine Sea, Japanese air and sea power was badly crippled, and the Imperial Navy was all but eliminated in a repeat engagement four months later. By the end of the year, *guerre de course* by American submarines and mines had devastated Japan's merchant shipping, cutting her supply of food and strategic resources, and long-range, heavy bombers of the Air Force's XXI Bomber Command were hammering cities on the empire's home islands at will.

The collapse of Japan's defensive perimeter spurred political changes in Tokyo. After nearly three years in office, Prime Minister Tojo Hideki resigned and General Koiso Kuniaki replaced him in July, 1944. With the American invasion of Okinawa the following April, that government also folded and the imperial mandate fell on retired Admiral Suzuki Kantaro. As Japan's prospects turned grim, a growing number of Japanese leaders became convinced that the war should end, and a peace faction quietly formed and gained strength inside and outside the government. For his part, Prime Minister Suzuki first believed Japan could fight on for two or three more years, but as he learned more about the strategic situation, he too concluded that Japan must soon sue for peace. But military leaders were adamant. Though many were resolved to the fact that Japan had lost the war, they were determined to fight one last battle for the home islands and repel the Allied invasion or, at least, inflict enough casualties on the enemy to force Washington to grant terms permitting Japan to retain its honor.

Indeed, the question of America's peace terms was a pivotal issue in Japan's decision to surrender. Military leaders insisted that Japan could not permit Allied forces to occupy their homeland, disarm their military services, try Japanese authorities as war criminals, or do anything that would violate the emperor's sovereign authority. As the strategic situation darkened, peace advocates became convinced that the Supreme Command's insistence on retaining control of the homeland and its defenses was unrealistic, and they realized the military's plan for a final, all-out battle was suicidal. Yet, even they were unwilling to surrender Japan to the Allies without assurances that the imperial dynasty would be preserved.

Allied leaders offered no such encouragement. From January, 1943, Franklin Roosevelt and Winston Churchill had resolved that Japan, along with Germany and Italy, must be forced to accept unconditional surrender. They formalized that policy in the Cairo Declaration later that November and remained true to its provisions throughout the war. In March, 1945, American military leaders intensified their efforts to compel Japan's submission by converting the aerial bombardment campaign from high explosive bombs to incendiaries, burning Japan's 66 largest cities and killing several hundred thousand people over the next five months. In the meantime, Germany was finally and thoroughly defeated during the first two weeks of May. Okinawa fell on June 22 at a cost of more than 12,000 American and 110,000 Japanese lives. Still, Japan did not surrender, though Tokyo did attempt to enlist Moscow's help in mediating a compromise settlement.

On August 6, an American B-29 dropped an atomic bomb on Hiroshima, destroying a major part of the city and killing about 70,000 people. Two days later, the Soviet Union issued a declaration of war and launched a combined arms assault into Manchuria, crashing through the lines of what remained of the once-proud Kwangtung Army. On August 9, the United States dropped a second atomic bomb, this time on Nagasaki, killing another 40,000 people and wounding as many more.

Following this sequence of events, Japanese leaders finally decided they must end the war, yet they could not agree on what, if any, conditions to attach to their acceptance of the Allied demand for surrender. When the debate extended into the early morning hours of August 10, Emperor Hirohito intervened and directed them to surrender with the sole condition that imperial sovereignty be preserved. That decision was transmitted to the United States by radio and via Swiss and Swedish intermediaries, but was rejected the following day. Meanwhile, the American military resumed conventional strategic bombing with a greater intensity than ever before. With Washington's rejection of Tokyo's bid for a conditional surrender, Japanese military leaders returned to their insistence that Japan remain free of occupation and forced disarmament. Once more the debate about how to end the war reached a deadlock, and once more the emperor intervened to settle the issue. On August 14, 1945, Japan finally transmitted its unconditional surrender to the United States.

The difficulty Allied leaders experienced in compelling Japan to surrender has caused considerable debate in the decades following the war. Many studies have sought to determine which variable was most instrumental in persuading Japanese leaders to give up. Contending theories offer such factors as the atomic bomb, conventional strategic bombing, the interdiction campaign, Soviet entry into the war, and the threat of imminent invasion as competing explanations for changes in Japanese behavior.[1] While such debate is certainly important, what may be more interesting, at least from a perspective of strategic culture, is not why the Japanese surrendered when they did, but why they did not surrender much earlier.

Why did Japan resist American efforts to compel her surrender for so long? They had clearly lost the war by the beginning of 1945. Efforts to prolong it only promised to erode Japan's strategic situation, further reducing what little bargaining power she may have had. Granted, the Allies were demanding unconditional surrender, a price for peace that no Japanese was willing to pay. But why didn't Japanese leaders at least try to open negotiations with Washington much earlier than they did? Why did they wait until they were virtually prostrate at the feet of the Allied military machine before trying to arrange terms and, even then, attempt to negotiate only through mediators? Other questions come to mind. After the surrender, some Japanese officials claimed the emperor wanted to end the war months, if not years, before he did. If that is true, why did he not speak up? Popular wisdom suggests that Imperial Japan had come to resemble its feudal forebear—that is, Hirohito had become a puppet of a military oligarchy and feared opposing it. But if that was the case, how could he stand up when he did, and why did military leaders obey his command to surrender? More recent scholarship suggests the emperor was an active participant in Japan's wartime decision-making process, and one prominent historian has even characterized him as a "fighting generalissimo," controlling if not personally directing Japan's military operations.[2] If such a portrait is accurate, why did Emperor Hirohito not stop the war before so many of his subjects died in vain?

In this chapter I examine events leading to the end of the Pacific war, focusing on the political developments that finally led to Japan's surrender. I demonstrate how the punishment- and denial-based solutions so frequently cited fail to adequately explain Japanese behavior during the final year of the war, and I show that balance-of-interest based explanations are even more deficient. Only when we evaluate the words and deeds of Japan's leaders in terms of their own strategic culture can we fully appreciate why they resisted American attempts to compel their surrender for so long and why they finally gave up when they did.

THE COLLAPSE OF AN EMPIRE

By early 1943, a growing number of people in and out of government in Tokyo were coming to believe Japan should find a way to end the war. Imperial forces were on the defensive in the Pacific, and with Germany's defeat at Stalingrad, the tide of war in Europe had clearly turned against Berlin, on whom Tokyo had staked its fortunes. But finding a diplomatic way out of the conflict would be no easy matter. As the nation was at war, foreign policy was not in the hands of the Foreign Ministry, but under control of the Supreme Command, and they saw the situation differently.[3] Army leaders maintained that the Russo-German struggle would eventually turn into a stalemate. This would prolong the European war, giving Japan time to fortify her position in the occupied territories. As the war proceeded, Britain and the United States would suffer ever-greater shipping losses, succumb to war weariness, and eventually, sue for peace.[4] Some navy officials were not so sanguine about Japan's ability to hold out while waiting for the Allies to tire of the war, but the army, backed by a group of navy hawks, dominated both the Supreme Command and the civilian government.[5] With General Tojo Hideki serving simultaneously as prime minister, war minister, and home minister, most Japanese were careful not to be heard saying anything that might suggest they did not fully support the war effort.[6]

Nevertheless, former prime minister Prince Konoe Fumimaro felt Tojo was leading Japan down a ruinous path, and he quietly and cautiously began talking to other influential people about what they might do about it. Konoe was convinced Japan was losing the war. Concerned that the social unrest that might accompany a military defeat would offer fertile ground for a communist uprising, he spoke to the empress's uncle, Prince Higashikuni, several times in 1942 and early 1943, trying to convince him of these dangers. Higashikuni expressed polite concern, but was noncommittal, so Konoe approached a couple of generals on the reserve list, Mazaki Jinzaburo and Obata Binshiro. Being *Kodo* faction officers purged from the army after the 1936 uprising, they readily agreed that Tojo, a *Tosei ha* leader, should be removed.[7] On the dubious strength of this backing, Konoe explained his concerns to Lord Keeper of the Privy Seal Kido Koichi and told him there was growing opposition to Tojo among political leaders and businessmen.[8] Kido had also become uneasy about directions the war was taking, and he was always alert for indications that domestic strife might threaten the monarchy, so he agreed to relay Konoe's concerns to the emperor. However, nothing came of this overture. Kido and Hirohito discussed the situation at length, but while the emperor, too, was disturbed about Japan's recent defeats and Germany's reverses in Europe, neither he nor the privy seal thought it wise to remove Tojo, the one man who seemed able to maintain unity between the army, navy, and government.[9]

Blunted in this gambit, Konoe set out to build an anti-Tojo faction within the *jushin* (senior statesmen), the body of former prime ministers who met when called upon to advise the emperor on subsequent prime-ministerial appointments. Unlike the *genro* (elder statesmen) whom they had replaced, the *jushin* had never attained the power to coordinate governmental activities, or even to advise the emperor on a regular basis; nonetheless, given the severity of the crisis that now confronted Japan, Konoe decided to work through this narrow avenue, available to him as a former prime minister, for influencing the throne. Ultimately, he hoped to maneuver the *jushin* into a position where it might influence the government as well. With that in mind, Konoe began secretly meeting with three other senior statesmen—Baron Hiranuma Kiichiro, Okada Keisuke, and Baron Wakatsuki Reijiro—and they began a series of discussions about the war situation and what might lie ahead for Japan. They soon agreed that the future looked grim—Tojo had set Japan on a dangerous course, one that could only be rectified by replacing him with a prime minister who might govern the nation in a more responsible manner. Unfortunately, given the general's political strength, that seemed an unlikely possibility in the near future. In the meantime, the *jushin* decided they would try to begin the process of political change by seeding the Tojo cabinet with ministers sensitive to their concerns.[10]

At first, they met with little success. Firmly entrenched in power, Prime Minister Tojo resisted Admiral Okada's bid to replace Navy Minister Admiral Shimada Shigataro with the more liberal Admiral Yonai Mitsumasa.[11] But as the strategic situation continued to deteriorate, Tojo became somewhat more responsive to the growing insistence that he "reorganize his cabinet in order to prosecute the war more effectively." In April, 1943, he conceded to appeals from the *jushin* and appointed the moderate Shigemitsu Mamaru as foreign minister.[12] Yet, this change had no effect on Japanese policy. In fact, Tojo consolidated his power in February, 1944, by dismissing Army Chief of Staff General Sugiyama and adding that post to his own portfolio while, simultaneously, having his navy minister, Admiral Shimada, dismiss Admiral Nagano and appoint himself as Navy Chief of Staff.[13] With the army and its pro-Tojo supporters evermore firmly in control of the Supreme Command, Japan remained on the same strategic course as before. Meanwhile, the Allies continued to assault the crumbling defensive perimeter of the island empire.[14]

The Fall of Tojo

In June, 1944, Japan suffered several disastrous military setbacks. The Imperial Navy's crushing defeat in the Battle of the Philippine Sea and the simultaneous emasculation of Japanese air power in the "Great Marianas Turkey Shoot" ceded the United States nearly undisputed control of the sea and air in the western Pacific.[15] The fall of Saipan quickly followed, signaling the breach of Japan's inner line of defense and providing the Americans a site for building a base in the Mariana Islands from which B-29 heavy bombers could reach the Japanese homeland.[16]

All of this spelled ruin for the Tojo government. Army propaganda had consistently denied Japan was losing the war. Military leaders had concealed defeats whenever possible and explained those they could not deny as deliberate moves in a strategic master plan devised and controlled by the Supreme Command. But the June debacles exposed the bankruptcy of Tojo's policies to the rest of the government, if not to the public, and it revealed the magnitude of the crisis facing the nation. With the Diet set firmly against him and antagonism building in the armed services, the prime minister struggled to regain his footing by reorganizing his cabinet and attempting to forge an alliance with the *jushin.* But the senior statesmen refused to throw him a lifeline and, instead, closed ranks, unanimously declining Tojo's gratuitous invitation to accept ministerial posts in his reconstructed government. The general's cabinet finally fell on July 18, 1944, three days after the resignation of Navy Minister Shimada.[17]

Koiso and the Supreme Council for the Direction of the War

Later that afternoon, the *jushin* met to formulate their recommendation on who the emperor should appoint to be the next prime minister. Theirs was not an easy task. Tojo had led the nation to the brink of destruction, and Yonai openly expressed his misgivings about the prospect of placing another military leader at the helm of state. Yet the pro-war clique still held sway in the armed forces, and it carried a great deal of influence in the bureaucracy and among the public at large. For the new cabinet to stand, the emperor would have to appoint someone acceptable to both the army and the navy. Moreover, given the crisis at hand, the next premier would have to be thoroughly familiar with military issues. After a lengthy discussion, the senior statesmen finally decided to nominate another general, but still could not agree on who would be the most suitable candidate.[18] Ultimately, they gave Privy Seal Kido three names from which to choose: Marshal Terauchi Hisaichi, the army's commander in the Phil-

ers, eager to prove the efficacy of strategic bombing, that this campaign was having little effect on Japan's ability to wage war.[40]

Consequently, in March the XXI Bomber Command scaled back its effort to destroy Japanese factories with high explosive bombs and turned instead to firebombing urban centers from low altitudes at night. On March 9, the first large-scale raid created a raging inferno that incinerated almost 16 square miles of Tokyo, killing more than 83,000 people and injuring 41,000 more.[41] Over the next five months, American B-29s dropped 104,000 tons of incendiaries, destroying an average of 40 percent of Japan's 66 largest cities.[42]

With Japan's cities being incinerated and her defensive perimeter collapsing, Koiso grew desperate to find a way out of Japan's strategic dilemma. This desperation may have clouded his judgment when he seized what he thought was an opportunity to readjust the balance of power in Asia. In mid-March he was contacted by Miao Pin, a Chinese who claimed to be a confidential emissary from Chiang Kai-shek. On Koiso's invitation, Miao traveled from Shanghai to Tokyo to present a proposition, purportedly from the Chungking government, that if Japan would withdraw from China and abandon the Nanking regime, Chiang would pull out of the Anglo-American alliance and cooperate with Japan against the communists. But Koiso's foray into diplomacy became his undoing. Both the Supreme Command and Foreign Minister Shigemitsu suspected Miao Pin was a fraud, and no one in the government was willing to grant him a hearing.[43] After several days, he returned to Shanghai empty handed, and Koiso, having argued fruitlessly for Japan to accept the "Chinese offer," was made to look the fool before his colleagues. With the Koiso government teetering, the United States provided the final shove on April 1 with the invasion of Okinawa. Koiso Kuniaki resigned on April 4, 1945.[44]

Suzuki Answers the Call

The *jushin* met the following day to determine who to nominate to be the next prime minister. As Tojo was now a senior statesman, he attended the meeting and quickly became an aggressive presence, insisting they should first decide whether Japan was to surrender or fight to the finish, then select a leader on that basis. He preferred they choose a general on the active list. But after a long discussion, the *jushin* decided that, in this time of crisis, the most important criterion in the selection of a new government should be its ability to win the confidence of the people. On Konoe's urging, they also agreed that the next prime minister should be free of any commitments or alignments from the past, and though he may be a military man, he could be from the retired list. With those criteria in mind, Baron Hiranuma nominated the aged president of the privy council, retired Admiral Suzuki Kantaro.[45] The other statesmen enthusiastically agreed.[46]

Admiral Suzuki had an impeccable reputation. A hero of the Russo-Japanese war, he was popular with the people, well liked by every major group in government, and a favorite of the emperor. The admiral was known to be a man of integrity and was fiercely loyal to the throne; but, at nearly 80 years of age, he had no experience in politics and was almost deaf. For these reasons, Suzuki tried to convince Marquis Kido that he was not up to the job. Kido turned his protests aside saying, "Japan's situation has become so critical that I, as lord keeper of the privy seal, must implore you to make a firm decision to save the nation."[47] While Kido's profession of confidence momentarily inspired the admiral, later that evening he demurred again, this time before the throne. But the emperor's mind was made up. After patiently hearing Suzuki out, Hirohito simply said, "Your unfamiliarity with politics is of no concern, nor does it matter that you are hard of hearing. Therefore, accept this command."[48] Suzuki Kantaro was now prime minister of the crumbling Japanese empire.[49]

Acutely aware of his political inexperience, Suzuki immediately consulted Kido and several of the *jushin* about who he should choose to fill his cabinet. On their advice, he retained peace advocate Yonai Mitsumasa as navy minister. However, instead of following Kido's guidance and reappointing Foreign Minister Shigemitsu, another member of the peace faction, Suzuki called on his close friend, Togo Shigenori, the man who had served as Tojo's foreign minister in late 1941 and early 1942.[50]

As Togo was known to have opposed the war, Kido decided he was a reasonable alternative to Shigemitsu; but when Suzuki approached the old diplomat, Togo hesitated. Before he could accept an appointment in Suzuki's government, Togo explained, he must first know what Suzuki thought Japan's chances were of continuing the war. In the course of a long discussion, Suzuki said he thought Japan could fight on for another two or three years. With that, Togo surprised his old friend by explaining that he feared Japan would be unable to continue fighting for even one more year, and, as there was such a difference in their opinions, he doubted they could achieve the mutual cooperation needed to work together. Therefore, he politely declined to join the Suzuki cabinet.[51]

Startled by this response, Suzuki proposed they talk again the following day. In the meantime, several influential peace advocates visited the former foreign minister, urging him to reconsider his decision, as the old admiral was uninformed on the strategic situation and needed guidance from someone reliable. As a result, Togo reluctantly met with Suzuki again and, in the course of another long discussion, convinced the prime minister to accept his arguments regarding Japan's prospects in the war. Moreover, the prime minister promised to grant Togo the freedom to seek peace, should an opportunity arise. With that assurance, Togo accepted the appointment.[52]

But despite his promise to Togo, Suzuki must have known that he lacked the freedom to chart any dramatically different direction in strategic policy. For his government to stand, the army had to provide a general on the active list to serve as war minister, and though the general staff offered Suzuki a capable and respected candidate, General Anami Korechika, their official approval only came with stringent conditions. Suzuki had to promise outgoing War Minister Sugiyama that the new cabinet would settle army-navy coordination problems, reorganize the nation for greater military effectiveness, and prosecute the war to the bitter end.[53] The prime minister may have had these commitments in mind on April 7, 1945, when he publicly announced the formation of his government and promised to give his life in Japan's defense, saying:

Now I stand at the head of the gallant nation, confident that though I fall at this my last post of service, all you people, a hundred million strong, will march over my lifeless body to overcome the unprecedented crisis that confronts our fatherland . . . . we must unite as one man and concentrate all effort on dealing the enemy a decisive blow. History has taught us that great nations do not always win, nor do small nations invariably lose, but whenever a small state has defeated a larger nation it has been by holding out to the last.[54]

Despite his tough rhetoric, Suzuki's behavior soon afterwards suggests he was less than certain about the wisdom of fighting to the bitter end. Whether influenced by Togo's arguments or simply sensitive about his lack of preparation for the job, one of Suzuki's first acts as prime minister was to order Chief Cabinet Secretary Sakomizu Hisatsune to conduct a thorough study to determine whether Japan's fighting abilities were sufficient to continue the war. Once completed, the findings testified that Japan was on the verge of national collapse, and Suzuki dutifully presented the report to the emperor.[55] However, the study was not finished until mid-May; in the meantime, newly appointed War Minister Anami had 400 people arrested, including a former ambassador to England, on suspicion of harboring "end-the-war sentiments."[56] Japan was still a long way from surrender.

Germany's Surrender Fuels Japanese Desperation

Soon after Suzuki took office, Privy Seal Kido funneled a flood of bad news to the emperor. The latest military reports suggested the situation in Okinawa looked hopeless; it was just a matter of time before Japanese resistance there collapsed. The naval situation was equally grim. For all practical purposes, what remained of the Japanese fleet was out of fuel, yet American aircraft continued to sink the idle ships wherever they were found in harbor. Meanwhile, food was growing scarce in the home islands, the air bombardment was intensifying, and, though army leaders continued to profess their faith in a climactic victory against an Allied invasion, reports reaching the emperor convinced him that the forces being prepared to meet that invasion were inadequately equipped. Then, on May 8, 1945, word reached Japan that Germany had surrendered. The war in Europe was over.[57]

Disastrous as this news was for Japan, it had no effect on the face Tokyo chose to show the world. On May 3, Suzuki attempted to prepare the Japanese public for Germany's imminent defeat with a statement insisting that "the changing situation in Europe," would only intensify Japan's commitment to prosecute the Pacific war to a successful conclusion. Adding that this changing situation had "in no respect been unexpected" by those in the Japanese government, he said he wanted "to take this opportunity to make known once again at home and abroad [his] faith in certain victory."[58] Six days later Tokyo responded to the news of Germany's surrender with a declaration that Japan would not change her national policy in the slightest way as her war aims were based on "self existence and self defense."[59]

Nevertheless, Germany's collapse did trigger subtle but important changes in the attitudes of Japanese leaders and the processes they used to make national policy. On May 11, 1945, the Supreme Council for the Direction of the War began a series of meetings to discuss the latest developments in the war situation. However, unlike meetings held in the past, attendance at these sessions was limited to the six principal members of the council—the premier; his foreign, war, and navy ministers; and the two military chiefs of staff.[60] The vice-ministers, vice-chiefs, and the many junior officers who made up the secretariat were excluded, and the proceedings were not disclosed to them.[61] In the relative safety of this confidential setting, the council began to openly discuss, for the first time, the possibility that, with Germany having been defeated, Japan might have to seek terms to end the war.[62]

But though the "Big Six" decision makers soon reached a general consensus that the war was lost, they still could not agree on how to end it. Togo wanted to sue for peace as soon as possible, and he scolded the others for not having opened negotiations through the Soviet Union before Germany's defeat. War Minister Anami, on the other hand, insisted that Tokyo not enter talks without first having achieved some success on the battlefield, as Japan would be forced to accept peace on humiliating terms. Togo warned that Japan would have to make substantial concessions in any case and even suggested that the empire might have to relinquish northern Manchuria to the Soviets and return to its pre-Russo-Japanese war boundaries. Nevertheless, Anami was adamant—Japan could not negotiate from a position of weakness. She must deal the Americans a costly blow before asking Moscow to mediate terms to end the war. With the foreign minister and war minister at an impasse on when to open negotiations, the Supreme Council decided, at least, to move in a direction in which they were all agreed. They would court the Russians in hopes of preventing the Soviet Union from entering the war against Japan.[63]

To that end, Togo asked a former prime minister and one-time ambassador to Moscow, Hirota Koki, to open a dialogue with Soviet Ambassador Jacob A. Malik.[64] Hirota enthusiastically agreed and contrived a "chance encounter" with the Russian on June 3 that led to a dinner engagement the following day. Over dinner Hirota expressed his personal, pro-Russian sympathies and asserted that all of Japan wanted improved relations between their two countries. Malik countered, saying Moscow had always believed the Japanese people were generally hostile towards the Soviet Union. He asked if Hirota's advance was an official representation from his government or simply his own opinions. Hirota said his words reflected the opinions of both his government and the Japanese people. Malik seemed unconvinced. He said that before they could proceed any further, he would have to consult with his superiors who would want to study the situation thoroughly. In other words, Hirota and the Japanese would have to wait on Moscow's response.[65]

Meanwhile, Japan's policy-making apparatus proceeded under its own momentum. Closed out of the Supreme Council's top-level discussions, the radical young officers at General Staff Headquarters developed their own "Fundamental Policy to be Followed Henceforth in the Conduct of the War." On June 6, 1945, the army called a full meeting of the Supreme Council to present the plan.[66] The Fundamental Policy was nothing short of a "fire-and-brimstone" call for "Japan's 'one hundred million' people, ever steadfast in their loyalty to their imperial father through all eternity, [to] arise together from the vantage ground of their sacred land to strike the invaders dead."[67] It was a brazen statement that the army and navy general staffs expected Japan to fight to the very last man, woman, and child, rather than surrender.[68] Togo argued vehemently against this official endorsement of national suicide; yet, though the Big Six had already privately agreed that the war was lost, no one else in the Supreme Council spoke out. Ultimately, the plan was accepted by consensus and presented to the Imperial Conference two days later where a silent and sullen emperor sanctioned it by his mere presence.[69]

Kido Acts to Save the Nation

The Fundamental Policy did not stand unchallenged. When Privy Seal Kido saw details of the suicidal plan, he realized he must act to save the nation and his sovereign. Embarking on a course that was not only un-precedented in his country's history, but completely contrary to the Jap-anese policy-making process, Kido decided to write his own plan of action and try to convince the emperor to sanction it *before* seeking the govern-ment's consensus-dependent approval.[70]

That day, Kido sketched out a "Tentative Plan to Cope with the Situa-tion." Citing the general staff's own study, "The Present State of National Power," the privy seal frankly stated that Japan was about to lose Oki-nawa, and, by the latter half of the year, the nation's war-making potential would be exhausted. Given the enemy's overwhelming air superiority, Kido continued, he could be expected to expand the firebombing cam-paign to include even small towns and villages throughout the country. Winter would then bring untold suffering and public unrest that the gov-ernment might be unable to control.[71] Moreover, Kido reasoned,

As it is plain that the principal aim of the enemy powers is to bring about the downfall of the military clique, it is desirable that the army should request peace and that the government should shape policies accordingly, in order to open dip-lomatic negotiations. But it is also plain that, in the prevailing circumstances, this is entirely out of the question. Should we, however, wait idly until an opportunity for action presents itself, we would be too late and the maintenance of the imperial house and of our national structure [*kokutai*] would become altogether impossible. Consequently, we must now appeal to the throne for guidance in ending the war quickly.[72]

Having laid this foundation, Kido then outlined a course of action that he hoped would guide Japan out of the war. He proposed that the emperor send Moscow a personal message for delivery to the Allies. Insisting the throne had always been interested in peace, this message would state that the emperor had decided, "in view of the impossibly heavy war damages [Japan had] sustained, to bring the war to a close on very generous terms."[73] Japan's terms were to include giving up all occupied territory, reducing her armed forces to the minimum required for home defense, and, if the Allies demanded, allowing Japanese troops in the occupied areas to be disarmed before returning to the homeland.[74]

During the next several days, the privy seal moved to put his program into effect. On June 9, he presented the "Tentative Plan" to Emperor Hi-rohito and obtained the sovereign's blessing.[75] As Suzuki and Yonai were busy quelling a storm in the Diet, four days passed before they saw the document. Both ministers were startled by the unorthodox nature of re-ceiving a policy proposal already sanctioned by the throne, but after some initial hesitation, threw in their support. Two days later, Kido approached Foreign Minister Togo who first responded to the initiative enthusiasti-cally, then, more cautiously, agreed to study it carefully. However, when

Kido presented the plan to War Minister Anami on June 18, the general reacted stiffly, reminding the privy seal that the army was committed to fighting a decisive battle.[76] Anami said he appreciated and shared the emperor's desire to end the war, but he believed negotiations would go better after giving the enemy a terrible beating.[77]

Nevertheless, with the emperor's desire to end the war now in evidence, Suzuki called a secret session of the Supreme Council's Big Six on June 18 to consider what steps they might take to bring about peace. War Minister Anami—supported by Army Chief Umezu Yoshijiro and, to Yonai's surprise, Navy Chief Toyoda Soemu—continued to insist on fighting a decisive battle and maintained that Japan should not enter direct talks with the Allies until that battle was engaged. However, the three diehards did agree not to obstruct efforts to put the Kido plan into effect. Consequently, the Supreme Council resolved to ask Moscow to mediate a settlement with the United States and Britain. This time they would not circumscribe the talks by efforts to achieve a nonaggression treaty or renew the neutrality pact; they would focus on trying to get Soviet leaders to broker an end to the war. Further agreeing that the minimum basis for peace was preservation of the throne and *kokutai*, the Supreme Council set early July as the deadline for sounding out the Russians and late September as their target for reaching a settlement.[78]

The Quest for Russian Mediation

Acting on this decision, Togo visited former Prime Minister Hirota the following day and urged him to resume his talks with Ambassador Malik according to the new priorities set forth by the Big Six. Next, he went to the Imperial Palace where he reported the council's decision to pursue Russian mediation and informed the throne of the Hirota-Malik talks. In response, Emperor Hirohito said that recent reports had convinced him that "military preparations, in both China and Japan, were so extremely inadequate as to make it necessary to end the war without delay."[79] Therefore, he urged the foreign minister to expedite the Hirota talks and do everything in his power to stop the war as soon as possible.[80]

On June 22, 1945, American authorities announced the conclusion of the Okinawa campaign, and, at Kido's urging, Emperor Hirohito summoned the Big Six to an Imperial Conference of the Supreme Council. Departing from the usual formalities, the emperor opened the conference with a carefully worded statement. While acknowledging the June 8 decision to fight to the bitter end, Hirohito said that Japan's situation was rapidly deteriorating both at home and abroad; therefore, it was now necessary to consider other methods for coping with the national crisis. He asked the council if they had given this matter any thought. In response, Togo informed him, once again, of the council's June 18 endorsement of the Hirota-Malik talks, but admitted that that effort had yielded no results to date. The emperor then asked when actual negotiations would begin in the Soviet Union. Togo said the Japanese envoy should be in Moscow before Russian leaders left for the upcoming Allied conference at Potsdam. Then Togo sat down, and Emperor Hirohito asked the rest of the council for their opinions on this plan. Suzuki and Yonai endorsed it without qualification. Anami said he did not object to attempts to save the situation, but he felt Japan should not appear desperate to achieve peace at any price, as that would only expose her weakness. General Umezu also urged caution, saying Japan should not rush into negotiations blindly. At this, the emperor pointedly asked his army chief if being overly cautious might not cost Japan her opportunity for peace. Stinging from this rebuke, Umezu abruptly adjusted course and agreed that negotiations should begin at once. The emperor closed the meeting by saying he wanted to proceed with the plan. The June 8 decision to fight to the bitter end was, therefore, appended by this secret imperial mandate to seek Soviet mediation to end the war.[81]

But the Japanese encountered one difficulty after another in their effort to get Soviet mediation. On June 24, Hirota met with Ambassador Malik and tried, once more, to interest the Russian in opening formal talks with Tokyo. Unfortunately, instead of following Togo's instructions and seeking Soviet mediation to end the war, Hirota resumed his campaign to persuade Moscow to brace up Japan's dwindling strategic prospects, either by treaty or by supplying Japan oil in return for lead, rubber, and tin. Malik expressed no interest in either of these proposals and informed Hirota that unless Japan had something concrete to offer, he saw no need for any further discussions. Five days later, Hirota returned with a written offer to neutralize Manchuria, give up Japan's fishing rights in Soviet waters, and discuss anything else the Russians might want to bring up, if they would grant Japan a nonaggression treaty and sell her oil. Showing little interest, Malik said he would forward the proposal to Moscow and they could talk again later; however, every time Hirota called upon the Soviet ambassador thereafter, he was told the Russian was indisposed due to illness.[82]

As June turned to July, Japanese leaders realized Malik was a dead end. On July 7, prompted by Kido, Emperor Hirohito summoned Suzuki to express his anxiety over the fact that peace talks with the Russians had not yet begun.[83] The emperor urged his prime minister to send a personal envoy directly to Moscow to open negotiations.[84] At Togo's and Suzuki's suggestion, the Big Six chose Prince Konoe for the job, and on July 12 the emperor called the former prime minister in and officially sanctioned his mission. Granting him free reign to negotiate on Japan's behalf, he secretly told Konoe to accept any terms he could get short of unconditional surrender. Konoe eagerly accepted the assignment and swore to serve the emperor to the best of his abilities.[85]

Unfortunately, Konoe would never have the opportunity to carry out his mission. On Togo's instructions, Ambassador Sato Naotake attempted to meet with Soviet Foreign Commissar Vyacheslav Molotov on July 12 to ask the Russians to accept the Konoe visit.[86] Sato was told the foreign commissar was indisposed, due to his imminent departure for Potsdam; he was then shuffled off to speak to Vice Foreign Commissar Alexander Lozovsky instead. When Sato asked Lozovsky to receive the imperial envoy, the Russian was courteous and attentive, but said it was impossible for him to respond to the request, as Stalin and Molotov were unavailable for consultation. He promised to forward the message to them at Potsdam. Five days later the Soviets informed Sato that, as there was no concrete proposal in the Japanese request, the purpose of the special mission was unclear. Therefore, the Soviet Union could neither accept nor decline the visit without more information.[87] In response, Togo directed Sato to tell the Soviets that the purpose of the mission was to ask them to mediate an end to the war. Togo added that specifics would be provided by Konoe himself, but he told Sato to emphasize that Japan could not accept unconditional surrender. Indeed, "the Yamato race would be forced to fight on as one man if this enemy demand remained."[88]

Togo's new instructions reached Sato on July 24, and the following day he met with Lozovsky again. This time he clearly explained that the purpose of Konoe's mission would be to end the war. He said that Japan could not accept unconditional surrender, but Prince Konoe would come prepared to discuss what terms Japan could accept; and if the Russians were willing to broker an agreement, Tokyo would be very generous with Moscow. Once again, the commissar seemed encouraging but was noncommittal, and he remained so in subsequent meetings. Meanwhile, on July 26, 1945, Truman, Churchill, and Chiang Kai-shek released the Potsdam Declaration demanding that Japan surrender immediately or face imminent destruction. Though Japanese leaders could not bring themselves to face it, their bid for Russian mediation had failed.[89]

From Potsdam to Apocalypse

At 6:00 A.M. on the morning of July 26, 1945, listening posts in Japan picked up a San Francisco broadcast of the Postdam Declaration. Throughout the day, officials at the Foreign Ministry, the Supreme Command, and other offices in the Japanese government and imperial court studied its provisions in detail.[90] The proclamation opened on an encouraging note— it said the leaders of the United States, Britain, and China had conferred and agreed that Japan should be given an opportunity to end the war— but little else in the text gave Japanese leaders much comfort. Citing the devastation recently visited upon Germany, the Allies warned that the forces being assembled against Japan were immeasurably greater than those that had been used against the Nazis. The message said it was time for Japan to reject the leadership of the militarists and listen to reason. Then it listed the Allied terms that included occupation, forced disarmament, forfeiture of all territories outside the Japanese homeland, war crimes trials, and replacement of the present regime with a truly democratic government. The declaration closed with the following words: "We call upon the government of Japan to proclaim now the unconditional surrender of all Japanese armed forces and to provide proper and adequate assurances of their good faith in such action. The alternative for Japan is prompt and utter destruction."[91]

Despite the joint communiqué's harsh tone, peace advocates in Japan found reason for encouragement. Whereas the Cairo Declaration had demanded the unconditional surrender of Japan, the proclamation coming from Postdam called, instead, for the unconditional surrender of all the Japanese armed forces. Moreover, though Potsdam's terms were severe, the Allies' decision to include them in the message indicated there would, indeed, be terms of peace; Japan would not be treated with complete ruthlessness. In fact, Togo felt the proclamation's wording left considerable room for negotiation concerning the status of the throne and Japan's future government. As he noted that Stalin had not signed the declaration even though he and Molotov were in Potsdam for the Allied conference, Togo believed his hopes for Soviet mediation were still alive.[92]

When he explained these points to the emperor the following morning, Hirohito said he considered the Potsdam terms acceptable, at least, in principle. The foreign minister found this reaction encouraging, but he knew only too well that the Supreme Command would not be willing to discuss ending the war on the basis of the Potsdam Declaration. He was right.[93]

Later that morning the Supreme Council for the Direction of the War met to discuss the Allies' demands and determine an appropriate course of action. It was a heated session, as the declaration's abrupt and threatening language offended diehards and moderates alike. Anami and the military chiefs insisted the government issue a stern rejection of the Potsdam Declaration and reiterate that Japan intended to fight on to victory. However, Togo strongly opposed rejecting it out of hand. Still counting on Soviet mediation, he knew that openly rejecting the Allied overture would cut Japan's last thread of hope for a negotiated settlement. The foreign minister argued fervently against this course and finally managed to sway the council when Prime Minister Suzuki weighed in on his side saying they should simply *mokusatsu*, or "take no notice of it," while they waited for word from Moscow.[94]

Unfortunately, *mokusatsu* is an expression that can have varying shades of meaning, and, deliberately or inadvertently, the Japanese press reported the Supreme Council's decision in a different light than it was meant. Japanese leaders had decided simply to not respond to the Allied demand, at least, for the time being; but newspaper headlines on the morning of July 28 openly declared that the government intended to *mokusatsu* the Potsdam Declaration. Taken in this context, *mokusatsu* does not simply mean to "ignore" or "take no notice" of something. It means to "treat it with silent contempt!"[95]

Granted this opening, military diehards renewed their efforts to openly reject the Potsdam Declaration. In response to the July 28 press reports, General Staff Headquarters received a flood of messages from army field commanders insisting that, for the sake of troop morale, the government issue a stern rejection of the Allied terms. With pressure mounting from the general staff, Anami, Umezu, and Toyoda began lobbying Prime Minister Suzuki to change his stance on the Potsdam Declaration and deliver a strong statement against it. The issue came to a head that morning at a meeting between the Supreme Command and the government, held weekly to coordinate routine administrative affairs. Togo was unable to attend the session, and without his support, Suzuki and Yonai were exposed to the combined assault of the diehards and their attending staff officers. Predictably, the old admiral buckled. At a press conference held late in the afternoon on July 28, the prime minister responded to a pre-planned question about the Potsdam Declaration by reading the following statement, prepared for him by a committee of army and navy staff officers: "I consider the joint proclamation of the three Powers to be a rehash of the Cairo Declaration. The government does not regard it as a thing of any great value; the government will just *mokusatsu* it. We will press forward resolutely to carry the war to a successful conclusion."[96]

Finally given a definitive position from the government, editors at Japan's Domei News Agency translated the Suzuki statement into multiple foreign languages and broadcast it to the world. Within hours, American radio and newspapers were announcing that Japan had rejected the Potsdam Declaration. President Truman, who received the news while still in Germany, consequently, authorized the use of the atomic bomb.[97]

Meanwhile, Japanese leaders fell into a lull as they waited for a conclusive answer from Ambassador Sato as to whether Moscow would mediate negotiations with the Allies. On July 30, Lozovsky told the ambassador he would have to wait for Molotov's return from Potsdam to learn whether the Soviets would accept the Konoe mission. Finally, on August 7, two days after Molotov's return from Germany, the Russians notified Sato that he was scheduled to see the foreign commissar. His appointment was set at 5:00 P.M. (11:00 P.M. Tokyo time) on August 8.[98]

Three Strokes of Doom

At 8:16 A.M. on the morning of August 6, 1945,

... the Tokyo control operator of the Japan Broadcasting Corporation noticed that the Hiroshima station had gone off the air. About 20 minutes later the Tokyo railway telegraph center realized that the main telegraph had stopped working just north of Hiroshima. From some railway stops within ten miles of the city, there came unofficial and confused reports of a terrible explosion ... [99]

Details were slow in reaching the capital. Throughout the remainder of the day, reports continued to filter in that some small number of enemy planes had wreaked devastating damage to the city of Hiroshima. The next morning a regional military commander's report informed Army Vice Chief of Staff Kawabe Torashiro that, "the whole city of Hiroshima was destroyed instantly by a single bomb."[100] Immediately, the Supreme Command threw a blanket of censorship over information about the Hiroshima bombing and hastily flew a team of military investigators and scientists to the scene for a first-hand report. In the meantime, Japanese listening posts monitored President Truman's announcement that Hiroshima had been destroyed by an atomic bomb, and they delivered the details to government officials, along with the American threat that, unless they promptly surrendered, they could "expect a rain of ruin from the air, the like of which has never been seen on this earth ... "[101]

As civilian officials learned more about the bombing, they became increasingly convinced that the time had come to accept the terms laid out in the Potsdam Declaration. At noon on August 7, Privy Seal Kido informed Emperor Hirohito that the Americans had dropped an atomic bomb on Hiroshima inflicting about 130,000 casualties.[102] Overwhelmed with grief, the emperor said, "under these circumstances, we must bow to the inevitable. No matter what happens to my safety, we must put an end to this war as speedily as possible so that this tragedy will not be repeated."[103] Later that afternoon, Foreign Minister Togo briefed the cabinet on the Hiroshima situation. Quoting American radio reports regarding the type of weapon used, he concluded: "this drastically alters the whole situation and offers the military ample grounds for ending the war."[104] But War Minister Anami stridently disagreed, saying that such a move was uncalled for, as the investigation had not even confirmed that the attack had been made with an atomic weapon.[105]

On August 8, the peace faction began to move more assertively. Late that afternoon Togo briefed the emperor on Truman's explanation of what had happened in Hiroshima, and he gravely explained the American threat to destroy the rest of Japan. Oppressed by the enormity of the situation, the foreign minister then took liberty to emphasize the urgent necessity of immediately ending the war on the basis of the Potsdam Declaration. The emperor wholeheartedly agreed, adding " . . . Japan should not miss the chance for peace by vain efforts to secure better terms. . . . all efforts should be concentrated on ending the fighting quickly. Tell the prime minister my thinking."[106] Togo did so at once, and, on his urging, Suzuki tried to convene an immediate meeting of the Supreme Council. Unfortunately, some of the military members were unavailable, so the session was put off until the following morning.[107]

Before the meeting could begin, a second major calamity struck Japan. On the evening of August 8, Ambassador Sato fulfilled his appointment with Foreign Commissar Molotov, expecting to be told whether Prince Konoe would be allowed to visit Moscow to plead Japan's case for mediation. Instead, the commissar abruptly read Sato an official document that asserted, as Japan had rejected the Potsdam Declaration, the Soviet Union had no choice but to honor the requests of its allies. As of August 9, 1945, the Soviet Union would be at war with Japan. Stunned but composed, Sato asked if he could send a cable informing his superiors of the situation. Molotov assured him he could, but the message never reached Tokyo. Nevertheless, during the early morning hours of August 9, Japanese listening posts monitored Russian radio announcements of the declaration, and, by dawn in Tokyo, Soviet forces had already crashed through the Kwangtung Army's defensive lines in Manchuria.[108]

When Emperor Hirohito heard that the Soviet Union had declared war, he felt more strongly than ever that Japan must immediately accept the terms of the Potsdam Declaration. Acting through Privy Seal Kido, he asked Suzuki to convene the Supreme Council at once. Subsequently, the Big Six assembled at 10:30 A.M., and the prime minister opened the meeting by declaring that the recent catastrophic events had made it impossible to continue the war. The time had come, therefore, to decide whether to accept the Allied ultimatum of July 26.[109]

In the discussion that followed, it soon became evident that, though none of the Big Six were opposed, in principle, to complying with the Allied demand to surrender, they were evenly divided over what conditions to attach to their acceptance of the Potsdam Declaration. Suzuki, Togo, and Yonai maintained that the Allied terms ought to be accepted in toto, provided the victors agreed to preserve the throne and kokutai. But Anami and the military chiefs argued that Japan had not yet been defeated, as the Imperial Army was still capable of inflicting enormous casualties on any enemy who might attempt to invade the homeland.[110] Therefore, they maintained, Japan should not settle for dishonorable terms. The three diehards insisted that, in addition to ensuring preservation of the throne, Japanese leaders must not allow the Allies to disarm their troops, occupy the homeland, or try any Japanese subject as a war criminal.[111] Togo knew the Allies would never accept such provisions, so he strongly objected to adding them. He believed quibbling over terms would cause the Allies to reject all of Japan's conditions and, consequently, endanger the throne. But the three diehards held out, and even though word arrived during the meeting that Nagasaki had suffered an atomic bombing at about 11:00 that morning, the council was still deadlocked when Suzuki adjourned it at 1:00 P.M.[112]

About an hour later, the prime minister convened an emergency cabinet meeting that had been scheduled for noon, but was postponed due to the long Supreme Council session. After Togo briefed the cabinet on the crisis at hand and the Big Six's secret activities during the preceding months, Admiral Yonai presented the case for accepting Allied terms with the one condition of preserving the throne. Anami then presented the opposing argument, emphasizing that the army was "still confident of being able to deal a decisive blow to the invaders when the homeland became the battlefield."[113] "Furthermore," he maintained, "the army will not submit to demobilization. Our men simply will not lay down their arms . . . [therefore] . . . there is really no alternative but to continue the war."[114]

General Umezu and Admiral Toyoda, the army and navy chiefs of staff, were not invited to this meeting, as they were not cabinet ministers; but if Suzuki, Togo, and Yonai thought they might, therefore, have the numerical strength to overpower Anami, they were mistaken. As the debate developed, several ministers tended to reject the peace faction's "defeatist" attitude. Two of them, Home Minister Abe Genki and Justice Minister Matsuzaka Hiromasa, clearly sided with the diehards. The argument continued throughout the afternoon and into the evening until, at about 10:00 P.M., Prime Minister Suzuki called for a vote. Nine cabinet ministers voted to surrender with the sole condition of preserving the throne, three voted to hold out for the additional terms, and three others held intermediate positions or were undecided. Though the peace faction had won a clear majority, the cabinet was unable reach consensus, so Suzuki called for an adjournment.[115]

The Emperor Commands a Conditional Surrender

In ordinary circumstances, if the prime minister was unable to foster a cabinet consensus on an important issue, Japanese custom dictated that he resign; but the circumstances now facing Japan were anything but ordinary. Having anticipated the deadlock in which the government now found itself, Suzuki, Togo, Kido, and Chief Cabinet Secretary Sakomizu had conspired the previous evening to take a step unprecedented in Japan's history—they would seek an imperial decision to break the stalemate. The following afternoon, they had explained their plan to the emperor, and he had concurred. Now, with both the Supreme Council and the cabinet locked in disagreement between peace advocates and die-

hards, Suzuki and Togo reported to the imperial palace, and Togo briefed
the throne on the day's developments.[116] Solemnly, Emperor Hirohito
agreed that the time had come to put the plan into effect, and he sanctioned Prime Minister Suzuki's order to convene an Imperial Conference
of the Supreme Council for the Direction of the War.[117]

General Umezu and Admiral Toyoda were both surprised and puzzled
when summoned for the Imperial Conference late that night. Granted,
Chief Cabinet Secretary Sakomizu had warned them the evening before
that an Imperial Conference might be called at any time, given the gravity
of the crisis at hand, and he persuaded them to sign a petition stating they
would make themselves available if called upon. But neither imagined a
conference might be convened in the emperor's presence without the
council first having reached a consensus. Presenting a divided opinion to
the throne was simply inconceivable. Nevertheless, Suzuki had summoned in the emperor's name, so they had no choice but to respond.[118]

Shortly before midnight on August 9, 1945, Prime Minister Suzuki convened the Imperial Conference in the bomb shelter adjoining the emperor's library. Besides the Supreme Council's Big Six, the conference was
attended by Privy Seal Kido, Chief Cabinet Secretary Sakomizu, and
Baron Hiranuma, president of the privy council. The meeting began with
Sakomizu reading the Potsdam Declaration, followed by the prime minister's summary of the day's events. Suzuki's tone was deeply apologetic
when he said that, although it was "unthinkable" to present the throne a
policy question without an accompanying recommendation, the emperor's government had been unable to reach a consensus.[119] As the situation demanded an immediate solution, it was necessary to submit the
issue to His Majesty for a decision.[120]

For the next two hours, Emperor Hirohito silently listened as the opposing factions restated the arguments they had presented so many times
before. Togo explained the peace faction's position, emphasizing his personal conviction that Japan's only chance of survival lay in accepting the
Potsdam terms immediately with the sole reservation that imperial sovereignty be preserved. He stressed that the Allies would interpret any
attempt to hold out for additional provisions as a refusal to surrender.
That would invite further destruction, ruin all chances of negotiation, and
endanger the throne. When Togo was finished, Suzuki called on Admiral
Yonai who only said he completely agreed with the foreign minister. But
General Anami had a great deal to say. Leaping to his feet, he declared
that he vehemently opposed Togo's position. Restating the diehard arguments at length, the war minister insisted that the outcome of the "Battle of Japan" could not be known until it was fought. In any case, "if Japan
were to surrender, she must insist on acceptance of her four conditions,
guaranteeing not only the integrity of the Imperial structure, but also Japan's right to disarm her own soldiers, conduct her own war trials, and

limit the forces of occupation."[121] Umezu continued in the same vein, emphasizing that, even with the Soviets in the war, Japan was more than a match for any enemy on her own soil. Accepting unconditional surrender would only dishonor the gallant Japanese dead.[122]

Protocol dictated that Suzuki next turn to the navy chief of staff, but, instead, he asked Privy Council President Baron Hiranuma for his opinion.[123] Unexpectedly granted the floor, Hiranuma launched into a series of probing questions that consumed more than half an hour. He first interrogated the foreign minister on details of the Soviet mediation effort, who the Allies might regard as war criminals, and Japan's prospects for disarming her own troops. Togo fielded the baron's questions nimbly and reemphasized his contention that the Allies would violently reject any attempt to hold out for terms such as self-disarmament.[124] Next, Hiranuma turned to the diehards and, after citing the litany of Japan's shortcomings, asked if military authorities were really confident in their ability to continue the war. Admitting they could not promise victory, Umezu said he believed the atomic threat could be checked by "proper antiaircraft measures," and Toyoda pointed out that, though Japan had long been on the defensive, military leaders had been hoarding their forces for a decisive battle—hereafter, they expected to counterattack.[125] Finally, after formally hearing both sides of the argument, Baron Hiranuma said he generally agreed with Togo, but emphasized that, should *kokutai* be put in jeopardy, Japan would have to fight to the death.[126]

Having given all the principals a chance to speak, Suzuki then brought the discussion to a close. Emphasizing that hours of debate had not yielded a consensus from the emperor's councilors, the prime minister declared that the gravity of the situation left him no alternative but to seek a decision from the throne. Turning to the emperor, he said, "your Imperial Majesty's decision is requested as to which proposal should be adopted— the one stated by the foreign minister or the one containing the four conditions."[127] With visible emotion, Emperor Hirohito stood and said:

I have given serious thought to the situation prevailing at home and abroad and have concluded that continuing the war can only mean destruction for the nation and a prolongation of bloodshed and cruelty in the world. I cannot bear to see my innocent people suffer any longer. Ending the war is the only way to restore world peace and to relieve the nation from the terrible distress with which it is burdened . . .

[paragraph omitted regarding the preparations to repel invasion falling short of expectations]

There are those who say that the key to national survival lies in a decisive battle in the homeland. The experiences of the past, however, show that there has always been a discrepancy between plans and performance. I do not believe that the discrepancy in the case of Kujukuri-hama [referring to inadequate preparations to repel invasion] can be rectified. Since this is the shape of things, how can we repel the invaders?

[paragraph omitted expressing regret in seeing Japanese soldiers disarmed and some tried as war criminals]

When I recall the feelings of my imperial grandsire, the Emperor Meiji, at the time of the triple intervention, I swallow my own tears and give my sanction to the proposal to accept the Allied proclamation on the basis outlined by the foreign minister.[128]

With that, the emperor left the room.

Allied Rejection and the Second Imperial Intervention

With the emperor's will so clearly stated, the Supreme Council had no choice but to accept the Potsdam Declaration with the sole provision that imperial sovereignty be maintained. Likewise, the cabinet unanimously endorsed the decision in a meeting immediately following the council session. Togo then composed surrender statements for transmission to the Allies via Swiss and Swedish intermediaries. The cables were sent early on August 10, 1945.[129] Later that morning Togo received Ambassador Malik who delivered the Soviet Union's official declaration of war.[130] After sternly pointing out that the neutrality pact between their countries was supposedly still in effect and Moscow had not responded to Tokyo's request for mediation to end the war, Togo accepted the Russian communiqué and asked Malik to inform his superiors that Japan had decided to accept the Potsdam Declaration. Concerned about the time it might take for Japan's surrender to reach the Allies, Togo also had the Domei News Agency broadcast an English translation of the surrender announcement in Morse code. That done, Japanese leaders had nothing more to do but anxiously await the Allied reply.[131]

They did not have to wait very long. Beginning about the time of Germany's defeat, American authorities had sporadically debated whether to grant Tokyo assurances that the emperor would be permitted to remain on the throne.[132] Though this issue had never been resolved, Japan's offer of conditional surrender forced a prompt decision now. In a hastily assembled meeting in the Oval Office, Secretary of War Henry Stimson, Navy Secretary James Forrestal, and White House Chief of Staff Admiral William Leahy urged the president to accept Japan's terms immediately. But Secretary of State James Byrnes objected. Wary of acting without consulting the Allies, he also did not want to concede anything that might give the Japanese some semblance of victory for fear of encouraging resistance to reforms later. On the other hand, neither Byrnes nor the others wanted to flatly reject Tokyo's offer and continue the war. Consequently, following the meeting, the secretary drafted a carefully worded response informing Japanese leaders that "from the moment of surrender, the authority of the emperor and the Japanese government to rule the state [would] be subject to the Supreme Commander of the Allied Powers who [would] take such steps as he [deemed] proper to effectuate the surrender terms."[133] While this statement vaguely implied that the Supreme Commander might, indeed, leave the emperor on the throne, Byrnes added, "the ultimate form of government of Japan [would], in accordance with the Potsdam Declaration, be established by the freely expressed will of the Japanese people."[134] Stimson and Forrestal liked the statement, and together they convinced Truman to release it after getting Allied concurrence later that evening.[135] Subsequently, the State Department released both Tokyo's offer and Washington's response for news broadcasts to the American public (and, hence, to Japan) and sent official replies to the Japanese through the Swedish and Swiss intermediaries.[136]

Japanese Foreign Ministry radios first picked up broadcasts of the American statement a little after midnight on August 12. Though disappointed by the wording, Foreign Minister Togo told Emperor Hirohito the following morning that he felt Japan had no alternative but to accept the Byrnes reply without further elaboration. The emperor agreed.[137] Unfortunately, military listening posts had also monitored the broadcasts and, urged on by their hawkish staffs, Umezu and Toyoda hurried to the palace that same morning insisting that Japan reject the American response as it implied the Allies would subordinate the emperor to the Supreme Commander.[138] Hirohito calmly told them that the government should wait until Washington's official answer arrived, then study the issue carefully before making a decision. The military chiefs were momentarily parried.[139]

But peace advocates soon faced more serious challenges. Baron Hiranuma, who's support for conditional surrender had been weak at best, considered the Byrnes statement completely unacceptable. So while Togo was at the palace, Hiranuma and War Minister Anami converged on Suzuki and convinced him that acceding to the American formula would jeopardize the throne. As a result, in a special cabinet meeting later that afternoon, Togo was mortified to hear the prime minister declare that Japan must continue the war if the Allies insisted on forcing disarmament on her. Togo fought back, but was unable to overcome the emerging coalition's arguments. He did manage, however, to stop a potentially catastrophic consensus from forming by convincing the ministers to shelve further discussion until they received Washington's official response through diplomatic channels. Immediately afterward, the foreign minister brought Suzuki back in line by sternly reminding him that the emperor was committed to accepting the Potsdam Declaration.[140]

The following morning, with the official American response in hand, Japanese leaders resumed their deliberations. In many respects, the discussions echoed those that had taken place several days before. Togo, supported by Suzuki and Yonai, maintained that the American stipulation that the authority to govern Japan would be "subject to" the Supreme Commander referred only to the administrative functions of state and, therefore, did not limit imperial sovereignty or threaten *kokutai*. But the diehards of the Supreme Council—Anami, Umezu, and Toyoda—insisted the "subject to" wording equated to "subordinate to." As the emperor was a living deity, subordinating him to any earthly authority was unacceptable.[141] Moreover, governing the nation according to the "freely expressed will of the people" would be incompatible with Japan's imperial structure. In sum, as the Americans were unwilling to guarantee the continuance of *kokutai*, Japan could not allow Allied forces to disarm her troops or occupy the homeland. She must fight to the bitter end.[142]

With the Supreme Council deadlocked once again, the Big Six adjourned and the debate was carried over to a meeting of the full cabinet. Just as before, the absence of Umezu and Toyoda was filled by the home and justice ministers, and the cabinet deadlocked with three diehards holding out against allowing the Allies to disarm Japanese forces or occupy the homeland. After several hours of fruitless debate, Prime Minister Suzuki closed the meeting with the statement that, though he had first found the Byrnes reply unacceptable, he now believed the wording did not suggest that American leaders had any malicious purpose in mind. As he also believed the emperor was committed to ending the war, he said he would, once again, seek an imperial decision.[143]

Remembering the outcome of the last imperial conference, the military chiefs did their best to avoid a repeat performance. When Sakomizu asked General Umezu and Admiral Toyoda to sign the petition making themselves available for the imperial summons, they did so only after getting the chief cabinet secretary to promise that no one would issue the order without consulting them first. Later that evening, they met with Togo in a last futile effort to convince him to see things from their perspective.[144] Finally, when Prime Minister Suzuki tried to convene the Supreme Council on the morning of August 14, Umezu said he would be unavailable until later that afternoon and Toyoda wanted to postpone the meeting indefinitely. However, developments unfolding that morning introduced a new sense of urgency to the deliberations.[145]

As Suzuki was trying to assemble the Supreme Council, one of the emperor's chamberlains brought Privy Seal Kido an Allied leaflet—one of millions just dropped on Japan—that disclosed the text of Tokyo's conditional surrender offer and Washington's response. Realizing this sudden revelation of Japan's secret bid for peace might cause a crisis when comprehended by the public, the secret police, and the military at large, Kido rushed to the emperor and convinced him that time had run out—he must immediately convene an imperial conference and firmly express his desire to accept the Potsdam Declaration as elaborated by the Byrnes reply.[146]

At about 10:50 A.M. on August 14, 1945, Emperor Hirohito walked into the air raid shelter beneath the imperial library and took his place before a combined conference of the Supreme Council, the cabinet, and other selected state officials. Suzuki opened the meeting, explaining that His Majesty had called the conference to hear his councilors evaluate the Allied reply and to permit those who dissented from the majority position to express their opinions. The prime minister summarized events leading to the conference and apologized to the emperor for delivering a divided opinion. Then he asked the diehards to present their arguments so the emperor could consider the issue and render a decision. Umezu spoke first, followed by Toyoda and Anami. Each of them presented brief but passionate statements stressing that Japan should not surrender under the terms laid out in the Byrnes reply, as they did not provide adequate assurances that *kokutai* would be preserved. Although none of them could promise that continuing the war would bring victory, the diehards insisted that Japan still maintained enough military potential to, at least, force the Allies to clarify their intentions regarding the status of the throne.[147]

When General Anami finished, Suzuki turned to the emperor and asked for his decision. Directly expressing his opinion for the second time in four days—indeed, the second time in all of Japan's history—Emperor Hirohito stood and said:

I have listened carefully to each of the arguments presented in opposition to the view that Japan should accept the Allied reply as it stands without further clarification or modification, but my own thoughts have not undergone any change. I have surveyed the conditions prevailing in Japan and in the world at large, and it is my belief that a continuation of the war promises nothing but additional destruction. I have studied the terms of the Allied reply and have concluded that they constitute a virtually complete acknowledgment of the position we maintained in the note dispatched several days ago. In short, I consider the reply to be acceptable . . .

[portion omitted discussing whether the Allies can be trusted and the difficulty of accepting disarmament and occupation and seeing Japanese subjects tried as war criminals]

In spite of these feelings, so difficult to bear, I can not endure the thought of letting my people suffer any longer. A continuation of the war would bring death to tens, perhaps even hundreds, of thousands of persons. The whole nation would be reduced to ashes. How then could I carry on the wishes of my imperial ancestors?

The decision I have reached is akin to the one forced upon my grandfather, the

Emperor Meiji, at the time of the triple intervention. As he endured the unendurable, so shall I, and so must you.

It is my desire that you, my ministers of state, accede to my wishes and forthwith accept the Allied reply. In order that the people may know of my decision, I request you to prepare at once an imperial rescript so that I may broadcast to the nation. Finally, I call upon each and every one of you to exert himself to the utmost so that we may meet the trying days which lie ahead.[148]

As Emperor Hirohito left the room, silent tears gave way to open weeping among his councilors. Several men slid to the floor in anguish. Nevertheless, they obeyed his command and delivered Japan's unconditional surrender to the Allies. That evening, junior army officers seized a portion of the imperial compound in a coup attempt aimed at preventing the broadcast of a recording of the emperor announcing Japan's surrender, but loyal military commanders suppressed it in short order.[149] The war was over. Compellence had finally succeeded.

ANALYSIS OF THE SURRENDER OF JAPAN

The surrender of Japan has confounded historians and political scientists for more than five decades. There were many reasons for Japanese leaders to capitulate in August, 1945. By evaluating the prospective costs and benefits of resisting Allied demands for surrender, one can readily understand why the Japanese were so motivated to end the conflict. Examining Japan's interests and comparing them to those of her adversaries reveals why the Allies were so determined to bring the war to a close, even if it meant devastating Japan in the process. This would suggest that Tokyo should have been even more motivated to end the war quickly to avoid ultimate destruction. But therein lies a problem. Though Japanese leaders had good reason to surrender when they did, there were ample reasons to submit long before that time, and one would wonder why the Japanese did not aggressively pursue a negotiated settlement months, if not years, before their near collapse at the end of the war.

The following analysis examines the behavior of Tokyo elites through the alternative lenses of punishment and denial theory, balance of interest theory, and the Japanese strategic culture profile to explain those actors' responses to efforts to compel Japan's surrender. It demonstrates that one must evaluate Japanese behavior from the perspective of their own strategic culture to fully appreciate why Japanese leaders held out for so long and why they finally gave up when they did.

Punishment and Denial—So Much Cost for So Little Benefit

Assessing this case in terms of punishment and denial presents some interesting challenges. However, unlike the previous cases in this study, the problem is not that the strategies employed were subtle or the coercive stimuli vague or weak, but that the strategies were multiple and the incentives so abundant and so powerful. Due to the overwhelming preponderance of force at their disposal, the Allies (principally the United States) could, and did, employ numerous potentially war-winning strategies simultaneously. They isolated or decisively defeated Japan's armies, destroyed her navy and air force, strangled and demolished her industries, and punished her population through extreme deprivation and relentless bombardment. Yet, Japanese leaders did not surrender until long after their strategic objectives had been irrefutably denied and their subjects had endured seemingly unendurable punishment. As a result, several competing punishment- and denial-based theories purport to explain what compelled Japan to surrender. The problem is not one of insufficient evidence but of too many variables, each offering an argument that seems persuasive on its own merits.

This problem is complicated by the fact that, though these arguments offer strong explanations for why Japan should have surrendered, none of them adequately captures the dynamics of Japan's complex decision-making process. For instance, popular wisdom holds that the atomic bombings so shocked Japanese leaders that they surrendered for fear of further punishment. At first blush, this appears to be a strong argument, as the bombings seemed to energize the peace faction, and the emperor first intervened shortly after Nagasaki. But theories focusing exclusively on the atomic bomb tend to ignore earlier developments that moved the Japanese toward surrender, while simultaneously failing to explain what held them back for so long. Indeed, peace advocates wanted to end the war long before Hiroshima. Yet, the diehards still objected to surrendering well after conceding the fact that the United States was using atomic weaponry. As Anami pointed out in cabinet deliberations on August 13, the atomic bomb seemed no more menacing to them than were the firebombings Japan had endured for months, and military authorities believed they could take adequate measures to mitigate the effects of atomic weapons. Clearly, to understand why compellence finally succeeded after so many months of failure, we must consider factors besides whether Japanese leaders were intimidated by the expectation of further punishment.

The Soviet declaration of war and plunge into Manchuria also coincided with Japan's surrender, and one could construct a plausible argument that these events convinced Japanese leaders that there was no further benefit in continuing the war. Manchuria was one of Japan's most important territorial possessions in terms of strategic location, colonization, and as a source of raw materials. One could posit that the Soviet army's rapid advance there convinced Japanese leaders they could not hold the region for much longer. This might also suggest they would soon lose their foothold elsewhere on the Asian continent, denying them all access to the strategic materials for which they originally went to war. But a closer examination of the evidence deflates these arguments. The interdiction campaign had effectively denied Japan the benefits of her continental possessions long before Russia entered the war. Though Anami once declared that Japan was not defeated so long as she held most of East Asia, by August even the diehards understood that the war was lost and Japan would have to relinquish all her overseas holdings to get any kind of negotiated peace. The issues holding up surrender were not resources and territory—they were abhorrence to forced disarmament, occupation, war crimes trials, and the threat to the throne.

Other popular arguments are even less credible when examined in light of the evidence. In *Japan's Struggle to Surrender,* the United States Strategic Bombing Survey concluded that, even without the atomic bombings or the Soviet attack, Japan would have surrendered before the Allied invasion, scheduled for November 1, 1945, due to effects of the conventional bombing and interdiction campaigns.[150] Counterfactual propositions like this one are difficult to assess. However, we must observe that while the survey authors attributed Japan's resistance to surrender before August, 1945, to a "time lapse between military impotence and political acceptance," they offered little rationale for why they believed political leaders would have accepted defeat after mid-August, but sometime before November 1.[151] The Strategic Bombing Survey was correct, however, in its conclusion that the threat of imminent Allied invasion had no coercive effect on Japan's military leaders.[152] In fact, accounts of top-level deliberations from the time Koiso proposed his Tennozan strategy until the emperor's second intervention consistently suggest that military leaders eagerly anticipated, even craved, a decisive battle on their home territory. Even after the Soviet declaration of war, the Supreme Command still believed Japan could inflict enough pain on an invasion force to persuade Allied leaders to soften their terms, allowing Japan to end the war with dignity.[153] On August 14, they virtually begged the emperor to allow them to prove their case.

Clearly, none of the popular punishment and denial theories offers an adequate explanation for Japan's behavior leading to the surrender. One reason for this deficiency is that many of these constructs treat the Japanese decision-making apparatus as a unitary rational-actor, abstractly calculating the costs of Allied attacks, real and anticipated, and arriving at a single conception of the costs of complying with Allied demands as compared to the benefits of continued resistance.[154] But, as case events reveal, Japanese decision makers were anything but unified in the latter portion of the war.

As the tide of battle turned against Japan, two key groups emerged from Tokyo's political elite, each with its own conception of the prospective costs and benefits of continuing the fight. One of these groups, the peace faction, first emerged in early 1943 and steadily gained strength as Axis defeats in the Pacific and Europe convinced a growing number of influential people that Japan could not win the war. Forming around Konoe in the *jushin*, Shigemitsu in the Foreign Ministry, and gradually, Kido in the imperial court, this group eventually managed to install some of its members in the decision-making councils of government, and it finally won Prime Minister Suzuki's vacillating support sometime late in the spring of 1945. More importantly, the peace faction seems to have gained the emperor's trust early on and, later, his active support. The other group was the diehard faction. Anchored in the military bureaucracy (particularly the army), this group dominated the government until the peace faction's emerging strength eventually enabled it to challenge that dominance, then invite the emperor to render a decision to end the war.[155]

It is important to note that both of these groups based their policy preferences on calculations of Japan's ability to achieve its strategic objectives; but, as their assessments of those prospects so often differed, so did the policies they preferred. When Midway and Stalingrad convinced founders of the peace faction that the tide of war had changed, they became convinced Japan should seek a negotiated settlement. Presumably, they believed ending the conflict then would enable Japan to retain greater benefits at less cost than would continuing a war with dwindling strategic prospects.[156] The Tojo clique, however, still maintained that Germany would curb the Russian counter-advance and Britain and the United States would eventually tire of the war. As this group firmly controlled the government and the secret police, the doves had no opportunity to even voice their concerns openly. In 1944, as Japan's fortunes went from bad to worse, peace advocates began revising their expectations of what Tokyo would have to relinquish to end the conflict—Shigemitsu recognized as early as January that unconditional surrender would be unavoidable—but Tojo, Koiso, and military leaders continued to insist that Japan could reap greater benefit by continuing her resistance than by yielding to Allied demands.

All of this suggests that, up to this point in the war, peace advocates and diehards were simply acting on differing assessments of Japan's prospects in the war. However, as the pressure on Tokyo grew extreme during the final year of conflict, both groups' behavior became more erratic and difficult to explain in terms of cost-benefit analysis.

In late 1944, Shigemitsu, who nine months earlier had told Kido the war was lost, tried to effect an impractical scheme to fight on by mediating a settlement between Germany and the Soviet Union, then forging a Russo-Japanese alliance. Two months later, he and a fellow peace advocate, Navy Minister Yonai, supported Koiso's ill-conceived plan to reverse the tide of defeat by fighting a Tennozan in the Philippines.

If this kind of behavior from peace advocates is puzzling, both factions behaved even more erratically as the pressure on them became more severe. When Berlin fell in early May, 1945, the Supreme Council's Big Six— diehards and peace advocates alike—concluded the war was lost. Yet, on June 6 and 8, they unanimously endorsed a suicidal plan to fight a climactic battle in the home islands, before agreeing to pursue mediation 10 days later after the emperor sanctioned Kido's "Tentative Plan" to end the war.[157]

As the war drew to a close, the diehard faction's behavior became more bizarre than ever. Denying the destructiveness of the atomic bomb, Anami, Umezu, and Toyoda argued passionately for continuing the fight, though Japan's war objectives had long since been conclusively denied and all available evidence suggested their climactic battle was doomed to failure. Even after the Soviet Army smashed through Japan's defensive lines in Manchuria, the diehards held out for a plan that would have subjected their own homeland to a devastating invasion. Though they obeyed the emperor's command to surrender on August 10, they returned to their suicidal stance when American leaders rejected Japan's terms. All the while, any one of them could have prolonged the war had he really wanted to do so—Anami could have resigned, bringing down the Suzuki government, and he, or either or the military chiefs, could have encouraged an insurrection among their radical subordinates.[158]

So, while a cost-benefit analysis focusing on individual groups produces a more refined picture of Japanese motives, it still leaves many questions unanswered. For instance, why did their perceptions of costs and benefits differ so dramatically? If a few individuals realized as early as 1943 that Japan was losing the war, why did the diehards refuse to accept that fact until May, 1945, long after their navy and air force had been destroyed and with American forces on their doorstep? After that, why could they not comprehend that continuing the fight until Japan's military potential was completely exhausted only promised to further reduce their negotiating posture and drive the ratio of costs to benefits ever higher? More importantly, why did both factions seem to vacillate periodically between commitments to fight a losing war and efforts to end it?

While the behavior of both political groups is certainly puzzling, the actions of Japan's nominal leaders, Prime Minister Suzuki and Emperor Hirohito, are no less baffling. Was Suzuki a hawk or a dove? Historians have never been sure. While publicly declaring time and again that he would lay down his life in a fight to the bitter end, he privately agreed with Togo that Japan would be unable to continue the war beyond the end of the year. When Germany was defeated, he told the nation that Japan would only fight harder, then he headed a Supreme Council meeting that concluded the war was lost. Soon after delivering the Sakomizu report informing the emperor that Japan was on the verge of collapse, he ardently championed the military staff's "Fundamental Policy," committing the nation to a suicidal last stand. Then, a few days later, he supported Kido's "Tentative Plan" to save Japan from that fate and called a secret session of the Big Six to put efforts to end the war back on track. Even during the final debate over terms of surrender, he confounded his colleagues by shifting his allegiance from the peace faction to the diehards and back again, largely depending on who confronted him last.

The emperor's behavior was almost as enigmatic as Suzuki's. According to Kase, Kido, and Shigemitsu, Emperor Hirohito said he wanted the war to end as early as March, 1943. Yet he continued to sanction the Tojo government, then conferred his mandate on two more prime ministers who stridently declared their determination to fight on to victory. As Herbert Bix argues, until June, 1945, he actively participated in strategic planning and persistently pressed military leaders to achieve a decisive victory.[159] On June 8, 1945, he sanctioned the general staff's "Fundamental Policy" to fight to the bitter end, then blessed Kido's "Tentative Plan" to seek a mediated settlement the following day.

While these fluctuations are difficult to explain, one thing is clear: both political factions seemed to base their policy preferences solely on assessments of Japan's chances of victory, but the grounds of debate differed in the imperial court. As the war drew to a close, concerns in the palace began to focus not only on whether Japanese forces were capable of repelling an enemy invasion, but also on the pain that Allied punishment was inflicting on the Japanese people. Kido's "Tentative Plan" lamented the suffering that winter would visit on the homeless victims of firebombing and worried that the government would be unable to control their unrest.[160] Emperor Hirohito's will to end the war was fortified when he learned of the carnage at Hiroshima. And when he twice commanded the government to surrender, he cited his people's suffering as well as his lack of faith in Japan's ability to repel an invasion. Indeed, the emperor may have first decided the war should end when he realized there was no benefit in further resistance, but he was finally compelled to act by the mounting costs of punishment. That raises one more question: why would the imperial court be more sensitive to punishment than either of the political groups that comprised the Japanese government?

In sum, an analysis of the costs and benefits facing Japan's decision makers offers a great deal of insight regarding what motivated them to end the war; however, it fails to explain why compellence succeeded when it did. It does not explain why the diehards were so slow to realize that nothing more could be gained by continuing the fight. Nor does it explain why, as the coercive pressure mounted, both groups seemed to waver in their commitment to end the conflict. Finally, it offers no insight as to why the imperial court would be sensitive to the costs of punishment while the other groups were so insensitive. Ultimately, no analyses based on

punishment or denial alone can precisely explain how Japan was compelled to surrender because, even when refined by focusing on the differing perspectives of individual groups, they all fail to capture the subtleties
of Japan's complex system of symbol, value, and social interaction.

The Balance of Interests in the Surrender of Japan

The balance of interests in this case explains Allied behavior quite well,
but it sheds little light on why Japanese leaders withheld surrender for so
long. American and British interests were relatively straightforward. In
keeping with the August, 1941, Atlantic Charter, Roosevelt and Churchill
were determined to end the war in such a way that would foster conditions conducive to stability, democracy, and free trade in the postwar
world.[161] That goal would require them to thoroughly defeat the Axis
Powers and restructure those governments. But early in the war, it was
uncertain whether Britain could hold out long enough to defeat Germany,
and Anglo-American leaders realized they would need extended cooperation from Soviet Russia, a country also victimized by Nazi aggression,
but who's ultimate goals contradicted the promotion of democracy and
free trade.

The peculiarities of this uneasy association had notable effects on Allied
behavior in both Europe and Asia. Stalin was incurably suspicious of
Anglo-American intentions. Hard pressed in the east, he persistently lobbied for Britain and the United States to open a second front with an
invasion of Western Europe. Roosevelt was inclined to oblige, but Churchill believed Allied power was inadequate for such an ambitious operation; therefore, he convinced the Americans to first attack the "soft
underbelly" of the Axis empire in North Africa instead. In early 1943,
following the successful Africa campaign, Churchill convinced Roosevelt
to put off a cross-channel invasion once again when they met at Casa-
blanca. But the president worried about how Stalin would receive this
decision, so he convinced his British colleague that they should close the
conference with a formal declaration that they would accept nothing less
than unconditional surrender from the Axis Powers. They formally issued
that demand to Japan later that November when they met with Chiang
Kai-shek in Cairo.[162]

As the war proceeded, Roosevelt was galvanized by the vision of a
United Nations, an international organization in which the Great Powers
would cooperate to maintain peace and stability in the postwar world. In
his conception, China would emerge from the war as a great democracy
and join the Allies as Asia's representative in that stabilizing body. Even
Soviet Russia would recognize the virtue of such a program and join the
movement as a responsible world citizen.[163] Truman may have shared that
dream when he became president following Roosevelt's death on April

12, 1945, but strains in the Alliance during the closing months of the war persuaded the new chief executive to be less trusting of his Soviet allies than had been his predecessor.

During the final months of the war, American interests focused more squarely on ending the conflict as soon as possible and ensuring that postwar Japan would never again tread a path of conquest. Unfortunately, those two objectives were not entirely compatible. American authorities generally agreed that, to curb future Japanese aggression, they would have to remove the military oligarchy from power and restructure the government in Tokyo. Of course, that precluded extending Japan any assurances that they would be able to maintain their existing form of government. But Joseph C. Grew, the assistant secretary of state and a former ambassador to Japan, strongly held that the war could be shortened if only Washington would reassure Tokyo that the Allies intended to preserve the imperial institution. On several occasions he urged President Truman to release a statement to that effect. Grew's convictions were generally shared by War Secretary Stimson, Assistant War Secretary John Mc-Cloy, Navy Secretary Forrestal, and White House Chief of Staff Admiral Leahy. However, a strong faction in the State Department maintained that preserving the cult of the emperor would perpetuate conditions that had first enabled the military oligarchy to come to power, and retired Secretary of State Cordell Hull cautioned Secretary Byrnes that the public would consider any retreat from unconditional surrender to be appeasement. Given this flood of conflicting advice, Truman was ambivalent and put off deciding the issue several times before receiving Japan's August 10 offer of conditional surrender.[164]

As 1945 dragged on with Japan holding out in the face of military defeat, geopolitical isolation, and intense bombardment, American authorities held little hope that Tokyo would capitulate before the November 1 invasion. Truman dreaded the 30,000 or more casualties his military chiefs told him to expect during the first 30 days of fighting on Japanese territory, but domestic pressure to end the war as quickly as possible convinced him he could not afford to wait for the uncertain results of merely continuing the blockade and aerial bombardment. Anticipating a bloody fight in the enemy homeland, Truman and his staff were eager for the Soviet Union to enter the war against Japan. Years later, Truman would recall: "As our forces in the Pacific were pushing ahead, paying a heavy toll in lives, the urgency of getting Russia into the war became more compelling. Russia's entry into the war would mean the saving of hundreds of thousands of American casualties."[165]

Meanwhile, American scientists scrambled to perfect the atomic bomb. Those on Truman's staff who knew of the project hoped it might provide the United States a weapon that would end the war before having to resort to a costly invasion. Beyond that, the atomic bomb seemed to offer "the opportunity to bring the world into a pattern in which the peace of the world and our civilization [could] be saved."[166] But some of the president's advisors were uneasy about the weapon's destructive potential. Concerned about the moral implications of this fearful new source of power, Stimson convinced President Truman to form the Interim Committee, a panel of civilian leaders in business, government, and science, to address the various political and ethical questions that having atomic weapons seemed to raise.[167]

Meeting in May, 1945, the committee set out to determine how the bomb should be used in the war against Japan and what international safeguards might later be necessary to control this new source of explosive power. Regarding the political issues, Stimson relayed three recommendations to President Truman in early June. First, the United States should use the bomb against Japan as soon as possible in hopes of saving the many American lives an invasion would cost. Second, to maximize the probability that an atomic bombing would convince Tokyo to surrender, the weapon should be used in a way that would make the greatest possible impression on both military and civilian witnesses in Japan. Therefore, the Interim Committee recommended a military target be chosen, surrounded by houses or other civilian buildings. Finally, the bomb should be dropped without prior warning to achieve the greatest possible shock effect and because the committee was not yet certain the device would actually work. As for the ethical questions, the committee recommended that the American government share the secrets of atomic energy with other nations if they, in turn, agreed to share further discoveries in the field and were willing to allow an international inspection committee to police such an accord.

Truman endorsed the committee's findings regarding use of the bomb against Japan, but was less sanguine about the wisdom of sharing atomic secrets with the Soviet Union. By June, 1945, friction had developed between Moscow and the Anglo-Americans over how they should administer the occupied countries in Europe—Truman was already beginning to question the viability of Roosevelt's dream of a cooperative, constructive United Nations. Consequently, though he liked the idea of sharing the moral responsibility for wielding atomic power, he suspected Moscow would be unwilling to submit to international control. On the other hand, the president did not want to expose himself to Russian charges that he had kept such an important development secret from a "trusting" ally. Therefore, during the Potsdam Conference, when the detonation of an atomic device in the New Mexican desert confirmed that America finally had a working bomb, Truman simply told Stalin that the United States now had a "new weapon of unusual destructive force." Seemingly unimpressed, Stalin only replied that he was glad to hear it and hoped America would "make good use of it against the Japanese."[168]

Given their many common interests, American authorities did not hesitate to share atomic secrets with their British counterparts; yet, British and American interests in Asia were not entirely synonymous. Although both governments hoped to construct a postwar world in which democracy and free trade would flourish, London also sought to regain Britain's lost colonies and revive her crumbling empire, a project for which Washington held little sympathy.[169] Motivated by these concerns, British leaders were eager to commit forces to the Pacific theater following Germany's defeat, and they petitioned American leaders for a voice in strategy formulation and the administration of liberated territories. However, American authorities were weary of the bickering over strategy they had encountered from the British in other theaters, and they feared that granting London a role in administering the occupation of Japan would open the door to a comparable demand from Moscow. As it turned out, American leaders consulted their British colleagues on nearly all strategic questions, and they even granted them a role in devising the strategy for liberating Southeast Asia. But British leaders recognized and accepted the reality of the situation. The United States had the preponderance of force in the theater. The Pacific war was an American war, and the conquest and occupation of Japan was going to be an American show.[170]

Soviet interests in the Second World War were coarse and direct. Beyond expelling the hated Germans from Russian territory and destroying the Nazi menace, Stalin sought to "extract the largest possible benefit—territorial, diplomatic, military, and economic—from the Red Army's eventual victory."[171] Stalin was well aware that American leaders were anxious to get Soviet participation in the war against Japan in order to reduce the toll of American casualties. Working that angle at Yalta in February, 1945, he obtained concessions from Roosevelt, ultimately resulting in the partition of Europe, in return for a promise to enter the war against Japan about three months after Germany's defeat. Yet the Soviets were more than eager to participate in the war in Asia. Manchuria and the Liaotung peninsula, with its deep, warm-water harbor at Port Arthur, were long-coveted prizes in Russia's geopolitical grand strategy. With the Kwangtung Army stripped of fuel, equipment, and capable soldiers, Japanese holdings in Manchuria were finally ripe for the taking. Moreover, a war with Japan would entitle the Soviet Union to other territorial acquisitions, and Stalin duly added the southern half of Sakhalin Island and the Kuriles, along with their oil deposits and rich fishing grounds, to the list of concessions he extracted from Roosevelt at Yalta.[172]

But if Stalin was so eager to enter the war against Japan, one might ask why Soviet authorities repeatedly put off answering Japanese requests for them to mediate an end to the war. Why did they not declare their hostile intentions earlier or, at least, definitively tell Tokyo that they would not plead Japan's case with the Allies? There are several answers to these questions. As Soviet authorities were busily engaged in redeploying men and materiel from Europe to the Manchurian border during the three months following Germany's surrender, they undoubtedly hoped to conceal their hand until they were certain they had a preponderance of force there. More importantly, Stalin wanted to maximize his gains by keeping everyone guessing about his intentions. At Potsdam, he reaffirmed his promise to enter the war, but linked that commitment to the successful resolution of certain "outstanding issues" with China. Then he tried to coerce concessions from Chiang Kai-shek concerning Soviet access to ports and railroads in Manchuria and the status of outer Mongolia.[173]

Thus, Stalin leveraged his commitment to enter the war against whatever concessions he could wrest from his allies. Yet, all of Moscow's objectives in Asia might have been lost had Japan surrendered before the Soviet Union declared war, and Tokyo's behavior strongly suggested that Japanese leaders considered the Russians their last hope for a mediated settlement. As far as Stalin and Molotov knew, had they openly refused Tokyo's overtures, the Japanese might have lost heart and surrendered prematurely. Then, Moscow would have been left holding an empty bag. Clearly, Soviet interests depended on Molotov's ability to string Tokyo along, keeping Japan in the war long enough for Stalin to wring concessions out of China and the Anglo-Americans while the Red Army redeployed along the Manchurian border.

All of this explains Allied behavior quite well, but what were Japan's interests in resisting attempts to compel her surrender? The objective for which Tokyo went to war was to break the "encirclement of the ABCD Powers"—that is, to break the Western Powers' monopoly on strategic resources, freeing the Japanese to expand their empire on the Asian continent. Early in the war, Japan's behavior served that interest quite well. Imperial forces seized the resource-rich regions of Southeast Asia and the Indies, drove the colonial Powers out of the western Pacific, and established a defensive perimeter thousands of miles from the home islands. But from 1943 onward, continuing the war was contrary to Tokyo's interests. The Allies persistently drove the defensive perimeter inward, both at sea and on the continent. Granted, Japanese military leaders may have convinced themselves that the early defeats were but temporary setbacks; however, by the end of 1944, none of them could deny that Japan's land, sea, and air forces had been irreparably crippled. How could any Japanese leader have believed continuing a war in such conditions served Japan's interests?

The stock answer, of course, is that the Allied demand for unconditional surrender raised the cost of compliance to such a level that the Japanese were willing to risk self-destruction rather than surrender the throne or abandon *kokutai*, their way of government. Indeed, that argument has merit. In the closing months of the war, both the diehards and the peace faction repeatedly stated they could not surrender without assurances that the Allies would preserve the throne. But, standing alone, the argument fails to provide a completely satisfactory explanation. After the war, members of both factions testified that, right up to the end, they did not believe the Allies were really serious in their demands for unconditional surrender.[174] Convinced the proclamations were mainly intended to bolster Chinese morale, Japanese leaders believed the Allies would be willing to negotiate terms if and when Tokyo decided to end the war. Even in August, 1945, after the peace faction had finally concluded that Japan had no alternative but to surrender unconditionally, Anami, Toyoda, and Umezu argued that, certainly, Allied leaders would be willing to grant Japan terms rather than suffer the casualties the Japanese could inflict on an invasion force. Clearly, the Allied demand for unconditional surrender was a serious impediment to ending the war, but it does not adequately explain why Tokyo did not, at least, attempt to open talks with the Allies long before August, 1945.

What may be more puzzling is why, when Japanese leaders finally decided to seek a negotiated settlement, they would trust Moscow to mediate on their behalf. Russia and Japan had been enemies for 50 years. Humiliated by St. Petersburg in the triple intervention, Japan had, in turn, humbled the Russians in 1905 when they destroyed two Russian fleets and took Port Arthur in the Russo-Japanese war. In the decades that followed, Russia and Japan had shared a tense coexistence in Northeast Asia, viciously competing for advantage on the continent, a competition that turned bloody on more than one occasion.[175] The rise of the Soviet Union had only added to the strain, as communism's goal of world proletarian domination directly threatened *kokutai*.

Now, with Japan on the verge of collapse, decision makers in Tokyo turned to their perennial enemy to rescue them from defeat. For some reason, Togo and the imperial court seemed to believe the Soviet Union would be willing to mediate a settlement on their behalf. Stranger still, military leaders, for a time, imagined they could solve their problems by mediating a settlement in Europe, and they were captivated with the possibility that Moscow might be willing to sell them strategic materials or sign a new treaty with Tokyo over the interests of Russia's allies. These ideas were absurd. What strategic analysis could have suggested to Japanese leaders that they could offer the Soviets anything more in Asia than the Red Army could simply take by entering the war on the Allied side? Yet, even after Moscow gave notice it was terminating the Russo-Japanese Neutrality Pact and with Soviet troops massing on the Manchurian border—a development of which Tokyo was fully aware—Japan's top decision makers, for some reason, could not seem to bring themselves to believe the Russians were about to attack.[176] Nor did anyone in Tokyo seem to realize that Malik, Lozovsky, and Molotov were deliberately stalling them concerning Japan's request for mediation.

These gross misperceptions suggest Japan's worldview was profoundly skewed. Such peculiar distortions cannot be fully explained by any objective analyses of costs, benefits, or interests. Only when we examine the strategic landscape through the lens of the symbols and values residing in Japan's unique strategic culture can we truly appreciate how Tokyo saw the world in 1945.

Strategic Culture and the Surrender of Japan

Events leading to the surrender of Japan clearly illustrate the powerful effects that factions and subcultures had on the imperial government's consensus-dependent policy-making process. As observed above, a number of Tokyo's civilian elite became convinced that Japan should end the war long before the military oligarchy reached the same conclusion. But a solid coalition of four of the Supreme Council's six principal decision makers—the prime minister, war minister, and the army and navy chiefs of staff—supported by a hawkish secretariat, consistently deterred the peace aspirations of Navy Minister Yonai and two consecutive foreign ministers, Shigemitsu and Togo. Only after the Supreme Council closed its sessions to the military staffs in May, 1945, did the diehards soften their stance enough to allow peace advocates to bring any notion of ending the war to the policy debate.

Yet, checking the consensus for war did not, in itself, bring about a decision for peace. Unable to agree on when and how to end the conflict, Japan's leaders squandered precious weeks seeking Soviet succor and mediation while the Allies concluded their plans for the final assault on the Japanese homeland. Even after the atomic bombings and the Soviet declaration of war, the councilors could not reach consensus on whether to surrender or fight on for better terms until the emperor twice intervened to settle the issue.

The irony behind the surrender of Japan is that all of Tokyo's key decision makers wanted to end the war months before they finally did, but the constraints of having to reach a unanimous decision on how to do so paralyzed their ability to act. This, in itself, explains a great deal about how culture affected the outcome of this case, but it still leaves many questions unanswered. To better understand the timing of events as well as the perceptions and motives behind the actions of individuals and factions, we must look more closely at the complex relationship between symbol and value in Japanese culture. More importantly, we must better understand how the group orientation in Japanese society governs individual behavior.

As I explained in chapter 3, decision making in Japan is a complex process in which group dynamics not only determine the outcome of any particular issue, but also compel each group member to support the policy ultimately chosen. In a Confucian society where group cohesiveness is a core value, decision makers are expected to champion whatever consensus emerges, even if they personally believe the decision is faulty or imprudent. Each member has an opinion, of course, but in Japan the individual's opinion loses consequence once a consensus begins to emerge. Consequently, when a strong majority begins to coalesce around a specific policy, not only do contenders stop resisting the tide of consensus, they often join their opponents in advocating the very policy they personally oppose, at least publicly and in group settings. Moreover, as every Japanese abhors personal confrontation, policy makers stay carefully attuned to their colleagues' positions on ongoing issues, avoiding challenges in areas in which a strong opposing coalition already exists.

These pressures explain much of the seemingly contradictory behavior exhibited by key members of the peace faction as they struggled to overcome the diehard stance during the last year of the war. In late 1944, while Shigemitsu and Yonai were secretly sponsoring Admiral Takagi's study on how to end the conflict, they still faced a strong coalition of diehards in the Supreme Council. Consequently, not only were they obliged to endorse Koiso's Tennozan strategy, but, as foreign minister, Shigemitsu was compelled to try to implement the council's bizarre scheme to mediate an end to the Russo-German war and court strategic favor in Moscow. Togo and Yonai faced similar imperatives the following June when the Supreme Council yielded to the pressure of radicals on the general staff and endorsed the "Fundamental Policy" to fight a climactic battle in Japan. In fact, even the most ardent peace advocates from within the *jushin*—Konoe, Okada, and Wakatsuki—were unwilling to speak out against the national consensus for continuing the war when the emperor consulted them individually in February, 1945.[177]

By the same token, Suzuki's seemingly erratic behavior becomes somewhat more reasonable when we consider, once again, the nature of leadership in Japan. As I have explained at a couple of points in this study, Japanese leaders do not lead in the Western sense of the word. The leader's role is to foster consensus among members of the group and sanction whatever position emerges, but, "above all, not to impose an independent will or even determine policy directions."[178] With this in mind, we can better comprehend how Suzuki could militantly champion a national consensus for fighting to the death, while simultaneously holding secret meetings to find a way to end the war. As head of state, he was obligated to support the established policy, even if decision makers were in the process of reevaluating that position. Likewise, his support of the "Fundamental Policy" on June 6 and 8 was not completely inconsistent with his endorsement of Kido's "Tentative Plan" several days later. In the first case, he simply carried forward the Supreme Council's consensus decision; in the second, he submitted to the Emperor's personal will, as expressed by Kido.[179] What is more difficult to explain is how Kido and the emperor could act in such an assertive fashion, not just in this instance, but during the surrender deliberations as well. I shall address that question later. In the meantime, let us examine the timing of when the diehards first entertained the possibility of ending the war.

Anami, Toyoda, and Umezu first conceded that the war was lost after Germany surrendered on May 8, 1945. At first blush, one might conclude that this change of heart reflected their conviction that the loss of a key ally substantially altered the strategic situation, but such was not the case. Japanese leaders knew Germany was defeated long before Berlin surrendered. With Soviet forces pressing from the east and Anglo-American forces rushing in from the west, Japanese diplomats in Switzerland and other neutral countries appraised Tokyo of Germany's imminent fall months before it came to pass. By May, 1945, the Pacific war had long since reached a critical stage—with Japan cut off from the mainland and hammered from the air, the Imperial Army was losing a bloody battle on Okinawa, the homeland's southern doorstep. Clearly, the fall of Berlin made little difference in Tokyo's strategic calculus.[180] But the event did make a difference in Japan's obligations in the Axis alliance.

In fact, Japan's strategic behavior from late 1944 onward suggests its military leaders already realized the war was lost; but, until the following May, the Supreme Council's freedom to maneuver was constrained by commitments Japan had made to refrain from making peace with Britain or America without Germany's consent. In December, 1944, with Japanese forces steadily losing ground in the Philippines, the general staff began transferring units from forward positions on the defensive perimeter back to the home islands.[181] Over the next several months, even as battles raged on Iwo Jima and Okinawa, they continued to move forces to the homeland in preparation for a climactic battle there.[182] All of this suggests the Supreme Command no longer had confidence in Japan's ability to stem the Allied advance; yet, military leaders were loath to even consider negotiating an end to the war. Owing, perhaps, to their Confucian sense of legalism, Japan's principal decision makers seemed resolved to abide by the letter of agreements Tokyo had signed with Berlin.[183]

But the Supreme Council abruptly changed course after Germany surrendered on May 8. With Germany fallen, the Tripartite Pact was null and void, and for the first time, the Big Six could move to end the war without betraying an ally. Subsequently, Anami and Umezu acquiesced to Togo's insistence that they close the sessions to the military staff, and beginning on May 11 they began discussing how they might bring the conflict to an end. Yet, it still took Japan another three months to effect a surrender. This final series of events speaks most loudly about the role culture played in the Supreme Council's efforts to end the war.

Japanese leaders were only able to move toward surrender when their frames of reference began to shift from their respective service or ministry *ie* (households) to a national *ie* headed by the emperor. As the strategic culture profile illustrates, Japanese tendencies toward cooperation or competition are determined by the frames of reference in which the participants find themselves. By the onset of the Second World War, the Japanese government had splintered into a number of separate households, each competing viciously with the others for policy advantage. When agency chiefs met to decide national policies, they came as leaders of their own *ie* and brought with them the rigid, parochial positions forged in the bottom-up, consensus-driven decision processes of those agencies.

Until May, 1945, this extreme factionalism resulted in a self-perpetuating consensus for continuing the war. Anami, Toyoda, Umezu, and their predecessors duly represented the militant positions driven by the extremists who controlled the War Ministry and the army and navy general staffs. Conversely, Navy Minister Yonai and Foreign Ministers Shigemitsu and Togo had greater latitude to pursue their own desires for peace, but were deterred by the strong coalition of diehards and, perhaps, by their own misgivings about violating the Tripartite Pact.[184]

But the councilors' frames of reference began to change in May, 1945. By agreeing to exclude the military-dominated secretariat from the council's proceedings, the Big Six took the first step in reorienting their attitudes and functions from being the heads of individual services and ministries to being members of a single, national-level *ie*, administered by the premier on behalf of the emperor. Isolated from their staffs, they became a functional group unto themselves, free to express opinions separate from their respective households.[185] This shift enabled the councilors to openly admit to one another that the war was lost and that they should find a way to end it. Nevertheless, this policy-making reorientation did not go unchallenged.

Responding in their own way to the heightened crisis following Germany's collapse, the military staffs developed their "Fundamental Policy" and called for a "full-dress" assembly of the Supreme Council. Placed, once again, before service members of the secretariat, the diehards reverted to their roles as heads of military households, and they ardently championed the combined staff's unanimously-endorsed document. In fact, Toyoda's behavior at this meeting offers fascinating testimony to the power of the group in Japanese society. Shortly before the session, the navy staff delivered a report estimating that Allied losses during an invasion would be somewhere in the range of 20 to 25 percent. Knowing these figures did not strongly support the navy general staff's corporate desire for a climactic battle—a position with which he did not personally agree, but was obliged to uphold—he pulled out his pen and changed the figures to 30 to 40 percent. Then, as he argued for the "Fundamental Policy" during the meeting, he impulsively reported the estimate of Allied losses to be 50 percent. After the war he explained:

Once the conference was underway, I suppose I must have felt like giving a round figure like "about one half" instead of a sharp estimate like 30 percent or 40 percent. I may have said 50 percent because I thought that the proposal to continue the war at all costs was as good as passed beyond reversal and that the use of pessimistic figures *would not be in harmony* with such a resolution . . . The fact is that *the conference decision was contrary to our true intentions* . . . there was such a crowd present that frank discussion was completely out of the question. And, as was the usual case at such meetings, there was for us no other way than to concur with extremely militant resolutions. [emphasis added][186]

The same group dynamics eventually forced Togo and Yonai to join the consensus, while Suzuki, as head of the council, orchestrated the affair. Two days later, they replayed the scenario for the emperor, who sat in abject silence, socially compelled to sanction the consensus-approved policy laid before him.

But this reversion to the old dynamic was short lived. Fearing that the self-perpetuating consensus that had locked the government in a seemingly irreversible decision for war would soon destroy Japan and the throne with it, Privy Seal Kido persuaded the emperor to sanction his "Tentative Plan." This bold stratagem so shocked members of the council that it abruptly returned their frames of reference to the national household. At Kido's urging, the emperor reinforced this newly adjusted mindset several days later by summoning the Big Six to an imperial conference and blessing their recent decision to resurrect the Soviet mediation plan. The die was cast. This series of events pointedly demonstrated to the Big Six, particularly the diehards, that they could no longer afford the luxury of passively relaying decisions made beneath them. Now, they were active participants in a national *ie*. They knew Japan faced a crisis of survival, and they realized the emperor was relying on them to solve it.

Unfortunately, this mental reorientation still did not resolve the council's deep-seated disagreements about how to end the war, disputes rooted in the differing perceptions and strategic preferences held within the constituent agencies. Certainly, each service or ministry looked to the emperor as the proverbial head of the family, and they all shared a common culture. But after decades of factional strife, each organization had also developed its own distinct subculture. These groups' perceptions and preferences were colored not only by the Japanese culture at large, but also by the symbols and values evolved in the insular environment of each specific organization.

Members of the peace faction had emerged largely from the civilian bureaucracy and from senior ranks of the prewar navy. The culture dominating most of the civilian ministries, particularly the foreign office, reflected the Confucian-based administrative values first embraced by the warrior bureaucrats during the Edo era. These men esteemed education, professional competence, and precise attention to details of law and procedure. Similarly, the interwar-period navy also valued education and competence, as naval warfare was complex and more technically demanding than combat between armies. The navy also prided itself in being worldly and sophisticated. A career at sea exposed navy officers to a range of cultural and political diversity unknown to most of their land-bound peers. Stemming from these values and experiences, members of the peace faction had both the will and the intellectual capacity to objectively assess Japan's prospects in the war. By 1945, they could see that continuing the struggle was suicidal.

But the mid-grade officers dominating Japan's wartime army and navy general staffs were cut from different stock. These men had ascended the ranks during the turbulent times of the previous two decades when *Kodo* (Imperial Way) propaganda stridently proclaimed it was Japan's manifest destiny to spread the emperor's divine righteousness across the face of Asia. Thoroughly inured in a warrior ethos that placed loyalty, courage, and self-sacrifice above all other virtues, they despised anyone who even suggested Japan might have to end the war in surrender. From their point of view, an unwavering commitment to *bushido* and faith in the emperor's divinity would assure Japan's ultimate victory, no matter how bleak the actual situation seemed. When all appeared lost, a Tennozan or a kamikaze (divine wind) would save the children of the sun from destruction. These men were true believers in the concept of spirit over matter.[187]

The general staffs' fanaticism placed Anami, Toyoda and Umezu in a very difficult position. Having recognized the war was lost, they conceded that it had to end. Therefore, they reluctantly accepted the steps taken by Togo, Kido, and finally, the emperor to forge an imperial *ie* devoted to resolving the national crisis. Yet, as heads of their own households, they still felt strongly obligated to carry forward the consensus position of the combined military staffs. So, though they cooperated in secret efforts to end the war, they maintained that the best way to do so—indeed, the only honorable way, unless a face-saving, mediated settlement could be arranged through Moscow—was by first fighting the climactic battle their subordinates so desired.

This clash of values explains the diehard faction's seemingly schizophrenic behavior during the last three months of the war. Their loyalty and obedience ultimately lay with the emperor and the *ie* formed around him to end the conflict, but their honor lay in a sense of obligation to their subordinates, an obligation to support the military's desperate desire to prove its worth by finally demonstrating the superiority of spirit over matter. In essence, the diehards found themselves in a paradox of contextual morality—a conflict between doing *chu*, service to the emperor, and fulfilling *giri*, the reciprocal obligation owed for the loyalty of those beneath them. Such a dilemma had a clear solution in Imperial Japan's culture—*chu* was a limitless duty that took precedence over all others. Yet that did not relieve these military leaders of the obligation to serve those institutions they represented. Consequently, in the very end, after Japan had lost everything but survival itself, Anami, Toyoda, and Umezu argued not for territory or some other tangible gain, but for terms that would win them, in addition to preservation of the throne, the one commodity the military held most dear. Efforts to avoid disarmament, occupation, and war crimes trials were firmly rooted in the military's obsessive desire to maintain face. For this, they would deny the enemy's might and even the destructiveness of the atomic bomb.

Members of the peace faction understood and sympathized with the position the diehards were in. In fact, they had the highest respect for the way General Anami comported himself throughout the surrender deliberations. After the war, former Ambassador to the United States Admiral Nomura Kichisaburo told Strategic Bombing Survey interrogators:

As a member of the cabinet [Anami] knew the real situation, but as head of the army he knew that there was a strong feeling in the army for continuing the war. Therefore, he was in a dilemma, and after signing the emperor's orders that they had taken the responsibility for ending the war, which all ministers must sign, he killed himself. He was in a very difficult position, being both a member of the cabinet and head of the army, and it was said that he acted truly like a gentleman.[188]

But the propensity for self-delusion was not confined to the military. Right up until the Red Army's plunge into Manchuria, the imperial court and members of both factions believed the Soviet Union would help Japan out of its difficulties, despite all evidence to the contrary. This catastrophic misperception was the product of several converging forces. First, the Russo-Japanese Neutrality Pact played on penchants in Tokyo to rely on legal technicality, giving Japanese leaders a false sense of security—surely, the Soviets would not attack while the treaty was still in force. More significantly, Japan's sense of propriety and international hierarchy and its leaders' desire to save face combined to convince Tokyo that they had no other place to turn.

Having lost the war, the Japanese were loath to negotiate directly with the victors. That would have entailed an immense loss of face, all the more so as the Allies were publicly demanding unconditional surrender. So, just as the Chinese had attempted to avoid direct negotiations with Tokyo at the end of the first Sino-Japanese war, Japanese leaders sought an intermediary through whom they could seek terms without having to face their conquerors directly. But finding the appropriate mediator presented a dilemma. The Supreme Council first considered approaching the Vatican, a source of moral authority whom they knew the Anglo-Americans respected. But, as the Pope had previously criticized Japan's conduct in the war, they doubted he would be willing to help them. Someone mentioned China, but Chiang Kai-shek had signed the Cairo Declaration, and Koiso's earlier flirtation with Chungking had caused Tokyo considerable embarrassment. They briefly considered Sweden and Switzerland, but the Big Six did not believe those nations had enough standing to command the Allies' respect. Only the Soviet Union seemed to have the necessary combination of prestige and diplomatic ties to present Japan's case to the Allies in a dignified way. In fact, Japanese leaders reasoned, given Russia's Great Power status, her position in Asia, and the Russo-Japanese Neutrality Pact, Moscow might even be offended if Tokyo turned to anyone else, and that would be dangerous. Ultimately, in their desperation to preserve the throne and avoid the humiliation of facing the Allies, Japanese leaders managed to convince themselves that the Russians were their friends and their only hope for a face-saving, negotiated settlement.[189]

That leads us, finally, to consider the role the Soviet declaration of war played in bringing about Japan's surrender, vis-à-vis the atomic bomb. As it turns out, both events dramatically influenced Japan's decision but, ironically, they did so in ways other than most scholars contend. Neither persuaded any political faction to substantially change its stance on ending the war—peace advocates were willing to accept most provisions of the Potsdam Declaration before August 6, yet diehards held out for additional terms even after August 9—but both events made a substantial impact on Japanese perceptions. The Soviet attack revealed the folly of Japan's overtures to Moscow, convincing both the emperor and the Big Six that there was no chance of achieving a face-saving, mediated settlement. Consequently, the event shocked and dispirited all of Japan's key decision makers, not because it changed the strategic equation, but because it confirmed once and for all the utter hopelessness of Tokyo's dreams of negotiating a peace with honor. Ironically, this revelation only increased the level of discord among elites in the Supreme Council and the cabinet. It strengthened the convictions of those who believed Japan's only hope now lay in surrender, but it intensified the commitment of those who insisted that Japan must end the war with dignity. With hopes for a mediated settlement crushed, the only path to honor now lay in the climactic battle. Consequently, Anami, Toyoda, and Umezu fervently argued for that policy until the very end. The atomic bomb, on the other hand, played a decisive role in bringing about Japan's surrender, but we can only appreciate that role once we understand why values in the imperial court differed from those held by other groups and how, to preserve Japan's core values, certain individuals conspired to circumvent traditional Japanese decision-making processes.

As observed in the cost-benefit analysis, both of Japan's key political factions based their policy preferences solely on estimates of the Allies' ability to deny Japan the benefits of continued resistance. In other words, both groups were concerned about Japan's prospects for winning or losing the war, but neither was sensitive to the suffering inflicted on the Japanese people by bombing and blockade. Those priorities can be explained by each faction's values. The diehards, enculturated in a warrior ethos that esteemed loyalty and self-sacrifice, considered death in the name of service a privilege. In their minds, the Japanese people were honored to suffer for the glory of the emperor and *kokutai*. The peace faction and the general public shared these *bushido*-based values though, perhaps, less fervently than the military. But the sense of public duty was augmented in civilian quarters by the traditional concept, *kanson minpi*, "official exhalted—people despised." Consequently, every Japanese official's notion of a subject's role in society revolved around obedience, service, and sacrifice. In this mindset, public suffering was never a significant factor in the government's decision calculus.

But Emperor Hirohito saw things differently. As spiritual and corporal father of the Japanese national family, the emperor felt deeply responsible for the well-being of his people. Consequently, as provisions grew scarce and the bombings intensified in the spring of 1945, he became increasingly agitated. Already doubtful of Japan's ability to win the war, the sharply escalated punishment threw an immense burden of cost on his shoulders, costs paid for benefits he had become increasingly convinced were irretrievably lost. On June 8, his anxiety turned to horror when the Supreme Council declared its unified resolve to sacrifice thousands of men, women, and children in a suicidal scheme to save Japan's military honor.[190]

Marquis Kido also was responsive to the costs of punishment, but for different reasons. As lord keeper of the privy seal, he was personally responsible for protecting the imperial institution and preserving *kokutai*. When he saw the "Fundamental Policy," he realized Hirohito had been forced to sanction a plan that, if carried out, would destroy Japan and the throne with it. At this point, Kido concluded that, despite the Supreme Council's earlier movement toward ending the war, the government was still captive to the general staffs' obsessive quest to regain face and honor. Therefore, the privy seal decided that, to save the throne, he must manipulate the government's decision-making process in a way that would circumvent the traditional, bottom-up flow of power and, thereby, defuse the forces driving Japan to its own destruction.

During the next three months, Kido diligently worked to sever the ties binding the Supreme Council to the military staffs. Playing on Hirohito's anxiety, he persuaded him to presanction the "Tentative Plan to Cope with the Situation," and he guided the emperor's efforts to revive and strengthen the imperial *ie*. Moreover, the privy seal was not alone in this project. He began exchanging notes and holding discussions with Togo, Yonai, Suzuki, and Chief Cabinet Secretary Sakomizu during the first half of June, preparing the ground for the emperor's intervention.[191] Ultimately, their coordinated efforts would be instrumental in manipulating the August deliberations, enabling Emperor Hirohito to order an unconditional surrender on the fourteenth.

But it is important to understand that Kido and the peace faction still could not have brought about Japan's surrender without the events that occurred between August 6 and 9. In the days leading up to the sixth, all of Japan's principal decision makers had fallen into a stupor waiting for Moscow's response to their pleas for Soviet mediation. Moreover, the military was so firmly wedded to plans to fight the climactic battle that it is doubtful that an imperial intervention would have been possible before that time. Hiroshima jolted the peace advocates out of their daze and so overwhelmed the emperor with grief that he wanted to end the war immediately. The Soviet declaration of war stiffened his resolve even further and, though it did not change the policy preferences of those yearning to save Japan's honor, it probably played a role in convincing field commanders to accept the imperially mandated surrender without taking "direct action" to continue the war. After the war, when Strategic Bombing Survey investigators asked Admiral Toyoda, "At what time during the course of the war would the navy have accepted an imperial rescript terminating the war?" he responded:

That is very difficult to answer because even on the 15th when the imperial rescript terminating the war was first issued, even then we found it difficult to hold down the front line forces who were all "raring to go," and it was very difficult to hold them back . . . I do not think it would be accurate to look upon the atomic bomb and the entry and participation of Soviet Russia into the war as direct causes for termination of the war, but I think that those two factors did enable us to bring the war to a termination without creating too great chaos in Japan.[192]

When pressed to elaborate, Toyoda said he was unsure if the navy would have obeyed an imperial rescript terminating the war any time prior to the intervention of Soviet Russia.[193]

Yet, even with the cataclysmic events that happened between August 6 and August 9, Japan could not have ended the war without an imperial rescript. As early as February, 1945, Admiral Takagi had concluded that imperial intervention would be necessary to persuade both the military and the Japanese people to accept peace. Allied demands for unconditional surrender had placed all of Japan's core values at risk. At the same time, the overwhelming onslaught of Allied military force placed the nation's continued existence in question. In the end, only a command from the emperor, the ultimate source of value in Imperial Japan's elaborate cosmology, could sufficiently unify the country's various factions to shoulder the risks entailed in opting for survival through surrender. But, ironically, imperial intervention, an event unprecedented in the history of Japan, was only possible when that nation faced a crisis equally unprecedented in its long history—the combined effects of total denial and overwhelming punishment.

CONCLUSION

Events leading to the surrender of Japan bear witness to the dramatic impact culture can have on the way national decision makers respond to coercive threat. By all reasonable measures, Japanese leaders should have been strongly motivated to seek peace by the end of 1944. The tide of battle had turned against them two and a half years earlier, and with their navy and air forces decimated, continuing the conflict clearly was not in Tokyo's interest. Further hostilities only jeopardized the gains made early in the war, eroding Japan's negotiating posture and exposing the Japanese people to ever-increasing punishment. Yet, Japanese leaders did not take meaningful steps to end the struggle until more than six months later.

Several factors combined to frustrate the hopes of those in Japan who sought to end the war. The dominance of a military oligarchy, driven by values that placed honor and face above national interest and public welfare, repeatedly deterred the peace aspirations of a growing faction of political elites who foresaw the calamity that lay ahead. Obsessive concern with keeping formal commitments to Berlin discouraged decision makers from seeking opportunities to negotiate a settlement until Germany had fallen and Japan was well on the road to disaster. Most importantly, Allied demands for unconditional surrender threatened Japan's core values and further impeded efforts to seek peace by making direct communication with the Allies extremely costly in terms of national pride and personal face.

Even after Japan's key decision makers concluded the war was lost and secretly agreed to end it, misperceptions, conflicting values, and peculiarities in the decision-making process inhibited their efforts to do so until the country neared the brink of destruction. Togo and Yonai had wanted to make peace for some time. Suzuki joined their ranks sometime in the spring of 1945. After Germany fell, Anami, Toyoda, and Umezu also conceded that Japan should end the war, but their duty to institutions that placed unwavering faith in the superiority of spirit over matter obligated them to insist that the military be permitted to regain its honor in a climactic battle for the homeland, should the Allies deny Japan the dignity of face-saving terms. Privy Seal Kido managed to bind these leaders together in a national *ie* devoted to resolving the crisis, but Soviet deceit and stalling paralyzed this newly formed household's will to act, as elites in both government and palace convinced themselves that Moscow held the key to Japan's salvation.

Only the combined effects of the atomic bombings and the Soviet attack had the necessary impact to jar Japanese leaders out of their torpor and bring about an unconditional surrender. The bombing of Hiroshima so grieved the emperor that he subsequently permitted Kido and the peace faction to maneuver him into position to intervene in the policy-making process. The Soviet declaration of war crushed Japanese hopes for a mediated settlement, further convincing peace advocates that Japan must surrender. Although that event only hardened the diehards' resolve to allow the military to seek honor in a climactic battle, it contributed to conditions that persuaded the military rank and file to accept the emperor's command to lay down their arms and yield to the Allies. Through it all, Japanese leaders remained absorbed in protecting the ultimate symbol of Japan's core values, the throne; but when the Allies refused their bid for a conditional surrender, they even relinquished that treasure. Seeing no further benefit in resistance and bearing the enormous weight of a level of punishment unparalleled in Japan's history, the emperor sacrificed *kokutai* for the only value that he, as father of the Japanese national family, held more dear—the survival of his people.

NOTES

1. American popular opinion holds that the atomic bombs so shocked and intimidated Japanese leaders that they felt compelled to throw in the towel for fear of further destruction. This argument has been expressed in books, such as Herbert Feis's *Japan Subdued* and numerous articles. Conversely, the United States Strategic Bombing Survey (USSBS) concluded that Japan would probably have surrendered before November 1, 1945, the date set for the invasion, even without the atomic bomb, due to the effects of conventional strategic bombing. Naval historians such as Kenneth J. Hagan contend that the interdiction campaign, waged primarily by submarines and secondarily by land- and carrier-based aviation, was America's most compelling weapon in the Pacific war. Most recently, Robert A. Pape has asserted that Japanese leaders were persuaded to surrender only after the Soviet plunge into Manchuria convinced them that they would be unable to inflict serious damage on an American invasion force. See Herbert Feis, *Japan Subdued: The Atomic Bomb and the End of the War in the Pacific* (Princeton, N.J.: Princeton University Press, 1961); Kenneth J. Hagan, *This People's Navy: The Making of American Sea Power* (New York: The Free Press, 1991); Robert A. Pape, *Bombing to Win: Air Power and Coercion in War* (Ithaca, N.Y.: Cornell University Press, 1996);

and USSBS, *Japan's Struggle to End the War* (Washington, D.C.: Government Printing Office, 1946).

2. Herbert P. Bix, "The Hirohito Emperor's 'Monologue' and the Problem of War Responsibility" *Journal of Japanese Studies* 18, No. 2 (Summer 1992): pp. 352–54.

3. For accounts from two of Japan's foreign ministers regarding how the Tojo Cabinet reorganized wartime diplomatic functions, see Shigenori Togo, *The Cause of Japan*, trans. and ed. by Fumihiko Togo and Ben Bruce Blakeney (New York: Simon and Schuster, 1956), pp. 250–55; Mamoru Shigemitsu, *Japan and Her Destiny: My Struggle for Peace*, trans. by Oswald White and ed. by Major General F.S.G. Piggott (New York: E.P. Dutton & Co., Inc., 1958), pp. 281–90 and 299–300.

4. Toshikazu Kase, *Journey to the Missouri* (New Haven, Conn.: Yale University Press, 1950), p. 68.

5. A few astute navy officers, such as Rear Admiral Takagi Sokichi, had noticed a serious trend emerging in Japan's merchant marine losses, a crucial area of concern for an island nation so dependent on imports. In fiscal year 1942 alone, 1,250 of Japan's 5,348 operable merchant ships were sunk, mostly by American submarines. During the same year, the Japanese were only able to build 362 replacement vessels and capture 377 others. This trend accelerated as the war progressed. See Jerome B. Cohen, *Japan's Economy in War and Reconstruction* (Minneapolis, Minn.: University of Minnesota Press, 1949), Table 32, p. 267.

6. The Home Ministry was in charge of maintaining internal security in Japan. Tojo had been chief of the *Kempeitai* (military secret police) while assigned to Kwangtung Army Headquarters in Manchuria during the 1930s. Later, while holding the War and Home Ministry portfolios, he reorganized security forces throughout Japan, increasing the efficiency of an already repressive police state.

7. Ben-Ami Shillony, *Politics and Culture in Wartime Japan* (Oxford: Clarendon Press, 1981), p. 52.

8. Koichi Kido, *The Diary of Marquis Kido, 1931–45: Selected Translations into English* (Frederick, Md.: University Publications of America, 1984), p. 350.

9. Ibid., p. 351. Before approaching the emperor, Kido met with Tojo who reassured him that he had both the war and domestic situation under control.

10. Robert J. C. Butow, *Japan's Decision to Surrender* (Stanford, Calif.: Stanford University Press, 1954), p. 16.

11. Shillony, p. 55.

12. Having served as ambassador to Moscow in 1936 and ambassador to London in 1938, Shigemitsu was considered a Soviet expert and was a diplomat whom the Japanese believed the West respected. See Kase, pp. 68–69; S. Woodburn Kirby, *The War Against Japan*, Volume V: *The Surrender of Japan* (London: Her Majesty's Stationary Office, 1969), 5:172; Shigemitsu, pp. 287–88.

13. Shillony, pp. 53–54.

14. Butow, p. 18; F. C. Jones, *Japan's New Order in East Asia: Its Rise and Fall, 1937–45* (Oxford: Oxford University Press, 1954), p. 423; Kase, pp. 68–69; Stephen S. Large, *Emperor Hirohito and Showa Japan: A Political Biography* (New York: Routledge, 1992), pp. 17–18; Shillony, pp. 55–56.

15. On June 19, 1944, during the Battle of the Philippine Sea, Admiral Ozawa Jisaburo sent 373 carrier-based planes in a four-wave attack on the U.S. Navy's

Task Force 58. Guided by radar and intercepts of Japanese tactical communications, U.S. Navy aviators shot down nearly 300 attacking aircraft at a loss of only 29 of their own. Dubbed by an American pilot the "Great Marianas Turkey Shoot," this defeat crippled Japanese aviation for the remainder of the war, as Japan had neglected to develop an aggressive training program to replace the loss of experienced pilots. See Ronald H. Spector, *Eagle Against the Sun: The American War with Japan* (New York: Vintage Books, 1985), pp. 307–8.

16. Herbert P. Bix, *Hirohito and the Making of Modern Japan* (New York: Perennial, 2000), pp. 475–76; Kirby, p. 5:172; Shigemitsu, pp. 311–12.

17. Butow, pp. 27–28; Jones, pp. 423–24; Shigemitsu, pp. 314–15; Shillony, pp. 63–64; USSBS, *Japan's Struggle*, pp. 2–3.

18. Shillony, pp. 64–65.

19. Kase says Tojo's real objection to Terauchi's nomination was because they were mortal enemies. See Kase, p. 83.

20. Butow, pp. 30–31; Jones, pp. 424–25; Kase, pp. 82–83; Shigemitsu, p. 319; Shillony, pp. 64–65.

21. Butow, p. 32; Jones, p. 425; Kase, pp. 83–84; Kirby, p. 5:173; Shillony, p. 65.

22. According to Koiso's testimony after the war, the emperor was vague as to what the relationship between he and Yonai would be and even which of them would be the prime minister. Koiso had to get clarification from Kido and Yonai after the imperial audience. See Butow, pp. 32–33; Large, pp. 119–20; Shigemitsu, p. 319.

23. Kase, pp. 84–85.

24. Ibid., pp. 86–87. Also see Butow, pp. 19–22 and 35–36; Shillony, pp. 66 and 68. After the war, Koiso testified that he did not seek the war portfolio during the formation of his cabinet, and, based on that testimony, Butow asserts that Tojo and Koiso did not quarrel over this issue. Yet, it is hard to explain the degree of animosity between Koiso and the army without accepting Kase's account.

25. Quotation from Butow, p. 38. Also see Butow, pp. 37–38; Jones, p. 426; Kase, pp. 88–89; Kirby, p. 5:173; Shigemitsu, pp. 319–320; Shillony, pp. 69–70; USSBS, *Japan's Struggle*, p. 4.

26. Jones, pp. 426–27; Kirby, pp. 5:173–74; Shigemitsu, pp. 295–96.

27. Takagi was a strategic analyst for the navy. He had first come to Yonai's attention in March, 1944, when Takagi confided to him the disturbing results of a study he had conducted the year before on orders of then Navy Minister Shimada. Takagi had been directed to examine the lessons of the war to date, but after an exhaustive review of the nation's military, industrial, and shipping losses, he concluded the war was lost and Japan must seek a negotiated peace. Fearful of taking these results to Shimada, Takagi passed them, instead, to Yonai and fellow peace advocate Vice Admiral Inouye Seibi. Yonai, in turn, informed the rest of the *jushin*. See Butow, pp. 20–22; USSBS *Japan's Struggle*, p. 3.

28. Butow, pp. 38–40; Kirby, p. 5:173; USSBS, *Japan's Struggle*, p. 3.

29. Butow, p. 41; Kase, pp. 92–97; Spector, pp. 426–42. Also see Haywood S. Hansell, Jr., *The Strategic Air War Against Germany and Japan: A Memoir* (Washington, D.C.: Office of Air Force History, United States Air Force, 1986), pp. 175–90.

30. Butow, p. 43.

31. Shigemitsu, p. 322.

32. Lester Brooks, *Behind Japan's Surrender: The Secret Struggle that Ended an*

Empire (New York: McGraw-Hill Book Company, 1968), pp. 128–29; Butow, pp. 42–43; Kase, pp. 96–98.

33. In fact, Koiso was in the antechamber of the Imperial Palace waiting to see the emperor when the war minister came in and whispered the news to him.

34. Brooks, pp. 129–30; Butow, pp. 43–44; Kase, pp. 98–100; Shillony, p. 73; USSBS, *Japan's Struggle*, p. 5.

35. Brooks, p. 131; Butow, pp. 44–46; Kase, p. 102.

36. Tojo asserted that the United States had fallen far short of its objectives. He also maintained that even if the Soviet Union joined in the war against Japan, it would not be able to commit enough force to the fight to make a difference. According to Tojo, Japan's biggest enemy was defeatism, and with determination, she could win. See Butow, pp. 46–47; Shillony, pp. 73–74.

37. Brooks, p. 131; Butow, pp. 46–50; Kase, p. 102; USSBS, *Japan's Struggle*, p. 5. According to *Japan's Struggle*, except for Tojo, the former prime ministers all asserted "that Japan faced certain defeat and should seek peace at once." However, as Butow points out, the notes taken by the attending grand chamberlain of the imperial household do not bear this out (see Butow, p. 46 n. 52). I could find no credible historian who agrees with the USSBS on this issue.

38. USSBS, *Summary Report (Pacific War)* (Washington, D.C.: U.S. Government Printing Office, 1946), p. 16.

39. Ibid.

40. Robert Frank Futrell, *Ideas, Concepts, and Doctrine: Basic Thinking in the United States Air Force, 1907–1960* (Maxwell AFB, AL: Air University Press, 1989), pp. 1:163–64; Michael S. Sherry, *The Rise of American Air Power: The Creation of Armageddon* (New Haven, Conn.: Yale University Press, 1987), pp. 266–73.

41. John Keegan, *The Second World War* (New York: Penguin Books, 1989), pp. 576–77; Spector, p. 505.

42. Shigemitsu, pp. 326–27; USSBS, *Summary Report*, pp. 16–17. As Sherry notes, USSBS calculations of deaths in Japan resulting from air raids of all types range from 268,157 in *Final Report Covering Air-Raid Protection and Allied Subjects in Japan* (Washington, D.C.: Government Printing Office, 1947), p. 197, to 900,000 in *The Effects of Strategic Bombing on Japanese Morale* (Washington, D.C.: Government Printing Office, 1947), pp. 194–95. See Sherry, p. 413 n. 43.

43. Butow, p. 51; Shigemitsu, pp. 331–33.

44. Bix, *Hirohito and the Making of Modern Japan*, pp. 492–93; Butow, pp. 51–54; Jones, p. 430; Kase, p. 108; Kirby, p. 5:174; Large, p. 120; Shigemitsu, pp. 341–42; Shillony, p. 76; USSBS, *Japan's Struggle*, p. 6.

45. Kase maintains that the outcome of this meeting was engineered in advance through a secret pact between Konoe, Okada, Wakatsuki, and Hiranuma to steer the discussion away from Tojo's preferred candidate, Marshal Hata Shunroku. See Kase, p. 114.

46. Butow, pp. 60–61; Jones, pp. 430–31; Kase, p. 114; Large, pp. 121–22; Shillony, pp. 77–78.

47. Quoted in Butow, p. 63.

48. Ibid., p. 64.

49. Butow, pp. 63–64; Jones, p. 431; Kase, p. 114; Kirby, p. 5:175; Shigemitsu, p. 353.

50. Butow, pp. 64–65; Kase, p. 121.

51. Butow, pp. 65–66; Kase, pp. 121–22; Shillony, p. 79; Togo, pp. 269–70.

52. Butow, pp. 66–67; Kase, p. 122; Shillony, p. 79; Togo, pp. 270–71.

53. See Butow, p. 65 n. 30; Shillony, p. 78.

54. Portion before ellipses quoted in Kase, p. 115; portion following ellipses paraphrased, ibid., p. 116.

55. USSBS, *Japan's Struggle*, p. 6. The report of the Sakomizu study is presented in its entirety as Appendix I to *Japan's Struggle*.

56. Butow, p. 75 n. 56.

57. Ibid., p. 76.

58. Ibid., p. 79.

59. Ibid. Also see Kase, p. 129.

60. Togo insisted on this change. The peace faction had been frustrated by the way the military staff officers who attended the meetings always seemed to dictate the agenda. As a result, Kase says "when the Suzuki cabinet took office we thought it imperative that the character of the Supreme War Council should be drastically changed." Togo recommended the change to Suzuki, Yonai, and, presumably, Toyoda. Meanwhile, Umezu convinced Anami that, considering the gravity of the issues being discussed, closed sessions were necessary to avoid leaks that might damage troop morale. See Butow, p. 82 n. 19; Kase, p. 145; Togo, pp. 282–83.

61. This development was important not only because it cut the young radical officers out of the information loop, but also because it created a vacuum that the peace faction could step in to fill. With the secretariat excluded, the six council members were left without administrative support. Consequently, peace advocates Kase, Matsudaira, Admiral Takagi, and army Colonel Matsutani Makoto stepped forward as a makeshift secretariat. Having met informally since January, 1945, these four men now shaped the Supreme Council's agenda. See Butow, p. 83 n. 20; Jones, p. 432; Kase, pp. 146–47; Kirby, p. 5:175; Togo, pp. 283–84.

62. Butow, pp. 81–84; Brooks, p. 137; Jones, p. 432; Kase, pp. 145–46; Kirby, p. 5:175; USSBS *Japan's Struggle*, pp. 6–7. Also see the interrogation of Navy Minister Yonai in USSBS, *Interrogations of Japanese Officials*, Volume II (Washington, D.C.: Government Printing Office, 1946), p. 2:332.

63. Brooks, pp. 137–39; Butow, pp. 83–85; Jones, pp. 432–33; Kase, pp. 169–70; Kirby, p. 5:177; Large, p. 122; Togo, pp. 284–87.

64. Togo, pp. 288–89.

65. Butow, pp. 90–92; Jones, p. 435; Kase, pp. 170–71; Shigemitsu, pp. 354–55.

66. Besides the six principal members of the Supreme Council, the June 6 meeting included the full secretariat, the chiefs of the various military affairs bureaus, the head of the cabinet coordinating bureau, the chief cabinet secretary, and the ministers of agriculture and munitions. See Brooks, p. 139.

67. Butow, p. 93.

68. Ironically, the proponents of "Fundamental Policy" attached two reports that supposedly supported their plan: "Estimate of the World Situation" and "The Present State of National Power." Far from lending support, the data in these reports reflected the reality that Japan could not possibly repel an Allied invasion. In fact, the figures provided in "National Power" plainly suggested that Japan would collapse, militarily and economically, sometime during the autumn. See Kase, pp. 172–73; Kirby, p. 5:178.

69. Brooks, pp. 139–42; Butow, pp. 93–94; Jones, pp. 435–36; Kase, pp. 171–73; Kirby, p. 5:177–78; Togo, pp. 290–92; USSBS, *Interrogations*, p. 2:320; USSBS, *Japan's Struggle*, p. 7.

70. Bix, *Hirohito and the Making of Modern Japan*, p. 493; Brooks, pp. 143–44; Kase, pp. 176–77; Large, p. 123.

71. Brooks, pp. 143–45; Butow, pp. 114–15; Kase, pp. 176–77; Kido, pp. 434–35.

72. Quoted in Kase, pp. 176–77.

73. Kido, p. 436.

74. Brooks, p. 146; Kase, p. 177; p. Kido, 436.

75. Bix, *Hirohito and the Making of Modern Japan*, p. 493; Butow, p. 114; Kase, p. 180; Large, p. 123.

76. In fact, during their discussion Anami subtly threatened Kido by casually asking what he thought of rumors that the privy seal was to be replaced. See Brooks, p. 149; Kido, p. 437.

77. Brooks, pp. 146–50; Butow, p. 114; Kase, pp. 180–81; pp. Kido, 436–37.

78. Brooks, p. 151; Butow, pp. 116–17; Kase, pp. 184–85; Kirby, p. 5:178; Shigemitsu, p. 357; Togo, p. 296.

79. Butow, p. 118.

80. Butow, p. 118; Kase, p. 185; Togo, pp. 296–97.

81. Bix, *Hirohito and the Making of Modern Japan*, p. 494; Brooks, pp. 151–53; Butow, pp. 119–20; Kase, pp. 185–86; Kido, pp. 437–38; Kirby, p. 5:178; Large, p. 123; Shillony, p. 85; Togo, pp. 297–98; USSBS, *Japan's Struggle*, p. 7.

82. Brooks, pp. 153–54; Butow, pp. 121–23; Kase, pp. 187–88; Togo, pp. 298 and 301.

83. Togo, p. 302.

84. Bix, p. 494.

85. Brooks, pp. 154–55; Butow, pp. 123–24; Feis, p. 54; Jones, p. 437; Kase, pp. 188–89; Kido, pp. 438–40; Kirby, p. 5:178; Large, p. 124; Shigemitsu, p. 357; Togo, pp. 304–8; USSBS, *Japan's Struggle*, p. 7.

86. However, for some reason, while Togo had Sato tell the Russians that Konoe would be coming to discuss bringing the war to an end, he explicitly instructed the ambassador not to tell them that Tokyo wanted Moscow to mediate a settlement or offer more than a hint that there would be something in it for the Soviet Union. Togo told Sato to say specifically: "We consider the maintenance of peace in Asia as one aspect of maintaining world peace. We have no intention of annexing or taking possession of the areas which we have been occupying as a result of war; we hope to terminate the war with a view to establishing and maintaining lasting world peace." See the 11 July 1945 telegrams from Togo to Sato in United States Department of State, *Foreign Relations of the United States, Diplomatic Papers: The Conference of Berlin (The Potsdam Papers), 1945* (hereafter referred to as FRUS *Potsdam Papers*) (Washington, D.C.: U.S. Government Printing Office, 1960), pp. 1:874–75.

87. Togo, p. 308.

88. Quoted in Brooks, p. 157 and Jones, p. 438. Also see Bix, *Hirohito and the Making of Modern Japan*, p. 507; Brooks, pp. 157–58; Butow, pp. 124–28; Feis, pp. 55–56, 64–65, and 92; Jones, pp. 437–38; Kase, pp. 193–94; Kirby, pp. 5:178–79; Togo, pp. 307–8.

89. Brooks, p. 157; Butow, p. 128; Feis, pp. 92–94; Jones, p. 438; Kase, p. 205; Kirby, p. 5:179; Large, p. 124.

90. Brooks, pp. 157–58; Feis, p. 95.

91. See the Postsdam Declaration in FRUS *Potsdam Papers*, pp. 2:1474–76.

92. Jones, p. 441; Feis, p. 95; Kase, pp. 209–10; Large, p. 124; Togo, pp. 311–12.

93. Jones, p. 441; Kase, p. 209.

94. Brooks, p. 160; Butow, pp. 143–45; Feis, pp. 95–96; Jones, p. 441; Togo, pp. 312–13.

95. Brooks, p. 161; Butow, pp. 145–46; Feis, p. 97; Kase, p. 211; Large, p. 124; Shigemitsu, p. 358.

96. Carried in the Tokyo *Asahi Shinbun* on Monday, July 30, 1945, and quoted in Butow, p. 148. Also see Bix, *Hirohito and the Making of Modern Japan*, pp. 500–501.

97. Brooks, p. 163; Feis, pp. 97–98; Large, p. 124; Shillony, p. 85; Togo, p. 314.

98. Brooks, p. 164; Butow, pp. 149–50 and 153; Togo, p. 314.

99. Postwar testimony of General Arisue Seizo, chief of army intelligence, concerning Tokyo's first indications of the atomic bombing of Hiroshima. Quoted in Brooks, p. 166.

100. Butow, pp. 150–51. After the war, Kawabe said he immediately suspected the damage at Hiroshima had been done by an atomic bomb, as Japan's leading physicist, Nishima Yoshio, had briefed him years earlier on the prospects of atomic energy.

101. Quoted in Butow, p. 151. Also see Brooks, pp. 166–68; Kase, p. 212; Kirby, p. 5:207; Shigemitsu, p. 359.

102. Kido, p. 443.

103. Kido's postwar testimony, quoted in Butow, p. 152 n. 35.

104. Brooks, p. 170.

105. Brooks, pp. 170–71; Feis, p. 113; Kirby, pp. 5:207–8; Togo, p. 315.

106. Brooks, p. 171. Also paraphrased in Togo, pp. 315–16.

107. Brooks, p. 171; Butow, pp. 152–53; Feis, p. 113; Kirby, p. 5:208.

108. Brooks, p. 172; Butow, pp. 157–58; Feis, pp. 114–15; Kase, pp. 123–24; Kirby, p. 5:208; Togo, p. 316; USSBS, *Japan's Surrender*, p. 8.

109. Bix, *Hirohito and the Making of Modern Japan*, pp. 511–12; Butow, pp. 159–60; Jones, p. 444; Kido, pp. 143–44. Togo maintains that it was he who opened the meeting with that statement. See Togo, p. 316.

110. General Umezu said, "If we are lucky, we will be able to repulse the invaders before they land. At any rate, I can say with assurance that we will be able to destroy the major part of an invading army, that is, we will be able to inflict extremely heavy casualties on the enemy." Quoted in Butow, p. 163. Also see Large, p. 125; Shillony, p. 85; Togo, p. 317.

111. Bix, *Hirohito and the Making of Modern Japan*, p. 512; Butow, pp. 161–62; Large, p. 125; Shigemitsu, p. 359; Togo, p. 317.

112. Butow, pp. 160–64; Feis, p. 119; Jones, p. 444; Kase, p. 231; Kido, p. 444; Kirby, pp. 5:208–9; Togo, p. 318; USSBS, *Japan's Surrender*, p. 8.

113. Kase, p. 231.

114. Quoted in Pacific War Research Society (PWRS), *Japan's Longest Day* (Tokyo: Kodansha International, Ltd., 1968), p. 27.

115. Bix, *Hirohito and the Making of Modern Japan*, p. 513; Butow, pp. 164–65; Jones, p. 444; Kase, pp. 231–33; PWRS, *Japan's Longest Day*, pp. 26–28; Togo, pp. 318–19, USSBS, *Japan's Struggle*, p. 8.

116. Togo, p. 319.

117. Butow, p. 165; Kido, p. 444; Kirby, p. 209; PWRS, *Japan's Longest Day*, pp. 28–30; Shigemitsu, p. 360.

118. Butow, p. 167.

119. Ibid., p. 169.

120. Butow, pp. 168–69; Kido, pp. 444–45; Kirby, p. 5:210; PWRS, *Japan's Longest Day*, pp. 31–32; Shigemitsu, p. 361; USSBS, *Japan's Struggle*, p. 8.

121. PWRS, *Japan's Longest Day*, p. 33.

122. Butow, p. 170; Kase, pp. 233–34; PWRS, *Japan's Longest Day*, p. 33.

123. Suzuki's error was probably a simple oversight caused by the stress of the situation. After Hiranuma yielded the floor, the prime minister returned to Toyoda who reiterated the diehard position and added that he could not be certain the navy would obey an order to surrender unless Japan disarmed her own troops. See Butow, p. 174; PWRS, *Japan's Longest Day*, p. 34.

124. Butow, pp. 171–72.

125. Ibid., p. 172.

126. Butow, pp. 171–73; Kase, p. 234; PWRS, *Japan's Longest Day*, p. 33; Togo, p. 320.

127. Butow, p. 175.

128. Ibid., pp. 175–76. No transcript exists of Emperor Hirohito's exact words. Butow constructed the account above from postwar testimonies of others at the meeting.

129. See these cables as relayed to U.S. authorities by Swedish and Swiss authorities in *Foreign Relations of the United States: 1945, The British Commonwealth, The Far East* (hereafter referred to as FRUS) (Washington: U.S. Government Printing Office, 1969) pp. 6:624–25 and 627.

130. Malik had requested an audience the morning before, but Togo was unavailable all day due to the many events cited above.

131. Brooks, pp. 173, 175–77, and 191–93; Butow, pp. 177–81 and 186; Jones, p. 445; Kase, pp. 238–39; Kirby, p. 5:210; PWRS, *Japan's Longest Day*, p. 35; Togo, pp. 321–23; USSBS, *Japan's Struggle*, p. 9.

132. I will address this in more detail when analyzing the balance of interests in this case.

133. See James F. Byrnes' letter, "The Secretary of State to the Swiss Chargé (Grassli), Washington, August 11, 1945" in FRUS, 6:631–32.

134. Ibid.

135. Butow pp. 191–92; Feis, pp. 122–23.

136. Butow, pp. 189–91 and 245; Feis, pp. 120–23; Jones, p. 146; Kirby, p. 5:211; PWRS, *Japan's Longest Day*, pp. 37–38, 41, and 42–43. Meanwhile, the combined American air forces of the army and navy intensified the conventional bombing campaign even further, culminating in a 1,014 plane bombardment on August 14. See Sherry, p. 345.

137. Togo, pp. 323–25.

138. Butow, p. 193.

139. Brooks, pp. 214–20; Butow, pp. 192–93; Feis, p. 127; Jones, pp. 446–47; Kase, p. 242; Kirby, p. 5:212; Large, p. 127; PWRS, *Japan's Longest Day*, pp. 46–48; Shillony, pp. 86–87.

140. Brooks, pp. 221–22 and 225–27; Butow, pp. 194–95; Feis, 127–28; Kase 243–44; PWRS, *Japan's Longest Day*, pp. 48–50; Togo, pp. 325–28.

141. See Toyoda's testimony in USSBS, *Interrogations*, p. 2:322.

142. Brooks, pp. 240–42; Butow, pp. 200–2; Feis, p. 129; Jones, p. 447; Kase, pp. 245–46; PWRS, *Japan's Longest Day*, p. 53; Togo, pp. 328–29.

143. Brooks, 250–51; Butow, p. 202; Kase, pp. 246–47; PWRS, *Japan's Longest Day*, p. 73; Togo, pp. 330–31.

144. Togo, pp. 331–32. Near the end of this meeting, Admiral Onishi Takijiro, creator of Japan's "Special Attack Corps" (*Kamikaze*), burst in and excitedly proclaimed that if Japan were only willing to sacrifice twenty million men in suicide attacks, victory would by hers. Togo calmly countered, "if only we had any real hope of victory, no one would for a moment think of accepting the Potsdam Declaration; but winning one battle will not win the war for us." On August 16, the day after the emperor announced Japan's surrender, Onishi himself committed *seppuku*, ritual suicide.

145. Brooks, pp. 252–54; Butow, pp. 204–6; Kase, p. 247.

146. Brooks, pp. 258–60; Butow, pp. 205–6; Feis, p. 130; Kido, p. 448; Kirby, p. 5:213; PWRS, *Japan's Longest Day*, p. 77; Shigemitsu, p. 362; USSBS, *Japan's Struggle*, p. 9.

147. Brooks, pp. 264–65; Butow, p. 207; Feis, pp. 130–31; Jones, pp. 447–48; Kase, p. 252; Kirby, pp. 5:213–14; PWRS, *Japan's Longest Day*, pp. 7–79; Togo, pp. 333–34; USSBS, *Japan's Struggle*, p. 9.

148. Butow, pp. 207–8. As in the case of the August 10 statement, Butow constructed the emperor's statement from postwar testimonies of others at the meeting, as no transcript exists of Emperor Hirohito's exact words.

149. For riveting accounts of the coup attempt, see Brooks and PWRS, *Japan's Longest Day*. Also see Shigemitsu, pp. 364–66.

150. USSBS, *Japan's Struggle*.

151. Ibid., p. 13.

152. Ibid., p. 12.

153. Robert Pape's argument that military leaders became convinced that Japan could not resist an invasion of the homeland after seeing the Soviet attack in Manchuria crush "Japan's premiere fighting force," the Kwangtung Army, does not square with the facts. By August, 1945, no one in the Supreme Command had any illusions that the Kwantung Army was a premiere fighting force. They had been siphoning off the best men and equipment from Manchuria for other fronts since 1942, and, starting in late 1944, they withdrew the remaining first-line units to reinforce the home islands in anticipation of a climactic battle there. Well aware that Kwangtung Army capabilities were disintegrating, the Supreme Command replaced its offensive war plans with a defensive strategy in September, 1944, then approved the field commander's April, 1945, request to allow Kwangtung forces to rely purely on delaying operations. Later that spring, the Supreme Command conscripted four new divisions and several independent brigades from among Japanese subjects living in China. That raised Kwangtung Army strength to an impressive total on paper; but, in fact, the new conscripts were almost completely

service lay in shouldering whatever shame was necessary to save the throne from imminent destruction.

In the imperial court, Marquis Kido's value interpretation paralleled that of the peace faction, but Emperor Hirohito's view was shaped by a broader cosmology. Though shackled by Japan's traditional decision-making process, he was free from the parochial concerns that tended to cloud other groups' interpretations of the strategic landscape. Consequently, before the war and throughout, his assessments of Japan's prospects of victory and defeat, though not always accurate, were frequently the most objective. Moreover, as emperor, he was both the spiritual father of the Japanese people and the corporeal representative of all the divine rulers that had preceded him. In the end, those roles colored his interpretation of values profoundly. For him, courage ultimately manifested as the stoic acceptance of whatever fate awaited him as he did what he felt he had to do to save his people and preserve the nation for future generations.[6]

But differences in value interpretation and perception are not limited to subcultural distinctions; there is also a temporal dimension. As table 7.1 illustrates, there is significant variance in the way Japanese leaders responded to compellent threats during the triple intervention as compared to their behavior in the latter two cases. This variance occurred because leaders in 1895 interpreted threats to their values differently than did leaders in 1941 and 1945. In the triple intervention, Japanese leaders put up only feeble resistance to the *Dreibund's* demand that they return the Liaotung peninsula, even though its conquest had been legitimized in the Treaty of Shimonoseki and sanctioned by Emperor Meiji. Returning the territory to China caused Tokyo tremendous loss of face; but, as Japanese leaders had not yet inflated the emperor myth to the proportions seen in later decades, they did not interpret the act as a threat to imperial infallibility or *kokutai*. Though the Japanese had already begun to equate building a continental empire with their core value of catching up with the West, acquiescing to the *Dreibund's* demand that they return Liaotung seemed less a threat to that value than the prospect of fighting a war with three Powers, all superior to them in the hierarchy of nations. In essence, they feared the Russian fleet, augmented by France and Germany, might cut them off from the mainland, jeopardizing *all* of Japan's continental holdings, and they made an expedient decision to curtail that threat.

This observation raises an important question, one parallel to questions that strategic culture theorists have raised in previous studies: was Japan's strategic culture more mythical or symbolic than operational? That is, did Japanese leaders use culture-based symbols and values to justify strategic behavior while standing independent of influence from those factors themselves? Put even more plainly, was the strategic culture of Imperial Japan a mere instrument to manipulate the masses? Certainly, there is abundant evidence that the Japanese government manipulated cultural symbols and values. As chapters 3 and 5 demonstrated, Meiji leaders deliberately encouraged the popular *kokutai* movement and reinterpreted the traditional concept of *ie* (household) to inspire patriotism and motivate greater sacrifice in the modernization campaign. Later, the ultranationalists built on this foundation, exploiting an inflated emperor myth to justify their program of continental aggression. But the exploitation of cultural symbols does not in itself suggest that individuals within the culture would not have acted on the values associated with those symbols even without official encouragement. A popular conservative backlash to Japan's "excessively Western orientation" was well underway even before Meiji leaders began to focus their indoctrination program on traditional themes. Moreover, throughout the period of this study, the Japanese public was remarkably responsive to militaristic propaganda—so much so that decision makers often felt compelled by the public's ardor for war. Martial virtue was a strong incentive in Japanese culture independent of government efforts to manipulate it. But the crucial question is whether Japanese leaders were influenced by their own strategic culture; this study's findings strongly suggest they were. Though they clearly manipulated cultural symbols and values to serve their own political ends, Japanese leaders were also prisoners of their own strategic culture.

On another issue, while the temporal variance in value interpretation does not invalidate the importance of understanding an adversary's core values, it does pose a separate challenge for the strategic culture theory. Those decision makers closest to the feudal experience seemed less bound to rigid, warrior value–based interpretations of world events than were their successors who governed generations later. Most Meiji statesmen were former samurai, yet they responded to the *Dreibund*'s challenge in a cautious, thoughtful manner. Conversely, though a greater percentage of Showa-era leaders were drawn from common stock, and though they governed more than half a century after the abolishment of feudalism, those leaders were more apt to characterize any international confrontation as a threat to their honor and to *kokutai*. Thus, they tended to react in ways contrary to Japan's greater interests.

Ironically, part of the answer to this dilemma may lie in the very fact that many Showa leaders lacked the aristocratic bearing their predecessors enjoyed. Historian Ronald Spector points out that the army became progressively more radical as the percentage of officers from lower middle-class backgrounds grew. That was partly because "these sons of petty landowners and small shopkeepers felt far less assured of their place in the social hierarchy than did the aristocratic lords of the Choshu and Satsuma clans who had dominated the army high command before World War I: they were thus all the more ready to embrace ideas which reassured them about their unique role in the nation."[7]

Yet, Japan's radical behavior in the latter cases requires more explanation than simply attributing it to class anxiety. I need not recount the complex social developments that simultaneously led to fascism and the inflation of *bushido, kokutai,* and the emperor myth, as I examined those issues extensively in chapter 5. Suffice to reiterate that Japanese fascism was largely an outgrowth of traditional warrior values. Its emergence was made possible by the Meiji-era fusion of spiritual and political authority in the person of the emperor and catalyzed in later decades by economic and social developments at home and abroad. The perversion of Japanese symbols and values that facilitated the rise of fascism led to conceptions of worldview and strategic preference among Japanese leaders in the 1940s that substantially differed from those of their predecessors in 1895. Consequently, where Meiji leaders had interpreted challenges to Japanese ambition in a very pragmatic sense, those who governed in the 1940s saw the world through distorted lenses created by exaggerated symbols and brittle values. They had become caricatures of their warrior forebears.

Interestingly, the differences between Japanese behavior in the triple intervention and the latter two cases do not bear out evenly across the 15 hypotheses. As one might expect from the foregoing discussion, hypotheses two, three, and four, those drawn from warrior virtues, show the greatest variance. Alternatively, hypotheses five through ten were drawn from more fundamental Confucian virtues; their outcomes suggest Japanese leaders interpreted those values somewhat more uniformly across cases. And the last five hypotheses yielded outcomes for case one that were even more similar to the other two cases. I developed those hypotheses by applying the strategic culture model to Confucian-based Japanese customs.

These results should come as no surprise. Confucian values were firmly rooted in Japanese society; in fact, they provided the foundation on which the martial virtues developed. Societal incentives to reinterpret these values were less intense than was the mounting pressure to inflate the martial ethos, so they survived the period of study largely unaffected aside from the government's efforts to redefine and intensify each subject's obligation to serve the emperor as a father. Consequently, while the outcomes of hypothesis eight (filial piety) reflect this change in the emperor's status, the findings of hypotheses concerning hierarchy, contextual morality, and *gekokujo* (usurping authority from incompetent leaders) suggest a more consistent interpretation of values across cases.

Hypothesis five captured the pivotal issue in the triple intervention. Japanese regard for the international hierarchy was the most significant factor in Tokyo's reaction to the *Dreibund*'s demands, overpowering the effects of other variables and driving unreasonably low correlations in hypotheses seven, eight, and nine. Meiji leaders did apply contextual morality in their dealings with Chinese and Korean authorities, and concerns about their filial obligation to serve the emperor competently were strong components in the desperation they felt when the Powers intervened. Yet, these concerns were overwhelmed by the shock Japanese leaders experienced when they realized three superior nations were "advising" them to return the Liaotung Peninsula.

Furthermore, the findings of hypothesis five suggest that Tokyo's conception of an international hierarchy persisted throughout the period of study. Japan's status vis-à-vis the Anglo-Americans was not an operative variable in the oil embargo or the surrender of Japan—by then, the inflated emperor myth had persuaded Japanese leaders that their nation was at least the equal of any other in the world, despite disparities in military power and industry. Yet, Japanese feelings of superiority and entitlement regarding China conditioned Tokyo's responses to Allied demands in both cases. Moreover, national power and prestige were central factors Japanese leaders considered when they sought a third-party nation to mediate a settlement with the Allies at the end of the war.

But the strongest correlation of findings across cases are observed in the last five hypotheses, those drawn from social customs relevant to Japanese decision making. Clearly, Confucian-based, consensus-dependent decision-making processes reduced Japan's political flexibility in all three cases by bloating and ossifying Tokyo's terms in proposed settlements to accommodate the demands of constituent groups. Group composition was a critical factor in each decision outcome. Individuals present were heard; those absent were unable to participate in shaping the consensus and, as the *mokusatsu* incident demonstrated dramatically, decisions could change from day to day with disastrous consequences.

This should serve to remind us that, while cultural norms define tendencies in worldview and ethos, every society is a collection of individuals with particular values and perceptions. No matter how culturally homogeneous a society is, one will always observe variance in individual ideas, preferences, and behaviors. Most people *usually* think and behave in ways circumscribed by cultural norms, but there are always those whose views and actions fall at either end of the bell curve; often these individuals find their way into leadership positions. In this study, the three most prominent foreign ministers come to mind: Mutsu Munemitsu in the triple intervention, Matsuoka Yosuke in events leading to the oil embargo, and Togo Shigenori at the surrender of Japan. These individuals were frequently more assertive and confrontational than Japanese cultural norms suggest is acceptable, and their behavior had notable effects on decision making in all three cases.

It is interesting to speculate as to why these three men behaved in ways that seemed to deviate from cultural norms. One possibility is that, for separate reasons, each did not consider himself in the mainstream of Japanese society. For instance, in his youth, Mutsu had opposed the Meiji government and was imprisoned for seven years as a political radical. After his release he decided his fortunes lay with supporting the system, and he entered the Japanese bureaucracy. Eventually, *genro* Ito Hirobumi recognized Mutsu's talent and invited him to join his cabinet as foreign minister. Although Mutsu wielded considerable influence there, he never felt fully accepted by other Meiji leaders, and he attacked them bitterly in his memoir, *Kenkenroku*. As for Matsuoka, he spent a considerable number of his early years in the United States where he was educated. That might account for his assertiveness and, perhaps, due to some negative experience there, the venom with which he seemed to regard America. Beyond that, one cannot help but notice that all three of these men were foreign ministers. It could be that the foreign ministry's functions fostered an organizational culture that valued assertiveness. On the other hand, all of this could be coincidence—after all, people are individuals.

Yet, Imperial Japan was a Confucian society that valued group preservation above all else, so decisions were always made by consensus. And the most powerful factor this study observed affecting consensus decisions are captured in hypothesis 15 which proposes that Japan's ability to respond to coercive threat is conditioned by its leaders' perceptions of the depth and breadth of the *ie* to which they belong. Japan's Meiji-era government was able to respond to the triple intervention promptly because seven of its most influential leaders had bonded into a household of personal retainers dedicated to serving the emperor. Later known as *genro* (elder statemen), these men coordinated the functions of governance by hammering out consensus decisions among themselves, legitimizing those decisions in the cabinet, then securing the emperor's sanction and enforcing compliance in the respective agencies they controlled. But by the onset of events leading to the oil embargo, the *genro* had passed from the scene and the Japanese government had splintered into a collection of petty fiefdoms. This political fragmentation confounded Tokyo's efforts to avoid war with the United States, as factional rivalry, intensified by Japan's bottom-up decision-making process, resulted in unreasonable proposals and provocative behavior that only served to raise Japanese-American tensions. Later, the same problem impeded Japanese efforts to end the war until Marquis Kido and Emperor Hirohito managed to forge an imperial *ie* to achieve that specific goal.

While the "household-frame-of-reference" model offers a great deal of explanatory power in terms of Japanese political behavior, it also raises some fundamental questions. First, how does the bottom-up nature of Japan's brand of consensus-driven decision making square with the directive aspects of governance by a small functional group at the top of a bureaucratic pyramid? If bottom-up decision making is as deeply rooted in Japan's Confucian-based society as this study suggests, then the various agencies that constituted the Meiji government would have to have operated along those lines. So, how were the *genro* able to function as a quasi-independent decision-making body and direct compliance beneath them? What determined when decisions would be developed as a grass-roots consensus and carried upward or when they would be made by the oligarchy and sent downward? Finally, how did these dynamics manifest themselves in the actions of the imperial *ie* forged among the "Big Six" policy makers who ended the Second World War?

Answers to the Meiji-era riddles lie in the nature of the elder statemen's relationship with the emperor and the time available to make decisions. Meiji institutions did, indeed, function according to bottom-up decision-making lines. Given time, each agency developed policies by cumulative consensus and passed them to its respective minister or service chief, who was often a *genro*. Each *genro*, in turn, generally made a good-faith effort to present his agency's concerns in the private sessions where national policies were made; however, he swore his primary allegiance not to the agency he nominally represented, but to the emperor and Japan.

Having guided Emperor Meiji through the trying times of imperial restoration, the elder statemen had a special relationship with their sovereign. Moreover, they felt a strong obligation to serve the greater interests of the nation above those of the agencies they headed.[8] Their subordinates understood this well; and though each ministry and service developed consensus positions on policies it preferred, they all faithfully carried out whatever plan the *genro* ultimately directed. Beyond that, they knew that if some crisis loomed, denying the agencies time to develop a bottom-up, consensus response, the *genro*, as the emperor's personal retainers, would decide what to do in their stead.

But this trusting relationship between emperor, minister, and bureaucrat had long since disintegrated by the Second World War. Ministers and service chiefs no longer bore the mantle of the emperor's personal retainers; they now saw themselves as heads of their own households. As such, they tended to represent their agencies' interests more narrowly, and their subordinates expected them to be faithful to the passive model of good Confucian leadership. Therefore, when the Big Six began to coalesce into an ad hoc imperial *ie* for the express purpose of seeking peace, they were forced to keep their activities secret, lest subordinates usurp their authority through "direct action." Just as Admiral Takagi had surmised in February, 1945, before the ministries and military services would obey any order to end the war, Emperor Hirohito would have to be directly involved. Without the cohesive bonds entailed in a nationally recognized imperial household, his was the only order the nation would follow without question.

All of this suggests that strategic decision making in Japan retained its feudal character throughout the imperial era. Despite the overlay of a Western-style, constitutional monarchy, a small circle of oligarchs governed Meiji Japan just as trusted retainers had administered the domains of warlords and shogun in bygone ages. As the *genro* passed from the scene, the lateral bonds of national government weakened. Then imperial institutions behaved in ways reminiscent of earlier periods in the nation's history when central authority had eroded. Like the feudal *han* (fiefdoms) from which they had emerged, the agencies that comprised Japan's modern, bureaucratic state became secretive, suspicious, and competitive.[9]

Ultimately, this tendency proved catastrophic—not just in the way it impacted the quality of Japanese responses to coercive threat, but in Tokyo's ability to even react to the crises presented in those threats. Indeed, this dynamic probably was the most dramatic aspect of how culture colored the way Imperial Japan responded to compellence.

ADDITIONAL FINDINGS AND IMPLICATIONS

Although it seems clear that strategic culture conditioned Imperial Japan's responses to coercive threat, it is important to remember that culture is only an intervening variable—it did not act independently. Though Japanese leaders perceived the external environment through lenses colored by their own symbols and values, international balances of interest were crucial considerations in their policy determinations. Although values were the fundamental substance with which they weighed the costs and benefits of resisting coercive pressure, the punishment and denial strategies Japan's adversaries employed ultimately drove the strategic calculations that produced compellence outcomes. Therefore, comparing case study findings in terms of how Japanese leaders responded to conceptions of interest, costs, and benefits will help us better understand the efficacy of theories associated with those factors. This analysis should also provide insights for constructing more effective compellence strategies in the future.

The balance of interests was a crucial consideration in Tokyo's response to the triple intervention, and it was an integral factor in Japan's behavior in the other two cases as well. Japanese leaders felt free to coerce exorbitant concessions from China following the first Sino-Japanese War largely because they believed Russia would not intervene and the other Powers had only minor interests in the region. Later, when Russia, France, and Germany all spoke up, the Japanese were so overwhelmed in their skewed

conception of the balance of power that they capitulated without testing
the ad hoc coalition's flimsy seams. Conceptions of interest also were important components in Japan's behavior leading to the Second World War.
As Tokyo believed Germany was emerging as the dominant power in
Europe, Japanese leaders were convinced Anglo-American interests in
Asia were minor enough that the Allies would be deterred from interfering with Japanese expansion once Tokyo aligned itself with Berlin. Continued misconceptions of Allied power and interests contributed to
Japan's decision to enter the war and prolonged Japanese suffering long
after continuing the struggle was no longer in Tokyo's interest.

These observations suggest that assessments of international balances
of interest are essential components in any compellence strategy. All national leaders are acutely sensitive to alignments in interest and shifts in
the balance of power. These considerations are among the first any government makes when facing a coercive threat, as decision makers attempt
to weigh the strength of the challenge facing them and determine what
they can do to counter or mitigate its effects. Therefore, these same deliberations should be an integral part of any process designed to develop a
compellent strategy. More than that, the strategy itself should incorporate
elements of coalition-building in an effort to shape the international strategic landscape in such a way that target-nation leaders feel isolated and
overwhelmed.

But interest assessments must be adjusted for culture, and the strategies
developed from such analyses must be culture-rational as well. It is not
enough to determine that one's own interests in a given issue are greater
than those of an adversary or that the military power at one's disposal
outstrips anything he can bring to bear. Compellence is in the eye of the
beholder. As Japan's responses to the oil embargo and attempts to compel
her surrender painfully illustrate, resolve and a preponderance of force of
do not equate to successful compellence if the adversary conceives a world
in which the balance of power is different or if acquiescence to the coercer's demands would threaten one or more of the adversary's core
values. On the other hand, Japan's behavior in the triple intervention suggests misconception can work both ways. If the coercer's power awes the
opponent and target leaders see no other way to protect a core value but
to comply with the coercer's demand, compellence may be remarkably
successful.

We must remember, however, that though such contextual analyses are
important, they do not comprise compellent strategies in themselves—the
coercer still must devise an effective way to bring coercive pressure to
bear on the adversary. That entails linking a threat of punishment or denial
to the way an adversary responds to some clearly articulated demand.
Here again, the case study findings inform us.

One of the more notable observations we can draw from the cases examined in this study is that coercion is a complex, interactive process. While scholars and theorists tend to focus on specific families of coercion theory—deterrence or compellence; punishment, denial, or interests—Japanese leaders clearly weighed all these factors in a comprehensive fashion as they developed their strategies before and after coercers issued their demands. Japanese political behavior in the first Sino-Japanese War illustrated how carefully leaders of less powerful nations attempt to balance interests and weigh anticipated costs and benefits in order to avoid being deterred from achieving their national objectives. Later, in response to the triple intervention, Meiji decision makers weighed both the potential costs of punishment *and* the possibility that the *Driebund* might deny them the fruits of their conquest and other interests in Asia—interests linked to Imperial Japan's core values. Events leading to the oil embargo brought to light the interactive nature of coercion. While Washington attempted to deter Japanese aggression in China, Tokyo focused on deterring American interference with Japanese efforts to expand on the continent. Finally, Japanese behavior in response to American efforts to compel surrender suggests political elites in Tokyo, to some extent, considered all the ways Allied actions inflicted costs on Japan and impeded her strategies, not just specific facets of punishment or denial as some theorists contend.

Yet, this study's findings do suggest that some coercive stimuli are more appropriate than others in certain circumstances. Threats of punishment and denial both have coercive effect, and most strategies should incorporate elements of both.[10] But denial-based strategies are often problematic, as it may be difficult to persuade an adversary that you can deny strategic objectives without actively moving to do so. In a deterrence scenario, posturing for denial can lead to confrontation, escalation, and war. Moreover, if the adversary has seized the initiative and compellence is required, it may not be possible to convince those leaders that they cannot achieve their goals without completely defeating their military forces, and that can be costly for both opponents. On the other hand, though threats of punishment may be a potent deterrent, Japan's conduct suggests that punishment may not be effective in compelling changes in ongoing adversary behavior unless target leaders have already begun to question whether they can achieve their objectives. For instance, in the months leading to Japan's surrender, Japanese leaders seemed willing to tolerate incredible costs so long as they believed there was some benefit in resisting. Moreover, their behavior suggests that this may be true even if the anticipated benefits are scaled down or different from those that first brought them to war. This attitude was not solely the province of the diehards. The peace faction, Marquis Kido, and the emperor all premised their desires to end the war with assertions that it was already lost. In fact, as late as the evening before the final surrender, Foreign Minister Togo told Admiral Onishi Takijiro, " . . . if only we had any real hope of victory, no one would for a moment think of accepting the Potsdam Declaration. . . ."[11] In sum, when a state is invested in a major conventional war, costs of punishment seem to become a factor only after a potent denial strategy has begun to take effect.

But we should hesitate to draw conclusions about the efficacies of punishment and denial based on this study alone. A single comparison of three cases is hardly an adequate basis for a universal inference of this sort. Moreover, as my earlier analysis suggests, Japan's unique culture may have made Japanese leaders more tolerant of punishment than decision makers would be in other countries.[12]

This qualification emphasizes, once again, the need to employ culture-based analyses in any effort to devise compellent strategies. Whether the coercer is trying to raise the cost of noncompliance or persuade an adversary he cannot achieve his objectives, a thorough understanding of the target's strategic culture must be central to that effort. Cultural symbols and values are fundamental determinants of costs and objectives, and behavioral patterns provide the mechanisms with which target-nation leaders respond to the coercers demands. That brings me to an additional finding.

To be effective, the coercer should tailor his demand to a form and substance most likely to induce compliance, given the target's unique strategic culture. National leaders cannot easily be compelled to jeopardize their core values—if a coercer's objectives range in that direction, he should expect dogged resistance, even war. On the other hand, if the strategy can be designed and communicated in such a way that persuades target leaders that only compliance will preserve a core value—as the *Dreibund* managed to do in the triple intervention and the United States finally managed to do at the end of the Second World War—then, the target will more likely acquiesce. Beyond that, target-nation leaders will be less apt to resist the coercer's demand if it is presented in a way that offers them a face-saving way to comply, a way that seems to protect their national honor and offer some benefit they can present to their people.[13] Once again, the "advice" the *Dreibund* tendered offers a good example. Though Tokyo suffered a tremendous loss of face in having to return territory to China—in fact, the public outcry in Japan brought down the Ito Cabinet—the collegial nature of the demand gave Japanese leaders the opportunity to make a voluntary gesture for the sake of a lasting peace. This aspect of the Powers' approach reflects a remarkable degree of cultural sensitivity.[14] Those who set out to craft coercive strategies in the future would do well to heed their example.

CRAFTING COERCIVE STRATEGIES BY GAMING
ADVERSARY BEHAVIOR

At several points in the foregoing section, I emphasized the importance of incorporating thorough, culture-sensitive analysis in any effort to develop coercive strategy. While few would question the wisdom of this advice, such an approach has rarely been attempted beyond simply bringing in regional specialists from the intelligence community to brief decision makers on what kind of behavior to expect from an adversary during a specific crisis. That is not enough. While this book focused on culture's role in compellence, the findings also suggest that compellence is but one possible phase in a complex, long-term relationship between two or more governments. This relationship extends across a spectrum of coercive interaction that includes deterrence, coercive diplomacy, compellence, and, potentially, war. Consequently, for a government to deal effectively with potential adversaries, it must devise long-term coercive strategies. These strategies should be developed from a perspective of how adversaries might react to various coercive stimuli at whatever level of confrontation currently exists.[15] Strategic culture-based analyses are integral to estimating those reactions.

But how do we incorporate strategic culture-based analysis into the strategy development process? One way is to game adversary behavior using regional specialists equipped with a model of an opposing government's strategic culture. Gaming is a technique the U.S. Department of Defense and its military services frequently use to explore new strategic concepts or weapons mixes. It involves forming teams of analysts with specialized knowledge and assigning them to work through specific strategic problems, sometimes using special quantitative or qualitative models. Often, the teams are given adversarial roles with different strategies or force structures. The conceptual "conflict" that follows informs planners about possible strengths and weaknesses of the approaches examined.[16]

Gaming offers an ideal venue for employing strategic culture models in the strategy development process. However, for gaming to be effective, it must link culture-sensitive regional specialists to the appropriate policy makers in an interactive forum. Effective coercion generally requires all of a nation's instruments of power—political and economic, as well as military—to be employed in a coordinated fashion. Therefore, the "players" should include, at a minimum, high-level representatives from the White House and the Departments of State, Commerce, and Defense, in addition to regional specialists drawn from the intelligence community, State, Defense, Commerce, and academia. Brought together for some period of time, these individuals would be divided into teams and asked to work through a strategy-development problem using a process depicted in figure 7.1.[17]

Preparation for a typical game begins with assessing all the relevant intelligence data available and profiling the adversary's strategic culture. Intelligence representatives gather and analyze data pertinent to the issue at hand; they develop a briefing on their findings and, if time permits, a written report. As this work progresses, a team of regional specialists from government and academia begin profiling the target nation's strategic culture, applying techniques similar to those used in chapter 3 of this book.[18] Drawing from the country's historical, religious, and philosophical background, they identify the symbols, values, and patterns of social behavior relevant to the target leaders' strategic decision-making processes. When the intelligence work-up becomes available, the regional team uses the strategic culture profile to interpret the contextual factors of the situation at hand in terms of how target leaders might perceive the world and what might likely be their strategic preferences, given the issues in question. The regional team also relates the target culture's social behaviors to whatever information is available about that state's strategic decision-making apparatus in an effort to determine how key individuals and groups interrelate to produce strategic behavior. Like the intelligence team, the regional team develops a briefing and a written report of their findings.[19]

On the first day of actual game play, all the participants assemble and are briefed on the game's purpose and construct, and the intelligence and regional teams present their assessments. Then the "Blue Team" gathers in a closed session. Representatives from the National Security Council

Figure 7.1
Generic Model for a Coercive Strategy Development Game

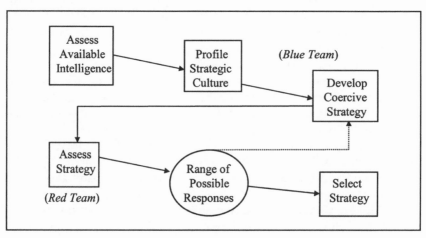

(NSC) staff (or other top-level executive officials) brief them on what objectives or "end states" the nation's top policy makers hope to achieve. Armed with the intelligence estimate and a notional profile of the adversary's worldview, strategic preferences, and decision-making processes, Blue Team members then attempt to develop a strategy to achieve the national objectives laid before them.[20]

Blue Team's job is to develop a strategy to coordinate and apply the national instruments of power in a way that maximizes the likelihood that the adversary's decisions will be consistent with our own objectives. The strategic culture work is central to this effort, since the essence of good coercive strategy is not simply to maximize the pressure one can bring to bear, but to apply pressure and possibly incentives in a way that maximizes the probability that the adversary will behave in ways one desires. Yet Blue Team must also address other concerns. For the proposed strategy to be of any use to policy makers, it must be technically feasible. It must also be politically acceptable to the public and to power centers within the Congress, the administration, and the bureaucracy. Finally, the strategy must be compatible with allies' interests and consistent with the impression we want to make on other third-party nations.[21] For these reasons, Blue Team should be made up of a mix of technical experts and high-level representatives of policy makers from all the federal departments cited earlier.

When Blue Team finishes developing its strategy, its representatives brief the reassembled group on the details, then "Red Team" begins its own closed session. Red Team's role is to evaluate Blue Team's proposed strategy in terms of the range of likely responses it might elicit from target-nation leaders.[22] The team should consist of regional specialists, and at least some of those who participated in developing the strategic culture profile should be present to guide other team members in its use. However, Red Team should have a different character from that of the group that created the profile. Whereas the nature of the profile team was quite academic, Red Team should be more functionally oriented. Players should be drawn from the intelligence community, the federal departments, and the military services. They should have as much knowledge as possible of the target-state institutions that correspond to their own and of the adversary's governmental functions at large. Language skill and in-country experience are also highly desirable.

It is important to emphasize that Red Team should not be expected to predict the adversary's behavior with any degree of precision.[23] Instead, they should be urged to develop two or more alternative response scenarios, predicated on the differing interpretations of worldview or strategic preference they believe target leaders might possibly conceive. Red Team should be encouraged to consider how adversary leaders might evaluate alternative outcomes to Blue's coercive challenge, given their value structure and conception of the strategic landscape. Will they be inclined to take risks, or will they be risk averse? Will they seek a short-term gain even if that bid jeopardizes greater, long-term interests, or will they take a more conservative approach to safeguarding their national destiny? Red Team should weigh all these issues and evaluate the impacts of changes to those variables as they develop their outcome scenarios.[24]

Moreover, Red Team should consider how the adversary's decision-making process might affect that state's response to Blue's coercive challenge. Do target leaders make strategic decisions by unilateral decree, by consensus among a select group of individuals, or by some other mechanism? Where are the power centers, and what are their relative strengths? Do the individuals or groups that comprise these centers seem to employ differing interpretations of worldview or cultural values? If so, how might these conflicting conceptions play out in the adversary's efforts to respond to coercion?

This is where the expertise of functionally oriented, regional specialists comes to bear most strongly. Military specialists will be most familiar with the values, attitudes, and decision dynamics in the adversary's military service that corresponds to their own; State Department analysts will best understand those aspects of the target state's diplomatic service. If information is available identifying which power centers have the most influence in the target's strategic decision-making process, players can make informed estimates of how subcultural factors might influence the adversary's response. Of course, information of this sort is often scanty, especially for very secretive states such as Vietnam and North Korea. In cases where little information is available, players must work on a more general level. In any event, as players work through the problem, they should be discouraged from formal role playing as that could lead to competitive bargaining within the team. Rather, they should dispassionately seek to understand how the target state's pathologies may affect its strategic reasoning, not bring those pathologies into their own analytical process.[25]

When Red Team has finished developing the scenarios its players believe best represent how the target state might respond to Blue's proposed coercion attempt, all the players reassemble and Red Team representatives brief their findings. They lay out the first scenario in detail, explaining how the target nation's perceptions and values might lead its leaders to the strategic preferences envisioned and how the state's decision-making process might produce the notional response. For each succeeding scenario, they specify which variable they are changing, explain why they think opposing leaders may interpret that factor differently, and assess the impact of that change on the scenario outcome. When all the alternative outcomes have been briefed, Red Team may rank-order them from most to least likely, if they choose. They may also advise Blue Team on how they might change their strategy to make it more effective. However, Red Team "should not be relied upon for high-confidence predictions and should not be encouraged to make them lightly."[26]

The end of Red Team's presentation signals the completion of one cycle of analysis. If the executive officials who called for the exercise are satisfied with Blue Team's strategy, given Red's assessment of the adversary's range of possible responses, they may deliver those results to policy makers who can use them to inform their own strategy development. On the other hand, if the Blue strategy is obviously flawed, and if time permits, game players may be directed to begin a second cycle of analysis—Blue Team members will then take the Red assessment and revise their existing strategy or develop an entirely new one, and Red Team will reassess it in turn. In the end, game administrators should write a comprehensive report detailing the process, products, and deliberations at every step of the exercise. This report can be used to guide efforts to modify the coercive strategy should subsequent events call for reassessment.

CULTURE AND COMPELLENCE IN THE TWENTY-FIRST CENTURY

We stand at the threshold of a new era. The world will change dramatically in the coming decades. Distances will shorten as information, goods, and people move at ever increasing speeds. Revolutionary developments in space and information technology, unfolding in a rapidly transforming commercial and geopolitical landscape, promise to make the twenty-first century one of tremendous opportunity and great peril.

Theorists differ widely on what will be the nature of the future security environment. Some claim that dramatic advances in technology will grant us nearly unconstrained access to space, reduce resource scarcity, and facilitate a global commercial interdependence so strong that war will be anachronistic for nearly all nations. Others maintain that commercial interdependence and information proliferation will seriously erode state sovereignty and make the lesser-developed world painfully aware of inequities in wealth. These trends, they say, will lead to envy, social disintegration, urban warfare, and anarchy.

No one can be certain which portrayal better describes the future world. But there are a couple of points of which we can be sure: first, for the foreseeable future, the community of nations will continue to turn to the United States as the principal guarantor of international stability. Second, to fulfill the obligations that naturally fall to a most powerful state that endeavors to base its policies on the principles of liberty, economic opportunity, and justice, American leaders will need the ability to shape the behavior of other world actors. They will need to orchestrate the instruments of national power in ways that deter aggression, and they will have to compel adversaries to readjust their behavior when deterrence fails. Deterrence and compellence are forms of coercion.

In this book, I have argued that coercion is a complex, interactive process involving two or more antagonists, each attempting to affect the other's behavior by manipulating their computation of potential costs and benefits in a complex strategic landscape of relative interest. But costs, benefits, and interests are not absolute values subject to objective measurement. Indeed, deterrence and compellence are in the eye of the beholder.

Japanese behavior in the triple intervention, the oil embargo, and efforts to compel her surrender all suggest we should employ culture-based analyses in any future efforts to devise coercive strategies. Symbols and values, firmly rooted in Japanese culture, colored Tokyo's worldview in all three cases and played central roles as Japanese leaders determined their strategic preferences. Centuries-old patterns of social behavior conditioned Tokyo's decision-making processes, profoundly impacting both the quality and the timing of Japanese responses to coercive threat. While these events took place between the late nineteenth and mid–twentieth centuries, there is no reason to suspect that future adversaries will behave in ways less subject to cultural conditioning. Therefore, any future coercive strategy should be built on a thorough understanding of the opponent's strategic culture.

NOTES

1. Several versions of this quotation are commonly attributed to Goering. The expression may have originated from a line in Hanns Johst's 1933 play, *Schlageter*, in which a character said: *"Wenn ich Kultur höre . . . entsichere ich meinen Browning!"* (Whenever I hear the word culture . . . I release the safety-catch of my Browning!)

2. Kenneth N. Waltz, *Man, the State, and War: A Theoretical Analysis* (New York: Columbia University Press, 1959) and *Theory of International Politics* (Reading, Mass.: Addison-Wesley, 1979).

3. Robert O. Keohane, *After Hegemony: Cooperation and Discord in the World Political Economy* (Princeton, N.J.: Princeton University Press, 1984); Robert O. Keohane and Joseph S. Nye, Jr., *Power and Interdependence*, 3rd ed. (Reading, Mass.: Addison-Wesley, 2000).

4. Brian Barry, *Sociologists, Economists, and Democracy* (Chicago: University of Chicago Press, 1979).

5. The ratings shown on this table are subjective approximations, not precise assessments. Each is open to debate when taken individually; yet considered collectively, they reveal trends and tendencies in Japanese behavior relevant to the issues at hand. I offer this table as a template to guide discussion in the comparative analysis, not as a semblance of rigorous scoring.

6. I must point out that this interpretation of Hirohito's motives contrasts

sharply with the one Herbert Bix presents in his Pulitzer Prize winning biography, *Hirohito and the Making of Modern Japan*. Bix paints Hirohito as a singularly self-interested man educated and indoctrinated to be an expansionist monarch determined to conquer Asia. Bix rightly dispels the emperor's popular image as a helpless, symbolic leader, who was a virtual puppet of Imperial Japan's military oligarchs and unaware of how his government was prosecuting the war. Drawing from previously unexamined documents, he ably demonstrates that the emperor was fully aware of Japan's political behavior and intimately involved in military planning even at the operational level. Based on Bix's evidence, it is clear that the emperor was an active participant in Japan's decision making process; *however*, Bix overstates that evidence when he portrays Hirohito as the driving force behind those decisions. Japanese decision making was a corporate process, versus the dominant-leader model that Bix's depiction implies. Hirohito was not powerless, but he was not omnipotent either. Although Hirohito was a nationalist with expansionist ambitions, as was nearly every other political actor in Japan's imperial government, the evidence does not confirm that he had the degree of callous disregard for the well-being of his subjects that Bix portrays. See Herbert P. Bix, *Hirohito and the Making of Modern Japan* (New York: Perennial, 2000).

7. Ronald H. Spector, *Eagle Against the Sun: The American War With Japan* (New York: Vintage Books, 1985), 84.

8. This national perspective is demonstrated by the frequency in which the elder statesmen rotated ministerial posts. As I pointed out in chapter 5, between 1885 and 1900, the seven main *genro* held a total of 40 ministerial positions between them. See Roger F. Hackett, "Political Modernization and the Meiji *Genro*," in Robert E. Ward (ed.), *Political Development in Modern Japan* (Princeton, N.J.: Princeton University Press, 1968), pp. 72 and 91.

9. In evoking this analogy I do not suggest that central authority weakened during the imperial era. While lateral bonds between agencies eroded, the Japanese government deliberately strengthened vertical bonds, tying each subject more strongly to the state and, nominally, the emperor.

10. I do not accept the narrow definition of punishment some scholars proffer—that punishment equates to attacking civilians. When I advocate using punishment as a coercive tool, I refer to deliberately inflicting costs on an adversary in ways that may or may not contribute to denial. For instance, a coercer may choose to destroy high-value military targets not directly supporting the adversary's strategy. Alternatively, the coercer may choose to defeat the adversary's strategy in a way that inflicts greater cost than would some other possible option, such as destroying an armor division versus immobilizing it by interdicting its fuel supply. For reasons both moral and strategic, I do not advocate attacking civilians directly, though I realize that some forms of punishment (blockade, embargo, infrastructure attacks, etc.) may have indirect collateral effects that impact civilians severely. Coercers must weigh these actions carefully in terms of discrimination and proportionality.

11. Lester Brooks, *Behind Japan's Surrender: The Secret Struggle that Ended an Empire* (New York: McGraw-Hill Book Company, 1968), p. 253.

12. To the extent that the shortcomings of punishment may be universal, possible reasons may revolve around "sunk costs" and other costs of compliance. Target-nation leaders may feel the blood and treasure they have already invested

in the contest make it imperative that they achieve some benefit, even though they anticipate suffering further costs. Moreover, the mounting costs of punishment often make political survival and even personal safety dependent on being able to convince fellow countrymen that the conflict was not in vain.

13. Of course, this is not always possible or desirable. Often, domestic constituents demand that adversaries be punished and humiliated for their misdeeds. Moreover, accommodation always carries with it the risk that adversaries or third parties will think the coercer is weak or uncommitted. All these considerations need to be weighed in careful, culture-sensitive analyses.

14. I suspect sensitivity to humiliation and shame is a trait common to all cultures in varying degrees. Yet, the Japanese are so sensitive to issues of "face" that Meiji leaders factored into their decision the possibility that resistance might lead to humiliation in the future that would be greater than that they would suffer in capitulating quickly. I am indebted to Thomas C. Schelling for pointing this out.

15. The best way to deal with a crisis is to avoid it; therefore, deterrence should be the starting point of any coercive strategy. When deterrence fails, or seems likely to fail, policy makers must devise more active forms of coercion. Yet, deterrence remains an important concern even after coercion takes a more confrontational form, and a fundamental objective of all coercive strategies should be to move the dispute back down the coercive spectrum toward simple deterrence.

16. The approach I use for this coercive strategy development game concept draws from opponent behavior modeling work Paul K. Davis and John Arquilla did at RAND Corporation a few years ago. See Paul K. Davis and John Arquilla, *Thinking About Opponent Behavior in Crisis and Conflict: A Generic Model for Analysis and Group Discussion* (RAND, N-3322-JS, 1991) and *Deterring or Coercing Opponents in Crisis: Lessons from the War with Saddam Hussein* (RAND, R-4111-JS, 1991). For a thorough treatment of the history of wargaming, see Peter P. Perla, *The Art of Wargaming* (Annapolis, Md.: Naval Institute Press, 1990). For information on how the military and civilian communities use simulations to develop and test innovative strategies, see Robert L. Bateman, III (ed.), *Digital War: A View from the Front Lines* (Novato, Calif.: Presidio Press, 1999); Michael Schrange, *Serious Play: How the World's Best Companies Simulate to Innovate* (Boston: Harvard Business School Press, 2000).

17. Typical war games last from two days to a week. The length of coercive strategy development games would largely depend on the time available to deal with the task at hand and the availability of key players. Efforts to explore long-term deterrence strategies would not be as time sensitive as games called to develop responses to sudden crises.

18. Ideally, this group would include historians, political scientists, economists, sociologists, and cultural anthropologists, all specializing in the region in question, teamed with other regional specialists from the intelligence community and other governmental departments. To the extent possible, the team should include individuals who speak the language and have lived in the country being profiled. Selected members of this team should also take part in "Red Team" deliberations; but that team will be constituted more along functional lines. I will address this in more detail later.

19. Whenever possible, players should be provided a game book a day or more before play begins. This book should outline the strategic problem the game is

called to address, include the intelligence and regional briefings and reports, and inform each player what his or her role in the game will be. This will facilitate a more efficient use of game time by encouraging players to begin thinking through the problem before they arrive.

20. In a crisis, it is doubtful that the NSC would simply sit back and wait for game players to assemble and develop strategy alternatives—the NSC itself would aggressively work the problem from its onset. In this case, we might anticipate that, if time permits gaming, administration officials will present not only a statement of strategic objectives, but a tentative strategy or set of alternative strategies they would like tested on Red Team. In these situations, Blue Team's function would probably entail fleshing out those strategies, examining them for technical and political feasibility, and formatting them for presentation to Red Team.

21. The format I describe here is a very simplified template for game design. More sophisticated versions might include some number of teams simulating other nations; regional specialists could play those positions, and strategic culture profiles could be developed to help guide their play in efforts to gauge potential third-party reactions to Blue Team's coercive strategies.

22. Red Team should not focus on trying to "defeat" Blue Team. In adversarial war games, opposing teams attempt to defeat one another in specific scenarios, and their efforts are adjudicated by an assessor team. But that approach will not work in a game where the objective is persuasion. A Red Team that is determined to "win" will only defeat the purpose and value of the exercise.

23. As Davis and Arquilla point out, "Given the extreme difficulty we have predicting political events in our own country, why should we ask regional specialists for high-confidence predictions about foreign countries or their leaders?" Davis and Arquilla, *Thinking About Opponent Behavior in Crisis and Conflict*, p. 22.

24. Davis and Arquilla emphasize that, though game theory and most other forms of decision analysis assume decision makers always seek to manipulate risks in ways that maximize their expected utility, the empirical record suggests they frequently behave otherwise. I agree. As the cases examined in this study seem to confirm, decision makers may take tremendous risks for short term gains if their conception of the strategic landscape fosters in them a sense of desperation and they perceive an opportunity to seize the initiative (oil embargo). Alternatively, they may avoid even moderate risk if they feel they have lost the initiative and their worldview and value structure suggests that yielding to a challenge, however distasteful, will be less costly in the long run than what they stand to lose in a confrontation (triple intervention). Davis and Arquilla offer several tools for systematically comparing such variables (e.g., influence diagrams, cognitive maps, and decision tables). These devices may be useful in gaming, but they should be approached with caution: plugging values into diagrams and tables produces formulaic outcomes that tend to inspire levels of confidence that may not be warrented. I suspect more accurate estimations of adversarial behavior can be developed by regional experts simply attempting to put themselves in the opponent's mindset, guided by a carefully constructed profile of his strategic culture, then working through the scenario in a qualitative, heuristic fashion. See Davis and Arquilla, *Thinking About Opponent Behavior in Crisis and Conflict*, pp. 12–20.

25. For instance, role-playing a regime ruled by a dominant, unitary actor could produce an analysis heavily weighted to the views of the analyst playing that

individual. On a lighter note, imagine gamers, role-playing Japan's struggle to end the Second World War, to unable complete their analysis due to an inability to reach a consensus decision.

26. Davis and Arquilla, *Thinking About Opponent Behavior in Crisis and Conflict*, p. 21.

Selected Bibliography

Akagi, Roy Hidemichi. *Japan's Foreign Relations 1542–1936: A Short History.* Tokyo: The Kokuseido Press, 1936.

Ala, Mohamad, and William P. Cordeiro. "Can We Learn Management Techniques from the Japanese Ringi Process?" *Business Forum* 24, Nos. 1, 2: 22–23.

Allison, Graham T. *Essence of Decision: Explaining the Cuban Missile Crisis.* New York: Harper Collins Publishers, 1971.

Allison, Graham T., and Philip Zelikow. *Essence of Decision: Explaining the Cuban Missle Crisis,* 2nd ed. New York: Longman, 1999.

American Diplomatic and Public Papers: The United States and China, Series III, *The Sino-Japanese War to the Russo-Japanese War 1894–1905,* Vols. 2 and 3, *The Sino-Japanese War I.* Wilmington, Del.: Scholarly Research, Inc., 1981.

Ball, Desmond. *Strategic Culture in the Asia-Pacific Region: With Some Implications for Regional Security Cooperation.* Canberra: Strategic and Defence Studies Centre, Australian National University, 1993.

Banerjee, Sanjoy. "Reproduction of Social Structures: An Artificial Intelligence Model." *Journal of Conflict Resolution* 30, No. 2 (June 1986): 225.

Barry, Brian. *Sociologists, Economists, and Democracy.* Chicago: University of Chicago Press, 1979.

Bateman, Robert L., III, ed. *Digital War: A View from the Front Lines.* Novato, Cailf.: Presidio Press, 1999.

Beasley, W. G. *Japanese Imperialism 1894–1945.* Oxford: Clarendon Press, 1987.

Bellah, Robert N. *Tokugawa Religion: The Values of Pre-Industrial Japan.* Boston: Beacon Press, 1957.

Benedict, Ruth C. *The Chrysanthemum and the Sword.* Boston: Houghton Mifflin, 1946.

Bergamini, David. *Japan's Imperial Conspiracy.* New York: William Morrow and Co., Inc., 1971.

Berger, Gordon M. "Politics and Mobilization in Japan, 1931–1945" in *The Cambridge History of Japan*, Vol. 6, *The Twentieth Century*. Cambridge: Cambridge University Press, 1988.

Bernstein, Barton J. "Compelling Japan to Surender Without the A-bomb, Soviet Entry, or Invasion: Reconsidering the US Bombing Survey's Early-Surrender Conclusions." *The Journal of Strategic Studies* 18, No. 2 (June 1985): 101–48.

Bix, Herbert P. "The Hirohito Emperor's 'Monologue' and the Problem of War Responsibility." *Journal of Japanese Studies* 18, No. 2 (Summer 1992): 352–54.

———. *Hirohito and the Making of Modern Japan*. New York: Perennial, 2000.

Blank, Stephen J., et al. *Conflict, Culture, and History: Regional Dimensions*. Maxwell AFB, AL: Air University Press, 1993.

Booth, Ken. *Strategy and Ethnocentrism*. New York: Holmes & Meier Publishers, Inc., 1979.

Booth, Ken, and Russell Trood. *Strategic Cultures in the Asia-Pacific Region*. New York: St. Martin's Press, 1999.

Borg, Dorothy, and Shumpei Okamoto, eds. *Pearl Harbor as History: Japanese-American Relations 1931–1941*. Editorial assistance by Dale K. A. Finlayson. New York: Columbia University Press, 1973.

Borofsky, Robert, ed. *Assessing Cultural Anthropology*. New York: McGraw-Hill, 1994.

Borton, Hugh. *Japan's Modern Century: From Perry to 1970*. New York: The Ronald Press Co., 1970.

Boyd, Robert, and Peter J. Richerson. *Culture and the Evolutionary Process*. Chicago: The University of Chicago Press, 1985.

Brinkley, F. *A History of the Japanese People: From the Earliest Times to the End of the Meiji Era*. New York: The Encyclopedia Britannica Co., 1914.

British Documents on Foreign Affairs: Reports and Papers From the Foreign Office Confidential Print. Part I, Series E, Vols. 4 and 5. Edited by Ian Nish. New York: University Publications of America, 1989.

Brodie, Bernard. *Strategy in the Missile Age*. Princeton, N.J.: Princeton University Press, 1991.

Brooks, Lester. *Behind Japan's Surrender: The Secret Struggle that Ended an Empire*. New York: McGraw-Hill Book Company, 1968.

Brown, Archie, ed. *Political Culture and Communist Studies*. Armonk, N.Y.: M. E. Sharpe, 1985.

Brown, Delmer M. *Nationalism in Japan: An Introductory Analysis*. Berkeley, Calif.: University of California Press, 1955.

Butow, Robert J. C. *Japan's Decision to Surrender*. Stanford, Calif.: Stanford University Press, 1954.

———. *Tojo and the Coming of the War*. Princeton, N.J.: Princeton University Press, 1961.

Byman, Daniel, Kenneth Pollack, and Matthew Waxman. "Coercing Saddam Hussein: Lessons from the Past." *Survival* 40, No. 3 (Autumn 1998): 127–51.

Byman, Daniel, Eric Larson, Kenneth Pollack, and Matthew Waxman. *The Coercive Use of Airpower*. Santa Monica, Calif.: RAND, 2000.

The Cambridge History of Japan, Vol. 6, *The Twentieth Century*. Cambridge: Cambridge University Press, 1988.

Cavendish, Richard. *The Eastern Religions*. New York: Arco Publications, 1980.

Cohen, Jerome B. *Japan's Economy in the War and Reconstruction*. Minneapolis, Minn.: University of Minnesota Press, 1949.

Conway, Martin A. *Cognitive Models of Memory*. Cambridge, Mass.: The MIT Press, 1997.

Coox, Alvin. "The Pacific War" in *The Cambridge History of Japan*, Vol. 6, *The Twentieth Century*. Cambridge: Cambridge University Press, 1988.

Craig, Gordon A., and Alexander L. George. *Force and Statecraft: Diplomatic Problems of Our Time*. New York: Oxford University Press, 1983.

Craig, William. *The Fall of Japan*. New York: The Dial Press, 1967.

Crowley, James B. *Japan's Quest for Autonomy: National Security and Foreign Policy 1930–1938*. Princeton, N.J.: Princeton University Press, 1966.

Davis, Paul K., and John Arquilla. *Deterring or Coercing Opponents in Crisis: Lessons from the War with Saddam Hussein*. RAND, R-4111-JS, 1991.

———. *Thinking About Opponent Behavior in Crisis and Conflict: A Generic Model for Analysis and Group Discussion*. RAND, N-3322-JS, 1991.

Dawes, Robyn M. *Rational Choice in an Uncertain World*. New York: Harcourt Brace & Company, 1988.

Dore, R. P., ed. *Aspects of Social Change in Modern Japan*. Princeton, N.J.: Princeton University Press, 1967.

Duus, Peter. *Feudalism in Japan*. New York: Alfred A. Knopf, 1969.

Earhart, H. Byron. *Religions of Japan*. San Francisco: Harper & Row Publishers, 1984.

Elder, Charles D., and Roger W. Cobb. *The Political Use of Symbols*. New York: Longman, 1983.

Ellsberg, Daniel. *Theory and Practice of Blackmail*. RAND, P-3883, 1968.

Enfield, Nick J. "The Theory of Cultural Logic: How Individuals Combine Social Intelligence with Semiotics to Create and Maintain Cultural Meaning." *Cultural Dynamics* 12, No. 1 (2000): 51–52.

Feis, Herbert. *The Road to Pearl Harbor: The Coming of the War between the United States and Japan*. Princeton, N.J.: Princeton University Press, 1950.

———. *Japan Subdued: The Atomic Bomb and the End of the War in the Pacific*. Princeton, N.J.: Princeton University Press, 1961.

Freedman, Lawrence, ed. *Strategic Coercion: Concepts and Cases*. Oxford: Oxford University Press, 1998.

Futrell, Robert Frank. *Ideas, Concepts, and Doctrine: Basic Thinking in the United States Air Force, 1907–1960*. Maxwell AFB, AL: Air University Press, 1989.

Garon, Sheldon. *Molding Japanese Minds: The State in Everyday Life*. Princeton, N.J.: Princeton University Press, 1997.

Geertz, Clifford, ed. *The Interpretation of Cultures*. New York: Basic Books, Inc., 1973.

George, Alexander L. "Case Studies and Theory Development: The Method of Structured, Focused Comparison." In Paul G. Lauren, ed. *Diplomacy: New Approaches in History, Theory, and Policy*. New York: The Free Press, 1979.

———. *Forceful Persuasion: Coercive Diplomacy as an Alternative to War*. Washington, D.C.: United States Institute of Peace, 1991.

George, Alexander L., David K. Hall, and William E. Simons. *The Limits of Coercive Diplomacy: Laos, Cuba, Vietnam*. Boston: Little, Brown & Co., 1971.

George, Alexander L., and William E. Simons, ed. *The Limits of Coercive Diplomacy*, 2nd ed. Boulder, Colo.: Westview Press, 1994.

George, Alexander L., and Richard Smoke. *Deterrence in American Foreign Policy: Theory and Practice*. New York: Columbia University Press, 1974.

Giffard, Sidney. *Japan Among the Powers, 1890–1990*. New Haven, Conn.: Yale University Press, 1994.

Goleman, Daniel. *Vital Lies, Simple Truths: The Psychology of Self-Deception*. New York: Simon & Schuster, 1985.

Gray, Colin. "National Styles in Strategy: The American Example." *International Security* 6, No. 2 (Fall 1981): 21–47.

———. "Comparative Strategic Culture." *Parameters* XIV, No. 4 (Winter 1984): 26–33.

———. *Nuclear Strategy and National Style*. Lanham, Md.: Hamilton Press, 1986.

———. *War, Peace, and Victory: Strategy and Statecraft for the Next Century*. New York: Simon and Schuster, 1990.

———. *Modern Strategy*. Oxford: Oxford University Press, 1999.

Grew, Joseph C. *Ten Years in Japan*. New York: Simon and Schuster, 1944.

Grinter, Lawrence E. "Cultural and Historical Influences in Sinic Asia: China, Japan, and Vietnam." In Stephen J. Blank, et al. *Conflict, Culture, and History: Regional Dimensions*. Maxwell AFB, AL: Air University Press, 1993.

Hagan, Kenneth J. *The People's Navy: The Making of American Sea Power*. New York: The Free Press, 1991.

Hanges, Paul J., Robert G. Lord, and Marcus W. Dickson. "An Information Processing Perspective on Leadership and Culture: A Case for Connectionist Architecture." *Applied Psychology: An International Review* 49, No. 1 (2000): 133–69.

Hansell, Haywood S., Jr. *The Strategic Air War Against Germany and Japan: A Memoir*. Washington, D.C.: Office of Air Force History, United States Air Force, 1986.

Harris, Marvin. *Cultural Materialism: The Struggle for a Science of Culture*. New York: Vintage Books, 1979.

Hata Ikuhiko. "Continental Expansion, 1905–1941." Translated by Alvin Coox, in *The Cambridge History of Japan*, Vol. 6, *The Twentieth Century*. Cambridge: Cambridge University Press, 1988.

Herzog, James H. *Closing the Open Door: American-Japanese Diplomatic Negotiations 1936–1941*. Annapolis, Md.: Naval Institute Press, 1973.

Higgins, E. Tory, and Richard M. Sorrentino, eds. *Handbook of Motivation and Cognition: Foundations of Social Behavior*, Volume 2. New York: The Guilford Press, 1990.

Hopfe, L. M. *Religions of the World*. Encino, Calif.: Glencoe Publishing Co., 1976.

Hosmer, Stephen T. *Psychological Effects of U.S. Air Operations in Four Wars, 1941–1991: Lessons for U.S. Commanders*. Santa Monica, Calif.: RAND, 1996.

Huntington, Sammuel P. "The Clash of Civilizations?" *Foreign Affairs* 72, No. 3 (Summer 1993): 67–80.

Ike, Nobutaka. *The Beginnings of Political Democracy in Japan*. Baltimore, Md.: Johns Hopkins University Press, 1950.

———. *Japanese Politics: Patron-Client Democracy*. New York: Alfred A. Knopf, 1957.

———, trans. and ed. *Japan's Decision for War: Records of the 1941 Policy Conferences*. Stanford, Calif.: Stanford University Press, 1967.

Ikl'e, Fred Charles. *Every War Must End*, Revised ed. New York: Columbia University Press, 1991.

International Military Tribunal, Far East, Tokyo, 1946–8. *Record of Proceedings, Exhibits, Judgement, Dissenting Judgements, Preliminary Interrogations, Miscellaneous Documents*. Volume 166.

Ishida, Takeshi. *Japanese Political Culture: Change and Continuity*. New Brunswick, N.J.: Transaction Books, 1983.

Ishida, Takeshi, and Ellis S. Krauss *Democracy in Japan*. Pittsburgh: University of Pittsburgh Press, 1989.

Jacobsen, Carl G., ed. *Strategic Power: USA/USSR*. New York: St. Martin's Press, 1990.

Janis, Irving. *Air War and Emotional Stress*. Santa Monica, Calif.: RAND, 1951.

Jansen, Marius B., ed. *Changing Japanese Attitudes Toward Modernization*. Princeton, N.J.: Princeton University Press, 1965.

Jervis, Robert. *Perception and Misperception in International Politics*. Princeton, N.J.: Princeton University Press, 1976.

———. "Why Nuclear Superiority Doesn't Matter." *Political Science Quarterly* 94 (Winter 1979): 617–33.

Johnston, Alistair Iain. *Cultural Realism: Strategic Culture and Grand Strategy in Chinese History*. Princeton, N.J.: Princeton University Press, 1995.

———. "Thinking About Strategic Culture." *International Security* 19, No. 4 (Spring 1995): 32–64.

Johnston Conover, Pamela, and Stanley Feldman. "How People Organize the Political World: A Schematic Model." *American Journal of Political Science* 28 (1984): 96.

Jones, F. C. *Japan's New Order in East Asia: Its Rise and Fall, 1937–45*. London: Oxford University Press, 1954.

Kajima, Morinosuke. *The Emergence of Japan as a World Power, 1895–1925*. Rutland, Vt.: Charles E. Tuttle Co., 1968.

———. *The Diplomacy of Japan 1894–1922*, Vol. 1, *Sino-Japanese War and Triple Intervention*. Tokyo: Kajima Institute of International Peace, 1976.

Kase, Toshikazu. *Journey to the Missouri*. New Haven, Conn.: Yale University Press, 1950.

Katzenstein, Peter J. *The Culture of National Security: Norms and Identity in World Politics*. New York: Columbia University Press, 1996.

Kecskemeti, Paul. *Strategic Surrender: The Politics of Victory and Defeat*. New York: Atheneum, 1964.

Keegan, John. *The Second World War*. New York: Penguin Books, 1989.

Keohane, Robert O. *After Hegemony: Cooperation and Discord in the World Political Economy*. Princeton, N.J.: Princeton University Press, 1984.

Keohane, Robert O., and Joseph S. Nye, Jr. *Power and Interdependence*, 3rd ed. Reading, Mass.: Addison-Wesley, 2000.

Kerr, Pauline. *Researching Security in East Asia: From "Strategic Culture" to "Security Culture."* Canberra: Strategic and Defence Studies Centre, Australian National University, 1998.

Khong, Yuen Foong. *Analogies at War: Korea, Munich, Dien Bien Phu, and the Vietnam Decisions of 1965*. Princeton, N.J.: Princeton University Press, 1992.

Kido, Koichi. *The Diary of Marquis Kido, 1931–45: Selected Translations into English.* Frederick, Md.: University Publications of America, 1984.

Kier, Elizabeth. "Culture and Military Doctrine: France Between the Wars." *International Security* 19, No. 4 (Spring 1995): 65–93.

———. *Imagining War: French and British Military Doctrine Between the Wars.* Princeton, N.J.: Princeton University Press, 1997.

Kingdon, John W. *Agendas, Alternatives, and Public Policies.* Boston: Little, Brown & Co., 1984.

Kirby, S. Woodburn. *The War Against Japan*, Vol. V, *The Surrender of Japan.* History of the Second World War United Kingdom Military Series, Sir James Butler, ed. London: Her Majesty's Stationary Office, 1969.

Klein, Bradley. "Hegemony and Strategic Culture: American Power Projection and Alliance Defence Politics." *Review of International Studies* 14 (1988): 133–48.

Klingberg, Frank. "Predicting the Termination of War: Battle Casualties and Population Losses." *Journal of Conflict Resolution* 10, No. 2 (1966): 129–171.

Krauss, Ellis S., Thomas P. Rohlen, Patricia G. Steinhoff, eds. *Conflict in Japan.* Berkeley, Calif.: University of California Press, 1984.

Kroeber, A. L., and Clyde Kluckhohn. *Culture: A Critical Review of Concepts and Definitions.* New York: Vintage Books, 1963.

Kuehl, Daniel T. "Airpower vs. Electricity: Electric Power as a Target for Strategic Air Operations." *The Journal of Strategic Studies* 18, No. 1 (Special Issue on Airpower Theory and Practice), (March 1995): 237–68.

Kupchan, Charles. *The Vulnerability of Empire.* Ithaca, N.Y.: Cornell University Press, 1994.

Laitin, David. "Political Culture and Political Preferences." *American Political Science Review* 82, No. 2: 589–98.

Large, Stephen S. *Emperor Hirohito and Showa Japan: A Political Biography.* New York: Routledge, 1992.

Lauren, Paul G. "Ultimata and Coercive Diplomacy." *International Studies Quarterly* 16, No. 2 (June 1972) pp. 131–65.

———, ed. *Diplomacy: New Approaches in History, Theory, and Policy.* New York: The Free Press, 1979.

Legro, Jeffrey. *Cooperation Under Fire: Anglo-German Restraint During World War II.* Ithaca, N.Y.: Cornell University Press, 1995.

Levi-Strauss, Claude. *Structural Anthropology.* Translated by Claire Jacobson and Brooke Grundfest Schoepf. New York: Basic Books, Inc., 1963.

Levy, Marion J., Jr. *The Structure of Society.* Princeton, N.J.: Princeton University Press, 1952.

Lord, Carnes. "American Strategic Culture." *Comparative Strategy* 5, No. 3: 269–93.

Luckham, Robin. "Armament Culture." *Alternatives* 10, No. 1 (1984): 1–44.

Mack, Andrew. "Why Big Nations Lose Small Wars." *World Politics* 27 (January 1975): 175–200.

March, James G. *A Primer on Decision Making: How Decisions Happen.* New York: The Free Press, 1994.

March, Robert M. *Reading the Japanese Mind: The Realities Behind Their Thoughts and Actions.* Tokyo: Kodansha International, 1996.

Martin, Curtis H., and Bruce Stronach. *Politics East and West: A Comparison of Japanese and British Political Culture.* Armonk, N.Y.: M. E. Sharpe, 1992.

Maruyama, Masao. *Thought and Behavior in Modern Japanese Politics*. Translated and edited by Ivan Morris. Oxford: Oxford University Press, 1969.

Mayo, Marlene, ed. *The Emergence of Imperial Japan: Self-Defense or Calculated Aggression?* Lexington, Mass.: D.C. Heath and Co., 1970.

Mishkin, Mortimer, and T. Appenzeller. "The Anatomy of Memory." *Scientific American* 256, No. 6 (June 1987): 80–89.

Moody, Peter R., Jr. *Tradition and Modernization in China and Japan*. Belmont, Calif.: Wadsworth Publishing Company, 1995.

Mueller, John. *Retreat from Doomsday: The Obsolescence of Major War*. New York: Basic Books, Inc., 1989.

Mueller, Karl. "Strategies of Coercion: Denial, Punishment, and the Future of Air Power." *Security Studies* 7, No. 3 (Spring 1998) pp. 182–228

Munch, Richard, and Neil J. Smelser, eds. *Theory of Culture*. Berkley, Calif.: University of California Press, 1992.

Murdoch, James. *A History of Japan*, Vol. 1: *From the Origins to the arrival of the Portuguese in 1542 A.D.* New York: Frederick Ungar Publishing Co., 1964.

Mutsu, Munemitsu. *Kenkenroku: A Diplomatic Record of the Sino-Japanese War, 1894–95*. Edited and translated with historical notes by Gordon Mark Berger. Tokyo: University of Tokyo Press, 1982.

Nakane, Chie. *Japanese Society*. Berkeley, Calif.: University of California Press, 1972.

Nakane, Chie, and Shinzaburo Oishi, eds. *Tokugawa Japan: The Social and Economic Antecedents of Modern Japan*. Translated and edited by Conrad Totman. Tokyo: University of Tokyo Press, 1990.

Needham, Rodney. *Structure and Sentiment: A Test Case in Social Anthropology*. Chicago: The University of Chicago Press, 1962.

Neustadt, Richard E., and Ernest R. May. *Thinking in Time: The Uses of History for Decision Makers*. New York: The Free Press, 1986.

Nish, Ian. *Japanese Foreign Policy 1869–1942: Kasumigaseki to Miyakezaka*. London: Routledge & Kegan Paul, 1977.

Nitobe, Inazo. *Japan: Some Phases of her Problems and Development*. New York: Charles Scribner's Sons, 1931.

———. *The Origins of the Russo-Japanese War*. London: Longman Group Ltd., 1985.

———. *Bushido: The Soul of Japan*. Rutland, Vt.; Tokyo: Charles E. Tuttle Co., 1941.

Norman, E. Herbert. *Japan's Emergence as a Modern State: Political and Economic Problems of the Meiji Period*. Westport, Conn.: Greenwood Press, 1940.

Okamoto, Shumpei. *The Japanese Oligarchy and the Russo-Japanese War*. New York: Columbia University Press, 1970.

Osgood, Robert E., and Robert W. Tucker. *Force, Order, and Justice*. Baltimore, Md.: Johns Hopkins University Press, 1967.

Pacific War Research Society. *Japan's Longest Day*. Tokyo: Kodansha International, Ltd., 1968.

Pandian, Jacob. *Anthropology and the Western Tradition: Toward an Authentic Anthropology*. Prospect Heights, Ill.: Waveland Press, Inc., 1985.

Pape, Robert A. "Coercive Air Power and the Vietnam War." *International Security* 15, No. 2 (Fall 1990): 101–46.

———. "Coercion and Military Strategy: Why Denial Works and Punishment Doesn't." *Journal of Strategic Studies* 15, No. 4 (December 1992): 423–75.

―――. *Bombing to Win: Air Power and Coercion in War*. Ithaca, N.Y.: Cornell University Press, 1996.

―――. "The Air Force Strikes Back: A Reply to Barry Watts and John Warden." *Secrurity Studies 7*, No. 2 (Winter 1997/98): 189–212.

―――. "The Limits of Precision-Guided Air Power." *Security Studies 7*, No. 2 (Winter 1997/98): 93–113.

Paxton, Robert O. *Vichy France: Old Guard and New Order 1940–1944*. New York: Columbia University Press, 1972.

Perla, Peter P. *The Art of Wargaming*. Annapolis, Md.: Naval Institute Press, 1990.

Pollack, Kenneth M. "The Influence of Arab Culture on Arab Military Effectiveness," Ph.D. diss., Massachusetts Institute of Technology, 1996.

Pye, Lucian W. *Asian Power and Politics: The Cultural Dimensions of Authority*. Cambridge, Mass.: The Belnap Press, 1985.

Quester, George H. *Deterrence Before Hiroshima: The Airpower Background of Modern Strategy*. New York: John Wiley & Sons, Inc., 1966.

―――. "Some Thoughts on Deterrence Failures." In Paul C. Stern, et al., eds. *Perspectives on Deterrence*. New York: Oxford University Press, 1989.

Reischauer, Edwin O. *The Japanese*. Cambridge, Mass.: The Belnap Press, 1977.

Reischauer, Edwin O., and Marius B. Jansen. *The Japanese Today: Change and Continuity*. Cambridge, Mass.: The Belnap Press, 1995.

Richardson, Bradley M. *The Political Culture of Japan*. Berkeley, Calif.: University of California Press, 1974.

Risse, Thomas, Stephen C. Ropp, and Kathryn Sikkink, eds. *The Power of Human Rights: International Norms and Domestic Change*. Cambridge: Cambridge University Press, 1999.

Rosen, Stephen Peter. "Military Effectiveness: Why Society Matters." *International Security 19*, No. 4 (Spring 1995): 5–31.

―――. *Societies and Military Power: India and Its Armies*. Ithaca, N.Y.: Cornell University Press, 1996.

The Russo-Japanese War: The Yalu. Report prepared in the historical section of the German general staff. Translated by Karl von Donat. London: Hugh Rees, Ltd., 1908.

Sansom, George B. *The Western World and Japan: A Study in the Interaction of European and Asiatic Cultures*. New York: Alfred A. Knopf, 1950.

―――. *A History of Japan to 1334*. Stanford, Calif.: Stanford University Press, 1958.

Schank, Roger C.,and Robert P. Abelson. *Scripts, Plans, Goals, and Understanding: An Inquiry into Human Knowledge Structures*. Hillsdale, N.J.: Lawrence Erlbaum Associates, 1977.

Schelling, Thomas C. "An Essay on Bargaining." *American Economic Review 46*, No. 3 (June 1956): 281–306.

―――. *The Strategy of Conflict*. Cambridge, Mass.: Harvard University Press, 1960.

―――. *Arms and Influence*. New Haven, Conn.: Yale University Press, 1966.

―――. *Choice and Consequence: Perspectives of an Errant Economist*. Cambridge, Mass.: Harvard University Press, 1984.

Schott, Richard L. "Administrative and Organization Behavior: Some Insights from Cognitive Psychology." *Administration and Society 23*, No. 1 (May 1991): 55.

Schrange, Michael. *Serious Play: How the World's Best Companies Simulate to Innovate.* Boston: Harvard Business School Press, 2000.

Shaffer, Ralph E., ed. *Toward Pearl Harbor: The Diplomatic Exchange Between Japan and the United States, 1899–1941.* New York: Markus Wiener Publishing, 1991.

Sharabi, Hisham, ed. *The Next Arab Decade: Alternative Futures.* Boulder, Colo.: Westview Press, 1988.

Sherry, Michael S. *The Rise of American Air Power: The Creation of Armageddon.* New Haven, Conn.: Yale University Press, 1987.

Shigemitsu, Mamoru. *Japan and Her Destiny: My Struggle for Peace.* Translated by Oswald White and edited by Major General F.S.G. Piggott. New York: E. P. Dutton & Co., Inc., 1958.

Shillony, Ben-Ami. *Politics and Culture in Wartime Japan.* Oxford: Clarendon Press, 1981.

Shultz, Richard H., Jr., and Robert L. Pfaltzgraff, Jr., eds. *The Future of Air Power in the Aftermath of the Gulf War.* Maxwell AFB, AL: Air University Press, 1992.

Sigal, Leon V. *Fighting to a Finish: The Politics of War Termination in the United States and Japan, 1945.* Ithaca, N.Y.: Cornell University Press, 1988.

Silberman, Bernard S., ed. *Japanese Character and Culture: A Book of Selected Readings.* Tuscon, Ariz.: The University of Arizona Press, 1962.

Simon, Herbert A. *Administrative Behavior: A Study of Decision-Making Processes in Administrative Organizations,* 4th ed. New York: The Free Press, 1997.

Smelser, Neil J., ed. *Theory of Culture.* Berkeley, Calif.: University of California Press, 1992.

Smith, Gaddis. *American Diplomacy During the Second World War: 1941–1945.* New York: John Wiley & Sons, Inc., 1965.

Smith, Hedrick. *The Power Game: How Washington Works.* New York: Ballantine Books, 1988.

Smith, Robert J., and Richard K. Beardsley, eds. *Japanese Culture: Its Development and Characteristics.* Chicago: Aldine Publishing Co., 1962.

Snyder, Glenn H., and Paul Diesling. *Conflict Among Nations.* Princeton, N.J.: Princeton University Press, 1977.

Snyder, Jack. *The Soviet Strategic Culture: Implications for Nuclear Options.* Santa Monica, Calif.: RAND R-2154-AF, 1977.

———. "Anarchy and Culture: Insights from the Anthropology of War." *International Organization* 56, No. 1 (Winter 2002): 7–45.

Sorokin, Pitirim A. *Society, Culture, and Personality: Their Structure and Dynamics.* New York: Cooper Square Publishers, Inc., 1969.

Sorrentino, Richard M., and E. Tory Higgins, eds. *Handbook of Motivation and Cognition: Foundations of Social Behavior.* New York: The Guilford Press, 1986.

Spector, Ronald H. *Eagle Against the Sun: The American War With Japan.* New York: Vintage Books, 1985.

Spiro, Rand, Bertram Bruce, and William Brewer, eds. *Theoretical Issues in Reading Comprehension.* Hillsdale, N.J.: Lawrence Erlbaum Associates, 1980.

Stein, Janice Gross. "Deterrence and Compellence in the Gulf. 1990–91: A Failed or Impossible Task?" *International Security* 17, No. 2 (Fall 1992): 147–79.

Stinchcombe, Arthur. *Constructing Social Theories.* Chicago: University of Chicago Press, 1968.

Storry, Richard. *A History of Modern Japan*. London: Cassell & Co., Ltd., 1960.

Strain, Frederick R. "Iran's Nuclear Strategy: Discerning Motivations, Strategic Culture, and Rationality." Essay on Strategy XIV, Institute for National Strategic Studies. Washington, D.C.: National Defense University (undated).

Straus, Claudia, and Naomi Quinn. *A Cognitive Theory of Cultural Meaning*. New York: Cambridge University Press, 1997.

Stuart, Reginald C. *War and American Thought: From the Revolution to the Monroe Doctrine*. Kent, Ohio: Kent State University Press, 1982.

Sullivan, Mark P. *The Mechanism for Strategic Coercion: Denial or Second Order Change?* Maxwell AFB, AL: Air University Press, 1995.

Sylvan, Donald A., and James E. Voss, eds. *Problem Representation in Foreign Policy Decision Making*. Cambridge: Cambridge University Press, 1998.

Takeuchi, Tatsui. *War and Diplomacy in the Japanese Empire*. New York: Russell & Russell, 1967.

Theis, Wallace. *When Governments Collide*. Berkeley, Calif.: University of California Press, 1980.

Togo, Shigenori. *The Cause of Japan*. Translated and edited by Fumihiko Togo and Ben Bruce Blakeney. New York: Simon and Schuster, 1956.

Truman, Harry S. *Memoirs by Harry S. Truman*, Vol. 1, *Year of Decisions*. Garden City, N.Y.: Doubleday & Company, Inc., 1955.

Tsunoda, Ryusaku, William T. de Bary, and Donald Keene. *Sources of Japanese Tradition*. New York: Columbia University Press, 1958.

United States Department of State. *Papers Relating to the Foreign Relations of the United States: Japan, 1931–1941*, Vols. I and II. Washington, D.C.: U.S. Government Printing Office, 1943.

———. *Peace and War: United States Foreign Policy, 1931–1941*. Washington, D.C.: U.S. Government Printing Office, 1943.

———. *Foreign Relations of the United States, Diplomatic Papers: The Conference of Berlin (The Potsdam Papers), 1945*. Washington, D.C.: Government Printing Office, 1960.

———. *Foreign Relations of the United States: 1945, The British Commonwealth, The Far East*. Washington, D.C.: Government Printing Office, 1969.

United States Strategic Bombing Survey. *Interrogations of Japanese Officials*, Vols. I and II. Washington, D.C.: U.S. Government Printing Office, 1946.

———. *Japan's Struggle to End the War*. Washington, D.C.: U.S. Government Printing Office, 1946.

———. *Summary Report (Pacific War)*. Washington, D.C.: U.S. Government Printing Office, 1946.

———. *The Effects of Strategic Bombing on Japanese Morale*. Washington, D.C.: Government Printing Office, 1947.

———. *Final Report Covering Air-Raid Protection and Allied Subjects in Japan*. Washington, D.C.: Government Printing Office, 1947.

Waltz, Kenneth N. *Man, the State, and War: A Theoretical Analysis*. New York, Columbia University Press, 1959.

———. *Theory of International Politics*. Reading, Mass.: Addison-Wesley, 1979.

Ward, Robert E., ed. *Political Development in Modern Japan*. Princeton, N.J.: Princeton University Press, 1968.

Warden, John. "Success in Modern War: A Response to Robert Pape's Bombing to Win." *Security Studies* 7, No. 2 (Winter 1997/98): 170–88.

Watts, Alan. *The Way of Zen.* New York: Vintage Books, 1985.

Waxman, Matthew C. "Coalitions and Limits on Coercive Diplomacy." *Strategic Review* 25, No. 1 (Winter 1997): 38–47.

———. "Coercion and the Dislocation of Authority: Emerging Intelligence Challenges." *International Journal of Intelligence and Counterintelligence* 10, No. 3 (Fall 1997): 317–31.

Weltzer, Peter. *Hirohito and War: Imperial Tradition and Military Decision Making in Prewar Japan.* Honolulu: University of Hawaii Press, 1998.

Wendt, Alexander. *Social Theory of International Politics.* Cambridge: Cambridge University Press, 1999.

Westenhoff, Charles M. "Airpower and Political Culture." *Airpower Journal* 11, No. 4 (Winter 1997): 39–50.

Wiegley, Russell F. *The American Way of War: A History of United States Military Strategy and Policy.* Bloomington, Ind.: Indiana University Press, 1973.

Wilson, James Q. *Bureacracy: What Government Agencies Do and Why They Do It.* New York: Basic Books, Inc., 1989.

Wilson, William Scot, trans. *Ideals of the Samurai: Writings of Japanese Warriors.* Burbank, Calif.: Ohara, 1982.

Witte, Serge. *The Memoirs of Count Witte.* Translated and edited by Sidney Harcave. Armonk, N.Y.: M. E. Sharpe, 1990.

Wolferen, Karel van. *The Enigma of Japanese Power: People and Politics in a Stateless Nation.* New York: Alfred A. Knopf, 1989.

Yamamura, Kozo, ed. *The Cambridge History of Japan,* Vol. 3, *Medieval Japan.* Cambridge: Cambridge University Press, 1990.

Yanaga, Chitoshi. *Japan Since Perry.* Westport, Conn.: Greenwood Press, 1949.

Zhao, Quansheng. *Japanese Policymaking—The Politics Behind the Politics: Informal Mechanisms and the Making of China Policy.* Westport, Conn.: Praeger, 1993.

Zola-Morgan, Stuart M., and Larry R. Squire. "The Primate Hippocamel Formation: Evidence for a Time-Limited Role in Memory Storage." *Science* 250, No. 4978 (12 October 1990): 288–90.

Index

About the Author

FORREST E. MORGAN is a policy analyst for the RAND Corporation. A recently retired Air Force officer, he has held such jobs as commander of a space operations detachment, staff officer at Headquarters Air Force Space Command and Headquarters United States Air Force. He is a graduate of the Air Force's prestigious strategy school, the School of Advanced Air and Space Studies and, after earning a doctorate in policy studies from the University of Maryland, College Park, returned to the SAASS as a member of the faculty.